The
Identification
and
Analysis
of
Chicano
Literature

Bilingual Press/Editorial Bilingüe

Studies in the Language and Literature of United States Hispanos

The Identification and Analysis of Chicano Literature

Edited by
Francisco Jiménez

Bilingual Press/Editorial Bilingüe
NEW YORK

ISBN: 0-916950-12-3
Printed simultaneously in a softcover edition. ISBN: 0-916950-11-5

Library of Congress Catalog Card Number: 78-67287

PRINTED IN THE UNITED STATES OF AMERICA

Cover design by Richard S. Haymes

Cover photo by Ede Rothaus

Acknowledgments

The editor wishes to thank the following publications for permission to reprint material appearing in this volume:

Caribe (Univ. of Hawaii, Manoa), for Roberto Cantú, "Degradación y regeneración en *Bless Me, Ultima*: el chicano y la vida nueva," *Caribe* (Spring 1976).

Cuadernos Americanos (Mexico), for Guillermo Rojas, "La prosa chicana: tres epígonos de la novela mexicana de la Revolución," *Cuadernos Americanos*, 44, 3 (May-June 1975), pp. 198-209.

Latin American Literary Review, for Carmen Salazar Parr, "Current Trends in Chicano Literary Criticism," *Latin American Literary Review*, 5, 10 (Spring-Summer 1977), pp. 8-15; and Charles M. Tatum, "Contemporary Chicano Prose Fiction: A Chronicle of Misery," *Latin American Literary Review*, 1, 2 (Spring 1973), pp. 7-17.

Mester, for Juan Rodríguez, "El desarrollo del cuento chicano: del folklore al tenebroso mundo del yo," *Mester*, 4, 1 (Nov. 1973), pp. 7-12.

Revista Chicano-Riqueña, for portions of Judy Salinas, "The Image of Woman in Chicano Literature," *Revista Chicano-Riqueña*, 4, 4 (otoño 1976), pp. 139-48.

World Literature Today (formerly *Books Abroad*), for Rolando Hinojosa, "Mexican-American Literature: Toward an Identification," *Books Abroad*, 49, 3 (Summer 1975), pp. 422-430; Tomás Rivera, "Chicano Literature: Fiesta of the Living," *Books Abroad*, 49, 3 (Summer 1975), pp. 439-452; and Charles M. Tatum, "Contemporary Chicano Prose Fiction: Its Ties to Mexican Literature," *Books Abroad*, 49, 3 (Summer 1975), pp. 431-38.

Oral versions of the following papers were presented at the Modern Language Association's Annual Conventions; San Francisco, December 29, 1975: Rolando Hinojosa, "Literatura Chicana: Background and Present Status of a Bicultural Expression"; José Antonio Villarreal, "Chicano Literature: Art and Politics from the Perspective of the Artist." New York, December 28, 1976: Luis Leal, "The Problem of Identifying Chicano Literature"; Rolando Hinojosa, "Chicano Literature: An American Literature in Transition"; Joseph Sommers, "Critical Approaches to Chicano Literature."

(Acknowledgments continue on page 411.)

For
Andrés Iduarte, Matt S. Meier,
Robert Penny, and
Susana Redondo de Feldman

TABLE OF CONTENTS

FORWARD

The idea for this volume originated in 1974 when I proposed that an on-going seminar on Chicano literary criticism be established as a regular annual meeting in the Modern Language Association of America. Such a seminar would serve as a valuable milieu for scholars, artists, and interested individuals to interact and share research strategies or methodologies and bibliographic resources in a field which had few established channels for professional interchange. My proposed seminar would focus on the development of critical approaches that could adequately encompass the different genres of Chicano literature, and it would provide a physical locale as well as an intellectual medium for scholarship and research in Chicano literature within the Modern Language Association.

My proposal was favorably received, and the first seminar on Chicano literary criticism was held at the annual meeting of the Modern Language Association in San Francisco on December 29, 1975. The principal participants, Roberto Cantú, Rolando Hinojosa, Tomás Rivera and José Antonio Villarreal were invited to present papers dealing with the general topic of "Critical Approaches to Chicano Literature."

The underlying theme of this first seminar was responsible scholarship. I felt that we should not only address ourselves to the creation of a distinct literature—Chicano literature, but that we should also contribute to the further richness of our art through the development of a body of responsible and honest criticism. I concluded that it was crucial to approach our literature from a critical perspective upon considering the fact that critics, in actuality, share in the process of forming a society's taste and upon reflecting on the strong probability that our literature would be read by a majority largely ignorant of the reality lived within our culture.

From this first seminar, then, evolved the idea for the two final sections of this volume, respectively entitled: "Critical Trends: An Overview" and "Critical Applications."

The general concept for the first two sections of this volume, "Toward an Identification of Chicano Literature" and "Origins, Background and Development," emerged from the second seminar held at the annual convention of the Modern Language Association in New York City on December 28, 1976. The participants, Rolando Hinojosa, Luis Leal, Arturo Madrid and Joseph Sommers, were to address the general topic "Toward an Identification of Chicano Literature." The purpose of this seminar was to begin the formulation of a viable definition-identification of Chicano literature, a definition that would trace the sources of this literature and specify its unique characteristics.

Several of the essays which appear in this volume were originally presented as papers at the two MLA seminars. A number of essays included in this collection not presented at the MLA conventions were solicited from established critics; others, already published, were selected for their quality and appropriateness to the scope of this volume. This collection, then, represents the best critics on Chicano literature, as well as the best essays published in scholarly journals such as *Cuadernos Americanos, Latin American Literary Review* and *World Literature Today*.

The aim of this volume is simply to make available a number of important and useful published and unpublished critical essays on Chicano literature not otherwise handy, and to provide some evidence of the vitality of scholarship on Chicano literature, an important part of America's literary heritage.

Certain generalizations about the contributors suggest themselves from their professional affiliations. All but one are university professors at institutions throughout the United States who have produced a body of critical work in both Latin American and Chicano literature. With few exceptions, these critics are known as creators in their own right. This combination of "poet-critic" enriches Chicano literary criticism, and the uniqueness of this criticism perhaps stems from its close alliance with the major Chicano literary experiments and achievements.

Justification should be provided for the omission in this volume of other fine critics of Chicano literature such as Juan Bruce-Novoa, Francisco Lomelí, Arturo Madrid, Frank Pino, Sergio Elizondo and Tino Villanueva. Their exclusion was based either on unsuccessful attempts to obtain reprint premission from journals in which their articles were first published or on the necessity for keeping a volume of this type within reasonable limits.

This collection of essays by no means exhausts the studies on Chicano literature as evidenced by the bibliography at the end of the volume, but it does give testimony to the variety and vitality of scholarship in this field. The studies are not intended to be viewed as independent essays, but rather to comprise a symposium in which it is hoped that the reader will now take part.

Finally, I should like to express my sincere thanks to several persons who have kindly and generously supported my editing of this book: to Gary D. Keller for his invaluable suggestions for improvements; to Karen S. Van Hooft for her supervision of the production of the manuscript; to Mary M. Keller and Gabriela Mora for their careful reading and correction of the essays; and to Katherine R. Martin and Celeste M. Fritchle for their helpful comments and clerical assistance.

FRANCISCO JIMENEZ
UNIVERSITY OF SANTA CLARA

I. Toward an Identification of Chicano Literature

Ya sabemos, según nos ha enseñado— o recorda-
do— la moderna filosofía que preguntarse por algo,
replantearse el existir de una cosa, es comenzar a
entenderla. Inclusive hacerse cuestión de uno mismo o de algo que nos atañe muy directamente, resulta más fértil que cualquier vana confianza, que
toda apresurada afirmación categórica. No es simplemente una regla filosófica: es una norma vital.

Guillermo de Torre, *Claves de la
literatura hispanoamericana*

THE PROBLEM OF IDENTIFYING CHICANO LITERATURE

Luis Leal

The simplest, but also the narrowest way of defining Chicano literature is to say that it is the literature written by Chicanos. This definition, although neat and precise, presents us with at least two problems. It is difficult to identify a particular author as being Chicano, and it focuses the attention of the critic upon the origin of the writer, rather than on the work itself. The reader must be familiar with the author's life, especially if he has a non-Spanish name as in the case of John Rechy. There may be such Chicano writers publishing literary works whose origins we are not aware of. It may be equally difficult to identify as Chicanos those writers with Spanish names, as, for instance, Amado Muro and Silvio Villavicencio. Muro was an American named Chester Seltzer married to a Mexican lady and using her maiden name, Amada Muro, as a pseudonym.[1] Villavicencio, on the other hand, is a young writer from Central America now living in Guadalajara, Mexico, who, as far as we know, has never been to the United States. Two of his stories appeared in the anthology *El Espejo/The Mirror*, considered as representative of Chicano writing.

No less important is the fact that there is no consensus of opinion as to who is a Chicano. To show how rapidly the meaning of Chicano has changed, I shall quote the two definitions given by Edward Simmen and published a year apart. In 1971 he defined the Chicano as "a dissatisfied American of Mexican descent whose ideas regarding his position in the social and economic order are, in general, considered to be liberal or radical and whose statements and actions are often extreme and sometimes violent."[2] One year later he defined as Chicano "an American of Mexican descent who attempts through peaceful, reasonable, and responsible means to correct the image of the Mexican-American and to improve the position of this minority in the American social structure."[3] Other definitions of the Chicano are extremely limited, both as to time and social philosophy.[4]

If we define the Chicano as this socially-oriented person, then only that literature written by him, but especially that in support of the social movement called *la causa*, initiated during the early sixties, is Chicano literature. The best example of this would be the plays of Luis Valdez, performed by the Teatro Campesino. Are we to say then that such works as Rudolfo Anaya's novel *Bless Me, Ultima,* Estela Portillo's drama, *The Day of the Swallows*, and others not dealing with social protest do not belong to Chicano literature? A broader definition is definitely in order, so that we may be able to include all aspects of that literature. The definition should be broad enough to cover not only the plays of Luis Valdez but also other works not dealing with social themes.

Those critics who are aware of the difficulty of reaching agreement as to who is a Chicano have turned to a different approach, the identification of Chicano literature by its intrinsic characteristics. This approach is more satisfying to the humanist, since he feels that defining the Chicano is a task for the social scientist, and not for the literary critic. As we said before, this approach has the advantage of focusing the critic's attention upon the work itself. But, here again, the characteristics of Chicano literature most often mentioned by critics give us an extremely narrow concept of that literature. Most of them apply to what is considered to be realistic literature. For instance, subject matter, it is said, must reflect the Chicano experience and deal with Chicano themes. It is for this reason that some critics exclude Floyd Salas' novel, *Tattoo the Wicked Cross*, from being classified purely as a Chicano novel.[5] Why should the Chicano experience be limited to the *campesino* struggle, the description of life in the barrio, or the social confrontation with the majority culture? Why can it not go beyond to include the universal nature of man?

Another often mentioned characteristic of Chicano literature is its sympathetic attitude towards *chicanismo*. One of the accomplishments of Chicano literature has indeed been the creation of a new image for the Mexican American. The Chicano, as revealed by that literature, is not the stereotyped creature portrayed by the mass media. The danger here is that, in order to avoid a negative presentation of the Chicano, the writer often falls into the trap of Manicheism and the lack of ambiguity. What Carlos Fuentes said about the Spanish American novel written before 1940 can very well be applied to Chicano literature. For him that novel was "caught in the net of the reality close at hand and can only reflect it. That surrounding reality demands a struggle in order to be changed, and that struggle demands an epic simplification: the exploited man, because he is exploited, is good; the exploiter, also intrinsically, is evil. This primitive gallery of heroes and villains, what literature has not had it?"[6] Manicheism, of course, can be avoided. Corky Gonzales does it by identifying the hero of his poem not only with Cuauhtémoc, Juárez, and Madero, but also with Cortés, Maximiliano, and Huerta. "Writing *I Am Joaquín*," he says in the Introduction to the poem,

> was a journey back through history, a painful self-evaluation, a wandering search for the people and, most of all, for my own identity. The totality of all social inequities and injustices had to come to the surface. All the while, the truth about our own flaws—the villains and the heroes had to ride together—in order to draw an honest, clear conclusion of what we were, who we are, and where we are going. *I Am Joaquín* became a historical essay, a social statement, a conclusion of our mestizaje, a welding of the oppressor (Spaniard) and the oppressed (Indian).[7]

Chicano literature, like all other literatures, can give expression to the universal through the regional. Over and above the social problems with which he is at present preoccupied, the Chicano is a human being facing the concerns of all humanity. And he is giving expression to this in an original style. By writing in a combination of English and Spanish he is creating new images. And the creation of a new image is precisely the problem that confronts the Chicano writer: for it is not easy to give universality to the regional or particular if the writer does not go beyond his immediate circumstance. The Chicano has to create a new synthesis out of history, tradition, and his everyday confrontation with the ever-changing culture in which he lives. But he cannot do so unless he creates mythical images. And that is just what the Chicano writer has been doing, as we can see in Rivera's "*. . . y no se lo tragó la tierra*," Méndez' *Peregrinos de Aztlán*, Anaya's *Bless Me, Ultima*, and other representative Chicano creations. Méndez' pilgrims inhabit a mythical Aztlán. With Aztlán, Alurista, Méndez and others have created a mythical place as important as the descriptions of the barrios that we find in Mario Suárez' short stories. The Chicano can identify as easily with Aztlán as he can with Señor Garza's barber shop, or Hinojosa's Klail City. This can be so because the myth of Aztlán was born out of history, having been the place where the Aztecs originated. And since the Chicano identifies readily with the prehispanic cultures of Mexico, the myth took hold of the people's imagination.

For these reasons, the new definitions of Chicano literature, which are not restricted only to social, realistic works, are much more satisfying, and can account not only for Chicano literature as it exists today, but for what is to be written in the future. A broad definition is necessary even to account for socially oriented Chicano literature where mythical and legendary elements are frequent. Otherwise, how can we analyze, in their totality, such poems as Alurista's *La Llorona* and Omar Salinas' *Aztec Angel,* or even poems of the barrio, such as Raúl Salinas' *A Trip Through the Mind Jail,* where we find this stanza:

> Neighborhood of Zaragoza Park
> where scary stories interspersed with
> inherited superstitions were exchanged
> waiting for midnight and the haunting
> lament of La Llorona—the weeping lady
> of our myth and folklore—who wept nightly,
> along the banks of Boggy Creek. . .[8]

In a very brief article published in *Mester* in 1973, Gustavo Segade says, "Chicano literature, then, refers to the historical, cultural, and mythical dialectic of the Chicano people. In its historical and cultural sense, Chicano literature is specific and unique; in its mythical sense, it is general and universal."[9] And Bruce-Novoa, with his original and challenging theory about the spatial nature of Chicano literature, has presented us with a significant definition worthy of consideration.

We can see then that in a relatively short time, Chicano literature has not only established itself as a significant part of minority literatures in the United States, and, at the same time, of literature in general, but has produced a criticism that has kept up with the rapid change taking place. In a few years, the identification of Chicano literature has progressed from the narrow, sociological definition to the broad, humanistic, and universal approach. Chicano literature by lifting the regional to a universal level has emerged from the barrio to take its place alongside the literatures of the world.

UNIVERSITY OF CALIFORNIA AT LOS ANGELES

Luis Leal

Notes

[1]See Gerald Haslam, "The Enigma of Amado Jesús Muro," *Western American Literature,* X (1975), pp. 3-9.

[2]Edward Simmen, ed., *The Chicano: From Caricature to Self-Portrait* (New York: New American Library, 1971), p. xiii.

[3]Edward Simmen, ed., *Pain and Promise: The Chicano Today* (New York: New American Library, 1972), pp. 55-56.

[4]For Luis Valdez, "being a Chicano means the utilization of one's total potentialities in the liberation of our people." But he adds: "In another sense, it means that Indio mysticism is merging with modern technology to create un hombre nuevo. A new man." Luis Valdez and Stan Steiner, eds., *Aztlán: An Anthology of Mexican American Literature* (New York: Alfred A. Knopf, 1972), p. xxx.

[5]See Teresa McKenna, "Three Novels: An Analysis," *Aztlán,* I, 2 (Fall, 1970), p. 55. ("Regrettably, *Tatoo the Wicked Cross* cannot be classified purely as a Chicano novel. The protagonist of the novel is not a Chicano but apparently someone who happens to have a possibly Spanish name [Aaron D'Aragon]. This ambiguity deserves exploration. Undeniably, the experience is one that many Chicanos have endured but the portrayal of this experience is not uniquely from the perspective of a Chicano.")

[6]Carlos Fuentes, *La nueva novela hispanoamericana* (México: Joaquín Mortiz, 1969), p. 14.

[7]Rodolfo Gonzales, *I Am Joaquín/ Yo soy Joaquín* (Toronto, New York, London: Bantam Pathfinder Editions, 1972), p. 1.

[8]Valdez and Steiner, *Aztlán...*pp. 341-42.

MEXICAN-AMERICAN LITERATURE:
TOWARD AN IDENTIFICATION

Rolando Hinojosa

Luis Leal wrote recently that Mexican-American literature is being written, published, and appraised at a rate which is truly phenomenal. As evidence of this fact there are already such established journals as *El Grito* and *Aztlán*, as well as the newer *Revista Chicano-Riqueña,* a Chicano-Puerto Rican effort published at Indiana University. Periodicals such as *Magazín, Con Safos* and *Regeneración* have been started, but their publication has been somewhat sporadic. The Modern Language Association of America included a workshop on Chicano literature at its convention in 1970; the Midwest MLA followed this by accepting a paper on Chicano literature for its 1971 session; and, in its December meeting of the same year, the American Association of Teachers of Spanish and Portuguese dedicated an entire section of its program to an examination of Mexican-American literature. In August 1973, in Mexico City, the program of AATSP included Mexican-American literature in its list of workshops and conferences held there for the year 1973. MLA followed this with a three-hour seminar on Chicano and other minority literatures, with Leslie Fiedler and Tomás Rivera as two of the participants. Other regional and national symposia which have dealt exclusively with Chicano literature and Chicano writers in the last twelve months include the Festival de Flor y Canto at the University of Southern California, the Chicano Short Story Symposium at Indiana University and the semester-long Brown Bag Seminar at the University of Texas at Austin. These publications, investigations, and symposia, together with a general increase of interest in Mexican-American literature, have given true meaning to what Philip D. Ortego has called a "Chicano Renaissance."

Serious professionals have naturally posed the questions: When does Mexican-American literature begin and to what area of literature does it belong? As yet, this two-part question has not been fully or widely answered, and so it may be helpful to look to history and language for the answers. Mexican-American literature may be considered a part of American literature; however, because it is sometimes written in Spanish, some may wish to categorize it as Mexican literature. The bilingual aspect that makes Chicano literature unique also makes it difficult to fit into this or that slot of the curriculum. The Chicano forms part of that American society which sometimes accepts and sometimes rejects him; this societal attitude is not so different from that of Mexico, which in times past has accepted and at times rejected the Mexican-American. Chicano literature has its roots in Mexican literature and in the Spanish language, but Chicanos are American citizens, educated for the most part in American schools and in the English language. The dual-language aspect of Chicano literature is, then, the first problem which must be faced by critics who wish to study this literature. These problems notwithstanding, however, first-rate criticism of Chicano literature does exist in both English and Spanish, as in the work of such specialists as Charles Tatum, Américo Paredes, and Arturo Madrid, among others. It is hoped that in time the ranks of critics may be swelled by other Chicano specialists who will be able to comment upon this dual phenomenon from a common ground based on a knowledge of both languages and to explain and evaluate Chicano literature from the Chicano perspective. This literature, like any other, needs critical insight and review and not merely cries of astonishment and surprise or only plaudits for its efforts.

There is no immediate nor—what is less likely—definitive answer as to where this literature properly belongs; this difficulty brings to mind the uncertain status of the Chicano or Mexican-American writer himself. Chicano literature, as an externalization of the will, has its roots in Mexican literature, and Mexican-American writers have their roots in Mexico as well—some deep, others superficial, but all sharing this same fundamental base. Roots, however, are not to be confused with the trunk of the tree itself or with the branches that spring from it. For, despite the Mexican influence, the Mexican-American writer lives in and is directly influenced by his life in the United States. To date, the one prevalent theme in Mexican-American writing is the Chicano's life in his native land, the United States.

Recently, Edward Simmen, the compiler and editor of *The Chicanos: From Caricature to Self-Portrait*, went on record as stating that Mexican-American literature did not come into existence until 1947. Simmen developed a social theory which asserts that the very structure of Chicano society did not permit the emergence of Chicano writing prior to that date, maintaining that the rich, educated minority of Chicanos was not interested in writing, that the poor were not trained for it and that the middle class was not inclined to such activity. These are stock characterizations and should be appreciated in that light. Any number of bibliographies on Chicano literature, however, such as those by Guillermo Rojas, Octavio V. Romano, Herminio Ríos, Lupe Castillo, and Joseph A. Clark Moreno disprove the 1947 thesis. This theory goes on to say that the Chicano is an American of Mexican descent and an individual of liberal or radical ideas in regard to the social and economic order whose actions are often violent. From this he concludes that the social and economic movement called "el movimiento" explains the recent origin of Chicano literature. I would counter this conclusion simply by referring to the previously mentioned bibliographies and to the very recent work by Frank Pino entitled *Mexican Americans: A Research Bibliography,* published in September 1974 in two 700-page volumes by the Latin American Center of Michigan State University.

Herminio Ríos, the literary editor of Quinto Sol Publications, identifies Mexican-American or Chicano literature as that written by Spanish-speaking inhabitants of the Southwest since 1848. I myself find the Southwest tag restrictive. Ríos's assertion stems from publications of poems, essays, articles and songs written and published in English and Spanish in the United States by Spanish-speaking American citizens from 1848 to the present. Luis Dávila, who has been chiefly responsible for the founding of the *Revista Chicano-Riqueña,* states that Chicano literature is that which is written by Americans of Mexican descent "regardless of what they might prefer to call themselves." Dávila does not restrict himself geographically nor does he set a specific date such as 1947 or 1848; but he does say, however, that this literature is of recent origin. In one of his articles he cites examples of the literary review, *El Amigo del Hogar*, which was published in Indiana Harbor, Indiana, between the years of 1924 and 1930. This review, incidentally, was the principal organ of information for the Mexican community in East Chicago. It is an established fact that Chicano literature in other parts of the United States goes back far-

Rolando Hinojosa

ther than 1924; for in 1911-12 the Lozano family of San Antonio founded and published *La Prensa*, a Spanish daily sent by rail to subscribers all over Texas. I myself sold this newspaper and some of its literary publications for some four or five years when I was growing up in the Rio Grande Valley of Texas. The publication lasted half a century and helped keep alive the Hispanic literary tradition in that part of the United States.

All this brings us to the matter of terminology and dates: the dates are worrisome, but suffice it to say for now that there is a long literary tradition behind what is being produced today. On the matter of terminology, "Chicano" and "Mexican-American" appear to be synonymous; one is neither more nor less militant than the other. *El Grito*, the Quinto Sol journal, is a stout defender of *chicanismo*; and it must be pointed out that this journal, founded by Chicanos, has the subtitle "A Journal of Contemporary Mexican American Thought." With the points of time and terminology at least touched upon—although I by no means claim to have the last word on the subject—let us turn our attention to the current movements in Chicano literature, beginning with the novel and going on to the theatre, the essay, poetry, the short story and returning, finally, to the novel.

The question of language as it pertains to this literature is worth noting for its important relationship to commercial considerations in marketing works for distribution to a wide audience, as envisioned by American publishers. Since these publishers have never been and still are not eminently disposed toward publishing a novel in Spanish or in any language other than English (with few notable exceptions), the Chicano writer has been forced to write in English. This is an unfortunate circumstance. The American publishing industry itself may be predisposed toward a stereotyped view of the Mexican-American as a result of the models propagated by O. Henry, Mark Twain, Bret Harte and others. Worse still, the work of a Mexican-American author often is subjected to certain excisions or revisions to conform to standards of salability. The first example that comes to mind is Richard Vásquez's *Chicano* (1970), which, to a considerable degree, has served as a misleading sociological interpretation of the Chicano whether he lives in California, Illinois or Texas. I seriously doubt that this was Vásquez's intent. I suspect, rather, that Vásquez's work may have undergone some depressingly insensitive editing. The novel's moderate success was due in part to the new market, and perhaps even more to the publishing house's ample advertising budget. Of prime consideration, of course, was the fact that Váquez wrote in

English. An earlier book, *Pocho* (1959) by José Antonio Villarreal, also in English, met with indifferent success until Doubleday reissued it recently in light of the recent wave of interest in Chicanos, primarily in the fields of history and sociology. An interesting and innovative novel with some universal appeal is Raimond Barrio's *The Plum, Plum Pickers* (1969), which may be more truly representative of the Chicano experience despite its restrictive agricultural setting. Barrio's literary sin is his lack of discipline in the presentation of argument and plot, and thus it is the Anglo who comes off as a stereotyped villain.

The dearth of Mexican-American publishers is another problem with which Chicano writers have had to contend, particularly if they wished to write in Spanish and generally if they wished to write of the Chicano experience in the United States for a predominantly Anglo audience. The problem again is twofold: which language is to be used and in which direction is the novel to go? That is, what should be the main thrust of the novel? Is it to be propagandistic, engagé, or strictly intramural (within the walls of the Chicano mind)? Is it to be exploratory within the writer's own narrow first-person concept? Should it be explanatory and didactic in order to teach others about Chicano life in the United States? And, always, is it to be commercial? The last question cannot be taken lightly, for in the eyes of editors and publishers, be they Mexican-American or not, it is too important to ignore.

One of the answers to this last question is obvious enough: with the advent of the interest fomented by Chicano assertiveness and by the establishment of Ethnic Studies departments, Chicano study centers and other similar programs, we have seen a rash of anthologies by such publishers as Harper & Row, Holt, and Houghton Mifflin dealing with Chicano literature. Since almost all are in English, I would suspect that their publication is in virtually every case attributable to financial prospects and considerations. Part of the proof lies in the books themselves. The selections for many of these anthologies are extremely poor in content, in style and in treatment of subject matter. In addition, the authors at times are not Chicanos but Mexican nationals or, in some cases, Anglo-Americans. The idea seems to be that once the words "Mexican-American" or "Chicano" are included in the title the race is on. One such unhappy choice is the novel *Viva Chicano* by Frank Bonham. Another is the anthology, *Mexican American Authors*, compiled by two Mexican-American educators who seem to have gone out of their way to produce a deadly book for

Houghton Mifflin. To date, the novel and the short story, in anthology form and in English, are the two principal genres that have interested American publishers. Chicanos who wished to bring out works in Spanish usually have had to arrange for private publication or seek out the few Chicano publishing houses in existence in this country.

For Chicano playwrights, who are naturally more interested in seeing their work come to life on a stage rather than in print, the situation is different. Chicano theatre not only received its first impetus from university and community groups but enjoys their continued support as well. Chicano theatre is actually a group of touring companies such as the *teatro campesino*, and thus it is theatre in the true sense: it appeals to the people; it must be seen and heard for effect; and it does not lend itself to quiet, reflective, personal reading. It is experimental, ironic, and sarcastic, and because of these restrictive tendencies it also leans toward didacticism. The *teatro campesino* pieces are presented in both Spanish and English and at times abound in Chicano locutions with appeal only to a limited audience. The prime mover behind all this activity is Luis Valdez, who lives and works in California; it is to his credit that Chicano playwrights have a narrow but active outlet for their work.

The Chicano essay, on the other hand, is almost always written in English, and there is no mistaking its thrust: it seeks at once to destroy the negative stereotypes of Mexican-American history and culture and to present the historical and the intellectual aspects of the Mexican-American which in some respects have led to the abovementioned renaissance in Chicano letters. The articles are sturdy, well-documented, and highly scholarly in their approach and concept. To date, some of the best essays by Mexican-Americans on Mexican-Americans are found in *Aztlán,* the journal published at UCLA, and in a volume entitled *Voices* (a new edition was issued in July 1973), published by Quinto Sol of Berkeley, California. These essays treat the modern state, anthropology, sociology, penal reform, historical myths, and matters pertaining to the Chicano and to his socioeconomic and educational position in the United States vis-à-vis misinformation and generalizations concerning Chicanos which have been passed from generation to generation throughout the country and even in some of our universities. It is not difficult to see that a number of these essayists received their university training in sociology, psychology, history, and other areas of the humanities. In view of this, responsible people should recognize the falseness of the claim that there are no trained professionals to investigate the Chicano citizenry from a Chicano perspective. On the other hand, Chicano fiction writers, like any other writers, may need no university training, although at the present time many of them have had most of their training in both Old World and New World literature—for the most part in graduate studies.

Chicano poetry is a free-wheeling genre. Some Mexican-American writers express themselves strictly in Spanish, others strictly in English, and still others in Spanish and English in the same poem, in the same verse, within a single thought. From the earliest published evidence, dating back to the 1840s, poetry has dominated the Chicano literary scene. This may be due in large measure to considerations of space. This particular genre, above all, can best illustrate a people's sensibility, and it can do so in a compressed form—in what John Donne once called "the force of few words." If there is a source from which the Chicano Renaissance directly springs, it is the poetic form. Three very brief selections from three Mexican-American poets will illustrate the type of work being done in this area. The first is taken from Corky Gonzales's *I am Joaquín,* a Chicano epic poem in English, later translated into Spanish and published in a bilingual edition in 1967. In it, Gonzales speaks of *La Raza* and writes that it has survived

> in the barrios of the city,
> in the suburbs of bigotry,
> in the mines of social snobbery,
> in the prisons of dejection,
> in the muck of exploitation
> and
> in the fierce heat of racial hatred.

The second example comes from Abelardo Delgado, and he too writes in English. These lines come from the *Chicano Manifesto* (1970):

> . . .there is one thing I wish
> you would do for us,
> in all your dealings with us,
> in all your institutions
> that affect our lives
> deal with us as you openly claim you can,
> justly. . .with love. . .with dignity.
> correct your own abuses on *la raza*
> for your own sake not for ours
> so you can have some peace of mind. . .

The third selection, by Alurista, is poetically bilingual in the sense

Rolando Hinojosa

that the combination of the two languages produces a startling and moving artistic effect, as in this passage from *El espejo / The Mirror*:

> Mis ojos hinchados
>   flooded with lágrimas
> de bronce
>   melting on the cheek bones
> of my concern
>   razgos indígenas
> the scars of history on my face
>   and the veins of my body
> that ache
>   vomito sangre
> y lloro libertad
>   I do not ask for freedom
> I am freedom.

Another bilingual work, *Perros y antiperros*, a recent Chicano epic poem by Sergio Elizondo, offers a wide-ranging set of experiences describing the travels of a young Mexican-American, whose encounters take him from the Rio Grande Valley to El Paso to California and elsewhere. In contrast to Corky Gonzales's strident outcry which spans the entire 400 years of Chicano history, *Perros y antiperros* recalls a more recent past as the poet wanders through the Chicano Southwest.

Second to poetry in abundance of literary output is the short story. Because of the recent publication of anthologies by American firms, Chicano prose is being more widely distributed than ever before. The short story is being written in English, in Spanish, sometimes in the Pachuco dialect, and occasionally even in bilingual form. Chicano short stories are varied in setting, thus forcing a disclaimer from those who have held that the agricultural motif is the only vein explored by this literary movement. The settings of these stories range from big city streets and rural communities to military life, educational institutions, and prison—in brief, wherever the Chicano experience has been felt and lived. The genre makes use of realistic language and dialogue perhaps better and to a greater extent than any other area of Chicano literature. The scenes of everyday life with their small, accidental joys, disappointments, and restraints are brought to life artistically through the varied use of the two languages by the characters and in the narrative itself. The Chicano perspective allows the reader a more faithful interpretation of background and setting, and the Mexican-American writer, by avoiding stereotypes, produces an effect that is both compelling and exciting in its presentation. One such Chicano short story is my own "Por esas cosas que pasan," which appeared originally in *El Grito* and later was included in the bilingual anthology *El Espejo/The Mirror.* (This anthology was published by Quinto Sol, to date the best channel for Chicano creativity in the visual and literary arts.) The original version of "Por estas cosas que pasan," as it appears in *El Grito*, begins with a fictional newspaper account in English of an unfortunate incident in a barroom. This is followed by a monologue in Spanish by the main character and then a taped interview with another character. There are, in addition, a letter from a defense attorney in Spanish and, finally, a deposition in English given by a Mexican-American some 28 to 29 years old and with a fifth-grade education. The story ends with another newspaper account in English. The work reaches its peak in the deposition, which I include here in full.

A DEPOSITION FREELY GIVEN

on this seventeenth day of March, 1970, by Mr. Gilberto Castañeda in room 218 of the Belken County Court House was duly taken, witnessed, and signed by Miss Helen Chacón, a legal interpreter and acting assistant deputy recorder for said County, as part of a criminal investigation assigned to Robert A. Chapman, assistant district attorney for the same County.

It is understood that Mr. Casteñeda is acting solely as a deponent and is not a party to any civil or criminal investigation, proceeding, or violation which may be alluded to in this deposition.

"Well, my name is Gilberto Casteñeda and I live at 169 South Hidalgo Street here in Klail. It is not my house; it belong to my mother-in-law, but I have live there since I marry Marta (Marta Cordero Casteñeda, 28, 169 South Hidalgo Street, Klail City) about three years ago.

I am working at the Royce-Fedders tomato packing shed as a grader. My brother-in-law, Balde Cordero, work there too. He pack tomatoes and don't get pay for the hour, he get pay for what he pack and since I am a grader I make sure he get the same class tomato and that way he pack faster; he just get a tomato with the right hand and he wrap it with the left. He pack a lug of tomatoes so fast you don't see it and he does it fast because I am a good grader.

Balde is a good man. His father, don Albino, my father-in-law who die up in Saginaw, Michigan when Marta and I, you know, go together. . .well, Balde is like don Albino, you understand? A good man. A right man. Me, I stay an orphan and when the Mejías take me when my father and mother die in that train wreck—near Flora, don Albino tell the Mejías I must go to the school. I go to First Ward Elementary where Mr. Gold is principal. In First Ward I am a friend of Balde and there I meet Marta too. Later, when I grow up I don't visit the house too much because of Marta, you know what I mean? Anyway,

Rolando Hinojosa

Balde is my friend and I have know him very well. . .maybe more than nobody else. He's a good man.

Well, last night Balde and I took a few beers in some of the places near where we live. We drink a couple here and a couple there, you know, and we save the *Aquí me quedo* on South Missouri for last. It is there that I tell Balde a joke about the drunk guy who is going to his house and he hear the clock in the corner make two sounds. You know that one? Well, this drunk guy he hear the clock go bong-bong and he say that the clock is wrong for it give one o'clock two time. Well, Balde think that is funny. . .Anyway, when I tell the joke in Spanish it's better. Well, there we are drinking a beer when Ernesto Tamez comes. Ernesto Tamez is like a woman, you know? Everytime he get in trouble he call his family to help him. . .that is the way it is with him. Well, that night he bother Balde again. More than one time Balde has stop me when Tamez begin to insult. That Balde is a man of patience. This time Ernesto bring a *vieja* (woman) and Balde don't say nothing, nothing, nothing. What happen is that things get spooky, you know. Ernesto talking and *burlándose de él* (ridiculing him) and at the same time he have the poor woman by the arm. And then something happen. I don't know what happen, but *something* happen and fast.

I don't know. I really don't know. It all happen so fast—the knife, the blood squirt all over my face and arms, the woman try to get away, a loud really loud scream, not a *grito* (local Mexican yell) but more a woman screaming, you know what I mean? and then Ernesto fall on the cement.

Right there I look at Balde and his face is like a mask in asleep, you understand? No angry, no surprise, nothing. In his left hand he have the knife and he shake his head like he say "yes" and then he take a deep breath before he walk to the door. Look, it happen so fast no one move for a while. Then Balde come in and go out of the place and when don Manuel (constable for precinct No. 21) come in, Balde just hand over the knife. Lucas Barrón, you know, el Chorreao (a nickname), well, he wash the blood and sweep the floor before don Manuel get there. Don Manuel just shake his head and tell Balde to go to the car and wait. Don Manuel he walk to the back to see Ernesto and on the way out one of the women, I think it is *la güera Balín* (Amelia Cortez, 23, no known address, this city), try to make a joke but don Manuel he say "no estés chingando" (shut the hell up, or words to that effect) and after that don Manuel go about his own business. Me, I go to the door but all I see is Balde looking at a house across the street and he don't even know I come to say good-bye. Anyway, this morning a little boy of Don Manuel say for me to come here and here I am."

Further deponent sayeth not.

Sworn to before me, this

17th day of March, 1970

Mexican-American Literature

/s/ *Helen Chacón*   /s/ *Gilberto Castañeda*

Helen Chacón   Gilberto Castañeda
Acting Asst. Deputy Recorder
Belken County

It is the novel form, however, that deserves special mention. Among the most recent Chicano novels is *Bless Me, Ultima* by Rudolfo Anaya (1971), winner of the 1972 Quinto Sol Award for Literature. Anaya's work takes place in New Mexico and treats the maturation of a young Chicano whose love for the desert and the mountains of his native state is the justification for the narrative's inclusion of tales of witchcraft and superstition. This is not magical realism but it is something similar. Anaya's direct style bears a resemblance to that of the contemporary American novel, but his treatment of his characters and their background—the mixture of fantasy and realism—is strictly Mexican-American: Chicanos are not simple, fun-loving, tradition-bound, lovable non-achievers or other mythical stereotypes such as those produced by John Steinbeck, but, rather, complex individuals like those found in any society. Tomás Rivera's *. . .y no se lo tragó la tierra (And the Earth Did Not Part)* is a 12-part work which presents a number of characters against a background of small Texas towns and migrant labor camps. There is no one central character save perhaps the young narrator who appears intermittently to join the various fragments comprising the novel. The final and longest chapter is a re-narration and a re-creation of the preceding events told in linear style. Rivera's work, written in Spanish with an English translation appended, and Anaya's novel, in English with relatively few Spanish expressions, represent two of the most recent forms of the Chicano novel and also have the distinction of being published by a Mexican-American press.

There are other novels as well, such as those by John Rechy, who identifies himself as a Chicano but who does not restrict himself to Chicano subjects. Another interesting book, *Las desventuras de un chicano*, is a strange work which points up the vulnerability of Chicano literature. It was published in Mexico and written by someone who calls himself Rogelio Leonardo Carpintero, which translates as Roger Leonard Carpenter. I have little proof to offer as yet, but as I read the book, it seemed to me to be the work of an Anglo with a university background in Spanish. It tells of the Chicano narrator's *desventuras* (misfortunes), as he labels them, and affects the sixteenth- and seventeenth-century picaresque style, which can be cumbersome.

17

Rolando Hinojosa

The novel is filled with example after example of the Chicano's misfortune in the United States, all unrelieved by dreams, accomplishments, humor, or inspiration and unresolved by any truly deep-seated tragedy centering on one event or on any one series of events that might serve as an aid to plot and to character development. It is a naive work, and for all its anti-war sentiment, it isn't especially "Chicano"; for this people are as divided on this issue as on any other, save one: we are what we are, and we don't need outside help in identifying ourselves. One further novel of particular interest, published in the Spring of 1974, is *Peregrinos de Aztlán* by Miguel Méndez of Tucson, Arizona. Méndez weaves a tapestry of the Spanish Southwest and the Mexican desert of Sonora, merging both with the Chicano's life in the United States as a background for the development of a tale of diverse themes and directions—poverty and suffering, ignominy and irony—in an attack on those Anglos and Chicanos who, in Méndez's view, lack a social conscience.

All genres, then, take off in different directions toward the same ultimate objective: a presentation of a heterogeneous people who form yet another distinct part of the United States. The year 1848 is a political starting point, as Luis Leal has pointed out, for prior to that date, Mexican-Americans did not exist in a legal sense—instead they were Mexicans or Texans or Americans. But let no one attach a magical power to the year 1848; the literary tradition was already there before that date.

UNIVERSITY OF MINNESOTA, MINNEAPOLIS

CHICANO LITERATURE:
FIESTA OF THE LIVING

Tomás Rivera

> Every poem we read is a recreation,
> that is, a ceremonial ritual, a fiesta.
> Octavio Paz, *The Labyrinth of Solitude*

I have been involved with Chicano literature for over six years. I have lived with its roots all my life, a life that for the most part has known no literature to represent it. For me the literary experience is one of total communion, an awesome awareness of the "other,"[1] of one's potential self. I have come to recognize my "other" in Chicano literature, but by this I do not mean to say that I find or reflect or faithfully render the Chicano experience. As a matter of fact, I would hope that what I write goes further. To claim that my own writing is representative of the Chicano experience is not my intention. Rather, I should like to focus on Chicano writing as a ritual of immortality, of awe in the face of the "other"—a ritual of the living, in a sense, a fiesta of the living.

To write is a total experience, like life itself. It is an original experience, like that of the complete and splendid act of sexual union, of birth, of death, of the joy one has in loving mankind, because of the feelings involved—compassion and brotherhood. Chicano writers are no different from other men who enter this total experience. I have known and have come to feel a bond with many of them: the majority I have met in person, and the others I have come to know through their works. I have felt their humanity. None has deceived me. I have found them to be truthful, ritualistic, in love with the "other" which each of them has found. Why do I feel this bond? Because I expect to do so? Or is it because they write of what I know? Not what I have learned, but what I know. Still, I have felt this same bond with other writers, although, I must confess, not as strongly and completely. I think we must return to the direct experience of life and our need for ritual. When I began my formal education and learned to read, I saw man manifested in so many words and with such evocative imagery that I came to expect that miracles, heroics, love and all human experience could be contained in words. I have found this to be the case in Walt Whitman, Hemingway, Shakespeare, Azuela, Cela, in Sábato, Machado, Guillén, Lorca. Even in the worst writings I have found an exact, pure desire to transform what is isolated in the mind into an external form. To perceive what people have done through this process and to come to realize that one's own family group or clan is not represented in literature is a serious and saddening realization. At twelve, I looked for books by my people, by my immediate people, and found very few. Very few accounts in fact existed. When I met Bartolo, our town's itinerant poet, and when on a visit to the Mexican side of the border, I also heard of him—for he would wander on both sides of the border to sell his poetry—I was engulfed with *alegría*. It was an exaltation brought on by the sudden sensation that my own life had relationships, that my own family had relationships, that the people I lived with had connections beyond those at the conscious level. It was Bartolo's poetry—or was it simply those papers that looked like his poetry—that gave me this awareness. I have previously mentioned his preoccupation with words, with their sound and with their relationship to communication in *". . .y no se lo tragó la tierra"*:

> Bartolo always came through town around December, when he felt that most of the people had returned from work in other states. He always sold his poems. They were almost completely sold out by the end of the first day because they mentioned the names of people in town. And when he read the poems out loud, it was a serious and emotional experience. I remember once he told the people to read his poems out loud because the voice was the love seed in the dark.[2]

Bartolo's poetry was my first contact with literature by my own people. It was to be my only contact for a long time. The bond that I felt with him and that I feel with other Chicano writers is the same. It is not pure nationality, Mexican, Chicano, Pocho, or otherwise; it is not because we take part in the same struggle against the same injustices; it is not because we come from the same environment or social class, although all these do manifest a *vigencia* of sorts. Is it not, rather, that we sense that we are part of the same ritual? Perhaps this is the case: a bond that comes from a feeling of uniqueness, from a common set of beliefs, from a sense of destiny. Yes, we sense a prophecy, and we sense a fulfillment of this prophecy. We have been alive since time began. We are not just living; we have been living for centuries. We must ritualize our existence through words. To me there is no greater joy than reading a creative work by a Chicano. I like to see my students come to feel this bond and to savor moments of immortality, of the total experience.

Yet, what is this bond? What brings it about? Is it just a sense of awareness? The creative act itself? Its product? One has to go beyond prophecy and ritual and seek the nature of this bond in the act of remembering. Remembering, because the past is what we have and it is all that we have. It is from the past that we are able to perceive, create and give life to our ritual; it is from this that we derive strength, that we can recognize our existence as human beings. I think we also come to the realization that life is perhaps not simply a relationship between the world, ourselves, and others, but, in addition, the discovery and recollection of the relationship of all these things. All societies have rituals of remembering. The Chicano is no different. The folklore traditions are based on remembering, retelling, and reliving.

La literatura chicana es un esfuerzo en darle forma, armonía y unidad a la vida Chicana porque se manifiesta ésta como vida que vale mientras esté sobre la tierra. Y así florecen el arte Chicano, la literatura Chicana, el drama—en fin se inventa y se futuriza el Chicano como un ser humanamente total. Esto es de gran importancia para el suroeste ya que es inconcebible la humanización de esta región sin la actuación propia de este segmento de la población de esta región. Pero, ¿por cuáles procesos se lleva a cabo la invención y la futurización?

En mi obra, . . .*tierra,* hice hincapié en los procesos del recuerdo, del descubrimiento y de la voluntad. Primeramente esto del recuerdo. Me refiero al método de narrar que usaba la gente. Es decir, recuerdo lo que ellos recordaban y la manera en que narraban. Siempre existía una manera de comprimir y exaltar una sensibilidad con mínimas palabras. También, existía constantemente el inventarle nuevas ocurrencias. Esto, claro está, es lo que elabora la tradición oral. Aunque muchos de aquellos padres que andaban en los trabajos eran analfabetos, el sistema narrativo predominaba. Siempre había alguien que sabía los cuentos viejos—del gigante moro, del negrito güerín, etc. Luego, había siempre aquellas personas que interpretaban películas, que narraban sobre partes distintas del mundo, y siempre los cuentos de Aladín y su lámpara maravillosa. De esta manera, en los campos migratorios, se desarrolló una literatura oral. La gente buscaba refugio no solamente en la iglesia, o con sus hermanos, sino también al

Tomás Rivera

sentarse en ruedo y escuchar y narrar y por medio de palabras escaparse a otros mundos, e inventarse también. Desde luego en los niños se desarrolló también una especie de mundo narrativo y en el tedio trabajo de cada día se cristalizaron mundos.

Las narraciones orales se formulaban también sobre México, o sobre las costumbres, sobre la revolución de 1910. También desde luego, se formulaban sobre lo fantasmagórico—los espantos, las ánimas, la llorona, el diablo, Juan sin miedo, las apariciones de mujeres con caras de caballo, los tesoros escondidos y las llamas que los anunciaban o las ánimas que los protegían. El pasado y el futuro se concretaban no como intrahistoria que se conoce casi siempre por medio del estudio sino como intrasensibilidad que se conoce por medio de la sensibilidad creada e imaginada. El recuerdo cada vez untado de imaginación fue capaz de proyectar esta intrasensibilidad.

Al recordar y al contar, el elemento imaginativo y la sensibilidad se elaboraron, se prepararon y se inventaron. Así, fue esto no solamente intrasensibilidad sino intrainventividad. Esta capacidad se les pasó a los niños. La capacidad inventiva se volvió realidad y de esta manera se fertilizó para el descubrimiento. El recuerdo revela una vida, revela una imaginación, y así es aun una especie de incubación.[3]

What I should like to discuss here is the ritual of remembering as a basis for a living culture for the Chicano of today. Chicano literature has many currents and facets, and within its complexity are contained distinct strata and orientations. In my perception, what Chicano writers strive for most is the capturing of a fast-disappearing past—the conserving of past experiences, real or imagined, through articulation. But to me the past is now, as well. There exists in Chicano literature both an external and an internal preoccupation with the past. I might add that it is not mere nostalgia brought about through a disillusionment with what has happened, nor a disorientation within a value system, nor the exploding of the myth of a moral government; but, rather, it is a ritual from which to derive and maintain a sense of humanity—a ritual of cleansing and a prophecy.

As stated before, I have known and have come to feel a bond with most Chicano writers. The poets cited below are personal acquaintances of mine, and whenever I read from their works, I participate fully in their intentions. For me they evoke my people. One comes to realize that we must love those with whom we live, those with whom we share.

La casa, el barrio, and *la lucha* are constant elements in the ritual of Chicano literature. I shall start with *la casa* as one of three parts in this ritual. *La casa* is to me the most beautiful word in the Spanish language. It evokes the constant refuge, the constant father, the constant mother. It contains the father, the mother, and the child. It is also beautiful because it demonstrates the strong connection between an image in the mind and an external form. The following poems recall for me those constant presences and this connection. The first is by Alurista, the most prolific of Chicano poets and one who has manifested and captured the binary spirit of the Chicano experience in his bilingual poetry.

la casa de mi padre

la casa de mi padre
    la de las alcobas mil
my people will sleep
    cama de piedra
tierra mojada—our floor
    y palmas verdes—our roof
the cantos
    corridos y jaranas
    boleros
    baladas tristes
and the melancholia of our passion
    to announce our arrival
la hacienda
    y sus portones abiertos
open and waiting for La Raza
    to swell
    in space
to draw from
    and shape
    dimensions three
en la casa de mi padre[4]

Continuing with the constant theme of *la casa*, the following is a poem by Ricardo Sánchez, a poet from El Paso, Texas. He begins his poem with the word "recuerdo." It is a poem dedicated to his father.

Recuerdo. . .

recuerdo un viejo fuerte,
con hombros anchos, alma llena,
y palabras que iluminaban mi vida

y tal hombre era
padre mío,
fuerte y cariñoso
como lamento cantado/llorado
su consejo amoroso declamado. . .
hombre maduro y macho,
sin temor al mundo él vivía;
padre mío

puro hombre
un chicano orgulloso. . .
en aquellos tiempos. . .
cuando
los militantes presentes
eran aún conservadores.
él ya era protestador. . .

east el paso lo respetaba,
barelas albuquerque lo conoció
       él entonces era azote,
       chicano que no se cuarteaba,

era Pedro Lucero Sánchez
       su madre era Gurulé por apellido,
y él fue
casi padre del barrio del diablo en el paso;

era yonquero de los mejores,
       a nadie se le postraba,
su mundo lo admiraba. . .
       ese hombre fue mi padre

lo que hoy me puede, carnales,
es tristeza del corazón—
el día que lo enterraron
yo estaba hundido en prisión. . .[5]

"La jefita" by José Montoya is representative of the many poems written about the Chicano mother, *abnegada,* whose great warmth and strength have contributed to the solidarity of the family. In the following poem, the poet also remembers that one person who provided strength—la jefita, the dear one, the dear little mother.

La jefita

When I remember the campos
    Y las noches and the sounds
Of those nights en carpas o
Vagones I remember my jefita's
    Palote
    Clik-clok; clik-clak-clok
    Y su tocesita.

(I swear, she never slept!)

Reluctant awakenings a la media
Noche y la luz prendida.
    PRRRRRRINNNNGGGGGG!
A noisy chorro missing the
    Basín.

¿Qué horas son, 'ama?
Es tarde mi hijito. Cover up

Your little brothers.
Y yo con pena but too sleepy,
    Go to bed little mother!
A maternal reply mingled with
The hissing of hot planchas
Y los frijoles de la hoya
boiling musically dando segunda
a los ruidos nocturnos and
The snores of the old man
    Lulling sounds y los perros
Ladrando—then the familiar
Hallucinations just before sleep.
    And my jefita was no more.
But by then it was time to get Up!
My old man had a chiflidito
That irritated the world to
Wakefulness.
    Wheeeeeeet! Wheeeeeeet!
¡Arriba, cabrones chavalos,
Huevones!
    Y todavía la pinche
    Noche oscura
Y la jefita slapping tortillas.
    ¡Prieta! Help with the lonches!
    ¡Caliéntale agua a tu 'apa!
(¡Me la rayo ese! My jefita never slept!)
Y en el fil, pulling her cien
Libras de algoda se sonreía
Mi jefe y decía,
    That woman—she only complains
    in her sleep.[6]

Then we come to the third person contained within the concept of *la casa*—the child. The following poem by Alurista recalls the Chicano infant. Alurista also proclaims he will ensure that the child will smile in the sun.

chicano infante

envidio tu sonrisa
    rojos labios
    tiernos
envidio tu pelo
    sedosos mechones
    húmedos
envidio tu sudor
    beautiful child

Tomás Rivera

```
brown eyed sun
    on the pyramid of joy
    contemplating
    Chicano infante
    niño de ilusión
envidio tu pureza
    tu candor
    tu gloria
tú eres feliz
    y lo serás
serás feliz
    y nadie
            ningún humano
nunca
    no lo permitiré
i won't allow it
i will protest
    i will yell
and you will hear
    and you will know
que no me dejo
and that you
you that are
    and your happiness spills
you will continue
    in your purity
    in your candor
    in your bliss
    in your happiness
objeto de mi envidia
tú eres
y lo serás
i will see to that
—you will smile (in the sun)⁷
```

These poems are representative of the Chicano poet's intent not only
to remember an obligation but to recall the sources of strength, the
original elements from which he came and from which he can once
again regain that strength.

El barrio is another beautiful word that evokes a constant element in the lives of Chicanos. I have yet to know a Chicano who dislikes or who is not moved by Raúl Salinas's "a trip through the mind
jail," wherein the *barrio* is an important protagonist in giving, conserving, and cleansing the poet. Every Chicano poet I have read has
written a poem directly or indirectly conceived with *el barrio* in mind.
Perhaps to some literary critics this would be a *flaqueza*, but again
the Chicano writer is involved in a ritual that takes him back to primal

and basic elements of a specific people. Of the many poems dedicated to the *barrio*, I have chosen two: one from Alurista, "nuestro barrio," and one by Raúl Salinas, "Journey II."

nuestro barrio

nuestro barrio
    en las tardes de paredes grabadas
    los amores de pedro con virginia
    en las tardes
        barriendo
dust about
    swept away in the wind of our breath
el suspiro de dios por nuestras calles
    gravel side streets of solitude
    the mobs from the tracks are coming
en la tarde
    mientras don josé barre su acera
    mientras dios respira vientos secos
        en el barrio sopla la vejez de chon
    y la juventud de juan madura
en la tarde de polvo
    el recuerdo de mi abuelo
    —de las flores en su tumba
    dust
        polvosas flores
blowing free to powdered cruces[8]

Journey II

They're tearing down the old school
    wherein i studied as a child
        Our Lady of Guadalupe. . .
Parochial prison / Internment camp for
    underprivileged Mexican kids,
        soon to be pummeled by
merciless wrecking ball.
    What do i remember best?
    What childhood mem'ries
cling stubbornly to the brain
    like bubble-gum under a table?

    Saturday afternoon Confession:
(it was no sweat giving up the li'l tadpole sins,
    spittin' out the big bullfrogs was the hassle.)
        unlit & cramped confessional closet
with only shadowy profile of Padre José,
    ever ready to impose heavy
        Our Father / Hail Mary sentence.
Catechism: Doctrina classes after school
    First Holy Communion Day!
        (i ingest

one of many sacraments to come
    & speak to the galaxies)
    white suit/padrino Chris/a ride in
        Posey's pre-war '38 Buick
The twins: Boffo & me fantasize,
    grown up—slaying dragons—planting corn
      if they would marry us.
Climbing, zooming heavenward, up rickety
    stairs into chamber of horrors/haunted
        house of learning. . .viewed by un-
suspecting boyzngirlz as transylvanian
    castle of doom.
        "No, 'Minga, those weren't black
ghosts flying around on lofty 5th floor
    balustrade, just Sisters' penguin-like
      habits; hanging out to dry."
The unforgettable recital: tribute to John Phillip
    Sousa, in abandoned subterranean lunchroom.
        All dress'd up like cadets. I played the
triangle. Big deal! The seamstress goofed on
    my uniform. Each time triangle went. . .ting!
      . . .oversized trousers slipped down
another inch. Trusty blue/gray lunchbox:
    opened many a coin slot
      on schoolyard bullies' heads.

Singing "God Bless America": would you believe?
    Competing for the lead with my friend Fernando. . .
The one who, like Nash & cousin Albino, never
    returned that Saturday; from gathering palms
        for Palm Sunday. . .crushed beneath grinding
locomotive wheels.
    How unreal it all seems now.
        They MUST have gone to heaven;
how could any God deny them entrance?
    Such beautiful people. . .young plants
      who never lived to blossom.
With their deaths life lost all meaning.
    Fernando: my competitor in song—Albino: cohort
    in chasing girls—Nash: (good ol' thoughtful
        Nash)
never once forgot my birthday.
    How unfair. . .unkindly
      they were stripped from my being.
"if only good people go to heaven when they die,
    i done blew my chance of ever seeing them again."

        Strutting birdbreast stuck way out, smoking
WINGS cigarettes. Great big eyes for Juanita what's-
her-name. Treating demure Catholic young ladies

to unpaid-for Kress's 5 & 10¢ birthstone rings
inducing them to smoke. . .too soon busted!
Reprimanded.
Forced to kneel prostrate before giant crucifix and
Sister Hermaneda. Tender knuckles kissed by
wooden ruler. Sorry, wrong rumba.
Carlin's Place: our crowd o' rowdies jitterbugging
me watching
"You got to ac-cen-tuate the positive, e-li-mi-nate the
negative, don' mes with Mr. in-between."
Sounds: Mercer, Woody & The Duke
"Couldn't make it without you, don't get around
much anymore."

A thousand merry harlequins dance happily/
nostalgically inside my head.
The families whose sons n' daughters
became priests & nuns.
I wonder what percentage of us
turned nomadic children
of the streets?
AGNES MARIE: because you were who you were
i'd name a daughter after you, i still possess the
comic valentine you sent me. The one of a
gawky/gangly gal in bathing suit & water-wings, which
read: "Lissen punk, you be mine or i'm sunk!"
So many times i've seen you as i turned a corner/
crossed a street, in so many different cities, but—
unlike Dante—the you i saw was never really you.

The 1st hip priest encountered—Father Busch—
Father Green was also pretty much aware;
in that long ago, before the era of NOW clergymen:
BRIGANTI & GOERTZ.
"Polished Pebbles": worn-out operetta
year-in-year-out performance by seniors
at uptight Knights of Columbus Hall.
To this day i've yet to know
who penned that lame libretto of corn!

The sandpile in back of Joseph's Garage
the little pasture at the French Legation:
first experiments with sex conducted there.
Josie luring us to Confederate Cemetery for
advanced lessons. i chicken out and run. So,
wherever you may be J., i apologize.
i just wasn't ready.

Sister Armela:
i've got news for you;
Ivory Soap Don't Taste Worth a Damn!

Tomás Rivera

And all i ever said was DAMN!!!
   The busted water fountain which i didn't bust.
      Ask God, He'll tell you i didn't do it.
Snitchin' Teresa said i did.

   E-X-P-U-L-S-I-O-N!

      Retaliation/paintbrush in hand/no longer
dull abandoned lunchroom. Red paint on sickly-green walls.
   Me an' my rappie—Joe Giddy—decorate the dingy
      cellar and defy the Gods.

"CATCH ME IF YOU CAN, YOU'LL NEVER TAKE
   ME
   ALIVE."-signed Mr. X. . ."GOD IS DEAD AND
      BURIED
IN THIS DINER THAT NEVER FED ANYONE." "THE
EASTSIDE TERRORS STRIKE AGAIN."
      Yeah, i did it,
   you shoulda' never kicked me out, father.
i loved the school in my own way.
Even if it was mostly prayers, i still learned something.
   There's still a couple of guys
      i'm pretty tight with/communicate with: like
Ol' St. Jude Thaddeus, who's had Miz' Hill
   on her knees there 36 years;
      & St. Dismas, he's one of the fellows.
He *knew* what was happening!

There's more. . .much more. . .an infinite voyage
   on a route paved with invaluable gems
      to treasure forever.
When i was out last time, i visited the old school
   once again. It had changed some. A section of
      the old spook house facade was gone, a modern
cracker-box was in its place. i would have lingered
   to catch a few vibrations of that other world, but
      i was a sick poet that day. My only concern
was the 4 caps of medicine someone had left under
   a rock for me. i thought of going back the next day.

   A prior commitment with the courts of law
made this impossible.
   i won't be there for the razing,
      but i'll return when i'm an aged, wizened man.
When freedom doves are on the wing again,
   i must go back and savor long the taste
      of spirits from another era (long before
the fall of innocence), upon my famished heart.

   And if there is a parking lot
      erected on that sacred spot

> i'll blow it up with dynamite
>
> and think of everything
>   it meant to me. . .⁹

The third element, *la lucha*, is not only linked to but encompasses *la casa* and *el barrio*. *La lucha* is a struggle of cultures, dignified and undignified, a struggle of man and that which he creates, a struggle to tear away one's own masks and discover oneself. Most of all it is the struggle with exterior and interior inconsistencies that both repress and call forth powerful, centuries-old human frailties. This struggle, this will to continue, is also a constant element of Chicano literature. The difficulty is maintaining a human base through the struggle as one confronts other men and one's own "other."

The following are three poems by two Chicano poets, Alurista and Sergio Elizondo. The poems by Alurista, "must be the season of the witch" and "mis ojos hinchados," are freedom cries in the struggle between cultures and technology. The poem "My Tale" is from a Chicano epic poem, *Perros y Anti-Perros* by Elizondo, in which a Chicano in remembering unmasks himself and becomes the sum of his own circumstances.

My Tale

I move now
to Augusts of Great Wars
that tremble my breast
and dance my heart.
In a French stable
    a stone shack
    wine from dark bottles
I celebrated my freedom.
Shoulder patches their thing,
rifles,
bread

I sing my Chicano epic,
Chingueasumadre the world
and long live the
    so-called American democracy!
a hundred skirmishes I leaped in
    where the "cousins" couldn't,
against other wretched men
    who owed me nothing.
in faith,
new lustre upon my bronze,
I prattled in English.
I chowed down in gringo,

Lots of down, lots of up
plenty of money,
I rode cars:
The Miller band took me,
in trombones and saxophones
to the arms of the first
and I said: "Aquí chingo."
They paraded all to hell
        in New York.
I and my body, alone.

Awaiting burial.
They denied me that in Three Rivers Texas.
The olive and arrow Eagle
buried me sacred.
But I and my ancient spirit
roam the land of my fathers.

        Brother, hand me the lira,
you with the twelve-string.
I have no hymn of glory. . .
let's see what we make of this.
I.
A soldier I went,
A man I returned.

        Dark through my parents'
                wings of passion,
        darker through the sun
                of my labors,
        white through the eyes
                of the Virgin,
        hot like the red chile.

She.
Rocks in the curves of her walking
Sings when she speaks.
In her brown skin
the sun burned the honey,
and
in her eyes,
the warmth of bees
that hover in the roses.

Friend: I have everything.
From now on,
the grapes that await me
        in the fields
friends of my harmony,
with tender hands
I caress as sisters.

Adam and Eve
two in one
in all these years
    they call history,
I am an Israeli
    of my vineyards.
I have a knife
for the sunglassed fatman
who guards my back
while silently
I work,
and peek ever slyly
at my girl.

Grapes of love
    I feel you leave me;
today I prefer
    my valiant self
and will no more complain.
Goodbye, goodbye, boss fatman,
I got things to do,
Chicana my soul,
gringos in my pockets,
a car at my side
like the eagle when I pounce
Now! Chingueasumadre, friend!
On the walls of my barrio
in big letters,
I write
so my eyes can delight:
I live, I enjoy, I fuck,
I love,
I take,
and on the corners
a 'Juana joint.
They cannot reach me,
I fly
and even if it is
the badges with new guns,
I leave them behind
and tell them
you-know-what
while I paint myself CON SAFOS.[10]

      must be the season of the witch

      must be the season of the witch
          la bruja
          la llorona
      she lost her children

and she cries
en las barrancas of industry
    her children
devoured by computers
and the gears
must be the season of the witch
    i hear huesos crack
in pain
    y lloros
la bruja pangs
    sus hijos han olvidado
la magia de durango
    y la de moctezuma
    —el huiclamina
must be the season of the witch
la bruja llora
sus hijos sufren; sin ella[11]

mis ojos hinchados .

mis ojos hinchados
    flooded with lágrimas
de bronce
melting on the cheek bones
of my concern
    razgos indígenas
the scars of history on my face
    and the veins of my body
that aches
    vomita sangre
y lloro libertad
    i do not ask for freedom
i am freedom
    no one
not even yahweh
    and his thunder
can pronounce
    and on a stone
la ley del hombre esculpir
    no puede
mi libertad
and the round tables
    of ice cream
        hot dog
    meat ball lovers meet
to rap
    and rap
and i hunger
    y mi boca está seca

el agua cristalina
  y la verdad
  transparent
in a jarro
  is never poured
dust gathers on the shoulders
  of dignitaries
y de dignidad
  no saben nada
muertos en el polvo
  they bite the earth
and return
  to dust[12]

   The ritual, the fiesta of the living I have presented here as a personal account of Chicano literature, may not be accepted by Chicano writers or critics; yet to me the act of writing is a personal ritual, a constant means of establishing contact with humanity and with one's origins. The ritual is simple yet complex. The bond is there, the cleansing is there, both for the Chicano writer and for his reader. The effects of the ritual are produced through simple forms such as *la casa* and *el barrio* and by the transgressive and ingressive concept of *la lucha*. Chicano literature presently dwells to a great degree on the past, whatever the genre, and is a remembering of our common human origins through the three specific elements discussed above. I do not think that literature is necessarily better when it speaks about man in general. Rather, I believe literature to be at its best when dealing with a specific individual. I do not mean that Chicano literature should have a "regional" or "costumbrista" basis but rather a profound *indagación* beyond these attitudes. It should, by drawing upon cultural origins, provide a perception of the world, of people, of oneself in awe of one's own life and its perplexities, its complexities, and its beauty. At present, Chicano literature is specific for the most part, and more and more provides a profound, lasting focus upon a personal perception. It beckons one to the source.

   I am like a drunkard, I suffer, I cry
   I say and recall
   May I never perish, may I never die!

   Where there is no death, where one wins I go:
   May I never perish, may I never die![13]

UNIVERSITY OF TEXAS, SAN ANTONIO

Tomás Rivera

Notes

[1]"In awe of the 'other' " implies specific and general philosophical points of view. I make reference to becoming cognizant of the expansive and evolving thought, in our era, on this matter; the "other" in the bosom of reason itself, as the object of the sentimental and instinctive ego, as the moral activity of the ego, as found in the dialectics of the subjective spirit and the dialectics of nature, as an invention of the ego, as phenomenological reflection, et cetera. See Laín Entralgo's *Teoría y realidad del otro.*

[2]Tomás Rivera, . . . *y no se lo tragó la tierra.* Berkeley, Ca., Quinto Sol, 1971, p. 163.

[3]Tomás Rivera, "Recuerdo, descubrimiento & voluntad" (From a paper presented at a Symposium on "Tomás Rivera and Chicano Literature," Indiana University, Bloomington, 14-15 April 1972).

[4]Alurista, "La casa de mi padre," *Floricanto en Aztlán,* Los Angeles, Chicano Cultural Center, UCLA, 1971, p. 27.

[5]Ricardo Sánchez, "Recuerdo," *Canto y grito mi liberación,* El Paso, Tx., MICTLA, 1971, p. 63.

[6]José Montoya, "La jefita," *Aztlán, An Anthology of Mexican American Literature,* edited by S. Steiner and L. Valdez, New York, Knopf, 1972, pp. 266-68.

[7]Alurista, "Chicano infante," *Aztlán,* p. 56.

[8]Ibid., "Nuestro barrio," p. 87.

[9]Raúl Salinas, "Journey II," *Voices of Aztlán, Chicano Literature of Today,* edited by D. Harth and L. Baldwin, New York, Mentor Press, 1974, pp. 192-196.

[10]Sergio Elizondo, "My Tale," *El espejo/ The Mirror,* edited by H. Ríos and O. Romano, 2nd ed., Berkeley, Ca., Quinto Sol, 1972, pp. 221-25.

[11]Alurista,"Must Be the Season of the Witch," *Aztlán,* p. 26.

[12]Alurista, "Mis ojos hinchados," *El grito,* Vol. 2, no. 1, p. 3.

[13]"Brief Song from the Nahuatl," translated by Rafael Jesús Gonzales, *El grito,* vol. 5, no. 1 (Fall, 1971), p. 14.

CHICANO LITERATURE:
AN AMERICAN LITERATURE
IN TRANSITION

Rolando Hinojosa

To say to a woman that you love her is not nearly enough. You usually have to spend a lifetime showing, explaining, and backing the testimony with evidential proofs. This evening I have fifteen minutes to talk about Chicano literature. I doubt if I can prove anything in fifteen minutes. Fortunately for you, I am the first speaker and I promise not to speed past the allotted time limit.

It is, however, a night session, and, if you wish, we can talk things out afterward. In that way, we'll comply with at least two MLA requirements: we stick to the subject at hand, and we speak to the faithful.

I am to speak to you tonight about Chicano Literature and about its identification; since the spirit of Roshomon prevails when the words Chicano and identification are mentioned in the same breath, I find that I may be taking my life in my hands. To begin with, Chicano literature as written by writers and as explained by them to other writers is one thing; what the general critics may say is something else; and, what some Chicano critics say is something else again.

To begin with, it is hoped that the following statement will set some minds at ease: I will not, in any way, speak to Villarreal's *Pocho*, to Vásquez's *Chicano*, to Villaseñor's *Macho*, nor to any literary characters in search of their identity. One reason is that much of what has been said and written about characters seeking an identity is like God's peace in that it passeth all understanding. Another is that many critics are still not aware of the convention of disguising first novels as memoirs. Thus, the authors are usually mistaken for protagonists of the novels. One more thing, whenever yet another form of the novel is used, those who should know better cast about and call *Tierra* a series of small narratives or short stories, or refer to *Estampas* as a series of vignettes in some instances or as a new form of literature. Flattering as this may be, both works, really, are novels true to the etymological sense of the word *novella*. As you can see, the spirit of Roshomon will continue to prevail as long as the penchant for classification is encouraged. This, of course, may be one of our curses as academicians.

I don't suppose that anyone has made a list of what characterizes Chicano literature in the order, say, that lists have been drawn up for characteristics of the Spanish picaresque novels: the first person narrator; hunger as a driving force; the serving of many masters; moralistic and didactic in intention; and so on. As you well know, these are some of the aspects of the picaresque novel at given times and places. As you also know, some aspects changed greatly from *Guzmán de Alfarache* to *El Periquillo Sarniento*. The changes in the form depended on the writer and on his talent to make changes while keeping a semblance of the original form. Also, the lists drawn up differed depending on who compiled them. To add to this, the lists did not necessarily identify the literature as much as they set down a list of characteristics for a trend in one genre, and then the lists underwent additions and deletions as time went by. Such a list would serve to characterize the different genres in Chicano literature, although its total identity would be a different matter. This, as in everything, would have to depend on the passage of time. And yet, for the present, there are some aspects of the whole of Chicano literature which can be identified: it is a United States literature and it is, at times, monolingual, bilingual, and, again at times, it is one which is sprinkled with words or phrases in Nahuatl. The latter, to be sure, is not as common as the other two languages, specifically, English and Spanish as used in the United States.

Another aspect for identification is the writers themselves. The writers of Chicano literature are usually of Mexican descent, and, for the most part, born in the United States. Notable exceptions to this would have to be made in the cases of Sergio Elizondo, Miguel Méndez, Herminio Ríos, Octavio Romano, Silvio Villavicencio, and others.

I shall now return to the first telling aspect of this literature: its consistent bilingual Spanish-English usage. To be sure, bilingualism is not the unique property of Chicano literature in this country. Its bilingual consistency as the one United States literature written by and about people of Mexican descent in this country, however, should leave few doubts as to its identity.

The necessity of wording the preceding statement in such a manner is brought about by what follows: There are some Chicanos who do not wish to be described as Chicano writers or tagged with labels of any kind. That they are Chicanos and that they write about Chicanos is coincidental, they say. What they don't say is that they may consider the word *Chicano* an opprobrium. If this is the case, the chances are very good indeed that it is an opprobrium and thus harmful or disparaging to them in a very personal way.

What these writers mean, I think, is that some writers who belong to an identifiable minority such as Philip Roth and Saul Bellow or Bernard Malamud write about Jews and are not considered as Jewish writers but rather as American writers. They may have a point there.

Some people just do not appreciate being labelled. Pío Baroja comes to mind immediately since he forsook the Generation of '98 label that Azorín heaped on him. Another and more immediate writer is Cela, and we all know what he did to discourage the *tremendismo* label.

This doesn't take me away from one point I wish to make about language use, and I will quote Casey Stengel: "I always heard it couldn't be done, but sometimes it don't always work." For example, Robert Graves has lived most of his life on Spanish soil, but who can argue that he is not an English poet and writer? Orwell is another example: he wrote in Paris about Paris and about the Civil War while in Spain, but he is, undeniably, an English writer. Then there is the Joseph Conrad question. Conrad was Polish born and is included, as he should be, in the body of English literature. On the other hand, there's Issac Bashevis Singer who is also Polish born, who became an American citizen, who writes in Yiddish and is then translated into English. What is he? Well, he's an American and a Jewish writer and, according to some, more Jewish than Roth, Bellow, or Malamud, but you couldn't hold my hand to the fire on that one.

It's a strong case for using language as an identifier. I'll now mention Jerzy Kosinsky, also Polish born, but whose works I read in English, so I must assume that he is an American writer. It seems to me that I am beating a very dead horse here, and what I am really saying is that language usage as the criterion for determining an identity label for writers applies to some but not to all.

I suppose that this happens in other areas of creativity: Irving Berlin is a Jew who writes American songs; Menasha Skulnik was a Jew who was a Jewish actor, and so on. I wonder if painters and sculptors have as much to say on this as writers and critics do? I should hope that they would not be as garrulous as I have been.

My main point is against being too categorical and precise. This identity business should not be rigorously scientific, and thus one must allow for flexibility. Listen to this rigid statement: Chicano literature shall be that which is written in Spanish or in Spanish and English in the same work, and those Chicanos who write only in English will not form part of Chicano literature. This may be very well for the classifiers, but it won't work. It's no good. Where does that put Rudolfo Anaya who calls himself a Chicano, as he should, of course, and who writes novels in English with very few Spanish expressions? And, where does that leave a few hundred aspiring Chicano poets whose principal language is English because they neither speak nor read Spanish fluently and yet insist on calling themselves Chicano writers?

One possible solution is to let each writer make a decision or several decisions, and then to allow critics to make their choices as well. Whether or not the two sides agree, I am convinced that it should not be fatal to the literature.

One of the difficulties in all of this is that some people who aim at the target expect to hit it bang center. It's a natural enough aspiration, I should imagine, but one not likely to happen with any degree of frequency.

As a writer, I like to come as close as possible to a hit, and I am happy when I come close. I may not be satisfied, and so I will aim again and then wait for another chance. Others are not content and wish to hit the bull's eye every time. It can't be done: We're dealing with people and with moving targets. All of us know what people are capable of anyway.

It may turn out that this literature will go away and thus stop bothering those smothered souls who don't know what to do with it or to make of it. I don't believe for one minute that it will go away; it will merely change, as all things change, *mutatis mutandis*.

UNIVERSITY OF MINNESOTA, MINNEAPOLIS

II. Origins, Background and Development

Everywhere we see the beginning of confusion, and we want a clue to some sound order and authority. This we can only get by going back upon the actual instincts and forces which rule our life, seeing them as they really are, connecting them with other instincts and forces, and enlarging our whole view and rule of life.

Matthew Arnold

LITERATURA CHICANA: BACKGROUND AND PRESENT STATUS OF A BILCULTURAL EXPRESSION

Rolando Hinojosa

Chicano literature as I will discuss it includes fiction as well as history, folklore, anthropology, and other genres which concern the various Chicano cultures in the United States.

José Antonio Villarreal's *Pocho* was first published by Doubleday in 1959; obviously, it was written before that date, but 1959 also marks the fifth year of the return from the Korean Conflict of the Chicano veteran. He was a different type from the World-War-II Mexican American veteran, from the World-War-I Latin American veteran, and from the Spanish-American-War Mexican as he has been variously called in the defense of his country. He was also different from the South Texas Mexican who fought in the American Civil War either as a volunteer for the North or as the hired hand and cowboy of the southern-bred ranch owners of South Texas.

Nineteen-fifty-nine is a representative year: Many of us were in our mid-twenties. We had finished our undergraduate work and, thanks to various G. I. Bills then in existence, many college graduates of the Generation of 1959 turned to teaching and to writing. This is in contrast with the preceding World-War-II generation, some of whom had gone after degrees in medicine and law while the majority had been shunted off and directed toward certificates in boat building out in the West Texas plains or in the mastery of woodcarving in plastic Los Angeles. It was a different time as well, but the appearance of *Pocho*, unheralded at first, and even subsequently, did set contemporary Chicano fiction literature in motion.

In the past sixteen years since the first printing of *Pocho,* other Chicanos have come forward as writers, printers, publishers, and distributors of Chicano literature. Over a year ago I said in Norman, Oklahoma that most of the Chicano literary reviews, journals, and newspapers were sporadic in their publication; this is still the case in December, 1975.

Among the better known Chicano houses was Quinto Sol. Quinto Sol lasted from 1967 until 1974; the best *El Grito* journals from Quinto Sol are not from the year 1974, as is well known. The original group of students and faculty that started it all has now scattered, and one of them, Andrés Ybarra, is dead. Quinto Sol is dead as well, but two new Chicano publishing houses have been announced by former Quinto Sol partners: Justa Publications by Herminio Ríos, and Tonatiuh International by Octavio Romano. Both are located across the bay from San Francisco in Berkeley, and we'll have to wait and see if Berkeley is big enough for both of them. We'll also have to wait and see before we can judge what their literary production will be.

The Chicano fiction writers are out there: a good number are quite talented; the larger number, as in any population group, are not. However, there is no lack of sincerity in what is being written and in what is being published. Sincerity is an admirable trait and one that most of us should attempt to cultivate along with some small amount of humility. I'll come back to sincerity in a minute.

While in Oklahoma, I also said that American publishing houses were quick to see that by using the word Chicano as a label or as a badge the sales in anthologies and other textbooks would reap profits for them. This statement still holds, and it is one which may hold fast for some time. This is their choice and their right as profit-seeking organizations, therefore I have little to say on the matter; while interesting points could be made against their use of the word Chicano, the exercise would be futile. One of the reasons is that if we bemoan the fact of their use of the term, as in *Chicano Voices, Voces Chicanas, Voces del barrio,* and *An Anthology of Mexican American Authors,* because some of the writers turn out to be Mexican nationals or precolumbians, then we must also bemoan the lack of sincerity of some Chicano compilers of anthologies and other materials who do just as bad a job.

On the matter of language, aside from the fact that some Chicanos write strictly in English while others prefer Spanish and some write and publish in both languages, and the fact that some critics prefer one language over the other and may even plumb for the use of Spanish alone and nothing else, the differences will best be settled by fiction writers themselves, and by the product they turn out. The languages will most probably coexist for some time, but, and this is a personal observation, I fear that Spanish will lose out in the long run. English, most certainly, will win out in the nonfiction areas of literature.

These differences, however, do not mean that Chicano literature is grasping for a sense of direction. Chicano literature, like all art forms, had its beginning for a definite reason. And, like any other art form, it will also lose its utilitarianism in time. There is evidence of this already. In so doing, it will develop a sense of multiple directions. This is where we are today in fiction and nonfiction.

This brings us back to sincerity and to those Chicano writers who masquerade as researchers. There are those Chicanos whose publications are an insult to scholarship and to scholarly research; I do not refer to the small publications, the sporadic, neighborhood publications with the spelling errata or to those that lack diacritical marks. No, these, for the most part, are sincere and committed publications, such as *Caracol* in San Antonio, and they manage to reach that portion of people who would not ordinarily read Chicano or any other literature.

Specifically, I refer to two Chicanos who have recently published a full-fledged dictionary of Chicano expressions with a total disregard for sound investigative research methodology; moreover, they appear to possess marginal knowledge of the steps involved in assembling a dictionary. They also demonstrate an appalling disrespect by their use of the word Chicano, which they debase by sticking it into the title so that every major or every jackleg university library will buy it, catalog it, and shelve it. This publication is almost impossible to read, and when the reviews start coming in, it's going to be criticized, and with justification.

Sincerity such as that exhibited by our low budget publications is one thing, mediocrity by professionals is something else. I daresay, however, that there are others whom you may know about. And bringing them to mind is one point of this paper.

It is our lot to be minority writers and charged, as all writers are charged, to write of specific problems with a universal appeal. The word minority is, of course, pejorative, and it will have to be dropped. We may write *Perros y antiperros, Ultima, Tamazunchale, Tierra* or *Peregrinos* in specifics, but always in relation to the universal. By the way, I really don't see how universality can be evaded in serious works. Critiqued or not, understood or not, loved or not, each work just mentioned is a study in general discipline toward a concentrated effort in explaining us to ourselves and to others as well. The faulty researcher, in his haste to publish, forsakes discipline and makes a passing effort at explaining Chicanos to Chicanos and usually succeeds in reinforcing stereotypes that, so help me God, hardly need reinforcing.

It isn't as if those sloppy Chicano researchers don't have other Chicanos to set examples for them as to what constitutes sound principles of documentation. For they do: There's the late George I. Sánchez, and now Américo Paredes, Arturo Madrid, Salvador Alvarez, Raymond Padilla, and Juan Gómez Quiñones, whose works are respected and sought out by serious scholars; there are also careful bibliographers such as Guillermo Rojas and Herminio Ríos to name but a few in various categories and disciplines. The models are there in full view.

If succeeding Chicano scholars don't exercise regard for accuracy in professional research, as the ones just mentioned certainly do, we'll continue to be no better off academically than we were prior to World War II; if we don't police ourselves, others will whether we like it or not for there is already good material on Chicanos being turned out, as in the cases of Richard Teschner and Roberto Galván, in a fine, unpretentious work called *Diccionario del español de Tejas* and a previous work by Teschner and associates: A bibliography on the Spanish spoken by Hispanos (Chicanos, Boricuas, and Cubanos) in the United States.

A serious consequence of poor researching may be that Chicano studies will wither. Since we are labeled as a minority group we may be also marked off *en masse* as deficient when it comes to digging for facts and in the performance of the highly detailed and laborious task of investigative research. If this continues, we'll play into the hands of those whose stereotyped opinions of us are already as hardened as tungsten steel.

Intramural parochialism in literary reviews, misdirection, and misrepresentation of ourselves by ourselves in investigative works will assure a continuance of fragmentation in the serious study of Chicano literature. It takes a certain amount of time to produce a fair piece of writing, but it takes much longer to produce something perennial; that, *lo perenne,* should be the present and continuing status of *la literatura chicana.*

As a writer I can only write about what I know, limited as that

Rolando Hinojosa

may be by the circumstances of time and experience. As a Chicano Ph.D., however, I have other responsibilities: I owe it to myself to speak this way about our own. I have done so publicly and in print and I believe that I must continue to do so.

UNIVERSITY OF MINNESOTA, MINNEAPOLIS

CONTEMPORARY CHICANO PROSE FICTION: ITS TIES TO MEXICAN LITERATURE

Charles M. Tatum

Literary historians and critics, like theologians of the Middle Ages who debated endlessly the question of how many angels could stand on the head of a pin, have expended a great deal of energy in the continuing polemic regarding national, ethnic, and minority literatures. For example, Herminio Ríos, in his introduction to Rolando Hinojosa's prizewinning work *Estampas del valle y otras obras,* points out that the very existence of Chicano literature is still being discussed hotly in some university circles.[1] In their time-honored study *Theory of Literature*, René Wellek and Austin Warren carefully outline the pitfalls of dealing with literature defined along national lines. They warn us that "the problem of 'nationality' and of distinct contributions of the individual nations, instead of being studied with theoretical clarity, has been blurred by nationalistic sentiment and racial theories."[2]

What Wellek and Warren say about national literatures can also be applied to ethnic or minority literatures in the United States. And in addition to difficulties cited by them, the problem of literary history and criticism is compounded when we begin to deal with relationships, similarities, borrowings, and influences of one body of literature on another: of African on Black American literature, for example, or of Mexican on Chicano literature. Yet, in spite of the difficulties which a comparative study might present, I would like to discuss in this paper, in a very general way, the ties of contemporary

Chicano prose fiction to Mexican literature. I will studiously avoid the consideration of the theoretical questions surrounding such an approach; nor do these questions unduly concern me. There is, after all, a clear precedent for this approach within the tradition of Hispanic literatures. Virtually every history of Latin American literature contains a lengthy section on Spanish Peninsular literary roots and heritage. For example, Enrique Anderson Imbert records for us the flowering of Spanish literary forms in the fertile soil of the New World.[3] In his *Historia de la literatura mexicana,* Carlos González Peña pays particular attention to the richness of the *crónica* and various tendencies of Spanish poetry which were transferred to the viceroyalty of New Spain and which prospered there during the colonial period.[4] Most historians of Latin American literature also acknowledge that until the late nineteenth century, with the advent of modernism, Latin American writers continued to rely heavily on their Peninsular counterparts for leadership in arts and letters.

On the other hand, along with these close ties between Spain and her colonies, Latin American literature has been characterized from the outset by the creation of its own hybrid poetry, drama, and prose fiction. Angel Rosenblat observes in his provocative essay on language in America that while Peninsular writers continued to look toward the written word—that is, the Spanish classics—as the model for their works, in Latin America writers sought to create their own forms of expression which would go hand-in-hand with their political and economic independence: "a través de toda la vida americana, desde la primera hora había un afán cada vez más vivo por encontrar la propia expresión, afán que ha alcanzado en los últimos años caracteres altamente espectaculares."[5]

This same process of striving for new literary forms and expression while remaining within a specific historical and cultural tradition can be observed in the relationship of Chicano to Mexican literature. However, it is important to note that while Latin American literary independence from the mother country, Spain, was accelerated by the independence movements of the early nineteenth century, Chicano literature received (and has continued to receive) a constant cultural infusion from Mexico dating from the Treaty of Guadalupe Hidalgo of 1848. Although large portions of Northern Mexico were ceded to the United States, after 1848 Mexicans on both sides of the newly created border continued to flow freely back and forth in large numbers in open defiance of the artificial boundaries between the two countries. Therefore, due to these historical and political circumstances, Chicano writers have always enjoyed a much closer relationship to Mexico than have Mexican writers to Spain, an ocean and a war of independence apart.

Although the focus of this study is contemporary Chicano prose fiction and its ties to Mexican literature, it is essential to keep in mind that, in general, Chicano literature has a long and proud tradition in this country which has maintained a vital and visible line of communication to Mexico. Contemporary Chicano writers are a part of this tradition and, at the same time, they have received and have responded to ideas from modern Mexican writers. Like *chasqui* (ancient Incan runners who carried news from one cultural center to another), successive waves of immigrants from Mexico since 1848 have continually revitalized the Mexican language, customs and literary traditions of the *barrios* of the Southwest and California. Chicano and Mexican writers have journeyed back and forth across the border, sharing forms, attitudes and concepts and constantly retying the cultural bonds between them.

Prior to 1848, traditional *cuentos* transmitted orally and concentrating on the elements of folk existence were the most popular literary forms used by Mexican writers living in the isolated areas of what was then Mexico's northern frontier.[6] As the settlement and population of today's Southwest and California grew, an increasing number of creative writers appeared, and by 1848 literary activity began to flourish. A number of newspapers and journals published not only the traditional *cuentos* but also other literary pieces such as poetry and *actos*—short dramatic works. After the conclusion of the war between the United States and Mexico, writers (now Mexican-American by token of their new citizenship) continued to rely heavily on forms, themes, motifs, and settings which were prevalent in Mexican literature. Of course, changes occurred, the most significant being the publication of works in English by writers such as Napoleón Vallejo, Andrew García, and Miguel Antonio Otero. The *cuadro de costumbres,* a literary form depicting local customs and language, was popular at this time in Mexico and was soon adopted by Chicano writers north of the border. The traditional *cuento* thus made an easy transition to the *cuadro* in this country. Along with poetry and the *actos* published in both English and Spanish, other Mexican forms had been transplanted successfully in Spanish-speaking areas of the United States. These forms were to remain viable and popular for decades as Chicano writers continued to practice their craft without a break in continuity with their Mexican cultural

49

Charles M. Tatum

heritage.

The period from about 1910 to 1940 is transitional for Chicano prose fiction and its relationship to various tendencies in Mexican literature. On one hand, writers who by this time were publishing almost entirely in English continued to hark back to nineteenth-century Mexican forms. They persisted in focusing on themes and using motifs from their rich Hispanic-Mexican past. For example, Arthur Campa, also a diligent researcher of Spanish folktales in the Southwest, was a prolific writer whose stories are shot through with folk piety and traditional respect for authority, both human and divine. He combines tone, setting, theme, and motif in a way that roots him firmly in the non-Anglo literary tradition kept alive in the American Southwest since 1848. Even as recently as the fifties and sixties, writers such as Fray Angélico Chávez, a New Mexican, have drawn heavily on the time-honored customs and legends of the poor folk who inhabit the isolated areas of Spanish-speaking parts of the United States. Chávez's "Hunchback Madonna" reminds us of Ignacio Altamirano's *costumbrista* works such as "La navidad en las montañas." For both writers, Chicano and Mexican, the mountains serve as a refuge for the *campesino* who finds shelter and tranquility there.

Concurrent with this persistence of nineteenth-century Mexican literary elements, Chicano works published from 1910 to 1940 began to reflect the social unrest among one of the country's fastest growing minorities. During the most violent phases of the Mexican Revolution (from about 1910 to 1926), large waves of immigrants from Mexico walked and rode north to the United States in search of security and employment. As Luis Leal observes: "The new immigrants brought new blood into the Mexican-American community and also reinforced the Mexican traditions. The same thing occurred in intellectual circles with the interchange of ideas among writers such as José Vasconcelos, Martín Luis Guzmán, Mariano Azuela, Ricardo Flores Magón, and others who lived in the United States."[7]

Chicano historians such as Rudolfo Anaya have carefully documented this interchange with Mexican intellectuals which, along with the steadily deteriorating social conditions for the masses of disenfranchised Chicanos, created a group consciousness which has carried over until today.[8] This increased awareness of the plight of more than six million people is reflected in the prose works of Chicano writers who published in the pages of the *Alianza* and the *LULAC News*, which enjoyed wide circulation in the twenties and the thirties.[9] These writers continued in the United States a new and vibrant

50

literary movement which had its roots in the novel of the Mexican Revolution. Mariano Azuela published his novel, *Los de abajo*, in 1915 in an El Paso, Texas newspaper. Other exiled Mexican writers lived and wrote in this country during and immediately following the Revolution. Although this period has not been well researched, it is reasonable to assume that in the urban centers of the Southwest and California, from about 1910 to 1940, Mexican and Chicano writers were drawn into close and frequent association, exchanged views and influenced one another's intellectual and literary development.

In Mexico, the novel of the Revolution represented a significant break with the literary past, and it was considered by other Latin American writers as a model for the description of national problems.[10] In the best tradition of *criollo* prose fiction, Mexican novelists, beginning with Azuela, began to deal with deeply-rooted social, political, and philosophical questions raised by years of bloodshed and civil strife. Leaving behind the Mexican *costumbrista* tradition, writers embarked on a new path of critical realism, and their representation of society rests firmly on a specific conception of the world around them. Azuela's *Los de abajo* is probably the best of the novels with its objective descriptions of the cyclical destruction brought on by the sweeping force of violence perpetrated by one group against another. Mexican novelists in the late twenties and thirties often turned toward journalistic accounts of battles and other settings of the Revolution. These accounts later degenerated into simplistic and superficial evaluations of the problems raised by the revolutionary period.[11]

The novel of the Revolution has greatly affected contemporary Mexican writers, and, at the same time, we can observe its influence on a group of Chicano novelists and short story writers who were writing in the late fifties and sixties in this country. Bearing in mind the heightened awareness which existed in the Chicano community after World War II, it is not surprising that the journalistic accounts which characterized the late novel of the Mexican Revolution should find favor among Chicano writers. The form cultivated by Martín Luis Guzmán, for example, was a perfect vehicle for Chicano writers who set out to present the lives of suffering and deprivation of thousands of Mexican nationals and Chicano United States citizens.

A cursory examination of Chicano prose fiction of the late fifties and sixties reveals that many authors deal directly with social, political, and economic problems plaguing urban and rural Chicanos.[12] Focusing mainly on the bitter experiences of this minority as it attempted to adjust to an alien Anglo culture, writers such as José Antonio Villarreal, Richard Vásquez, and Amado Muro utilize an external, descriptive approach. Characters, while portrayed vividly, are often flat and stereotyped, representative sociological figures rather than multifaceted fictional beings. But in spite of this and other weaknesses, works such as *Pocho* and *Chicano* are important to the development of Chicano prose fiction, just as López y Fuentes and Guzmán are important to the development of modern Mexican literature. And in a similar way, these Chicano works are cathartic, providing a release from accumulated suffering and frustration of generations of Chicanos, just as the novels of the Mexican Revolution allowed Mexicans to express their horror of the bloodbath their country endured.

Many writers cover in their works a period of Chicano history which begins early in this century and continues even now, in the urban *barrios* and the rural fields of the Southwest and California. The Depression, riots of the thirties and the forties, strikes, and the civil rights movement serve as the backdrop against which we see a whole culture in the process of transformation and adaptation to new ways and problems of daily existence. What is referred to euphemistically as "acculturation" and "assimilation" is refocused for us in these works as survival based on the abandonment of traditions and language. The varied experiences of several generations are retold, allowing the reader to draw his own conclusions regarding the history of Chicanos in this country.

Just as Mexican writers of the thirties and forties tended to reflect in their works the social and political turmoil of their time, many Chicano writers also mirror the exterior as well as the emotional state of their people during a period of rising consciousness. *Chicano* by Richard Vásquez is a good example. In this novel, the author traces the changing social conditions and attitudes of successive generations of a Chicano family in this country from about 1915 to 1960. From the initial disillusionment and isolation of Héctor Sandoval in his new and unfamiliar role as immigrant, through the teenage Angelina who realizes that her white skin is an asset in Anglo society, to Mariana's renewed pride in her ancestral culture, Vásquez gives us an overview of an historical period much as the Mexican novelists of the thirties and the forties do in their works. Writing mainly from personal experience, authors such as José Villarreal, Richard Vásquez, Amado Muro, Mario Suárez, and Genaro González create a group consciousness, a Chicano consciousness, just as Mexican writers of the Revolution directed their creative efforts toward a national consciousness, to the questions most immediately at hand.[13]

Chicano prose fiction of the late fifties and sixties seems to be dominated by a view of the historical past as it examines a wide spectrum of immigrant and native Chicano experiences on a mainly social level. In the end, this operates as a conceptual limitation, because missing from many of the works are the complexities of individual psyches, the consideration of problems which are not purely social in nature, and introspection. While they have great value as documentaries, as good journalistic accounts of a people's history, they are surpassed artistically by works published more recently.

Raymond Barrio's *The Plum, Plum Pickers* (1969) is such a work. In the best tradition of Mexican proletarian literature of the Revolution, this novel has been heralded by one critic as the most significant novel of the decade in American literature.[14] Although this description is probably too enthusiastic, Barrio does portray, often poignantly, the struggle of a migrant family in the fictitious town of Drawbridge, California. The novel contains all the elements of the farm workers' movement to gain freedom from the wall of indebtedness, hunger, and sickness which surrounds them. Barrio presents an enriched multiple view of the Chicano while rejecting the flat, stereotyped characters of many earlier writers. Although he does not deviate from the basically sociological point of view of these writers, he does greatly enhance the vividness and credibility of the migrant experience through his sensitive characterization.

Barrio's novel goes a long way toward freeing contemporary Chicano prose fiction from the essentially journalistic overview of the minority experience. The novel of the Mexican Revolution continues to serve as a model, but writers such as Rolando Hinojosa and Tomás Rivera have been far more successful than Barrio in experimenting with new forms and bringing to bear on their works a different conceptual framework. They have achieved this, however, without abandoning the struggle of *La Raza*.

Chicano prose fiction published within the last three years is, among many other things, a confluence, a coming together of several rich traditions of Mexican and Chicano literature to form a unique reservoir of native Mexican Indian myth, Hispanic customs and beliefs, a proletarian view of life in a dominant Anglo society, and a far-reaching exploration of the Chicano psyche. Nineteenth-century *costumbrismo* and the social protest literature of the Mexican Revolution are integrated into recent Chicano works but not in their original forms. They are given new depth and vitality in the context of Chicano language by Chicano writers who are conscious of both the social experience and traditions of their people and the artistic demands of their craft. They fit Luis Dávila's description of the sensitive Chicano writer who rejects extremes and morally simplistic choices of painting the Chicano as simpleminded and pliantly folkloric or elevating him miraculously to social sanctity and epic heroism. Dávila says: "The sensitive Chicano writer looks around, and he discovers only partial truths. Absolute truths are not easy to identify anymore. What's more he soon finds that his ethnic characters are more human, if he allows them to indulge their fantasies, even though they later stumble, falter or lose. They can aspire to be cosmos shakers, but this does not mean that they will not have feet of clay."[15]

Both Rolando Hinojosa and Tomás Rivera embody this description of the Chicano writer. In addition, their works are excellent examples of the ties that continue to exist between contemporary Chicano writers and Mexican literature of both the past and the present. Hinojosa and Rivera have been recognized by Quinto Sol Publications for the high degree of artistic achievement of their award-winning works. Rivera received the Quinto Sol literary prize in 1971 for his *". . .y no se lo tragó la tierra,"* and Hinojosa won it in 1973 for his *Estampas del valle y otras obras.* These works stand out not only because of their artistic merit but also because they reflect poignantly the customs, language, and social injustices against Chicanos. This combination of art and sensitivity to social conditions draws them close to contemporary Mexican writers, especially Juan Rulfo.

It would be foolhardy to suggest that recent Chicano prose fiction has followed faithfully the rapidly changing tendencies and emphases of modern Mexican fiction or that it has received exclusively Mexican or even Latin American influence. But while no cause-and-effect relationship between the two bodies of literature exists, there are similarities which can be discerned between recent Chicano works and some published in Mexico within the last twenty years. At the same time, writers like Hinojosa and Rivera continue to draw on a whole tradition of Mexican and Chicano literature.

Hinojosa's *Estampas del valle y otras obras* consists of a series of brief sketches which defy precise literary classification, although they do resemble the skillfully created *estampas* of the Mexican writer Julio Torri. Neither "short story" nor "vignette" adequately describes Hinojosa's *estampas*, which contain a little of both while at the same time reminding us of the *cuadros de costumbres* in their depiction of customs, traditions, celebrations, speech, and representative social types. However, the *estampas* transcend the *cuadro*, which is often limited to a physical description of the external aspects of reality. The *estampas* display a broad range in tone, from humor to a terse, direct presentation reminiscent of Rulfo's *El llano en llamas*. One important linguistic aspect of the *estampas*, as well as of another of Hinojosa's short works, "Por esas cosas que pasan," can be seen in Rulfo's collection of short stories. Hinojosa's repeated use of expressions which communicate a deeply felt resignation to the natural course of life is similar to the technique which the Mexican writer employs. For example, in his story "Es que somos muy pobres," Rulfo repeats certain details and phrases to heighten the utter despair of a Mexican family who has lost its cow in a flood. Through the child-narrator's repetition of the phrase "es que somos muy pobres," Rulfo conveys to the reader the family's tenuous rural existence, which is at the mercy of both natural and human acts. Hinojosa also begins and ends many of his *estampas* with such an expression which serves to set the tone or to reinforce the dominant feeling contained within them. The most effective use of the technique of the brief repeated phrase is seen in his short work "Por esas cosas que pasan." As in Rulfo's story, the title of this selection sets the tone of resignation to a course of events over which the characters seem powerless to exert any control.

In *El llano en llamas* Rulfo's rural dwellers are often manipulated by socio-economic and political forces which are concentrated far from them in the provincial capitals and large cities. Unlike many of the novelists of the Revolution, this Mexican author does not cry out indignantly through his characters, demanding the destruction of the oppressive institutions which continue to exploit the peasants. In a similar way, Hinojosa refers to the Anglo world indirectly, never stating explicitly the relationship which exists between that world and the Chicano community of Klail City, Texas, and its environs, which provide the setting for his work.

Rulfo's stories are rooted in Mexican reality: the aridity and abandonment of that forsaken part of the state of Jalisco, his birthplace; the continuing exploitation of the Mexican peasant by postrevolutionary *caudillos*; the deep-seated fatalism and the cycle of suffering, guilt, and violence in the lives of his characters. Yet Rulfo transforms this Mexican setting through the accumulation and juxtaposition of details, nuance of language and tone, and many other techniques which cannot be discussed in this short study. He transforms the specific Mexican setting by obscuring temporal and spatial delineations while at the same time remaining firmly grounded in a Mexican social and cultural context.

Rulfo, along with Sherwood Anderson and William Faulkner, is one of Rivera's acknowledged masters.[16] Like Rulfo, Rivera draws heavily on the daily lives of the people he knows best, while at the same time elevating their fears, struggles, and beliefs beyond the level of social protest literature. Rivera does not ignore the cause of *La Raza*; rather, he gives it greater force and credibility through the creation of characters with many more dimensions than those of Vásquez or Villarreal. Like Rulfo, Rivera has rejected the stock sociological or historical model of pamphleteering literature in favor of (in his own words) "an artistic world that is created, in which the literary characters must move, speak, and feel as true and complex creations."[17]

Like the Mexican writer, Rivera seeks to reveal a psychic center in his characters. Their exterior actions and truncated speech become, at the same time, manifestations and symptoms of that interior life. As in *El llano en llamas*, in *". . .y no se lo tragó la tierra"* Rivera succeeds in obliterating limits of time and space to create in their place a consciousness, an identity in the young protagonist who is central to many of the stories of the collection. Again, as in Rulfo's work, each story contributes to the creation of this central consciousness which, in turn, gives unity and focus to the Chicano reality pervading the entire collection.

The Chicano writer has undergone a rapid change in the last few years. The trajectory of his development can be characterized as one which approaches total subjective interiorization coupled with thematic and esthetic complexity in his works. Expression rather than description is now basic to the novels and short stories of recent Chicano writers. Although most of them have rejected the simplistic solutions and shallow characterization of earlier Mexican and Chicano writers, they remain committed to the struggle of their people.

Like Mexican literature since about 1950, contemporary Chicano prose fiction has a new orientation which has burgeoned into a rich and varied body of literature. It merits the attention and study of serious scholars of American, Latin American, and comparative literature. Its relationship to other bodies of literature, while often elusive and difficult to pinpoint, should become the focus of future investigation.

HOLY CROSS COLLEGE

Ties to Mexican Literature

Notes

[1] Herminio Ríos, *Estampas del valle y otras obras*, Berkeley, Ca., Quinto Sol Publications, 1973, p. iv.

[2] René Wellek and Austin Warren, *Theory of Literature*, New York, Harcourt, Brace, and World, 1956, pp. 40-41.

[3] Enrique Anderson Imbert, *Historia de la literatura hispanoamericana*, vol. 1, Mexico City, Fondo de Cultura Económica, 1970, pp. 17-56, passim.

[4] Carlos González Peña, *Historia de la literatura mexicana*, Mexico City, Editorial Porrúa, 1969, p. 15.

[5] Angel Rosenblat, *Lengua literaria y lengua popular en América*, Caracas, Cuadernos del Instituto de Filología Andrés Bello, 1969, p. 7.

[6] See Philip Ortego, "Background of Mexican American Literature," (unpublished Ph.D. dissertation, University of New Mexico, 1971), Chapters 1 and 2.

[7] Luis Leal, "Mexican American Literature: A Historical Perspective," *Revista Chicano-Riqueña*, vol. 1, p. 39.

[8] See Rudolfo Anaya, *Occupied America: The Chicano's Struggle for Liberation*, New York, Canfield Press, 1972, especially Chapter 6.

[9] Leal, p. 39.

[10] Aldalbert Dessau, *La novela de la revolución mexicana*, Mexico City, Fondo de Cultura Económica, 1972, p. 11.

[11] Joseph Sommers, *After the Storm: Landmarks of the Modern Mexican Novel*, Albuquerque, University of New Mexico Press, 1968, pp. 34-35.

[12] For a more complete discussion of Chicano prose fiction during this period, see my article, "Contemporary Chicano Prose Fiction: A Chronicle of Misery," *Latin American Literary Review*, vol. 1, no. 2, pp. 7-17.

[13] Sommers, p. 34.

[14] The comment was made by Philip Ortego, currently Assistant to the President, Metro College, Denver, Colorado.

[15] Luis Dávila, "Chicano Fantasy Through a Glass Darkly," a paper presented at the XVI Congreso del Instituto Internacional de Literatura Iberoamericana, held at Michigan State University on 30 August 1973. The quote is taken from p. 3 of the text of the paper.

[16] A comment made by Juan Rodríguez in his paper on the Chicano Short Story read at the August 1973 conference on Chicano literature held in Mexico City. The quote is from a tape of his paper.

[17] Tomás Rivera, "Into the Labyrinth: The Chicano in Literature," a paper presented at the conference on Chicano literature held 7-8 October 1971 at Pan American University in Edinburg, Texas. The quote is taken from p. 22 of the text of the paper.

EL DESARROLLO DEL CUENTO CHICANO: DEL FOLKLORE AL TENEBROSO MUNDO DEL YO

Juan Rodríguez

Durante las dos últimas décadas se observa en el ámbito de las sociedades más complejas del mundo, un rebrote de inusitado vigor de las inquietudes que afectan a los llamados grupos minoritarios.[1] El fenómeno se manifiesta por la creciente conciencia que estos conglomerados adquieren de su pasado, de su destino y de sus derechos para exigir de los sectores dirigentes, su autodeterminación. Este hecho social general, parece revestir relieves más notables en los Estados Unidos de América del Norte, en donde genera proyecciones altamente interesantes en el seno de la atmósfera cultural del momento y en la actividad literaria consecuente.

Ninguna persona imparcial e inteligente juzgará el fenómeno como producto espontáneo y debido exclusivamente a razones del momento histórico actual. La verdad es que no hay movimiento social de repercusión que suceda sin un período, las más veces largo, de gestación. Esto vale tanto para las causas extrínsecas como las intrínsecas de cualquier movimiento social. En otras palabras, cualquier confrontación social significativa no nace a raíz de un solo abuso particular contra un individuo, sino de abusos generalizados a través del tiempo contra un conglomerado de individuos, agrupados según los caprichos arbitrarios de las clases dirigentes. Asimismo, la transgresión va cobrando magnitud al minar, al fragmentar, a medida del tiempo, el espíritu, la psicología de un pueblo entero.

Ciñéndonos al caso singular del chicano, el quebrantamiento

El desarrollo del cuento chicano

psicológico nació como resultado ineluctable de dos factores principales. Primero, la región habitada por la mayoría de los chicanos, el mítico Aztlán, ha conocido, aun desde los tiempos prehispánicos, un aislamiento natural, pues ya es una inmensa llanura árida, ya una inhóspita paramera con hitos montañosos, cicatrizada por escasos y pequeños oasis. El segundo factor surge al realizarse el sueño dorado del Coloso del Norte, a saber, la conquista de casi la mitad del territorio mexicano. Con ello los habitantes de esta región, los futuros chicanos, experimentaron sobre las limitaciones naturales, un aislamiento político, económico, social y, de peores consecuencias, sufrieron una separación cultural.

Por razones consabidas el invasor expresamente determinó extirpar el cordón umbilical que nutría al chicano desde el sur de la frontera convencional. Negándole al chicano el uso del idioma nativo, inició el anglosajón una violenta campaña anti-mexicana tanto para convencer al conquistado de la superioridad yanqui en todos los campos y sentidos como para inculcar en la mente del agredido la idea de su innata inferioridad. Así pues, el anglosajón logró apartar al chicano de su historia, de su cultura, de su centro vital, de su *raison d'être*, sometiéndole a un aislamiento psicológico, es decir, depositándolo en el mundo vertiginoso del enajenamiento.

El éxito casi rotundo de la campaña yanqui contra los chicanos se verifica en la ausencia de una literatura viable, con fueros de revelar la existencia efectiva del chicano. Esta lamentable situación es comprensible si recalcamos el hecho de que poco a poco se le vino prohibiendo al chicano, bajo pena nunca en proporción con el delito, el empleo de su lengua nativa. No sorprende, por lo tanto, la divergencia subsecuente del idioma español en estas regiones, pues el uso severamente limitado a los círculos íntimos en la mayoría de los casos, aseguró un retraimiento lingüístico. Naturalmente la supresión lingüística, acompañada de la pérdida del control de los medios de comunicación, principalmente los periódicos, disminuyó la eficacia de la comunicación entre los chicanos, de suerte que se extremó su alienación. El hecho cobra relieve al considerar el efecto que esto tuvo en el desarrollo de la literatura del pueblo "mexicano" conquistado.

Primero se debilita el dinamismo de la literatura escrita en español. Luego se cambia de público lector, es decir, los escritores chicanos empiezan a escribir para un público anglo-parlante. Con esto vienen los cambios más profundos, los de temática, por ejemplo. Se crea así una especie de vacío en el cual fue relativamente fácil crear

59

imágenes falsas y tergiversadas de la realidad chicana, imágenes que los prejuicios anglosajones exigían.

No obstante los desmesurados caprichos ajenos, el chicano sobrevivió sufriendo, armado de su tenacidad e ingenio, ambos manifestados en el fraguar de su jerga peculiar. En virtud del espíritu perenne de resistencia, brotaron de las entrañas del pueblo desahuciado, los cronistas, los autores improvisados, cuya mayor aportación a la Raza, hasta ahora, ha sido el haber substraído la victoria de una derrota irremediable. El autor chicano ha conseguido para el pueblo la victoria del reconocimiento de sí mismo, de la afirmación, la de la humildad y la resistencia, la del *awareness*. Decididamente los mejores autores chicanos percibieron que el chicano no estaba solo, y ateniéndose a ello lo arrebataron del anonimato insoportable para hacerlo contemporáneo de todos los hombres.

He aquí pues el postulado básico de toda la literatura chicana: testimoniar la vida particular y, por consiguiente, universal del chicano para asegurarle su sitio correspondiente en la familia de la raza humana, sitio que le pertenece por derecho propio, no por decretos divinos, ni por amenazas diabólicas. En el fondo, la obsesión de los autores chicanos, a despecho de su dilatada heterogeneidad artística, se traduce en un conato frenético de otorgarle amplio cauce a la expresión de *su* conciencia de la realidad, conciencia que en su intención es sinónima a la del pueblo que los produjo. De improviso percibimos la firme coincidencia ideológica de una actividad vital y la creación estética. La literatura chicana está comprometida a darle forma artística a la vida enajenada del pueblo. En resumidas cuentas los nuestros procuran devolverle la razón a la vida chicana, y de esa manera permitirle seguir su propio desarrollo.

Ahora bien, conforme a nuestro criterio, esta coincidencia ideológica en los escritores chicanos realmente señala el génesis de la literatura chicana, fenómeno cuyos perfiles exactos aparecen desde las dos últimas décadas. Conforme al mismo criterio, la diversa literatura producida en las antiguas tierras mexicanas y escrita por "mexicanos" antes de las fechas aludidas, se reconoce como precursora del *corpus* que llamamos literatura chicana. Aclaramos este punto, no tanto para añadir nuestro parecer a la polémica al respecto que actualmente se discute entre los conocedores de la literatura chicana, sino para advertir que los cuentos y cuentistas aquí discutidos caen más o menos dentro de esos límites temporales.

No es de sorprender que el cuento, ya sea en prosa o en verso, haya sido la forma prístina de la expresión artística chicana, pues la rica tradición oral resistió considerablemente la incursión cultural del agresor. Además, puesto que la memoria es una reserva invicta de la derrota, los primeros cuentos volvían a esa fuente para suscitar escenas y personajes que el tiempo y una realidad cada vez peor hacían más atrayentes.

Lógicamente, ante la actitud anti-mexicana del anglosajón, los primeros cuentistas, aquéllos que por razones de clase social ya tenían la oportunidad de rozarse con el anglo y de utilizar sus medios publicitarios, tomaron una actitud defensiva ante la embestida cultural sajona, pues se proponían justificar la presencia "mexicana" en este país acudiendo a la presentación de nuestro folklore. Algunos, quizás por la influencia nociva de los muchos cuentos anglosajones del mismo tiempo, llegaron hasta la exageración romántica del folklore, ofuscando así nuestros auténticos valores humanos e hiriendo la realidad tanto como los perversos estereotipos que en nuestro vacío literario los falsos cronistas nos habían forjado. "Count La Cerda's Treasure",[2] de la nuevo-mexicana Nina Otero, por ejemplo, contiene todas las características de una visión hollywoodesca: Un Conde de la Cerda, en busca del tesoro del Gran Quivira, hiere a su contrincante en un lío amoroso; pero al ser encarcelado logra la libertad gracias a su hermano, quien aparece oportunamente con mucha plata para facilitar el rescate. El desenlace deja saber el desquicio mental del Conde, mas eso no impide que el pueblo siga creyendo en la leyenda del tesoro del Conde.

Con todo, la mayoría de los cuentos de esta primera etapa concierne más a la presentación pintoresca y costumbrista de nuestro pasado inmediato. Américo Paredes ("The Hammond and the Beans"), Jovita González ("Among My People"), Amado Muro ("Mala Torres"), Sabine Ulibarrí ("Tierra Amarilla"), Josephina Niggli ("The Street of the Three Crosses"), Josefina Escajeda ("Tales From San Elizario") y Arturo Campa ("The Cell of Heavenly Justice"), entre otros, si bien escriben para un lector anglosajón, logran rescatar y preservar del olvido algunos matices de nuestro vivir contaminado por la neurosis social del ambiente en que existimos.

Quien raya a mayor altura en este primer grupo de cuentistas chicanos es Mario Suárez. Sirviéndose de las vecindades chicanas de Tucsón, Arizona, como fondo, Suárez expresa la vida y milagros de algunos personajes típicos del barrio. Mas su realismo se distingue del de sus coetáneos por la fuerte añoranza del pasado y por el firme sostenimiento de la validez de nuestro modo de vivir. Asimismo supera Suárez la mera exhibición de nuestro pasado y de nuestras cos-

Juan Rodríguez

tumbres, los cuales la mayoría anglosajona había tachado de *quaint* (de apariencia anticuada y extraña, pero no desagradable) y que los otros autores chicanos al caer en la trampa, se vieron forzados a defender con inútiles disculpas. Ante la embestida cultural, Suárez patentiza, sin exagerar, los valores sencillos pero muy humanos que le han permitido al chicano sobrevivir en un ambiente social inhóspito. Su cuento "Señor Garza" descubre el ancho sentido filantrópico de éste, quien además de ser propietario, peluquero principal, cajero y conserje de Garza's Barber Shop, es el San Francisco de la comarca. El éxito económico de su peluquería no le menoscaba su sentido humano de la realidad, pues sin lugar a duda "the shop will never own Garza".[3]

El énfasis en los auténticos valores chicanos en vez del hincapié en lo exótico o "extraño" de nuestro folklore y costumbres, trastoca diametralmente la actitud que antes nutría la literatura chicana respecto a los anglos. Si antes se tomaba una actitud defensiva, con Suárez se consigue la ofensiva; ahora serían los anglos quienes tendrían que defender su modo de vivir ante la aparente "superioridad" de la cultura chicana, tal como la presentaban los cronistas chicanos. Asimismo divulga esta nueva posición literaria un cuidado por incluir al chicano mismo entre sus lectores. Cesa por consiguiente el estrechísimo empeño de justificarnos ante el invasor, y nace la más sana de las tareas, la de definirnos ante nosotros mismos y ante el mundo entero.

Al intentar la dramatización del ansia de definición personal, el cuentista necesariamente fue obligado a indagar en la circunstancia sufrida del pueblo. En este segundo paso el cuento abandona las narraciones plácidas de adornadas fachadas, para acusar con vehemencia las razones externas del enajenamiento. Tras el nuevo motivo, lo que apenas intuía el primer grupo de escritores toma perfiles exactos, a saber, se manifiesta la concurrencia de una profunda conciencia social y la creación estética de jóvenes quienes se veían en el proceso dinámico de apropiarse del futuro. Con nuevos principios el cuentista chicano ahora escribe de espaldas al anglosajón y de plena cara a la Raza.

De los muchos que colaboran en este segundo grupo, pues es el más numeroso, nos atrevemos a colocar entre los más hábiles a Genero González ("Un hijo del Sol"), Javier Alba ("The Sacred Spot"), J.L. Navarro ("East Los Angeles: Passing Time"), Octavio Romano ("A Rosary for Doña Marina"), Carlos G. Vélez ("So Farewell Hope") y Nick C. Vaca. Este californiano con su cuento "The Purchase"[4] señala bien la ruta del cuento chicano en su segunda etapa.

El desarrollo del cuento chicano

Acercándose los días navideños, doña Lupe, viuda dependiente del cheque mensual del gobierno, inesperadamente descubre el "maravilloso" sistema de compras conocido como *lay-away*. Incómoda por la invariabilidad de sus regalos a los hijos, a saber, toallitas y pañuelos bordados por su propia mano y paciencia, doña Lupe domina el temor de presentarse en la tienda con sus dos palabras de inglés, y aparta los regalos para su familia. El día en que entrega el penúltimo pago, su entusiasmo y alegría ante el indudable éxito de su proyecto la llevan a acariciar las muchas chucherías que se exhiben sobre los mostradores. Pero al salir ella de la tienda, un joven dependiente la registra, injustamente acusándola de robo. Sus lágrimas de pena y orgullo la acompañan hasta el apartamento, donde a la una de la madrugada, por fin, se sienta a bordar toallitas y pañuelos.

Afortunadamente los mejores de nuestros cuentistas han superado esa fase en que a menudo el *slogan* y el programa, impuestos por el férreo compromiso social, sacrificaban la belleza artística. Y lo insólito del caso está en que el fenómeno se realizó casi de la noche a la mañana. En este sentido, el cuento chicano se ha revolucionado más que evolucionado. Sin embargo, en su madurez el afán de los cuentistas chicanos es, *en principio*, el mismo que llevó a los primeros cuentistas chicanos a escribir: buscar y expresar nuestra completa realidad. Pero en vez de buscar la verdad por fuera, en el sufrimiento físico, al cuentista sazonado le conmueve nombrar, para así dominar, el dolor psíquico, el que únicamente puede aprehenderse desde el interior, donde se encuentran los mitos y los símbolos de lo que somos. En efecto, los cuentos de esta última etapa representan un descenso al propio y tenebroso mundo del yo, y una marcha atrás en el tiempo hasta el origen del dilema no sólo del chicano sino del hombre mismo. Si bien es verdad que estos cuentos se escriben, como diría Octavio Paz, desde la condición chicana, no sobre ella, aún persevera la protesta social, y con mayor impacto, gracias a la fina sutileza con la cual se manifiesta.

Lo que sí desaparece es el inglés. Dedicados no tanto a reflejar la realidad como a crearla, los integrantes de este grupo, a diferencia de los del primer y segundo grupos, optan por expresarse en español, cuyos extremos los determinan el barroco y metafórico lenguaje de Miguel Méndez—quien también domina el caló ("Taller de imágenes, pase" y "El buen chuco")—y el lacónico, sencillo pero igualmente bello lenguaje de Tomás Rivera. El cambio de idioma en la expresión literaria, significa más allá de una postura ideológica, un querer recuperar el pasado auténtico del pueblo.

Juan Rodríguez

Realmente cada escritor de este grupo merecería un estudio monográfico, ya por su madurez artística, ya por su sólida influencia en las letras chicanas. Muy pronto tendrán que realizarse dichos trabajos, para perfilar y elucidar las raíces y la sustancia de la labor literaria de Aristeo Brito ("En el principio. . ."), Rolando Hinojosa (*Estampas del Valle*), Miguel Méndez, Tomás Rivera, así como la de otros jóvenes escritores chicanos, cuyos talentos apuntan hacia el auge de nuestra literatura. Por el momento, forzoso es limitarnos a la discusión de los cuentos de Tomás Rivera.

De la aparente plétora de autores chicanos que publican a partir de los 60, uno más que nadie ha acaparado la atención de sectores dentro y fuera de la esfera chicana. Tomás Rivera, además de ganar en 1970 el primer premio anual Quinto Sol de esa ya reconocida casa editorial, ha sido invitado en numerosas ocasiones a participar en discusiones literarias, llevadas a cabo por distinguidas organizaciones regionales, nacionales e internacionales, dedicadas al estudio y promoción de la literatura. Esta acolada se la debe Rivera exclusivamente a una pequeña colección de cuentos, . . . *Y no se lo tragó la tierra*, publicada en 1971.

No obstante la reciente aparición de su obra, Tomás Rivera delata, tanto en sus comentarios como en su obra, la mucha reflexión dedicada a su arte. Acertadamente ha dicho, por ejemplo, que "the spontaneous vitality of Chicano literature expresses itself as a life which not only exists but also wants to be (ser and estar). El ser is life, el estar is the form". Luego sintetiza: "So we find Chicano literature and Chicanos in fiction as simply life in search of form".[5] Por supuesto, ninguna obra cumple tan religiosamente con ese planteamiento como la del propio Rivera. En . . . *Y no se lo tragó la tierra*, las vidas esparcidas por el suelo sofocante de un pueblo anónimo, incomunicado y sin rumbo fijo salvo el de la muerte, llegan a conocer la forma, el órden y la expresión a través del recuerdo del protagonista, un joven sensible sacudido por la angustia de ver a inocentes olvidados bajo el yugo de la miseria. Los ojos y los oídos de la memoria del joven últimamente son la criba en la cual los granos desparramados, las vidas del pueblo, se aúnan, se purifican, para encauzarse en la corriente de la humanidad, donde pertenecen, donde está su forma, su razón de ser.

Para lograr tan laudable empresa, Rivera, como sus maestros Sherwood Anderson, William Faulkner y Juan Rulfo, se acerca a la vida psíquica de los personajes, y considera las acciones externas de éstos sólo como manifestaciones sintomáticas o simbólicas de esa

vida íntima. Consecuentemente en "El año perdido", el cuento introductorio de la colección, se presenta al protagonista de la obra como
un joven de aguda sensibilidad, ensimismado sobremanera, pues
está debajo de una casa, cuyo refugio le arrulla y lo separa de las formas habituales de la vida, permitiéndole contemplar los repliegues
y profundidades de su ser.

Tras el agudo enfoque exclusivamente sobre el estado psíquico
del protagonista, Rivera establece los límites dentro de los cuales se
verifica toda la acción de los catorce cuentos y las trece brevísimas
anécdotas imbricadas entre ellos, que constituyen la obra. Efectiva-
mente crea Rivera un centro de conciencia, como diría Henry James,
al cual le entrega el poder omnisciente tradicionalmente acaparado
por el autor. De esta manera aniquila el tiempo y el espacio, porque
en verdad el joven habita el mundo de la imaginación, más allá del
tiempo cronológico, en el tiempo íntimo, inmensurable salvo por las
emociones y sentimientos más personales y profundos.

Dentro de ese mundo imaginado, fantasmagórico, el problema
urgente del protagonista se resuelve en encontrar a "alguien que le
llamaba por su nombre".[6] De este modo se plasma súbitamente la
búsqueda de la identidad, como el acicate que forzosamente, en vista
del estado psíquico del joven, le empuja hasta el pleno centro del
mundo vertiginoso de la creación verbal. Porque, recalquemos, no se
trata de acciones sino de pensamientos, cuya realización depende
exclusivamente de las palabras. Por eso, al procurar fijar el pasado,
le importaba sobremanera al protagonista encontrar las palabras.
"A veces trataba de recordar y ya para cuando creía que se estaba
aclarando todo un poco se le perdían las palabras" (p. 1).

En tal caso el ansia de definición personal se manifiesta como
un frenético recorrido por un mundo verbal sumamente enmaraña-
do. En el proceso desaforado la línea divisoria entre la realidad y la
mera invención de los recuerdos se aniquila por completo. "Luego
ya no supo si lo que pensaba había pasado o no" (p. 1).

Siendo así, el protagonista llega a pleno conocimiento de su capacidad inventiva, revelación ambivalente porque a la vez que le resuelve la crisis de identidad, le compromete irremediablemente a la
acción. Al precisar la cuestión reparamos en que si al principio el joven acude al exterior en busca de su identidad, el fracaso patente en
su dar "una vuelta entera, y así (quedar) donde mismo" (p. 1), al lado
de su certidumbre infalible de haber sido "él a quien llamaban" (p. 1),
le impelen a indagar en sí mismo. En el ámbito interior encuentra el
éxito pero también el terror porque "se dio cuenta de que él mismo

Juan Rodríguez

se había llamado" (p. 1). La anonadadora conclusión es ineludible:
¡Su existencia, su identidad, son meramente productos de su propia
invención verbal! Por consiguiente él no existe independiente de sí
mismo, de su actividad mental.

Instigado por esta comprensión del problema, se dedicaría a colocar en rigurosa tela de juicio todas sus creencias, sus experiencias,
en fin, toda su vida para cerciorarse de la realidad de las cosas. Con
ese propósito, determina recordar, relacionar, ensanchar, aun inven-
tar su vida. Bajo esta luz, las narraciones subsiguientes a "El año perdido" forman solamente una minúscula parte de este designio total.

La estremecedora revelación, empero, encierra mayor trascendencia, especialmente en lo que atañe al alma, al objeto o motor principal de la obra de Rivera. A partir de su entendimiento particular de
la realidad, el joven protagonista de "El año perdido" asume absoluta
responsabilidad de su vida. En otras palabras, el proceso inventivo
concomitantemente desenfrena su voluntad y a la vez le entrega el
máximo y exclusivo poder sobre la determinación de su propio destino. De improviso aparecen nítidamente el meollo del complejo te-
mático de ... *Y no se lo tragó la tierra* y el mensaje de Rivera al pueblo
subyugado: Cada quien es dueño de su destino; nada existe más allá
de la percepción y valorización del hombre.

Como comprueba la lectura de los otros cuentos de la colección,
asevera el autor que el temido poder del Diablo ("La noche estaba
plateada"), de Dios ("...Y no se lo tragó la tierra"), de los elementos
naturales (el sol en toda la obra) y del patrón ("Los niños no se aguantaron"), que estos poderes como algo inamovible y fatal, no existen
independiente del hombre, que existen dentro del hombre, como
creencia, como vicio, como un elemento roedor, puesto allí por otros
para debilitarlo con el miedo a toda rebelión. Independiente del hombre mismo, asegura Rivera, no existen los poderes que hasta ahora
hemos tenido como invencibles, más allá de toda protesta, de toda
oposición. Pone en duda, pues, la existencia de un mundo estático,
inalterable, con poderes establecidos para siempre, poderes como el
sol, el patrón, la iglesia, Dios, el diablo, etc. Desde esta perspectiva
Rivera es uno de los autores más revolucionarios y modernos entre
nosotros.

En resumen, así como el impresionante personaje que ha creado
en "El año perdido", ése cuyo recuerdo reconstruye al hombre dividido por el temor y el sufrimiento, Tomás Rivera, como autor, también recuerda a su pueblo para darle forma. Metido en él acaricia la
esperanza de encontrar su propia forma, porque sabe que el sentido

de esa forma, es el sentido de su vida y de su comprensión de la realidad.

Tal ha sido el desarrollo del cuento chicano. Su trayectoria se caracteriza por la interiorización subjetiva y la complicación estilística y temática. El cuento chicano en su madurez tiende más hacia la expresión que hacia la descripción de la realidad. Aún comprometidos al movimiento social, los mejores cuentistas de hoy en día no pretenden convertir a sus personajes y situaciones en emblemas o modelos de la protesta social; prefieren afilar y afinar la protesta para lastimar más hondo. En fin, pretenden definir el presente a base del pasado para forjar el futuro. Ansían plasmar una imagen trascendental y completa de la realidad que viven y que los cicatriza y, al mismo tiempo, anhelan que sirva esa imagen como testimonio de su intento para marcar, a su vez, esa misma realidad.

UNIVERSITY OF CALIFORNIA AT BERKELEY

Notas

[1]Reimpreso aquí, este artículo, originalmente escrito durante el verano de 1973, representaba en ese entonces un esfuerzo por parte nuestra de encauzar los varios cuentos chicanos que se venían publicando por aquí y por allí, para mejor entender el desarrollo de este género dentro de nuestro mundo literario. Es decir, nuestro ensayo pretende interpretar el desarrollo del cuento chicano a base de los cuentos ya conocidos, pues en esos días todavía no emprendíamos las investigaciones que descubrirían las raíces y el proceso histórico del florecimiento del cuento chicano. En la actualidad, ya bien adelantadas dichas investigaciones y apoyadas de otra manera de ver la realidad social y literaria, tenemos la tentación de cambiar sustancialmente lo que escribimos en 1973. Pero no lo hacemos porque creemos que el trabajo, tal como fue escrito originalmente, todavía mantiene cierto valor.

[2]Nina Otero, "Count La Cerda's Treasure", en *Old Spain in Our Southwest* (New York: Harcourt Brace Jovanovich, 1936).

[3]Mario Suárez, "Señor Garza", *Arizona Quarterly* (Summer 1974).

[4]Nick C. Vaca, "The Purchase", *El Espejo/ The Mirror* (Berkeley: Quinto Sol Publications, 1969).

[5]Tomás Rivera, "Into the Labyrinth: The Chicano in Literature", *New Voices in Literature: The Mexican-American* (Edinburg, Texas: Pan American University, 1971), p. 24.

[6]Rivera, ... *Y no se lo tragó la tierra* (Berkeley: Quinto Sol Publications, 1971), p.1. De aquí en adelante los números de las páginas citadas de esta obra aparecerán entre paréntesis inmediatamente después de la cita en el texto.

LA POESIA CHICANA:
UNA NUEVA TRAYECTORIA

Salvador Rodríguez del Pino

A pesar de que la poesía es el género más abundante dentro de la literatura chicana, poco se ha escrito acerca de ella de manera comprensiva. Existen varios artículos publicados sobre la poesía, pero éstos, en su mayoría, estudian un solo poeta y su obra, sin tratar el género en su totalidad. Sin embargo, esta deficiencia crítica está por ser expertamente fortalecida dentro de poco tiempo ya que he tenido la oportunidad de leer varios excelentes manuscritos inéditos en donde se profundiza, se clasifica y se juzga, dentro de ciertos modelos críticos, la poesía chicana y sus diversas perspectivas. Esta aportación al corpus de la crítica chicana será valiosa tanto para el investigador como para el estudiante de la literatura chicana. En este breve estudio sobre la poesía chicana, he consultado estos manuscritos así como también las entrevistas personales con varios poetas chicanos quienes me dieron una orientación sobre sus obras y sus ideologías. A éstos les agradezco el interés que me han brindado y espero que con este breve estudio aporte y cumpla con mi obligación de investigador de la literatura chicana. A pesar de tanto material leído y estudiado, me propondré solamente tratar brevemente ciertos aspectos de la poesía chicana que puedan servir como fondo para enmarcar lo que yo llamo en este estudio "la nueva trayectoria" en la poesía chicana.

Las trayectorias tradicionales

Al igual que en todos los países hispanoamericanos, el pueblo chicano posee una larga y antigua tradición poética enraizada en el sentir popular de su gente y en la tradición poética hispana. Dentro de la tradición hispana traída de España y de México, la poesía chicana empleó las mismas formas de la tradición oral de los pueblos hispanoamericanos, o sean *las trovas, los romances* y, como en México, su madre patria, *los corridos.* Pero la sensibilidad poética chicana es tan diversa como el chicano mismo y tan diversa su realidad y experiencia como lo es en los demás pueblos hermanos de Latinoamérica. Sin embargo, históricamente, la poesía chicana ha seguido, como en todas estas literaturas nacionales, dos trayectorias socioculturales: (1) la popular—el pueblo que preserva la tradición oral y ancestral, y (2) la culta, o sea la poesía escrita basándose en las formas *literarias* tradicionales más refinadas en el culto de la palabra florida y empleando un simbolismo que refleje su propia mitología y raíces históricas. Dentro de la primera trayectoria encontramos las trovas y coplas del pueblo trabajador, del pueblo consciente de su opresión cultural, la del hombre que necesita cantar su propio sentimiento y lamento sobre el mundo físico y espiritual que lo rodea. Dentro de la segunda trayectoria se encuentran dos grupos: los poetas conscientes de la poética y sus reglas clásicas y aquéllos que han tenido una formación literaria ya sea dentro del condicionamiento angloamericano o latinoamericano. No puede haber una clasificación determinante de poetas en los dos grupos puesto que algunos de ellos fluctúan entre las dos trayectorias, y podemos encontrar a un obrero o campesino consciente de la expresión culta poética, o podemos tener un profesional académico que emplee la expresión popular como elemento de identificación con el pueblo y con sus raíces comunes.

Perspectiva histórica

Para comprender mejor estas dos trayectorias dentro de la poesía chicana, es preciso trazar, aunque brevemente, una perspectiva histórica y así poder apreciar su diversidad lingüística y social. Para empezar, hay que tener en cuenta que la poesía chicana no es un producto reciente que nació con "El movimiento". Tampoco podemos desprenderla de su nueva condición que originó una nueva conciencia al encontrarse el pueblo en calidad de conquistados y relegados a una realidad de extranjeros en una nación que ya no era de ellos.

Los vestigios de la poesía chicana se remontan a los comienzos del siglo diecisiete cuando Gaspar Pérez de Villagrá escribe en verso la *Historia de la Nuevo México.*[1] Este largo poema histórico fue publicado en 1610 en Alcalá, España, y consiste en 34 cantos que dan una crónica de las hazañas heroicas de Don Juan de Oñate y la subsecuente dominación del pueblo Acoma. A pesar de que esta obra es más un documento histórico que literario, no podemos ignorar su rica descripción poética, como lo atestiguan algunos críticos como Luis González Obregón.[2] Con la aparición de esta obra se empieza a dar relación de realidades netamente americanas y específicamente de Nuevo México. Los colonizadores nuevomexicanos continúan la tradición oral española en sus pastorelas, posadas y autos sacramentales que eran recogidos en cuadernos que se repartían a los participantes para ser cantados y guardados por ellos para su memorización y perpetuación de estos eventos sociales y religiosos. Muchos de estos parlamentos eran improvisados y reflejaban su propio medio ambiente y realidad social en el enclave al que pertenecían: semi-aislado y en poca comunicación con el resto de la colonia de la Nueva España. Este aislamiento empezó a producir cambios profundos que poco a poco fueron moldeando la base de su propia identidad lingüística y la realización de un mundo en el cual la lucha era constante en contra del medio ambiente y pueblos hostiles. La importación de romances de España por las expediciones que incursaban en el norte, trajo nuevas formas que fueron acogidas con entusiasmo transformándolas e incorporándolas rápidamente a su propia situación de vida y estilo. Este procedimiento popular de estilo poético estaba basado en una perspectiva que incluía: (1) el empleo del lenguaje popular como expresión poética; (2) énfasis de la narrativa en la estructura y contenido y (3) la inclusión de su propia situación humana.[3] La tradición oral en Nuevo México continuó a través de todo el período colonial implantando una tradición cultural hispánica que se aferró a todas las facetas de eventos sociales y religiosos que eran muy comunes y frecuentes, con el intento de aliviar la árdua tarea de la vida fronteriza y el áspero ambiente.

En el período mexicano (1810-1848), los colonos se establecieron en clases sociales claramente separadas: los rancheros, los criollos, los vaqueros y la gente del pueblo, mestizos e indígenas. En California, la élite compuesta por los rancheros y religiosos que guardaban la tradición española era la "gente de razón" que tenazmente luchaba por retener su cultura hispánica en contra de las incursiones de los yankees que ya habían infiltrado en Texas y ahora en California. Durante este período la poesía escrita y difundida se vuelve elitista, apoyada por las clases dirigentes y apegadas a conservar su legacía cultural. Santa Fe en Nuevo México y Santa Bárbara en California surgen como centros culturales y la cultura popular y espontánea ya está claramente separada y excluida de los centros culturales. Sin embargo, el pueblo no deja de crear sus propias formas y ahora hay individuos que se aventuran a dar funciones para el pueblo en donde las tandas de clara rebelión social son finamente disfrazadas en autos sacramentales y se improvisan entremeses en contra de algún personaje opresor del pueblo. Pero las arengas de algún orador espontáneo no iban dirigidas solamente en contra de su propia gente, sino que el pueblo ya tenía conciencia de otra cultura distinta y ajena que poco a poco se iba filtrando, alterando la vida social, política y cultural hasta que culminó en la completa marginación del pueblo al perder México su territorio a la insaciable onda de expansionismo yankee. Otra de las formas de la cultura popular en esa época fueron los llamados "torneos poéticos" en donde los trovadores populares de una región se enfrentaban con otros por medio de un alarde de coplas espontáneas para determinar quién era el mejor cantador de trovas y de cómo respondía a los desafíos de los otros trovadores. Uno de los más conocidos por su elegancia en las trovas era "El Viejo Vilmas". Sus trovas fueron recogidas en un escrito llamado *Los Trovos del Viejo Vilmas*.[4] En una serie de versos se relatan los torneos poéticos en que participaba y ganaba Vilmas y hasta se documenta su justa poética con el gran trovador mexicano "El Negrito Poeta".[5]

En la trayectoria culta se destacan los californios Joaquín Buelna, cuya obra mayor fue su *Loa a la Virgen del Refugio,*[6] y el militar Guillermo Zúñiga, autor de un romance histórico intitulado *La Batalla de los Tulares* en donde como participante relata la rebelión de una tribu de indios de Santa Bárbara en contra de los colonos mestizos.[7] En esta obra de Zúñiga ya se perfilan indicios de nuevos elementos opresivos al negar el autor su propia condición de mestizo y alabar las hazañas de opresión en contra de los indios y colonos nuevos.[8]

El año 1848 es un punto de partida para la poesía mexicoamericana. La realidad de encontrarse bajo una nueva nación con diferentes leyes y cultura, distrajo al pueblo de su continuación elitista en la poesía al dedicarse a luchar por mantener lo que les pertenecía y en ajustarse a una nueva condición de ciudadanos de segunda clase. Empiezan entonces a aparecer algunos poemas de protesta puestos como relleno en los periódicos fronterizos y aun en algunos de Santa Fe, pero su producción no es abundante puesto que en estos periódicos y panfletos se encuentra la poesía lírica de tipo romántico en mayor número que la de protesta.[9] Sin embargo, este estado de tensión creado por la confluencia de culturas, asienta una de las bases de la poesía chicana contemporánea: la poesía de protesta y la temática de la opresión.[10] José M. Vigil, un poeta contribuyente al *Nuevo Mundo,* periódico publicado en San Francisco, California durante la época de la guerra civil americana, debe ser considerado como antecesor de este tipo de poesía.[11]

Entre 1910 y la Segunda Guerra Mundial, proliferan los "periódicos de barrio" y éstos llegan a un número impresionante debido al aislamiento en que se encontraba la población mexicoamericana en relación a la prensa mexicana. La aparente trayectoria poética en estos periódicos de barrio renueva las dos trayectorias ya antes establecidas: la popular, ahora de protesta, y la culta todavía afianzada a una orientación conservadora que reflejaba los valores artísticos de la clase media y de la moral católica.[12] Pero de entre estos dos niveles, sobresale una voz disidente que es la de Gabriel de la Riva en San Francisco, California. Según Herminio Ríos en su introducción al libro *"...y no se lo tragó la tierra"* de Tomás Rivera: "Las obras poéticas de Gabriel de la Riva reflejan un amplio conocimiento de la mitología griega y a la vez reflejan un profundo entendimiento al igual que una simpatía para con la lucha mexicoamericana de su época."[13]

Al encontrarse los Estados Unidos envuelto en la Segunda Guerra Mundial, la frontera se abre para dejar entrar la segunda gran oleada de inmigración mexicana. Los Estados Unidos necesitan trabajadores para mantener su maquinaria bélica y para cosechar sus campos. Los mexicanos y los chicanos se concentran en las ciudades ahora en mayor número y llegan a formar el más bajo nivel de la clase trabajadora. Esta gran concentración de raza en las ciudades da comienzo a los llamados ghettos y barrios en donde la explotación desmesurada de este pueblo, engendra los famosos Zoot Suit Riots de 1943. Esta confrontación abierta con el orden establecido produce por primera vez una palpable solidaridad del pueblo chicano que experimenta con sangre la brutal discriminación racial que había venido sufriendo en diferentes formas por casi un siglo. Como un velo rasgado, la rebeldía abierta de los Pachucos descubre al pueblo chicano su tradición y legacía cultural que ya casi estaba en el olvido. Pero este descubrimiento también despertó la conciencia de que había entre ellos una nueva estética, cultura y orientación filosófica que se comunicaba con un lenguaje diferente que no era ni mexicano ni anglosajón; era una amalgama de los dos, como ellos mismos lo eran. Después de la guerra, los chicanos que regresaron se dieron cuenta de que nada había cambiado; que todavía tenían que seguir la lucha por su propia tierra. Mas ahora, el chicano se encontró con la opción de la educación del G.I. Bill y varios de ellos entraron en las universidades en busca de un mejoramiento social y económico. No hubo mucha actividad poética durante este tiempo aunque existen varios poemas como los escritos por Servando Cárdenas y distribuidos en Corpus Christi.[14] Estos poemas tienen como tema al Pachuco, pero éste no se encuentra idealizado o mitificado sino meramente descrito en su comportamiento y lenguaje. Estas descripciones son irónicas y burlescas y tienden a reafirmar los antiguos valores mexicanos que según el poeta yacían olvidados y descartados.[15] A pesar de esta inactividad literaria, los chicanos empiezan a renovar su lucha política, económica y social por todo el suroeste y en las fiestas del Cinco de Mayo y 16 de Septiembre, los declamadores populares tientan el afán patriótico del pueblo recitando a poetas mexicanos como López Velarde.

Después de esta aparente calma e inactividad de los cincuenta, la fermentación política y cultural está ya implantada en un pueblo ahora consciente de fervor nacionalista. La explosión militante de los chicanos en los sesenta no fue espontánea como muchas veces parecía en la prensa; fue la culminación de un largo y penoso proceso histórico como se ha visto en lo anterior. Pero ahora se desborda en todos los frentes: en lo político, en lo económico, en lo social y en lo cultural.

La Poesía Chicana a partir del Movimiento

Como consecuencia natural de la brecha abierta por el "movimiento negro", el chicano se abandera con los slogans del "movimiento chicano" y de *La causa*. En los campos surgen los Chávez y en las ciudades los Corky Gonzales; en el campo literario y cultural surge un "renacimiento" sin antecedentes en la historia del pueblo chicano.[16] La conciencia del chicano ya había sido fundamentalmente alterada por los nuevos dirigentes que exigían cambios radicales en la situación del pueblo y, para difundir esta nueva conciencia, se empezó a imprimir un sinnúmero de panfletos, "newsletters" y periódicos locales que llevaban la palabra al pueblo. La poesía en estos impresos fue abundante y espontánea. Ya no la empleaban como simple relleno sino que ahora desempeñaba la función de hacer oír la indignación del pueblo en una forma literaria históricamente propicia para la sensibilidad requerida. El corrido también predominó en los periódicos rurales ya que éste era una de las formas que más se adaptaba para ser contada y cantada durante las peregrinaciones que hacían los huelguistas en Sacramento y en las caminatas a zonas agrícolas del estado que debían oír el mensaje. Luis Valdez adoptó el corrido como fondo musical a sus actos teatrales funcionando como coro que comentaba la representación sugiriendo a los huelguistas posibles soluciones necesarias y animándolos a la acción social. *El Mal-*

criado, periódico publicado en Delano, California y dedicado a *La causa*, recoge muchos de estos corridos y poemas de los campesinos y huelguistas de esta región. Por primera vez la voz del campesino es capturada en estos periódicos rurales que empiezan a aparecer por todos los rincones del suroeste: *El Gallo* de Colorado, *Los Muertos Hablan* de Laredo, Texas, *Ya Mero* de McAllen, Texas y *Sal si Puedes* de Santa Bárbara, California. La claridad de su mensaje propone un lenguaje de expresión popular que postula una nueva poética que proyecta la realidad que unifica el lenguaje y el mensaje. Las masas campesinas, históricamente relegadas a un trasfondo invisiblemente literario, encuentran una apertura en estas publicaciones y una oportunidad para exponer lo que siempre había estado encerrado y vedado en ellos: su propia expresión poética. En forma de paráfrasis de lo que dijo Octavio Paz en *El laberinto de la soledad:* al descubrirse el lenguaje chicano, se creó la poesía chicana. Las palabras y expresiones del pueblo, siempre tomadas como vulgares por las clases dominantes, son ahora el vehículo que nos hace penetrar en un mundo que solamente puede ser explicado y descrito en su propio lenguaje. La expresión poética ya no es la palabra florida, resonante, afectada, sino la simple, desnuda e hiriente de la realidad. La poesía de protesta renace llena de slogans, repeticiones e imitaciones, pero el pueblo la acoge como eco de su propio sentir. El Pachuco y el "vato loco" se idealizan como símbolos de rebeldía y protesta y el caló o el lenguaje pachuco predominó y funcionó como lenguaje de expresión poética. Un ejemplo de esta clase de poesía popular es el poema anónimo que puede representar el sentimiento prevalente durante el pujante "renacimiento literario chicano" acoplado con *La causa* de Delano:

Ahora es cuando Raza

Ahora es cuando Raza
Ya basta
es tiempo de despertar
los gabachos nos comen el mandado
y nosotros no tenemos guebos pa quejar
En Delano ya se a visto que se puede
aunque nos den en la madre por tratar
y si tienes miedo o piensas que te duele
haste a un lado pal que quiera jalar
Nomás cuando tengamos la justicia
no digas "ya vencimos" sin luchar
porque sino jalamos parejos
mas vale ni siquiera empezar[17]

Notamos en este poema anónimo una preocupación por la forma, por la rima para que "parezca" poema. También se notará que no tiene palabras en inglés y esto supone que el autor quería expresarse en español para dar a entender que todavía lo hablaba y que conocía la tradición poética hispana del género. Sin embargo, se podría decir que este poema trata de seguir la forma del corrido ya que ésta era la forma más popular y conocida y que también se podía cantar para ser aprendida y divulgada. Se nota además en este poema, que no contiene muchas palabras del caló urbano porque el español empleado, aunque con faltas de ortografía y "vulgarismos", es perfectamente entendido por cualquiera que hable español. Deduzco que el autor de este poema era un "mexicano" trabajador de los campos de Delano que apenas estaba cobrando conciencia de "lo chicano".

Los que empezaron a darse cuenta de una forma diferente con la posibilidad de una poética chicana fueron aquéllos que reconocieron el alcance que podría tener una poesía escrita en los dos idiomas del chicano. Al principio, esta clase de poesía era un poco burda al no percibirse un procedimiento sistemático en el empleo de las palabras en ambos idiomas sin ton ni son. Pero para 1968 se publica, por primera vez, una serie de diez poemas escritos por Alurista en forma bilingüe sorprendentemente bien manejada. Al estudiar más detenidamente estos poemas bilingües publicados en *El Grito*, se da uno cuenta de que dentro de ese bilingüismo están intercaladas otras expresiones dialectales como el Black English, el caló urbano, el *slang* americano y el habla del pachuco. Entonces, ya no basta entender los dos idiomas, el inglés y el español, sino que también hay que conocer los diferentes dialectos y expresiones chicanas para comprender estos poemas en su totalidad. Hablando sobre esta nueva forma de expresión bilingüe que Alurista ya estaba proponiendo, Jesús Maldonado dice:

> Por esta razón la Poesía Chicana es un arte único. No es posible comprenderle sin saber inglés y español. Lo esencial, la mera papa de la poesía de Alurista está precisamente en el "piquete" de las palabras. . . Si no saben estas cositas, pos, ni pa' cuando que puedan saborear la Poesía Chicana como se debe saborear toda obra poética.[18]

Con la publicación de *Floricanto*, la poesía chicana adquiere un tono innovador y vanguardista a través de la forma poética, ya concientemente creada; el lenguaje bilingüe y sus expresiones persiguen una forma estética en la posición y contra-posición de la expresión

lingüística al alcanzar estos elementos la intensidad de expresión
que conlleva el hábil empleo de las palabras. Con esta innovación
estilística, Alurista crea un vívido mosaico de imágenes duales super-
impuestas en varias dimensiones perceptibles solamente al iniciado
en la experiencia chicana. Herminio Ríos hace este comentario:

> Cuando Alurista escribe: Mis ojos hinchados flooded with lágrimas
> de bronce. . ./, la tensión e intensidad que adquiere la palabra "flood-
> ed" al llenar un espacio lingüístico dentro de una estructura sintác-
> tica extranjera, se le da a la imagen un valor expresivo que no lo hu-
> biera tenido sin esta intrusión sintáctica. En vez de una simple
> "flood", Alurista crea un diluvio de "lágrimas de bronce". Y éstas
> son lágrimas de bronce porque Alurista escribe acerca de un pueblo
> de bronce; él siente el sufrimiento de su pueblo de bronce. Además
> de esto, la intrusión sintáctica de "flooded" intensifica la metáfora
> "lágrimas de bronce" y esta imagen nos hace sentir la inmensidad
> de ese sufrimiento infinitamente más intenso.[19]

El bilingüismo en el habla chicana ha sido siempre un elemento normal de expresión para el chicano desde que se encontraron las dos
lenguas, y es por esto que se justifica que para llegar poéticamente
al alma chicana, al poeta se le impone una obligación estructural para
ser comprensible a los lectores chicanos. Sin embargo, la intrusión
lingüística del inglés no se superimpone para crear un poema inglés
con intrusión del español; estos poemas son claramente identifica-
bles como poemas en español reforzados con expresiones inglesas y
pachuquismos para recrear la realidad lingüística del chicano. Veamos un poema como ejemplo representativo de esta afinación lingüística escrito por otro de los maestros del bilingüismo, José Montoya:

Early Pieces

>   Tony junior fue el que nos dijo
>   El hijo de Don Antonio
>   The ruco who runs the old
>   Beer joint across from the chino
>   Que la Rosa the new cantinera the
>   One who was a wetback
>   Was doing it with all
>   The chavalitos, just don't tell!
>   So me and Meño y el culerio carnal de
>   La coja went over
>   Like we were shining
>   Shoes y no habia nadie and she's in
>   There alone reading a funnybook moving
>   Her lips and she yells,
>   No hay nadie, mas tarde, eh?
>   And she lifts her dress a little

And we look embarrassed at
Each other and she goes back
   To the comic and moving her lips.
We stand there todos escamaus and confused
   Then we run off to Meño's
   Garage and when the other vatitos
Get there we start bragging how we got
It from the wetback cantinera and Tony
   Junior looks surprized so we
   All laugh and sit down to jack off.[20]

Para un bilingüe, este poema de Montoya se lee con un ritmo que no se pierde aun zigzagueando del inglés al español; es más, el inglés ni se notaría si no estuviera uno consciente de la presencia de los dos idiomas. El español y el inglés fluyen poéticamente y forman una unidad lingüística que unifica estructuralmente al poema y funde las metáforas y las imágenes en un concierto de mensaje y forma.

Uno de los poemas sobresalientes durante el período de "El movimiento" es *Yo soy Joaquín* de Rodolfo "Corky" Gonzales. Publicado por primera vez en 1967 como "una épica del pueblo mexicoamericano", *Yo soy Joaquín* se ha distinguido desde entonces como el poema más famoso y representativo de "El movimiento". Gonzales unifica al pueblo chicano con el pueblo mexicano por medio de sus raíces comunes, por la invocación de mitos ancestrales y de las leyendas de personajes heroicos como Cuauhtémoc, Hidalgo, Villa y Zapata, fundiéndolos en símbolos comunes de los dos pueblos. Pero la realidad divergente del chicano es manifestada en la pluralidad del pueblo chicano:

Peleo con revolucionarios
      contra mí mismo
Yo soy Rural
    ordinario y bruto
Yo soy el indio montañero
     superior a todos.
El galope truenoroso son mis caballos.
El chirrido de ametralladoras
   es muerte para todos que son yo:
     yaqui
      tarahumara
     chamula
      zapoteca
       mestizo
        español[21]

Este poema le descubre su identidad y sus raíces al chicano; ya no es él el desheredado de México y América. Ahora sabe lo que siempre había sospechado y sentido: que no solamente basta cargar el peso de sus antepasados en la sangre, sino que hay que admitirlo orgullosamente y aceptar la obligación ancestral de continuar la lucha para la perpetuación. *Yo soy Joaquín* fue escrito enteramente en inglés con el propósito de darle mayor difusión, pues ya no era el campesino o el obrero que escribía para sus compañeros; era ahora la voz del chicano en general: el urbano, el campesino, el obrero, el estudiante, el blanco, el mestizo y el indio.

Al empezar la década de los setenta, el furor nacionalista incitado por "El movimiento" ya había llegado a la cumbre en la tragedia del *Moratorium* en Los Angeles. Tenía que haber un cambio de dirección tanto en el campo político como en el cultural. La formación de programas de estudios chicanos en varias universidades y colegios inyecta nuevas esperanzas de solidificar la lucha en todos los frentes. La literatura chicana tenía que estudiarse, pero hasta entonces era muy vaga, difusa y difícil de conseguir. Los poetas del Movimiento tenían que afianzar sus conquistas, crecer artísticamente y ofrecer al pueblo un arte verdaderamente chicano. Hacía falta un nacionalismo cultural que siguiera el postulado de Franz Fanon en su libro *The Wretched of the Earth*. Los primeros años de los setenta, el "renacimiento literario" dentro de la poesía fue incrementado por la aparición de los libros de Alurista, Ricardo Sánchez, Omar Salinas, José Montoya y Tino Villanueva. Abelardo Delgado, a quien podemos considerar el precursor de los poetas del Movimiento, ya había venido publicando varias colecciones siguiendo las formas tradicionales, pero con la publicación de *Chicano* (1969), impreso por él mismo, Abelardo se une a la nueva forma chicana, sobre todo con "Stupid America", uno de los poemas más comentados y recitados de la poesía chicana. Estos poetas de los setenta son ya más pulidos, conscientes de la forma bilingüe y del contenido con impacto. La mitología indígena se sobrepone a la greco-romana o se funde con ella. Las formas tradicionales respiran nuevas incursiones e intentos de innovación. Las imágenes se vuelven más complejas al mezclarse toda clase de expresión conocida por el chicano; el poeta se preocupa por encontrar una estética que mejor represente por sí misma el universo artístico y cultural del chicano. Durante este período se separan, se bifurcan y se juntan como una doble hélice en espiral las dos trayectorias socioculturales determinantes dentro de la poesía popular y la poesía refinadamente artística.

Los poetas de La Nueva Trayectoria

Llamo poetas de "La Nueva Trayectoria" a aquellos que conscientemente buscan, dentro de las formas poéticas tradicionales, nuevos modelos, nuevas creaciones de metáforas personales usando la expresión chicana para crear imágenes dentro de una realidad artísticamente chicana que fije nuestra sensibilidad dentro del mosaico artístico universal. Estos poetas no son los espontáneos de las manifestaciones o los trovadores del sentimiento popular del momento; éstos son los que han leído y estudiado la poesía internacional, los que se han formado con estilos poéticos desde los clásicos como Homero hasta la poesía "Beat" de Ginsberg. Estos son los poetas que tratan de encontrar un nuevo estilo en la fusión de la forma-contenido. Los que tratan de alcanzar universalidad sin dejar de pisar sus raíces. La mayoría de estos poetas han sido instruidos en las universidades americanas y poseen las artes necesarias para su tarea poética. Con pocas excepciones, notablemente la de Miguel Méndez, encontramos los autodidactas comparablemente hábiles en este arte. En varios de estos poetas se notan influencias de poetas latinoamericanos, americanos, franceses y aun orientales. Unos lo confiesan, otros no; pero estas influencias son las que los proyectan en la trayectoria hacia lo universal, pues al estar conscientes de estas formas e influencias, estos artífices tratan de encontrar dentro de ello la mera esencia del arte chicano. *Perros y Anti-Perros* de Sergio Elizondo puede partir de *Poemas y antipoemas* de Nicanor Parra. Alurista admite influencia de *Trece poetas del mundo azteca* de León Portilla, y varios de ellos rinden homenaje a Pablo Neruda. Algunos se vuelven indigenistas, como Aristeo Brito y Miguel Méndez, y tratan de revivir ese pasado envuelto en la neblina del misterio impregnando de sabor poético a los nombres y palabras del náhuatl, maya o yaqui; palabras que por su difícil pronunciación inyectan a la forma poética el carácter místico y esotérico de una mitología ajena a la poesía universal. Me sería imposible dar en este estudio un ejemplo de cada uno de estos poetas a quienes clasifico dentro de esta trayectoria, pero intentaré dar una flexible categorización de ellos según sus tendencias o habilidades para crear imágenes rescatadas de la experiencia chicana ya sea en forma tradicional o popular. Hay varias posibilidades de otras clasificaciones como la separación según las influencias de las literaturas nacionales en las cuales han sido instruidos y que les han proporcionado los medios con los cuales recrear esas imágenes. Pero en esta clasificación tendríamos el problema de que en algunos poetas se ven influencias mexicanas y americanas, y en otros se dan las tres: la mexicana, la americana y la chicana. Sin embargo, por el momento, esta clasificación según las influencias es la más adaptable ya que me parece la más fácil de identificar. La influencia americana proviene de poetas anglosajones, ya sean de los Estados Unidos, Inglaterra, Canadá o cualquier otra nación en que se hable el inglés; la mexicana incluye toda la tradición hispanoamericana, y la chicana, que parte de estas dos, convierte esa dualidad en una influencia única.

Los poetas de influencia claramente americana (incluyendo la poesía "Beat") son Tino Villanueva, Ricardo Sánchez, Juan Gómez-Quiñones, Raúl Salinas, Bernice Zamora y Juan Felipe Herrera. Un ejemplo representativo de esta categoría puede ser un poema de Tino Villanueva:

Catharsis

Into the page-stuffed night
in Pavlovian-like response at
                    semester's end
I go groping through
        Lorca's New York surrealism
        Whitman's symbology,
                    greenboard formulas,
        and untangling dangling participles by
        midnight tick-tock alarm clock.
In late Fall and Spring comes this
        ritual of grotesque notebooks,
thoughts surrounded by underlined
                    paragraphs of future.
And shortly,
            early rays come solid through the
curtains in my cram. . . cram. . . cramming for a
final classroom catharsis—
with only the morning sun for breakfast,
            turning the pages in habitual
syndrome with cigarette,
                    I yield to nausea.[22]

En este poema de Villanueva, sacado de su libro *Hay otra voz*, se pueden distinguir claramente las influencias de la literatura universal y su condicionamiento en las universidades americanas. Las referencias a Pavlov, Lorca y Whitman refuerzan las imágenes del mundo con el cual tiene que contender. Las expresiones "page-stuffed", "Pavlovian-like" and "cram. . .cram. . .cramming" denotan la influencia de la poesía americana contemporánea, notablemente la

"Beat", pero su última frase "I yield to nausea" es la catarsis esperada de alguien no preparado para vivir en un mundo que no contiene sus propias raíces. Este poema me recuerda la misma "nausea" del cuento de Nick Vaca, "A Week in the Life of Manuel Hernández", donde la metamorfosis gradual de chicano a profesional académico resulta en una náusea fatal al darse cuenta de que "algo falta" cuando uno trata de moldearse y caber en un mundo que no es el suyo.

Los poetas de influencia mexicana (incluyendo el indigenismo) son: Sergio Elizondo, Abelardo, Miguel Méndez, Aristeo Brito y Alurista. Un poema dentro de esta clasificación en donde se converge hábilmente la mitología judeocristiana con la náhuatl es el logrado poema de Alurista de su colección *El Ombligo de Aztlán:*

> *Bronze Rape*
>
> la india se arrodillaba
>   en el río
> a recoger agua iba
>   mujer de fibra
> bronze tez apenas
>   notables are the round
>   moons of your breasts
> and hair dark flowing
>   to the breath and
>   will of the ehecatl, padre
>   del viento
>   y de la aventura alada
>   que prendió al criollo
>   en su bronzeada caída
> kissed her forehead
>   and raped the silence
> of the trickle, trickle, trickle
> of the stream
>   pulling the ground
>   to her dark plumaje screaming
> el mestizo
>   ante el altar
> nació sin padre
>   pero sí con mucha madre[23]

Este poema es una hermosa imagen sobre las raíces divinas del mestizo en donde Alurista ha tomado un cuadro representativo de la "Anunciación de la Virgen María" y lo traspuso con imágenes indígenas evocando en conjunto todas las imágenes de este tipo en el arte universal: las representaciones por varios pintores de la "Anunciación" y aun las clásicas representaciones greco-romanas sobre la violación divina que produce a un semi-dios, tales como "Leda y el Cisne" o la violación de Diana por Apolo. En este poema de Alurista, la núbil virgen es una india de "bronze tez apenas / notables are the round / moons of your breasts" quien ha sido seleccionada por "ehecatl, padre / del viento", una deidad del panteón náhuatl y padre de los dioses. El Espíritu Santo está representado por "la aventura alada / que prendió al criollo / en su bronzeada caída" y la intervención divina de la violación ocurre en la metáfora "kissed her forehead / and raped the silence. . ." La consumación de este acto divino es la unión del cielo (lo divino) con la tierra (lo humano): "pulling the ground / to her dark plumaje". Y la consecuencia, el nacimiento violento del mestizo: "screaming / el mestizo / ante el altar / nació sin padre / pero sí con mucha madre". Y esto, en efecto, en nuestra raza mestiza es la realidad: el padre español, considerado por los indígenas como un dios, viola a la india (en esta imagen no solamente se incluye lo sexual, sino también la cultura, la lengua y la civilización indígena) de la cual nace el mestizo repudiado por el padre pero que retiene todo en su madre indígena. La doble imagen de la metáfora "pero sí con mucha madre" es interpretada en dos niveles: (1) el tener el mestizo sus raíces y valores en lo indígena y (2) el de tener "mucha madre" (valentía) para sobrevivir la explotación y opresión proveniente de su propio padre.

En su tercer libro *Timespace Huracán*, Alurista es indudablemente más indigenista, empleando voces mayas y náhuatl, inclusive usando la numerología maya para subdividir las estrofas. Pero al virar más al indigenismo, Alurista se aleja al mismo tiempo del sistema anglosajón como algo que ya no se puede salvar o que no tiene redención. Si él antes escribía la palabra América con *K*, ahora la escribe con dos y hasta con tres *kaes:* "amerikkka / klan de penny yankee".[24] Si su temática penetra ahora más en lo indigenista, la forma que él emplea es un alarde de experimentación de modelos: desde las coplas hasta el Hai-ku. Alurista usa estas formas básicas pero continúa reestructurándolas en sus propias versiones con diferentes toques gráficos y estilísticos en lo que él mismo llama "poesía lapidaria". Según Alurista: "Lapidary poetry is like beads. I bring myself to an economy of language and I use a number of principles in poetry, especially the hai-ku, except that I use the pivot line which is the pivot line in the seventeenth syllable form and use it at the beginning or at the end and sometimes I use it over and over again".[25] A continuación es un ejemplo de su libro *Timespace Huracán* en donde Alurista emplea una de sus formas favoritas, la espiral:

In lak'ech

tú eres la vida
   el sol y la luz
   tú eres la tierra
     la raza y la flor
   tú eres el arco
        de lluvia y de amor
   tú eres aurora
          rocío luchador
   tú eres sudores
           de manos labor
     caminas veredas
      valles de creación
dadores de la vida
   la tuna sin espinas
   la causa libertaria
     da su miel
inlak'ech
   inlak'ech
     inlak'ech
       inlak'ech
    mi otro yó tú eres
   tú eres mi otro yó
     reflejo humanizante
   conciencia de la unión
inlak'ech
   inlak'ech
     inlak'ech
       inlak'ech
   unión amerindia
cadenas ya no más se abren las fronteras
   se apaga la opresión
del árbol de la vida
   la fuente de armonía
   marchítase'l imperio
     brota la paz[26]

La forma espiral es para Alurista el símbolo del pensamiento maya: todo se mueve en espiral o en forma serpentina conteniendo en ella movimiento y medida. Desde *Floricanto* hasta *Timespace Huracán* se nota claramente la dinámica estilística y formalista de Alurista que no cesa ni cesará hasta que tal vez se llene de experimentar y jugar con todas las formas poéticas pero sin dejar la temática del indigenismo y la opresión.

Otro poeta dentro de esta clasificación cuyas imágenes brotan del mismo suelo del desierto y su naturaleza inhóspita en donde la planta más fuerte es la que sobrevive a pesar del ambiente es Miguel

Salvador Rodríguez del Pino

Méndez y su poema épico *Los Criaderos Humanos.* Méndez es un mago al crear imágenes ilusionistas por medio de metáforas que aparentemente parecen rebuscadas pero que tienen la sencillez de una creación espontánea: "Voces superficiales de arena me golpean con la fiebre negra de palabras hundidas en la tierra".[27] Esta "Epica de los desamparados" es un poema de sesenta páginas en el cual Méndez hace un peregrinaje por una tierra "que se traga a la tierra". Es un peregrinaje sin fin, tal vez una "muerte sin fin" como la de Gorostiza.

Los poetas de influencia chicana (incluyendo Black Poetry) son la mayoría de los citados, pero principalmente José Montoya, Omar Salinas, Alurista y casi todas las poetisas chicanas. Estos rescatadores de imágenes que considero netamente chicanas hacen brotar recuerdos e imágenes por medio de metáforas compuestas de inconfundibles expresiones chicanas y otros dialectos de las minorías americanas que solamente un chicano comprendería en su totalidad. Aparte de la forma bilingüemente expresiva, estos poetas evocan y hacen vibrar de nuevo el mero palpitar de esa esencia chicana elusiva para el que no comprende. Recurro de nuevo a José Montoya para recrear en su poema líricamente narrado las voces, lugares y acontecimientos del barrio; pero es su casi apoteosis del Pachuco lo que sobresale en su poema, "El Louie", que reproduzco aquí en fragmentos que sobresalen para identificar a los poetas de esta clasificación:

El Louie

Evocación del tiempo:	Hoy enterraron al Louie And San Pedro o sanpinche are in for it. And those times of the forties and the early fifties lost un vato de atole.
Descripción del Pachuco:	Kind of slim and drawn, there toward the end, aging fast from too much booze y la vida dura. But class to the end. En Sanjo you'd see him sporting a dark topcoat playing in his fantasy the role of Bogart, Cagney or Raft.

. . . .

Wow, is that el Louie
Mire, comadre, ahí va el hijo de Lola!

La poesía chicana

Los barrios y el pueblo:

Era de Fowler el vato
carnal del Candi y el
Ponchi—Los Rodríguez—
The Westside knew 'em
and Selma, even Gilroy

La paradoja del chicano:

Hoy enterraron al Louie.
His death was an insult
porque no murió en acción—
no lo mataron los vatos,
ni los gooks en Korea.
He died alone in a rented
room—perhaps like a
Bogart movie.

The end was a cruel hoax.
But his life had been
remarkable!

Vato de atole, el Louie Rodríguez.[28]

Las poetisas chicanas

Como mencioné anteriormente, considero a las poetisas chicanas dentro de la clasificación de lo chicano con la excepción de Bernice Zamora quien tiene doble clasificación con la categoría americana. Estas mujeres poetas tienen también la distinción de pertenecer a una doble minoría: la chicana y la de la mujer. Estas poetisas chicanas se meten con fervor en los dos campos tratando una doble temática, la opresión del sistema y la temática de la opresión de la tradición machista chicana, herencia de la cultura mexicana. Estas mujeres evocan con sensibles recuerdos la vida familiar del barrio y lo pintan con una ternura nostálgica para preservar y conservar esas imágenes que tal vez se pierdan para siempre; pero, a la misma vez, están tratando de romper esas tradiciones de su herencia que históricamente las han oprimido dentro de su propio pueblo. Es la lucha irreconciliable: preservar y desechar lo que vale y lo que no debe perdurar. Algunas de ellas como Bernice Zamora y Virginia Cunningham emplean un lenguaje más directo y a veces estridente "sin rodeos" para resaltar la urgencia de su mensaje.

Los temas predominantes en esta poesía son dirigidos en contra de la violación y discriminación sexual y en contra de la tradición mexicana que relega a la mujer como un miembro pasivo ante el hombre y la sociedad; pero en la expresión se nota la voz amarga y dulce de una dualidad que todavía no acepta la completa emancipación. Margarita Cota Cárdenas y Angela de Hoyos conservan esas imágenes del barrio, imágenes nostálgicas e irónicas a la vez, conmovedoras y punzantes, una amargura dulce de lo que fue pero que no debe seguir. Bernice Zamora ha tenido la distinción o el dudable halago de que su poesía "parece haber sido escrita por un hombre".[29] Confieso la falta de no haber estudiado más detenidamente a estas poetisas dignas de un estudio profundo dentro de la poesía chicana y de la mujer. Evangelina Vigil e Inés Tovar son otras que se deben mencionar como innovadoras de un estilo a que los poetas chicanos todavía no han llegado.

En revistas tales como *Caracol, De Colores* y *Mango* se nota una predominancia de poetas chicanas. Más y más sus voces se están alzando, pero sospecho que aun dentro de las publicaciones chicanas, estas poetisas aún encuentran cierta discriminación velada al tratar de publicar sus libros. Tenemos todavía la mentalidad de que la mujer poeta debe tratar temas dulces y tiernos como Elizabeth Browning y que no tienen lugar en la poesía de protesta, mucho menos sobre sus derechos de mujer. Para muchos críticos y escritores chicanos o mexicanos, la única mujer digna de ser llamada poetisa es Sor Juana Inés de la Cruz, en quien comienza y termina la poesía escrita por una mujer. Sin embargo, se notará una contradicción al darse uno cuenta de que los primeros premios en concursos literarios chicanos, los primeros lugares han sido ganados por mujeres. Se sospecha una leve inclinación por borrar el estigma de la discriminación en contra de la mujer, ya sea fidedigna o causada por un remordimiento. Pero a pesar de esta laguna en la poesía chicana, veremos en los próximos años un torrente de poesía escrita por mujeres que no más esperan que se desate ese nudo gordiano que aparentemente tienen las publicaciones chicanas y americanas.

Restless Serpents es una colección de Bernice Zamora publicada en complicidad con José Antonio Burciaga, un pintor y muralista que promete como poeta pero que no he tenido el gusto de estudiar. La poesía de Zamora es pulida y calculada. Sus influencias vienen como en fisión de átomos y ella las absorbe con ilusoria facilidad para darles formas, innovadas o tradicionales, con una expresión callada pero penetrante de simbolismo. Su poema "Pico Blanco" es para mí uno de sus más reveladores de su ideología como mujer y como chicana:

Pico Blanco

On your "steep sea-wave of marble"
I stand—mad Cassandra, screeching

perhaps, but straining my eyes
to catch a glimpse of the "great king,
cold and austere," or the "pale
hunchback shuffling along corridors,"
or Azevedo's three giant Indians
stepping over the Ventana Mountains
These are the stewards of *your* estate.
You will, I hope, entertain the blond
harlot while I search for mine.
Never mind cousin Christ. He will
rise above America's adoration for
blood in the corners.

"Poor bitch," you say. Indeed I am;
but I am not mumbling to my people
or to my gods. I am chipping the
crust of the Pico Blanco.
Your stewards could help—or you,
Jeffers; then you and I could vacillate
breaking the crust—You and I, Jeffers.[30]

Queda todavía mucho por estudiar. La poesía chicana se extiende y se multiplica espoleada por el nacionalismo y la identidad. Pero la poesía chicana está llegando a niveles de pulimiento artístico por poetas que han ya publicado varios libros y se puede, entonces, apreciar la dinámica creativa que está sacando a la poesía chicana de una adolescencia mediocre para convertirse en sólido y maduro arte nacional de un pueblo cuya lucha se convierte en arte por medio de una ambición obsesiva de supervivencia. Si se estudia por etapas, la poesía chicana tendrá que ser vista por medio de otra perspectiva diferente a la mía pues como hemos visto, las trayectorias de las cuales yo he hablado aparecen y desaparecen dentro de varias épocas históricas. Como dice Tomás Rivera: "La literatura chicana se puede dividir en tres etapas, a partir del movimiento: conservación, lucha e invención".[31] Durante la primera etapa los escritores y poetas trataban de conservar su herencia chicana y escribían sobre acontecimientos pasados como hechos que debían ser recordados y preservados. En la segunda etapa, la protesta, lucha por conservar esa identidad junto con el derecho de ser diferentes pero iguales dentro de la pluralidad americana; la tercera, la invención, es la etapa en que se encuentra actualmente la literatura chicana puesto que ya se ha podido conservar nuestra herencia y estamos conscientes de ella. Esta etapa de invención es el alejamiento de modelos imitativos, los escritores y poetas están ahora creando e inventando una literatura que parte de lo chicano pero que incluye ahora la calidad de lo hu-

Salvador Rodríguez del Pino

mano universal. Otros escritores podrán clasificar a la literatura chicana sobre otras categorías, lícitamente clasificadas, como "la generación inventiva" o "los escritores de la Nueva Conciencia", pero espero que esta clasificación que yo he usado sirva como punto de partida a la realización de que la literatura chicana y más la poesía chicana posee ahora una conciencia definitivamente diferente, temática y formalmente, de los llamados Poetas del Movimiento.

UNIVERSITY OF CALIFORNIA, SANTA BARBARA

Notas

[1]Gaspar de Villagrá, *Historia de la Nuevo México* (México: Museo Nacional, 1900).

[2]Luis González Obregón, "Introducción" a la *Historia de la Nuevo México* de Gaspar de Villagrá (México: Museo Nacional, 1900).

[3]Tomás Ybarra-Frausto, "La poesía chicana". Manuscrito inédito.

[4]Aurelio M. Espinosa, "Los Trovos del Viejo Vilmas", *The Journal of American Folklore,* Vol. XXVII (abril-junio, 1974).

[5]N. León, *El Negrito Poeta mexicano y sus populares versos: Contribución para el folklore nacional* (México: Imprenta del Museo Nacional, 1921).

[6]Los escritos de Joaquín Buelna están en el "Buelna Manuscript", CC-23, en la Biblioteca Bancroft, Berkeley, California.

[7]Aparecen en el Lugo Manuscript, CD-118, en la Biblioteca Bancroft de Berkeley, California.

[8]Ybarra-Frausto, op. cit., p. 9.

[9]Herminio Ríos y Lupe Castillo, "Toward a True Chicano Bibliography: Mexican-American Newspapers: 1848-1942". *El Grito,* 3:4 (Summer, 1970).

[10]Joseph Sommers, "Critical Approaches to Chicano Literature". Presentado en la Modern Language Association, Nueva York, diciembre de 1976, e incluido en la sección III de esta colección.

[11]Los poemas de José M. Vigil aparecen en varios números de *El Nuevo Mundo* desde el año 1848 hasta 1864. Hemeroteca de la Ciudad de San Francisco.

[12]Ybarra-Frausto, op. cit. p. 18.

[13]Herminio Ríos, "Introducción" al libro de Tomás Rivera . . .*y no se lo tragó la tierra* (Berkeley, California: Quinto Sol Publications, Inc., 1971), p. viii.

[14]Ybarra-Frausto, op. cit., p. 26.

[15]Ibid., p. 26.

[16]Philip D. Ortego y José A. Carrasco, "Chicanos and American Literature". En *Searching for America,* editado por Ernece B. Kelly (Urbana, Illinois: 1972).

[17]Este poema anónimo apareció en *Chilam Balam,* sin número (Santa Bárbara, California: 1969).

[18]Jesús Maldonado, *Poesía Chicana: Alurista el mero chingón*. Monograph Series of the Centro de Estudios Chicanos, No. 1 (Seattle, Washington: 1971).

[19]Herminio Ríos, book review of *Chicano* by Richard Vásquez. *El Grito,* 3:3 (Spring, 1970), p. 67.

[20]José Montoya, *El sol y los de abajo* (San Francisco, California: Ediciones Pocho-Che, 1972), p. 1.

[21]Rodolfo Gonzales, *I am Joaquín/ Yo soy Joaquín* (New York: Bantam Books, 1972), p. 39.

[22]Tino Villanueva, *Hay otra voz* (New York: Colección Mensaje, sin fecha), p. 9.

[23]Alurista, "The Poetry of Alurista", *El Grito,* 3:1 (Fall, 1968).

[24]Alurista, *Timespace Huracán* (Albuquerque, New Mexico: Pajarito Publications, 1976), p. 17.

[25]Salvador Rodríguez del Pino, Entrevista con Alurista. Grabada el 20 de abril de 1977.

[26]Alurista, *Timespace Huracán*, p. 32.

[27]Miguel Méndez, *Los Criaderos Humanos* (Tucson, Arizona: Editorial Peregrinos, 1975), p. 3.

[28]José Montoya, "El Louie". En *Rascatripas,* II (Oakland, California: 1970).

[29]Bernice Zamora, Conferencia sobre "Imágenes chicanas y la literatura latinoamericana" (Santa Bárbara, California, 26 mayo, 1977).

[30]Bernice Zamora, *Restless Serpents* (Menlo Park, California: Diseños Literarios, 1976).

[31]Tomás Rivera, "La novela chicana: forma en busca de vida". Conferencia presentada en Santa Bárbara, California, 31 mayo, 1977.

FROM THE TEMPLE TO THE ARENA:
TEATRO CHICANO TODAY

Jorge A. Huerta

The year is 1965, in the very birthpangs of the campesino revolution in California, when a young Chicano named Luis Miguel Valdez goes to César Chávez in Delano and asks if he might work with the union, employing theatre to educate the campesinos about the need for unionization. It is a far cry from the first indígena rituals which marked the beginning of theatre in America so many centuries ago. But yet it is a ritual; a ceremony of expulsion of the evil Tezcatlipoca in the form of the wealthy and repressive California growers. In a small pink house in Delano, Luis Valdez becomes the leader of a movement that will reach hundreds of thousands of people in the United States, Latin America, and other parts of the world: Teatro Chicano.

Luis Valdez was born into a campesino family in the rich and fertile Valle de San Joaquín in 1940, and even as a child was impressed by theatrics and the dramatic experience. Early in his childhood, he began to explore theatre through puppet shows and entertainments he and his friends would mount in the family backyard. He suffered the inadequate education a migrant worker's children are heir to: a continual move from one place to another, barely giving the student time to get acclimated to his new surroundings when the family moves once again, following the crops and the meager existence this form of labor provides. But Luis was somehow different, and he managed to win a scholarship to college where he studied English and dramatic literature. His first play, *The Theft*, written when he was an undergraduate, won him a prize and Valdez was launched on a career that would bring him and his mission international fame.

Just before going to Delano in 1965, Valdez had worked for a year with the radical street theatre, the San Francisco Mime Troupe, and had discovered *commedia dell'arte* being employed in the twentieth century in order to educate the public about social injustices and political reforms. Thus, when Valdez went to César Chávez and asked if he could somehow help in the struggle, he was not certain of what he would do, but he had the seeds of experience with the Mime Troupe firmly implanted and knew he would somehow try to adapt his experiences to the farmworker's struggle.

When Valdez met with a group of huelguistas for the first time, he brought some signs and masks with him, hoping that he could get the campesinos to portray their own realities. The crowd was curious to see who this fervent young man was, and how he might help them. "You can't talk about theatre," he thought to himself, "you have to *do* it." So he asked the group what it was they were going through and which were the experiences they wished to share with others. Immediately, a campesina began relating an experience she had undergone with another campesino who was an esquirol, and Luis interrupted her and asked if she could demonstrate what occurred. "Here's a sign that says 'campesina,' " he told the group, "and here's another which says 'esquirol.' Who saw what happened to the señora and wants to play the esquirol?" "Yo lo vi," said a modest looking campesino, and he jumped up to put on the sign which would label him a scab. Knowing the importance of masks, Valdez then gave the gentleman a comic mask and asked him to put it on. Everyone laughed at the man's transformation, and behind that cover of protection this humble campesino who had never been on a stage in his life became, for the moment, an actor.

During the couple's re-enactment of the conflict between the huelguista and the esquirol, the audience members bellowed at the humor of the representation. These people knew from personal experience what was being presented, and had the satisfaction of seeing the huelguista win in the end. Valdez had hit upon the means of telling other campesinos, who were as yet uninvolved in the huelga, what it was all about. The short improvisations they began to create became the actos: political skits which are the mainstay of Teatro Chicano today.

The acto, which got its name out of expediency, for there was no time to worry about semantics or labels when there was a union to be organized, has as its purpose two goals: to educate and entertain. Thus the acto runs the risk of becoming a political tract, with little or no entertainment value, or a comic skit whose message is obscured by its concern with arousing a laugh. However, when based on the personal experiences of those creating it, coupled with the proper direction, the acto can be an extremely effective tool. Under the guidance of Luis Valdez, the Teatro Campesino was born, nurtured by the participants' common experiences and the perfect form of expression for these non-theatre people, the acto.

Early Development of the Teatro

The Teatro developed actos about various aspects of their struggle, always bearing in mind the audience they were directing themselves to. The typical campesino in California is usually Mexican, Chicano, or Filipino, and many do not understand English, so the Teatro had to be linguistically versatile, able to perform in either or both Spanish and English. Farce and exaggeration are important to the success of the acto and therefore this physicality made the message perfectly clear. Signs and masks also left no doubt in the audiences' minds as to who the heros and villains were. The actos became modern morality plays, demonstrating the evils of the growers as opposed to the honest efforts of the hardworking campesinos.

It is probably no coincidence that this resurgence of Chicano drama occurred as it did, for the Chicano/Mexicano has a deep tradition in religious theatre since pre-Conquest times. César Chávez, being a Roman Catholic, always marched behind a banner of the Virgin of Guadalupe, a symbol of utmost importance in most humble families. Following the huelga efforts from town to town, marching behind the banner of Mexico's Patron Saint, the Teatro Campesino became a symbol of the new missionaries retracing the footsteps of the first California friars, but with a new message of social justice for the campesino.

When the Teatro Campesino took its program of actos and huelga songs to Stanford University in order to earn some much-needed revenue, they discovered that the college crowd received them with enthusiasm and empathy. Here was a way to take the message of what Chávez and his troops were fighting for out of the campo and into the cities, thus spreading the word and bringing recognition of the struggle. The Teatro thus began to tour college and university campuses where they could earn monies and educate the public as well. A national tour was arranged, and the Teatro Campesino found itself in a little theatre in Greenwich Village, New York performing for the awed crowds of New Yorkers who hadn't seen such down-to-earth political theatre since the 1930s when *Waiting for Lefty* caused such an uproar. The Teatro performed on the steps of the Senate for the Subcommittee on Migrant Labor and brought invaluable national attention to the growing efforts of the Union. The group was awarded an "Obie" for its work in New York and was invited to participate in the *Théâtre des Nations* in Nancy, France in 1967.

After the second year of being the theatrical arm of the Union, the Teatro decided to leave the organization and begin an existence of its own, not hampered by the daily conflicting needs of a union. It was simply a matter of improving their craft, and growing beyond the rural struggles to other experiences common to the Chicano/Mexicano as well. The Teatro established a small community cultural center in Del Rey, then in Fresno, and finally settled in San Juan Bautista, California.

Meanwhile, the seeds of creativity that the group had sown wherever it had performed began to sprout and other groups began popping up in California, Texas, and other parts of the United States. Other Chicanos had seen the power of the acto and the teatro form and decided that they, too, could employ the styles of Teatro Campesino to educate La Raza about common problems and possible solutions.

Annual Festivals

By 1970, five years after the birth of the Teatro Campesino, Valdez's group hosted a national Festival de los Teatros Chicanos and sixteen groups from all parts of the United States attended. The participating groups included Teatro del Piojo, from Seattle, Washington; Teatro Mestizo, San Diego, California; Grupo Mascarones, Mexico City; Teatro Aztlán, San Fernando, California; and Teatro Bilingüe, El Paso, Texas—groups which are still in existence. Most of the other groups have not survived, but there have been many to take their places over the years.

The first festival demonstrated the great need for a yearly gathering in which teatros could come together and share their common problems and goals and learn from one another. The Teatro Campesino was the leading group and was the only teatro which was involved in full-time theatrical activities. All of the other groups were student-oriented and thus suffered from the inconsistencies that part-time involvement can create. The problems most groups generally recognized were lack of training and the need for material to produce.

Most of the groups were imitating their only role model to date, the Campesino, and there was very little experimentation beyond the basic acto form. But the festival was a great success in that it brought together for the first time Chicanos, Mexicanos, and Puerto Ricans who were all trying to express themselves through teatro.

The tradition of holding an annual festival continued the following year with the Teatro Campesino again hosting the event, this time in Santa Cruz, California. The number of groups was growing, and the Teatro Movement was becoming more than a sometime thing, so the directors met in the spring of 1971 to form TENAZ, El Teatro Nacional de Aztlán. This coalition assumed the responsibility of co-ordinating national and regional festivals, publications, and most importantly, communication between groups. The directors agreed to meet four times yearly to discuss matters of common interest and to plan the next year's festival, to be hosted by Teatro de la Gente, in San Jose, California.

The San Jose festival brought together over twenty-five groups, and when a list of all known teatros was compiled, the total came to fifty-five groups in all parts of the U.S. The time had come to move out of California and when the Mascarones of Mexico City, along with CLETA-UNAM, asked to host the 1974 festival in Mexico City, the teatros unanimously agreed to go to their ancestral land and hold El Quinto Festival de los Teatros Chicanos—Primer Encuentro Latinoamericano en la capital de México.

El Quinto Festival was the largest undertaking yet for TENAZ, and when it opened on June 24, 1974 at the Pyramid of the Moon in Teotihuacán, there were thirty-five Chicano and seventeen Latin American groups in attendance. This two-week event was a culture shock for all concerned, and when it was over, the groups returned to their respective homes, revitalized and eager to continue their work. The encounter between the participants from all parts of Latin America (including the U.S.) raised many questions about the purpose of political theatre, especially for those groups which were "in the belly of the monster," as it were, but it was recognized that each group had problems particular to its home base. Though there were regional differences, the participants had much to share with each other and much to learn.

El Sexto Festival was held in San Antonio, Texas, hosted by El Teatro de los Barrios, and it brought together thirty groups from the United States, as well as the ever active Mascarones. This festival had as its theme "Encuentro con el Barrio," and thus the performing groups went to different barrios each night to share their craft with the residents. El Pueblo responded very favorably as they witnessed the diversity of the growing Teatro Movement. Groups presented obras concerned with drugs, education, La Migra, racism, and any of the other problems Chicanos and Latinos face in the U.S. The problems remained the same as in 1965, but it was the evolving technique that demonstrated the growth of the different teatros. Though most were still presenting actos, some of the groups had developed in their acting styles and direction to the point that one could no longer say they were "cheap imitations" of El Teatro Campesino.

Other Teatros Emerge

While the world famous Teatro Campesino continues to evolve and express the neo-Maya philosophy of Luis Valdez, it remains the symbol, for many, of what Teatro Chicano is all about. Yet there are well over seventy-five teatros throughout the U.S. expressing their particular realities. From the Teatro Desengaño del Pueblo, of Gary, Indiana, an urban Chicano and Puerto Rican group which is composed of both children and adults, to the Teatro de los Pobres of El Paso, which presents Mexican and Spanish classics in their native tongue—all are a part of the Teatro Movement.

The Chicano college student in the U.S. is different from the ordinary white, middle and upper middle class student in many respects, not the least of which is finances. It was only when the government decided to throw the minorities a few "huesos" in the form of financial aid, that any appreciable number of Chicanos were able to attend institutions of higher learning. The majority of Chicanos in the colleges and universities are receiving financial assistance and come from very humble backgrounds. Generally educated in inferior barrio high schools, these students are often not as prepared for the college scene as their white counterparts are. College can be a shock for anyone, and the university atmosphere is certainly a jolt to most Chicanos who manage to get in. Away from their familiar surroundings, in a world they never thought they'd get a glimpse of, the Chicano students search for ways of holding onto their culture, and teatro, for some, is that connection.

Most of the Chicanos who form teatros on their campuses are not formal students of theatre, and herein lies a major problem in the development of teatro as an art form. Not having training in theatrical techniques, styles of acting and playwriting, the students who attempt to organize teatros find themselves at a disadvantage. The national and regional festivals sponsored by TENAZ are helpful, but infrequent, and teatros find themselves searching for directors and actors who have some knowledge of theatre and teatro in particular. Teatro members are urged to take as many drama courses as they can manage, in order to add to the collective pool of knowledge within their groups. A few Chicanos with formal training in theatre are now teaching at the college level, but their numbers are minimal.

Many student teatros feel the necessity to work in the community and participate in some form of community center, conducting workshops and performances for residents of the barrio. At times, this becomes a case of the blind leading the blind, but usually the teatro members have had sufficient experience in teatro to pass their knowledge on to younger high school students, and certainly to the children, who are often their best, if most vocal, audience. Teatro appeals to all ages, but since the younger people have more time to get involved in such activities, some teatros find themselves spawning younger groups. Because of the transience of students, the teatros are constantly in search of new blood, and their workshops are often a basic training for new members and musicians.

The Roles of Music and Dance

Music has always been an important part of Chicano/Mexicano culture, and teatro has reflected this in its integration of corridos, and sometimes, the regional dances of Mexico. Indeed, in the early years many teatros began their careers as ballets folklóricos, recreating for enthusiastic audiences the dances of Jalisco, Veracruz, Michoacán, and other regions of Mexico. No one is threatened by folkdances, and thus dance groups had access to many places a political theatre group would not have been invited to: elementary and high schools, churches, and community meetings, for example. While some of the older dance groups remain strictly ballets folklóricos, others have joined the ranks of TENAZ and have shed the costumes of the baile for those of the acto or play. In making the transition from dance group to teatro, some groups presented "tandas de variedad" in which they would alternate songs, dances, and actos. This technique is especially effective for community gatherings, but requires a rather large company of actor/singer/dancers.

In the early stages of the Teatro Movement, Chicanos sometimes criticized the dance groups for not being political or not having a social message to convey. Today most groups agree that the baile is an excellent prologue to the politics; a sort of "foot in the door" which endears an audience with its grace and beauty, breaking down the public's barriers before surprising them with a call for social justice. Though the national festivals have not had the participation of dance groups for a few years, the regional festivals will usually offer a local ballet folklórico in their presentations.

Song has been with Teatro since the Teatro Campesino first altered the words of a popular corrido to tell of the huelga in the fields:

> El picket sign, el picket sign
> Lo llevo por todo el día,
> El picket sign, el picket sign,
> Conmigo toda la vida.

The rhythm of the livelier corridos brought a sense of joy and hope to an otherwise bleak situation, allowing the campesinos to sing with the teatro and proclaim their growing independence from the farm owners.

Eventually the corridos became dramatized and added a new form to Teatro. While the singer sang his narration, actor/dancers in stylized Kabuki-like makeup would pantomime the words that were being sung. Sometimes the actors would take over the narration and speak the lines of the song as their characters would. If, for example, the singer sang: "Y luego dijo Rosita: '¿Por qué me has engañado?'," the actress playing "Rosita" would say: "¿Por qué me has engañado?" The stylized movement was sometimes in slow motion to accent the action or sometimes dance-like. The total effect of the corrido is a blend of all the elements of the theatre, making a cultural, artistic, and political comment the audience can relate to on its own terms. If the words of a popular corrido have been changed to suit the needs of the moment, the audience is forced to pay even greater attention to what is being said.

The Teatro Campesino employed a very Brechtian technique by completely altering the words of the popular "De Colores." As the singers sang the revised version of the song, the audience, conditioned to sing the traditional words, had to listen carefully to the new lines, and because they were so different, were often more affected by them. In its original form, "De Colores" says:

> De colores; de colores se visten los campos en la primavera.
> De colores; de colores son los pajarillos que vienen de afuera.
> De colores; de colores es el arco iris que vemos lucir.
> CORO
> Y por eso los grandes amores de muchos colores me gustan a mí.

But the altered version made the audience cheer with recognition:

> De colores; de colores se visten los ricos con nuestro dinero.
> Mi salario; mi salario enriquece las bolsas de tantos coyotes.
> El coyote; el coyote acecha la siembra de los campesinos que luchan aquí;
> CORO
> Y por eso los grandes rencores de pocos colores me sobran a mí.

The lovely melody, soft and gentle, is here contrasted with the bitter words which express one of the major forms of discrimination the campesino suffers under: the farm labor contractor, or coyote, as he has been called by the campesinos. In calling for a union hiring hall, the huelguistas were asking to abolish the old system in which the farm labor contractor is free to exploit the workers by offering them jobs and then transporting them in usually unsafe trucks and buses to their stoop labor for less than minimal wages, collecting a handsome salary for himself.

Few teatros do not employ song and music in some form in their presentations. Teatro de la Gente, in their recent "Corrido de Juan Endrogado," dramatize and narrate in song the experiences of a young Chicano who is sucked in by the drug scene and is eventually killed but comes back in spirit to kill the pusher, who is dressed like "Uncle Sam." The narrator/singer is always at stage right during the corrido, commenting upon the action in song and telling the audience what is going to happen through the lyrics. This group's corrido goes beyond the original experimentation in dance and stylized makeup and adds much more dialogue from the characters. But the music seems always present, adding to the atmosphere of the particular scene. If the action deals with Chicanos, the background song might be a popular Chicano tune; if the action moves to the ambiente of the drug scene, the music alters accordingly.

Technical Considerations

Because of limited budgets, most teatros do not get involved in complex technical demands for their presentations. Often performing on flatbed trucks or on the very edges of a picketed field, the Teatro Campesino had no time, space or money to be elaborate with their scenery and lighting in the early days. Often the lighting was provided by the sun itself or by car headlights if at night. The acto's simplicity and expediency enable the form to accept minimal technical facilities and works better with an economical setting. As the Campesino and other groups have evolved, they have begun to employ lights and scenic effects, but since all of the teatros are travelling companies, their equipment must be kept at a minimum. Here is true theatre of poverty, and the teatros have adapted well to the limitations.

There are few, if any, barrios with well-equipped theatres in their midst, and if teatros are to continue the tradition of performing for the community, la gente del pueblo, they will often have to perform in grammar school cafeterias, parks, gymnasiums, and the worst non-theatrical conditions. Thus teatros must remain rather simple in their scenic demands. The real livelihood of the teatros depends upon performances in colleges and universities that can afford to pay anywhere from $300.00 to $2,000.00 for a performance, depending on the group. Following the tradition set by the Campesino, most groups will perform on a campus, which is almost always far from the local barrios, and then arrange a free performance in the community. This pattern has given the teatros a sense of civic contribution while also allowing them to earn some money to continue their work.

The basic scenery for most teatros is a flat cloth backdrop, usually hung on pipes that can be disassembled for travel. The backdrops vary but may have a large mural depicting some aspect of the Chicano in the U.S. or simply the name of the particular group. Some groups have attempted semi-realistic dramas calling for furniture and props and often simply gather up whatever they can at each performance site rather than travel with couches, tables, and chairs. If the groups find themselves in an auditorium with the proper equipment, they might take advantage of it. Though accustomed to performing with no light changes at all during a particular play, El Teatro de la Esperanza of Santa Barbara, California employed the lights in a college theatre when they discovered they had them. Most groups do not have portable lighting equipment to tour with and thus design shows that can function without this "luxury."

Again, the teatros lack a certain amount of training in the utilization of sophisticated scenery and lighting. Sometimes, when a group finds that it has a dimmer board at its disposal, the members do not know how to take full advantage of these electronic systems. Since most theatre staff technicians are not Spanish-speaking, they too find themselves limited when attempting to follow cues that are not in English. Always seeking additional members, most teatros cannot afford to travel with a technician who is not also in the production and are again at a loss.

Jorge A. Huerta

The Chicano Audience

For the moment then, Teatro Chicano is really in its infant stages, adapting to the world of "theatre" with all of the mistakes and short-comings that any new venture will create. Teatro remains a theatre of poverty that is striving to grow artistically and politically as the groups and the audience itself become accustomed to the genre. Amazed at the very presence of Chicano actors and actresses on a stage, re-creating their own realities, the Chicano audience is very undemanding of its teatros. A Chicano audience will jump to its feet at the close of a production not only because they enjoyed the presentation, but because of the pride that seeing their own people on-stage can create. We are not accustomed to seeing ourselves represented by the media in anything but a negative light, and the change brought about by teatros is awesome for our audiences.

Chicano audiences are not patronizing and are certainly not the typical white middle-class public that frequents most theatrical events in the U.S. Chicanos have not passed through the tradition of theatre parties and opening nights and go to a teatro presentation not knowing what to expect, but knowing that they are going to see something related to their own experiences. When those realities present themselves on the stage, therefore, the audience does not sit dumbly in its seats. Bertolt Brecht called for an audience that would comment upon the action, discussing the events represented and questioning their causes and effects. If the great German playwright and theorist were alive today, he might find his perfect public in a Chicano audience.

Audience members most affected by teatro presentations will sometimes yell at the actors, either reinforcing what has been said, or sometimes trying to negate the message. Most often the comments are affirmative, but once, when a man in the audience stood up and told the actors that he was not a vendido (the subject of the acto), the actor said: "Who said we were talking about you?" More than likely, the man did have his sell-out tendencies and the acto hit too close to home, succeeding in its purpose: to arouse the consciousness of the people. Unfortunately, teatro presentations remain mostly theatre for the initiated, and the real culprits of the actos and plays are seldom in the audience.

There have been occasions when a teatro has been performing on the edges of the fields, in front of the police, dramatizing their mistreatment of the farmworkers, and the effect on the audience has been more than dramatic. With the visible threat of the law officers' presence, there is the sense that one is viewing a real situation, not a dramatization. The audience might find itself not knowing who to look at, the actors or the police. Other "villains" who might find themselves in the audience of a teatro presentation are high school teachers and counselors, and their reactions are usually predictable: try to stop the program, or condemn all Chicanos and teatros as instigators or "commies" or both.

Our audiences are always a reflection of the community and are composed of the ever present niños, scrambling onto the stage to get a better look, the teenagers sitting cautiously at the rear, the parents of the children telling them to be quiet, the viejitos, laughing at the dirty jokes; the proverbial drunk, commenting on the action—all of them attentive and interested in what is being said. The noises of the children have become part of any teatro presentation, comic or serious, and the teatros have learned to expect and accept the little people, though at times the noise can be distracting to the actors. But the audience never seems to be dismayed, as children are always with us, and give a Chicano gathering of any kind its finishing touch. When an actor who has never performed before complains about the noise during a rehearsal, he is quickly reminded that he had better be able to act with more noise than that if he's going to perform for our people!

"Guadalupe"

It may seem absurd to an observer that the Chicano/Mexicano must be told of oppression, but this is the battle all teatros face. The media in this country are so effective that even the poor sometimes think that they too can someday become the "Brady Bunch," laughing their way through life, free from cares. The "American Dream" seems a reality to many, and it may be that the dream is what keeps the people going from day to day. If the people are not aspiring to the goals of the dominant society, they are probably convinced that they must stay where they are on the socio-economic ladder, living from day to day with little or no hope for the future.

A major problem within the Chicano Movement is the need to help the Mexicanos understand what it is we are struggling for. The vast majority of Mexicanos who come to this country, legally or illegally, are seeking their nirvana and are amazed at the Chicanos' complaints. "If you think this is bad," a Mexicano might say to a dissenting Chicano, "you should see how we were living in Mexico." Of course the Mexicano is correct; conditions in the U.S. are far better than for the poor in Mexico, but when compared to the living standards of whites and even Blacks in this country, the Chicano/Mexicano is only a few points above the unfortunate Native American on the socio-economic scale. Yes, some of us have "made it" in the professional world, but the vast majority of our people have not, and this injustice is what teatros are attempting to convey to their audiences.

El Teatro de la Esperanza, for example, collectively created an obra entitled "Guadalupe," an obra which toured California and Mexico in the summer of 1974. The obra was videotaped for channel 13 in Mexico City, and was aired nationally in a 90-minute special in August and December of the same year. This work will serve as an example of how a teatro attempts to dramatize a message and what that message is.

Guadalupe, California is a small town of under 2,000 people northeast of Santa Barbara. It is a campesino town, and 80% of its population is Chicano/Mexicano—the cheap pool of labor needed to plant, harvest, and process the crops. The main street of Guadalupe resembles a Mexican town, lined with cantinas, restaurants, and one cine. There is one small park in town and no other recreational facilities for the children or adults. The Pacific Ocean is close by, but nobody seems to go there except for tourists and some surfers.

At first glance, Guadalupe looks peaceful enough; there is a fairly new tract of homes across the tracks, the typical stucco boxes California is infamous for, and they appear comfortable. It is only when one approaches these dwellings that their shoddy construction and cheap materials become apparent. Walls are cracking, doors and windows have broken, plumbing has gone out. If someone is renting one of these houses, there is little chance of getting any repairs done; if a family is buying its own home, well, things cost money, and there is very little of that in Guadalupe.

Guadalupe remained another anonymous rural town until some parents attempted to organize themselves to fight for better schooling for their children in 1972. Advised by a local leader of Chávez's Farmworker's Union, the parents began holding meetings and discussing the miserable conditions they were all living under, especially their children, who were often physically mistreated, and worse, were somehow not completing their schooling and were generally unmotivated by their anglo teachers and administrators. The controlling interests in the town, seeing that trouble was brewing, arranged to have a meeting in which a local vendido, Melchior O'Campo, was scheduled to speak against the United Farmworkers and the Chicano Movement in general. Events developed as planned, and a few weeks after the meeting, in which the people had not allowed O'Campo to continue his libels, ten of the most active members of the parents' committee were arrested on charges of "disrupting the meeting." After months of harrassment, three of the men were jailed for five to forty-five days, and most of the people were placed on probation. The city fathers succeeded in frightening most of the community into submission, and little changed in Guadalupe until a report was published by the California State Advisory Committee to the United States Commission on Civil Rights in April of 1973.

The report was entitled: *The Schools of Guadalupe. . .A Legacy of Educational Oppression,* and it exposed in documented detail how the people of Guadalupe, especially the children in the schools, were being oppressed. Only sixty miles from Teatro de la Esperanza's home base, the group saw in this pueblecito all the material needed for an obra, and more. Using the "Report" as a starting point, the teatro members began to research the town, its inhabitants, and the incidents that had led to the mass arrest in 1972. The group began its investigation in January of 1974, two years after the arrests, and discovered that little had changed for the people of Guadalupe. Teatro members interviewed adult residents and school children, and spent as much time as possible with the people in an effort to grasp as fully as possible the temper of the town and its inhabitants. The group even found itself attending a Sunday Mass in order to hear for themselves the village priest, a Spaniard who had come there forty years prior, and who invariably spoke against the Union, and anything that might disrupt the status quo. "If you follow César Chávez," the cura was known to say, "you will go straight to hell!"

Beginning with the basic acto form, the teatro members improvised situations that were described in the "Report" and, after reaching a common vision, one of the members would script the scene and bring back the written scene for review and analysis. Various songs and corridos were studied for their adaptability to the situations, and new lyrics were written to better convey the message of the piece. Working with an outline that showed the evolution of the incidents that led up to the arrest, the teatro members created a one-hour production composed of thirteen scenes, with opening and closing songs and corridos and other types of music to introduce each scene.

During this time the teatro was composed of twelve members, so actors played more than one role, changing a shirt, scarf or hat, etc., to denote a change of character. The major figures of the plot were the parents who organized El Comité de Padres, and the story followed their first discussions of the problems while working in the fields and in the packing house to the point of their arrest after the O'Campo meeting. After the entire group sang its introductory song, which was an adaptation of the opening song in the Chilean folk cantata, "Santa María de Iquiqui," the actors promptly became campesinos working in the fields. Brief quotes that had relevance to the ensuing scene were given in Spanish and English and, after some sort of musical introduction, the scene would begin. The first scene in the fields was accompanied throughout by the corrido "Valentín," but with new lyrics:

> Voy a cantar un corrido
> de un pueblo muy escondido;
> llamábase Guadalupe, y de repente
> fue muy conocido.

> Toda la gente del pueblo
> trabaja entre los files
> día tras día sudando, y siempre no tienen
> pa' pagar los biles. . .

Following each new verse, the actors would dialogue about the particular problem that had just been expressed in song. After the singer/narrator sang

> La educación de los niños
> no vale ni un centavo;
> sólo ayuda al gringo, y'al Mexicano
> lo echa 'un lado.

an actress portraying one of the mothers talked with her "son" about why he didn't want to go to school. In a few moments, the mood was set for the various aspects of oppression these people lived under: drugs and alcohol, inadequate education and mistreatment of the children in the schools, the insensitive priest, police brutality and bribery, and the oppression of the growers and city fathers.

The teatro premiered the work on Cinco de Mayo, 1974 at a local college and immediately won the favor of its audience with its combination of drama, song, and narration. The majority of the group had been together for four years and had achieved the discipline and dedication to allow themselves to collectively create a production of this kind. Probably the most exciting presentation was the first time the group took the play to Guadalupe itself. Everyone knew that the teatro had been investigating their lives, and when the group arrived an hour before the show was set up, the auditorium was already buzzing with the early arrivals who did not want to miss a seat. When the show began, over three hundred people jammed into the small gymnasium in the park to see themselves onstage. Even the priest was there, but he soon left when he realized that he, too, was in the show, and not in a pleasant light.

The group had changed the names of the characters in the play, but the audience knew who was who on stage and delighted in the knowledge of that reality. They laughed and cried, knowing that things were still basically the same in their town and wondering if this one-hour dramatization of their plight might bring some change in their lives. Already the local chief of police had been incarcerated for accepting bribes and the Superintendent of Schools had resigned, but they wondered if things would really change. There is some change in Guadalupe in 1976, but the wheels of progress turn slowly, slowly.

What the teatro had discovered early in their investigation of Guadalupe was that this town was a microcosm of any Chicano / Mexicano barrio in the U.S. The names, the people, the places were different, but the problems were always the same, whether urban or rural. The majority of the Chicanos are urban, and at first the teatro thought it should dramatize the problems of the city but then realized that they were one and the same.

No matter where the group took its obra, during the customary question-and-answer period after every show, the audience always verified that their reality was the same. After one memorable presentation in a barrio in Los Angeles, a lady in the audience stood up to say: "You know, I went to Hillside School around the corner twenty years ago, and I knew these things happened then, but I had no idea that they were still occurring in other places." Immediately, another woman in the audience replied with "Señora, that's still happening at Hillside!" The closing discussions with the public were always exciting for the teatro because they afforded them an opportunity to hear feedback from the Pueblo and know where it had succeeded or failed in its purpose. The incident in Los Angeles was very rewarding for the teatro members because it demonstrated how the production had enabled a member of another community to educate her peers by bringing the issue right down to their doorstep. The teatro could act and sing all day about the problems in Guadalupe, but until the audience realized that these problems were theirs too, the major purpose had not been achieved.

Jorge A. Huerta

In keeping with the tradition of Teatro and the portability of the obra, there was no scenery for "Guadalupe." The actors sometimes used a muslin backdrop with the group's name on it or any other neutral background. The actors never left the performance area, sitting at the sidelines like a basketball team while the scenes were in progress. The actors onstage had to hold the attention of their public so as not to let any motion of an actor changing a shirt or other costume detract from the scene. With the correct energy level, the actors usually kept up a pace that did not let the audience be distracted by anything other than the message. The group wanted the audience to see them not so much as actors, but as "demonstrators" who were able to jump in and out of a character in order to better get the message across, just as someone who is describing an auto accident might assume the "characters" he is talking about to better illustrate what happened. Once again, the inspiration for this technique came from Bertolt Brecht, and it generally was successful. Like Brecht, the group did not want its audience to be taken in by the emotions of the situation and forget the *causes*. The teatro members hoped that by not separating themselves as "actors" they might have a better chance of communicating with their public.

Unlike the early actos of the Teatro Campesino, "Guadalupe" could not call for simple solutions. There were more problems being exposed, and though each was different from the other, still they were inter-related. The poor schooling led to a general apathy, which caused the children to drop out of school and therefore have no earning capacity above that of unskilled labor in the fields, and on and on. It can be said that one major solution to the problems exposed would be unity, but the methods of reaching that unity are difficult to define. Even after all that has happened in Guadalupe, the people are yet ununited in toto. Perhaps complete unity for the Chicano/Mexicano is an unrealistic goal, but the teatros are still calling for it nontheless. Even as the Teatro de la Esperanza was creating its obra, the group realized that there were no easy solutions and that their major purpose would be in exposing the problems and hoping the communities would take some sort of action. That seems the least a political theatre can hope for.

The Chicanos and Mexicanos

When the Teatro toured Mexico, in the summer of 1974, it performed in ejidos in Veracruz, schools and streets in Oaxaca, and universities and prisons in the rumbos of the capital. The first lesson the group learned was that the language would have to be altered to at least 90% Spanish if the Pueblo Mexicano was going to understand the obra entirely. For some of the actors who were not completely bilingual this posed a problem, but with enough practice and performance they adapted well. The group had not created "Guadalupe" as a street theatre piece, since it was mostly serious in style, so when they found themselves performing in the streets of a colonia in Oaxaca, they quickly revised the piece and left out the scenes that were the quietest. This turned out to be a wise decision, as the noises of the barrio, coupled with the chattering of the children, made it very difficult for much of the dialogue to be distinguished. Nonetheless, the presentation was a success, and the group was applauded and cheered for its presentation. If there is one dictum which most teatros must learn to follow, it is: adaptability. Groups will often find themselves in places and situations which are totally unexpected and must improvise if they are to succeed. Of course some Chicanos say that the only method of survival "in the belly of the monster" is to improvise, so we may have an inherent ability to do so.

In their discussions with the audiences in Mexico, the Teatro members realized that although the obra was telling them that things aren't that great on the "other side," they seemed much better than in Mexico, and one play wasn't going to dissuade anyone in need from crossing the line p'al otro la'o. Of course there were always the questions about what makes the Chicano different from the Mexicano, aside from the fact that they don't speak Spanish the same. "That's what we're trying to illustrate in this obra," the actors would respond and know that the only illustration of the disparity between the Chicano and the Mexicano was in the actual experience of living in the United States.

In recent years, with the recession and job shortage, the undocumented Mexican has become the scapegoat of the system and our Mexican brothers are being blamed for the lack of employment and any other failure of free enterprise to keep the people working. As with the mass deportations of Mexicanos in the 1930s, the Immigration Bureau is again deporting thousands of "illegals." Organizations in the U.S. are fighting this system and attempting to educate the Mexicanos about their rights and how to go about securing their papers. The media and government have been very successful in making the Chicano believe that the illegals are the cause of their problems and thus have heightened the differences between the two groups. Mexicanos are amazed to find that many Chicanos not only do not understand them, but actually dislike them, calling them "wetbacks," "T.J.'s," "mojados," and the like. These Chicanos have fallen into the trap set for them and in many instances have succeeded in alienating the Mexicanos from the Movimiento Chicano. Neither side really understands the other and both find it very difficult to dialogue under such adverse conditions. Totally duped by the System, the vendidos, or established Mexican-Americans, are generally unconcerned about helping illegals and might even assist the "Migra" in finding and deporting these unfortunate brothers and sisters.

It can be generally stated that those Chicanos who are involved in the Movement are not opposed to the illegals and are trying to help the cause. Thus many teatros have dealt with the problem of the interrelationship between the Chicano and Mexicano and have exposed such racist laws as the Kennedy-Rodino Bill and the Dixon-Arnett Law—legislation that ensures the rights of the employers, while ignoring the rights of the undocumented workers. Teatro de la Esperanza's "Guadalupe" touches upon the problems of communication between the two groups, and Teatro de los Niños of Pasadena, California created a puppet show entitled "Beauty and La Migra" which depicts the brutality of the "Migra" and the helplessness of the Mexicano.

Teatro de los Niños, directed by Vibiana Aparicio Chamberlain, is composed of children who create their own statements about their realities in this country. Mrs. Chamberlain often participates in the productions, the only adult among the little people, but she allows the children to say what they want to say in their own manner. Their actos deal with children's perceptions of birth and death, insensitive teachers, and generally what is is like to be a Chicano child in an urban setting. Thus, the group created "Beauty and La Migra" to make their audience aware of a problem which they had experienced.

"Beauty and La Migra," whose title is a take-off on "Beauty and the Beast," a popular fairy tale, depicts an immigration officer harassing a Mexicana because she does not show him her papers. Physical violence is important in the use of puppets, and the audience responds with mixed emotions of laughter and disgust when the "Migra" hits the "Mexicana." The "Migra" offers to make her his domestic worker as a bribe, and she agrees in order to stay in the U.S. He wants her to cook him "hot dogs, hamburgers, and apple pie," but she can only cook Mexican food and concocts her hottest chile for him. Like a pig, the "Migra" gulps down his dinner before he realizes what it is, and keels over from the chile, thus ending the acto with cheers from the audience and a chant from the puppets: "¡Raza Sí, Migra No! ¡Raza Sí, Migra No!"

The solution offered by "Beauty and La Migra" is fanciful, but the short acto serves the purpose of exposing a child's view of the problem and a somewhat cathartic enjoyment of the solution. Vicariously, the audience members enjoy seeing the "Migra" destroyed and find themselves taken in by the message. Many people have yet to be educated about the "Migra" and, while this acto does not offer a realistic conclusion, its exposure of the problem is the important matter here. Hopefully the adults in the audience will create their own solutions and act upon them.

The Chicanos and Other Latinos

While the Chicanos and Mexicanos are discovering their differences in the southwestern states, the Chicanos and Latinos in the Midwest are realizing that their backgrounds are unique. Teatro Desengaño del Pueblo, of Gary, Indiana, is a Chicano and Puerto Rican group that symbolizes the growing need for some awareness between the Latinos in this section of the country. Their actos attempt to illustrate the similarities between the Spanish-speaking people of the Midwest, and offer solutions of unity and acceptance of one another. This group is composed of adults as well as children, sometimes acting side-by-side, sometimes apart, but always with a vitality that endears them to their audience. Isolated from the rest of the Chicanos and Mexicanos in the U.S., the Raza in the Midwest find themselves constantly searching for their roots and attempting to maintain their culture. There are hundreds of thousands of Chicanos and Mexicanos in this region, and groups such as the "Desengaño del Pueblo" are working to make the Raza in other parts of the U.S. aware of the struggles in Detroit, Chicago, and other urban and rural centers in the Great Lakes area.

Because of the different demographic conditions, teatros in the Midwest welcome the participation of non-Latinos in their groups, a practice which might meet with disdain in Texas and some trepidation in California. Often termed "cultural nationalists," people in the early stages of the Chicano Movement reversed the racism their people had suffered in the hands of the Anglo and hated back with a vehemence that is only now beginning to wane. In the formative years of the Teatro Movement, non-Chicanos were *personae non gratae* at the festivals and certainly suspect if in a teatro. Indeed, there are still very few non-Chicanos/Mexicanos participating in teatros, although those that are have been accepted.

Political Allegiance

Reflecting the political climate of the Chicano Movement in general, teatros have varying degrees of political allegiance, ranging from the so-called "indigenistas" to the Marxist-Leninist teatros—from cultural nationalism to the Third World. Thus, if a teatro claims to be Third World, this should be reflected in its ethnic make-up, but few groups have more than one non-Chicano in their ranks, and except for the Puerto Rican groups, Blacks are unheard of. The language is, of course, a major deterrent for a non-Chicano who is not bilingual, and eventually the groups may be able to recruit more people of the Third World into their ranks who can communicate in Spanish.

For the moment, however, the major audience of all teatros is La Raza, and anyone who joins a teatro must recognize that a play in Spanish is going to have its greatest impact on a Chicano/Mexicano audience. Thus, a Black actor who wants to deal with the problems of his people might find a better outlet in one of the Black groups which exposes their concerns. When the Puerto Rican Teatro Calle Cuatro of Manhattan's Lower East Side ghetto performed in the barrios of San Antonio, Texas, the audience was completely involved in their obra, which was in Spanish. Here were actors and actresses who appeared to be Black Americans, but who spoke in the language of the Mexicano about problems which beset any immigrant to this country. Few Puerto Ricans live in the Southwest, and thus their presence was an interesting experience for the teatro members and the audiences.

An all white group from Minnesota, the Alive and Trucking Theater Company, participated in the Sexto Festival in San Antonio and was warmly received by the audience. Its message dealt with the universal problem of unemployment, which everybody could relate to, and the group was probably more acceptable in a Chicano/Mexicano park because it was participating in a Chicano activity. It is difficult to speculate how the group would have been accepted in the southern reaches of Texas, apart from the festival, but their acceptance in San Antonio lead observers to feel that the trend is moving toward acceptance of non-Chicanos/Mexicanos in the Movement.

Teatros must never forget their audience, its likes and dislikes. Recognizing the deep spirituality of the Chicano/Mexicano, the Teatro Campesino adapted the sixteenth-century play, *Las Cuatro Apariciones de la Virgen de Guadalupe a Juan Diego,* in 1971. Aware that many of our people can be found in church on Sunday morning, the Teatro knew that this ancient obra would allow them entrance to a place where politics has few supporters. The local priests were thrilled to have a teatro perform this play on December 12, and welcomed the Teatro into its sanctuary. Prior to this, the audience usually came to the Teatro somewhat aware of the fact that this group was political. On December 12, 1971, however, the Teatro went to the people, into their territory, and amazed and delighted them.

Not content to simply present the play in its original state, the Teatro carefully analyzed it for its contemporary application and altered the situation to reflect the present colonization of the people. The "priests" and "friars" in the play began to debate whether the "Indios" were considered worthy of baptism. But it was too late, for the audience was already completely taken by this energetic group of actors and singers who began their presentation with new lyrics to the chorus of "La Feria de las Flores":

> Aquí vengo a saludarte,
> Virgen Santa, Madre mía;
> Mi bella Guadalupana,
> Causa de nuestra alegría.

With a beautiful morena actress playing the image of the Virgen and the sincerity of the group's reverence to Her, the audience knew that the Teatro was going to treat their Virgen with respect and was not distressed by the realistic portrayal of the original friars. The Teatro Campesino had won the day and the parishioners, and now have more invitations from local churches than they can manage. At first critical of such a move on the part of the Teatro Campesino, other groups eventually began to follow their example, discovering in their own areas that this was, indeed, an excellent way to win over an audience. "If the people do not come to the Teatro," states the "Tenaz Manifesto," "then the Teatro must go to the people."

"La Gran Carpa"

Attempting to link the Chicanos' past with their present, the Teatro Campesino collectively created "La Gran Carpa de los Rasqua-chis," evolving this obra between 1972 and 1974. "La Carpa" was per-haps one of the finest of the Teatro's presentations to date, hailed by many as totally innovative and exciting theatre. This work became a combination of the acto, corrido, and ritual and expressed in song, dialogue and action the experiences of one "Jesús Pelado Rasquachi," who comes to the U.S. seeking his fortune, only to find misery, hu-miliation, and ultimate death. The work began with "Christ" carry-ing his cross, and ended with "Jesucristo/Quetzalcoatl" and "La Virgen María," hand-in-hand, reciting:

> In Lak 'Ech.
> Tú eres mi otro yo.
> Si amo y respeto a ti,
> Amo y respeto a mí mismo.
> Si hago daño a ti,
> Hago Daño a mí.
> In Lak 'Ech.

Then the entire group would sing the indigenous power song, "Es-trella del Oriente":

> Estrella del Oriente
> Que nos dio su Santa Luz.
> Es Hora que sigamos el camino de la Cruz.

This work was highly criticized by those who felt that the solu-tion being offered was a return to the Church. Yet, within the obra the Church itself was represented by an actor in a burlap bishop's robe and mitre with huge dollar signs painted on it and a sign that said, "St. Boss's Church." The Teatro was calling for a return to spir-ituality as a possible means to a greater understanding of ourselves and our situation, not a return to an oppressive church that had help-ed initiate the colonization of America, and obviously continued it. What is most important, perhaps, as an analysis of an obra's effective-ness, is the response of its audience, and the Raza loved "La Gran Carpa."

"La Gran Carpa" demonstrated how the Mexicano/Chicano is being exploited at every turn in this country. "Jesús Rasquachi" has to follow the crops after bribing a border official to let him cross; he gets married and his children are taken in by the System; when he can no longer work and has to go to the welfare office for financial assistance his pride is finally broken and he dies, another casualty of the "American Dream." The obra was rife with examples of the injustices the Chicano/Mexicano suffers in the hands of a government and people who do not understand us, nor care to.

With an almost continual musical accompaniment, "La Gran Carpa" moved so swiftly the audience had to be very attentive to grasp every thought. Employing a large backdrop of burlap potato sacks sewn together, the acting space in front of this neutral background was never empty. Actors would change roles with the flip of a mask or a hat, and suddenly become another character, almost dancing onstage from behind the backdrop to begin a new episode in the lives of the "Familia Rasquachi." This obra became a "superacto," having grown beyond the short, comical skit to a theatrical statement with no easy solutions. The problems were exposed, the personages introduced; it was now up to the audience to take from it what they could and apply it to their own lives. In Lak 'Ech is a very personal thing, and how this Maya philosophy would adapt to the Chicanos' contemporary situation was never clearly defined, but it probably will never be.

Economic Survival

For the Teatro Campesino, the only full-time Chicano Teatro living and working collectively, their lifestyle reaches towards a Neo-Maya communal experience, growing their own food and animals, living off the land as much as possible in a small rural town in central California. This group preaches a respect for La Tierra Nuestra Madre and attempts to put their philosophy into daily practice. Members of the group are paid very modestly, and everyone contributes to the collective as a performer, office worker, babysitter, farmer, etc., on their forty acres. The group dreams of one day living on their little piece of land in their own homes, but for the moment, members rent separate apartments and houses in town, if married, or live in the modest house the Teatro is buying. The group's funding is generated by their yearly tours in the fall and spring, sales of books and records, and a few television contracts they have received.

None of the other teatros have the fame and experience of the Campesino and must survive on modest fees when they perform as well as maintain full or part-time jobs or student status. Many of the student members of teatros must also work to stay in school, and this adds to the burden of their commitments. As can be expected, the teatros are continually struggling for mere survival. Some groups, such as Teatro de la Esperanza, have received small grants from the

Jorge A. Huerta

National Endowment for the Arts and the California Arts Council, but most groups do not have the organization and permanence that must be apparent before they can apply for subsidies. Some groups reject the thought of federal or state funding altogether, fearing that they might be controlled by the hands that feed them. Of course, this is always a danger, but as more liberals are elected to office, and with the Kafkaesque enormity of the federal bureaucracy, it is often possible to receive federal monies and continue being a political theatre.

In one instance, a group that had been receiving federal funding was reviewed by a Washington committee, none of whom understood Spanish. Thus these bureaucrats were delighted at the seemingly "quaint" presentations by the teatro, unaware that some of the dialogue was calling for revolution and an end to the then popular Vietnam War. Perhaps the government is too large to learn the language of its colonized, and this is certainly to the advantage of teatros that can communicate in two idioms. The example of the sixteenth-century indígenas duping the Spaniards by speaking their own tongue parallels the Chicanos' experience in the U.S., adding to the similarities between our peoples.

Publications

Although the Chicano can trace his theatrical heritage to the days when the indígenas practiced a ritual drama with every sacrificial ceremony, through to the Spanish religious theatre of the Conquest which continues to this day, we have few published full-length plays. The Teatro Campesino and Teatro de la Esperanza published anthologies of their most successful actos, along with a collection of works published by the now defunct *El Grito* journal, and an anthology of mediocre works by Nepthalí de León, but none of these publications included what can be termed a full-length realistic play. Roberto Garza has recently published an anthology of actos and plays entitled *Contemporary Chicano Theatre* which includes the one realistic three-act play ever published by a Chicano, *The Day of the Swallows*, by Estella Portillo.

Sra. Portillo is the only person, male or female, to have expressed in traditional theatre terms a drama dealing with the life of La Raza. Though the play takes place in a small Mexican village, the people and situations are such that it could also happen in a small Chicano community as well. Indeed, the play is universal, dealing with a woman's suppressed lesbianism in a man's world, threatening to her for

114

its violence and lust. This play is written in the realistic style of Williams or Miller, calling for well-developed characters who reflect the complexity of the human spirit caught in a web of intrigues and duplicity.

The protagonist of *Day of the Swallows*, "Josefa," is the town's image of virtue, helping the less fortunate as she maintains her vocation of making fine lace. Having rescued a young woman from the whorehouse, "Josefa" has apparently been caught making love to the woman by a young boy of the village. In her moment of guilt, "Josefa" cuts out the boy's tongue, hoping to silence him forever; but she can no longer maintain the facade, so she tells her good friend the priest of the incident and is left alone to drown herself in the lake.

Day of the Swallows is as intricate as the lace which plays such an important part in the play. Mrs. Portillo has created people that live and breathe the air we do and, in doing so, has reflected another aspect of the Chicano/Mexicano experience. Unlike the acto, which has its major purpose of educating the public about certain issues, sometimes offering concrete solutions, Portillo's play assumes the responsibility of reflecting a reality which for some may be difficult to understand, but which must be discussed nonetheless. Performed in her native El Paso, Texas, Portillo's play raised some eyebrows, but was nevertheless accepted and applauded by its Chicano audience.

Conclusion

After witnessing Teatro de la Esperanza's production of a one-act play about brujerías, Enrique Buenaventura said to the group: "As you study the complexity of la vida Chicana your teatro will reflect that complexity in its obras." Slowly, and often, awkwardly, the Teatros of Aztlán are grasping their complex realities in theatrical terms and beginning to express those realities through a medium that has great potential. Contemporary Teatro Chicano was born alongside the most effective and enduring arm of the Chicano Movement—the United Farmworkers—and continues to evolve.

The Teatro Movement is moving, exposing the past and present frustrations and dreams of our people in their language, on their terms. While the politicians and newsmen celebrated the Bicentennial, teatros were touring the country telling the real story behind the "American Dream." The people are ready for truths now, more than ever, and hopefully the teatros will provide a creative and exciting means to that end.

UNIVERSITY OF CALIFORNIA, SAN DIEGO

DRAMATIC PRINCIPLES OF
THE TEATRO CAMPESINO

Francisco Jiménez

> How could a better ending be arranged?
> Could one change people? Can the world
>   be changed?
> Would new gods do the trick? Will atheism?
> Moral rearmament? Materialism?
> It is for you to find a way, my friends,
> To help good men arrive at happy ends.
> *You* write the happy ending to the play.
> There must, there must, there's got to be
>   a way.[1]

During the 1950s the aims of the off-Broadway theatre groups were essentially to present a variety of plays of high quality that would be both entertaining and stimulating. Almost none of these groups were politically oriented or deeply involved with social issues. Thus, they were concerned primarily with artistic excellence rather than with commitment to a social or political position.[2]

The status quo attitude toward theatre of the 1950s, however, was succeeded in the 1960s by an almost diametrically opposed posture. Instead of detachment, commitment to social and political issues became the vogue. Theatre groups organized for the specific purpose of using the theatre as a weapon through which to initiate change. The San Francisco Mime Theatre, for example, formulated the following policy: "We are committed to change not to art. We have tried to cut through the aristocratic and square notion of what theatre is and risk our egos to keep the search open for better ways of making theatre in content and in style, a living. . .force."[3] Similarly, Peter Schumann of the Bread and Puppet Theatre states: "I think the trouble with the legitimate theatre or academic theatre and so on is that they. . .have nothing to say."[4]

Discussing the major differences between the current generation of dramatists and those of the past, Oscar G. Brockett observes that "many of our dramatists wish to be relevant and care little about creating enduring art works. Consequently, many of the questions asked in the past about the nature and purposes of art seem to them irrelevant. The experience *now*, the effect *now* is to them the important thing, and to be concerned about art in the traditional sense is elitist, snobbish, and escapist."[5]

Thus, the dominant note of contemporary drama is an urgency for change. Theatre is viewed as a propagandistic tool and as a weapon to be used against all elements deemed harmful or detrimental to society.

The Teatro Campesino, the most successful of Chicano theatres,[6] falls within the historical framework of the 1960s and forms an integral part of contemporary drama. It is in this context that I wish to discuss the dramatic principles of the Teatro Campesino and the forces and ideas that have gone into its making. It is not my purpose either to advocate or to denounce the principles of this theatre. I wish merely to generate understanding so that audiences might approach it knowledgeably, for worthwhile judgments depend upon informed opinion rather than on prejudices and impressions.

Luis Valdez,[7] the founder of the Teatro Campesino, was imbued with the philosophy of art that prevailed in the 1960s. Like Bertolt Brecht, whom he read while studying English at San José State University, Valdez believes theatre should serve as an instrument of change in society. In an interview with Beth Bagby in 1967, he expressed a strong desire for a theatre of commitment to awaken a social conscience that would hopefully lead to change. "The idea that really excites me about the future of teatro, and American theatre," he states, "is a theatre of political change. . . .I am talking about really influencing people, and I sense a hunger in art for this. We're into a political age; we're going to go further into it because social problems are increasing."[8]

Just as he views theatre as a tool to initiate change, Valdez equates art with propaganda: "I sometimes think the best propaganda comes through and is merged with the best art. In the theatre, art is communication and propaganda; but organizing and politics and teaching are nothing but that, communication. So the more artful you are, not arty, artful, the more propagandistic you are."[9]

This view of art is a crucial issue, for how Luis Valdez conceives the purpose of art and, therefore, of the theatre determines its content and form. In his own words: "The nature of chicanismo calls for a revolutionary turn in the arts as well as in society. Chicano theatre must be revolutionary in technique as well as content. It must be popular, subject to no other critics except the pueblo itself, but it must also educate the pueblo toward an appreciation of social change, on and off the stage."[10]

Objectives

Keenly aware of the potential inherent in theatre for reaching large Chicano audiences, and for influencing them to initiate change, Luis Valdez founded the Teatro Campesino in 1965.[11] Initially, the theatre had one specific, political goal—the organization of farm workers. For two years the Teatro Campesino was actively involved in the everyday struggles of the farm workers' strike. It joined the strikers on marches to Sacramento, California, publicizing the *Huelga* (strike) and gathering public support for the farm workers union (National Farm Workers Association).

The Teatro Campesino broadened its objectives in 1967 when it established El Centro Campesino Cultural in Del Rey, California. This cultural center was designed to impart to students a sense of pride about being Chicano through a variety of courses dealing with Chicano culture. To this end the Teatro Campesino was utilized with so much success that it shifted its focus from the farm workers to Chicano culture in all its ramifications. The common denominator, however, remained political. As Luis Valdez states: "El movimiento [Chicano] progresa día tras día y nosotros tenemos que seguir un paso adelante con nuestros mensajes políticos. Actuamos no para la gloria falsa de un aplauso, sino para educar, informar y unir La Raza."[12] This political statement of purpose summarizes the ideological base upon which the Teatro Campesino exists today. Stated briefly, the farm workers theatre has five principal objectives: (1) to serve as the voice of the *barrios*, the community of the oppressed; (2) to inform the Chicano of the negative conditions that exist to oppress him; (3) to politicize the Chicano so he can overcome the existing conditions of oppression; (4) to inform the Chicano of his rich heritage so as to instill in him pride in his culture; and (5) to strengthen the

Francisco Jiménez

Chicano's heart by communicating spiritual values such as love, hope, and kindness.

In broader terms, the Teatro Campesino proposes to raise the consciousness of the Chicano and restore his spiritual harmony by destroying what Luis Valdez describes as "an internal struggle in the very corazón of our people."[13] According to Valdez, this spiritual unrest also calls for revolutionary change which can be accomplished through the theatre. He states: "Our belief in God, the church, the social role of women—these must be subject to examination and re-definition on some kind of public forum. And that again means tea-tro."[14]

Content

Since the immediate goal of the Teatro Campesino was the or-ganization of the farm workers, the content of its first *actos* (plays) deals exclusively with *La Huelga*. Actos such as *Las dos Caras del Patroncito* (1965) and *Quinta Temporada* (1966)[15] dramatize the socio-economic and political plight of the *campesinos* and their struggles against agri-business. For the most part these early plays are comedies, characterized by "bittersweet humor." Luis Valdez explains:

> We use comedy because it stems from a necessary situation—the ne-cessity of lifting the morale of our strikers, who have been on strike for seventeen months. When they go to a meeting it's long and drawn out, so we do comedy with the intention of making them laugh—but with a purpose. We try to make social points, not in spite of the com-edy, but through it. This leads us into satire and slapstick, and some-times very close to the underlying tragedy of it all—the fact that hu-man beings have been wasted in farm labor for generations.[16]

With the success of El Centro Campesino Cultural and the un-ionization of the farm workers (NFWA), the Teatro Campesino broadened its repertoire to include everything and anything related to Chicano culture. As Luis Valdez states: "Pachucos, campesinos, low-riders, pintos, chavalonas, familias, cuñados, tíos, Mexican-Americans—all of the human essence of the barrio—is starting to appear in the mirror of our theatre. With them come the joys, suffer-ings, disappointments, and aspirations of our gente."[17] Thus the tea-tro has developed and performed plays that deal with a variety of Chicano-related themes: acculturation (*Los Vendidos*, 1967); Chica-no militants (*The Militants*, 1969); education (*No Sacó Nada de la*

Escuela, 1969); Vietnam (*Vietnam Campesino,* 1970; *Soldado Raso,* 1971); etc.

These more recent plays, like the earlier ones, are characterized by humor and satire which Luis Valdez considers to be the major assets and weapons of his theatre.[18] *Los Vendidos,* performed at Elysian Park in East Los Angeles best illustrates the manner in which Luis Valdez handles humor. The setting is "Honest Sancho's Shop" where representative Chicano types are sold: farm workers, Pachucos, Revolutionaries, and Mexican-Americans. Sancho, the owner of the store, introduces each type to Miss JIM-enez, a secretary from Governor Reagan's office who wishes to purchase a Chicano for the administration. After rejecting the farm worker because he is too unsophisticated, Miss JIM-enez asks for an urban model.

SANCHO: Ah, from the city! Step right back. Over here in this corner of the shop is exactly what you're looking for. Introducing our new 1969 JOHNNY PACHUCO model! This is our fast-back model. Streamlined. Built for speed, lowriding, city life. Take a look at some of these features. Mag shoes, dual exhausts, green chartreuse paint-job, dark-tint windshield, a little poof on top. Let me just turn him on. *(Snap. Johnny walks to stage center with a Pachuco bounce)*
SECRETARY: What was that?
SANCHO: That, señorita, was the Chicano shuffle.
SECRETARY: Okay, what does he do?
SANCHO: Anything and everything necessary for city life. For instance, survival: He knife fights. *(Snap. Johnny pulls out switchblade and swings at secretary)*

Secretary screams

SANCHO: He dances. *(Snap)*
JOHNNY: *(Singing)* Angel Baby, my Angel Baby. . .*(Snap)*

... ...

SECRETARY: Economical?
SANCHO: Nickles and dimes. You can keep Johnny running on hamburgers, Taco Bell tacos, Lucky Lager [sic] beer, thunderbird wine, yesca. . .
SANCHO: He steals. *(Snap. Johnny rushes the secretary and steals her purse)*
JOHNNY: Dame esa bolsa, vieja! *(He grabs the purse and runs. Snap by Sancho. He stops)*

> *Secretary: runs after Johnny and grabs purse away from him, kicking him as she goes.*

SECRETARY: No, no, no! We can't have any *more* thieves in the State Administration. Put him back.

Miss JIM-enez is then introduced to the Mexican-American model who possesses all the characteristics sought for by her employer, the State Capital. Again, Sancho describes him:

SANCHO: He just came in this morning. Ain't he a beauty? Feast your eyes on him! Sturdy US STEEL frame, streamlined, modern. As a matter of fact, he is built exactly like our Anglo models except that he comes in a variety of darker shades: naughahide, leather, or leatherette.

SECRETARY: Naughahide.

SANCHO: Well, we'll just write that down. Yes, señorita, this model represents the apex of American engineering! He is bilingual, college educated, ambitious! Say the word "acculturate" and he accelerates. He is intelligent, well-mannered, clean-. . .

SECRETARY: How about boards, does he function on boards?

SANCHO: You name them he is on them. Parole boards, draft boards, school boards, taco quality control boards, surf boards, two by fours.[19]

As expected, Miss JIM-enez purchases the Mexican-American. However, when she exits the shop we discover that the Chicano models are real, and that Sancho, the salesman, is a mannequin.

Form

Responding to a demand for different forms to express the growing political and cultural consciousness of the Chicanos, the Teatro Campesino has developed two principal dramatic structures: the *acto* and the *mito*.

The term *acto* was employed by Luis Valdez to define the short, improvised dramatic scenes performed by the Teatro Campesino during the farm workers strike. Although the *acto* is very similar to a skit, Valdez decided against using that name because he needed a Spanish term to which La Raza could relate.[20]

The *acto* is not uniquely Chicano in form. Other radical drama groups such as the Bread and Puppet Theatre and the San Francisco Mime Troupe also utilize this dramatic structure. However, the *acto* is unique in content for it deals exclusively with Chicano themes.

According to the founder of the Teatro Campesino, the form of the *acto* developed naturally, without plan. He states: "The actos were born quite matter of factly in Delano. Nacieron hambrientos de la realidad. . .The reality of campesinos on strike had become dramatic. . .and so the actos merely reflected the reality. Huelguistas portrayed Huelguistas, drawing their improvised dialogue from real words they exchanged with the esquiroles (scabs) in the fields every day."[21]

Valdez also affirms that "actos are created collectively, through improvisation by a group," and that "the reality reflected in an acto is a social reality."[22] Thus, the major emphasis in the acto is not the ideology of the individual artist or playwright, but the collective consciousness of La Raza. For this reason the actos do not treat the problems of specific individuals (for as Luis Valdez has said: "Who responds [nowadays] to Tennessee Williams or Arthur Miller picking his liver apart?")[23] but rather those issues that affect specific Chicano groups such as the Pachucos or campesinos. Correspondingly, the characters portrayed are not drawn as individuals but are treated instead as representatives of specific groups or types. Many of the characters, such as John Pachuco, Juan Raza, and la Chicana bear the names of the groups they represent. According to Valdez "the teatro archtypes [sic] symbolize the desired unity and group identity through Chicano heroes and heroines. One character can thus represent the entire Raza, and the Chicano audience will gladly respond to his triumphs or defeats."[24]

The *mito* (myth) is an evolving dramatic form whose content is the cosmic vision of pre-Columbian Indian civilizations. "The FORM of our mitos," states Luis Valdez, "is evolving from something-resembling-a play to something-that-feels-like ritual. At the center of our mitos so far (as opposed to the actos) is a story—a parable (parábola) that unravels like a flower indio-fashion to reveal the total significance of a certain event. And that vision of totality is what truly defines a mito. In other words, the CONTENT of a mito is the Indio Vision of the Universe. And that vision is religious, as well as political, cultural, social, personal, etc. It is total."[25]

The *mito* "revives" the legends and myths of the Mayan and Aztec civilizations through words, music, color, and visual symbology. Its function is to serve as an instrument in the evolution and spiritualization of La Raza.[26]

Although the *acto* and *mito* differ in content, they complement each other. Luis Valdez poetically describes their contrasting and balancing qualities as "day goes into night, el sol la sombra, la vida la muerte, el pájaro la serpiente. . .Los actos y los mitos; one through the eyes of man; the other through the eyes of God."[27]

Francisco Jiménez

Style and technique

In creating the Teatro Campesino, Luis Valdez was confronted by the fact that the farm workers, the audience he was trying to reach, knew nothing about drama. This factor, to a large degree, determined the style and the technique Valdez was to adopt for his theatre.

From the very beginning, Luis Valdez discovered that traditional theatre would not appeal to the farm workers since "most of them had never been to a play as such."[28] Thus Valdez turned to forms of entertainment that would attract the campesinos. In his search he came upon the *Commedia dell'arte*, a style which characterized the San Francisco Mime Troupe, a drama group Valdez had worked with during his studies at San José State University. "I figured," he states, "that if any theatre could turn on farm workers, it would be that type of theatre—outside, that lively, that bawdy."[29] His supposition was correct. The *Commedia dell'arte* style proved so successful in communicating with the farm workers that Valdez continued to borrow styles and techniques from other forms of popular entertainment such as puppet shows, vaudeville, parades, and carnival side shows. Speaking at the 1973 Theatre Festival at San José State University, Valdez credited theatre groups, both historical and contemporary, as having contributed to the success of his theatre. He cited Old Comedy, the choral work of such groups as the Mascarones of Mexico, the Bread and Puppet Theatre, the Open Theatre, the Living Theatre, the agit-prop drama of the thirties, and the San Francisco Mime Troupe. Of these groups, the last seems to have had the greatest influence on the development of the Teatro Campesino's style and technique.

From the San Francisco Mime Troupe, one of the oldest of the contemporary political theatres and one of the most varied in its use of popular entertainment forms and techniques, Luis Valdez adopted the principle "that your dramatic situation, the thing you're trying to portray on the stage, must be very close to the reality that is off the stage."[30] The practice of this tenet significantly enhances communication, for the audience can easily relate to the performance since whatever is on stage is closely related to their experience.

The production of *Quinta Temporada* (The Fifth Season) is an excellent example to illustrate the practice of this principle. In this acto, Summer, the harvest season, is portrayed by a man dressed in an ordinary workshirt and khaki hat; both garments are completely covered with bright green paper money of different denominations.

With arms outstretched, Summer comes on stage. The farm worker immediately attacks the season and begins to pick off the bills as rapidly as possible, stuffing them in his back pocket. The portrayal of Summer as a "money tree" is an image easily understood by the farm worker who views the Summer as the time to make money. The effectiveness of this dramatic theory is attested to by Luis Valdez. He states: "I've noticed one thing about audiences. When they see something they recognize as reality, they laugh. Here in the Teatro we sometimes work up imitations—of personalities, animals, or incidents. Impersonations are funny, why? Just because the impersonation itself comes so close to the reality. People say, 'Yes, that's the way it is,' and they laugh. If it's a reality they recognize as their own, they'll laugh and perhaps tears will come to their eyes."[31]

The images employed to represent a reality, the Summer for example, are usually symbolic, emblematic presentations of what the audience experiences or has experienced.

Like the Mime Troupe theatre, the Teatro Campesino uses no sets, few props, and few devices—an old pair of pants, a wine bottle, pair of dark glasses, a mask.[32] The advantage in this scarcity of materials is that performances can be staged anywhere—in the streets, the fields, the back of a truck. As Valdez remarks: "Real theatre lies in the excited laughter (or silence) of recognition in the audience, not in all the paraphernalia on the stage. . .; minus actors, the entire theatre can be packed in one trunk."[33]

Luis Valdez also appropriated from the San Francisco Mime Troupe an acting technique similar to mime[34] in which the most powerful means of communication is the actor's body. By employing his body as his tool, the actor can portray man's humanity or inhumanity to his fellow man. Explaining this dramatic technique, Valdez gives the following example which illustrates the importance of the body as an expressive device: "You take the figure of DiGiorgio standing on the back of two farm workers. The response of the audience is to the very real situation of one human being standing on two others. That type of fakery is not imitation. It's a theatrical reality that will hold up on the flatbed of a truck. You don't need fancy lights or a curtain. This is what we're working toward—this type of reality."[35]

Since the actors do not have access to amplification, they must project the image they are trying to portray with only their physical being. Thus, in order to make their image clearer to their spectators, they magnify all their actions—their gestures, movements and physical reactions. The actors also justify emotionally the motivations behind their actions—that is, they experience the emotion then amplify the result. This task is not difficult to accomplish since most actors play roles they have actually lived, and their performances reflect the most intimate understanding of everyday events in the fields or barrios from which they come. As Luis Valdez remarks: "Being free to act out as they will, to infuse a character type with real thought and feeling, the farm workers of the teatro have expressed the human complexity of the grape strike."[36]

Today, Luis Valdez maintains that any style or technique that might prove effective in reaching the theatre's objectives will be utilized. He therefore urges Chicano theatre people to be knowledgeable in the styles and techniques of earlier drama and to keep abreast of new developments, for everything that can be appropriated is enormously advantageous to the creation of productions. Furthermore, the eclectic nature of the Teatro Campesino allows it to remain open to changing political circumstances and permits it to adapt to unforseen circumstances through improvisation.

Language

By necessity, the Teatro Campesino's material is bilingual. Some actors as well as some Chicano spectators speak little or no English, while others barely understand Spanish. Thus dialogue fluctuates between English and Spanish and is peppered with *pochismos*, a sort of "Spanglish" known as *pocho* or *caló*.[37] Wherever either language is not understood, there is little visual doubt as to the significance of an event. For example, Felipe Cantú, a "star" actor of the Teatro Campesino who resembles a Mexican version of Ben Turpin, speaks no English. However, he reacts so totally with his voice, face, and body that one hardly notices he has no lines. "His wild extravagant Cantinflas-like comic style needs no words," affirms Luis Valdez.[38]

When the Teatro Campesino was first founded in 1965, the actors often wore signs, most often in Spanish, that designated the character's name or role. The signs were employed to communicate the content of the theatre since most of the farm workers had never been to a play. This practice of utilizing signs to identify characters continues today, though with less frequency.

Music is another art form used by the Teatro Campesino to communicate its message. Performances are often accompanied by *corridos* whose music is taken from old ballads familiar to Chicano audiences. These songs are usually sung in Spanish and introduced with English explanations.

Actors

Originally, all the actors of the Teatro Campesino were farm workers, and the performances were improvised by the campesinos themselves. Their willingness to actively participate in the theatre was due to the nature of the Teatro Campesino itself. As Luis Valdez explains: "The teatro appeals to its actors for the same reason it appeals to its audience. It explores the meaning of a social movement without asking its participants to read or write. It is a learning experience with no formal prerequisites. This is all-important because most farm workers have never had a chance to go to school and are alienated by class-rooms, blackboards, and the formal teacher-student approach."[39]

Today, the actors, ranging in age from 18 to 44, vary tremendously in their degree of education, but they have one thing in common—all of them have experienced life in the fields or in the barrio, whence their effectiveness in acting out real life situations.

Audience

Strongly influenced by Brecht, who envisioned a theatre in which the audience would play a vital and active role, Luis Valdez insists that "audience participation is no cute production trick; it is a pre-established, preassumed privilege."[40]

The belief in and practice of this privilege is so strong that sharing a performance with the audience has become natural to the Teatro Campesino. Often, the actors may even go out into the streets in parade-like fashion and seek out an audience that would not voluntarily attend a theatre.[41]

The purpose of urging interaction between the audience and actors is that it creates a feeling of community. This sense of communion enhances the theatre's effectiveness in what Luis Valdez terms as "turning on crowds." He states: "We think of our spiritual purpose in terms of turning on crowds. We know when we're not turning on the crowd. From a show business point of view that is bad enough, but when you're trying to excite crowds to go out on strike or to support you, it gains added significance."[42]

The intercourse between actors and audience is encouraged by keeping the performance open to improvising so that the performer

Francisco Jiménez

can respond directly to spectators and to situations that may arise in the immediate area during the performance.

Funding

The Teatro Campesino is self-supporting and independent. It survives on funds generated by performing at various colleges and universities around the country, and by the sale of posters, records, magazines, and books of playscripts.

None of the participants receives any pay. They freely devote their time and energies to promoting their cause and to making the Teatro a success. Their food and lodging is often provided by sympathizers, especially when the group in on a cross-country tour.

Influences of the Teatro Campesino

Inspired by the efforts of the Teatro Campesino, other Chicano theatre groups have emerged, many at colleges and universities. These include: El Teatro Urbano (San José, California); El Teatro Popular de la Vida y Muerte (Long Beach, California); Chicanito de Tiburcio Vásquez (Santa Bárbara, California); Teatro Aztlán (Northridge, California); Teatro del Barrio Chicano (Los Angeles, California); Teatro de los Barrios (San Antonio, Texas); Teatro Rasquachi (Colorado College, Colorado Springs); Teatro de los Estudiantes (University of Michigan, Ann Arbor); Teatro de la Gente (San José State University, California); Teatro Calcetín (Oakland, California); Teatro Mestizo (San Diego, California); Espíritu de Aztlán (Anaheim, California); Teatro de la Esperanza (Goleta, California); Teatro de las Chicanas, Los Topos (Berkeley, California); Hijos del Sol (Berkeley, California); Teatro Urbano (Los Angeles, California); Conciencia Mexicayotl (University of California, Irvine); Teatro Chicano de Sacramento (California State University, Sacramento); Teatro de los Niños (Pasadena, California); Teatro Machete (Los Angeles, California); and Teatro Popular del Barrio (San Diego, California).

The appearance of so many Chicano theatres precipitated the First Chicano Festival which was sponsored in 1970 by the Teatro Campesino in order to provide concentrated seminars in theatre, with cross-pollination of ideas and techniques. Representatives from various parts of the country and Mexico participated, including Los Reveladores del Tercer Mundo from New York City, Teatro Bilingual from El Paso, Texas, and Los Mascarones from Mexico City.

The success of the Festival has encouraged a similar annual

gathering of theatres.[43] The Fourth Festival de los Teatros Chicanos was held at San José State University on June 15, 1973. The purpose of the festival was to consolidate, reveal, and define contemporary theatrical achievements in the context of Chicanos coming to political and cultural power. The most important result of this festival was the drafting of the TENAZ (Teatro Nacional de Aztlán) MANI-FESTO which established common goals for all theatres. It reads:

> El Teatro Chicano was born of the social struggle of la Raza; given birth by trabajadores who remain trabajadores. Este es un renaci-miento: de lo viejo sale lo nuevo. Teatro es el espejo y el espíritu del Movimiento. Es el espejo de Tezcatlipoca que ilumina the evil we are surrounded by; es el Espíritu de Quetzalcoatl en que hallamos la bondad y la esperanza de la Raza. Teatro es la voz de los barrios, de la comunidad, de los de abajo, de los humildes, de los rasquachis.

> Los Trabajadores del Teatro Nacional de Aztlán are committed to a way of Life/Struggle ayudándole [sic] a la gente a entender el por qué [sic] de sus problemas sociales individuales and to search for solutions. Que sea nuestro Teatro el arco iris humano: let [sic] it create Teatro para toda [sic] la palomía—para niños, jóvenes, viejos, mu-jeres, estudiantes, obreros, campesinos y hasta para los tapados. Debe nutrirse de las raíces culturales de nuestros antepasados para sembrar semillas de liberación en el presente y para cosechar en el futuro la victoria de nuestros pueblos.

> La organización de TENAZ, which will work with all oppressed peo-ples, must develop a humane revolutionary alternative to commercial theatre and mass media. It is also necessary that we work and unite with all theatres struggling for liberation donde quiera, particular-mente en Latinoamérica. It should serve as a tool in the Life/Struggle of la Raza by developing Teatros as community organizations.

> El Teatro debe ir al pueblo y no el pueblo al Teatro.[44]

Although most Chicano theatres have a common ideology as expressed in the TENAZ MANIFESTO, there is some diversity among them in form, style, and convention. Los Topos, for example, a theatre group founded in a classroom at Laney College in Oakland, California, is multicultural. Members of the cast include Chicanos, blacks, and orientals. Rather than perform just for Chicanos, Los Topos entertains in "middle class" areas with the intent of passing on Chicano news that "is not adequately covered by the daily news media."[45]

Among the myriad of Chicano theatres, there is also a Teatro de los Niños, a children's theatre in which Chicano children celebrate their culture and disclose their perception of it to adults. This com-

Francisco Jiménez

munication between generations reinforces unity among the various Chicano social groupings.

Conclusion

In our discussion of the dramatic principles of the Teatro Campesino, one thing becomes clear—the Teatro is eclectic and, therefore, difficult to categorize. Many persons attuned to traditional theatre might be disturbed by this fact and might be inclined to dismiss this theatre as misguided. However, instead of dismissing it because it fails to fit into established and easily understood categories, one must look to it for esthetic values and for insights into Chicano culture.

UNIVERSITY OF SANTA CLARA

Notes

[1] Epilogue to *The Good Woman of Setzuan* in *Parables for the Theatre: Two Plays by Bertolt Brecht,* trans. Eric Bentley (Minneapolis, 1961).

[2] Oscar G. Brockett, *Perspectives on Contemporary Theatre* (Baton Rouge: Louisiana State University, 1971), p. 71.

[3] *Program for Radical Theatre Festival,* San Francisco State Univerity (September, 1968), p. 12.

[4] Ibid., pp. 24-25.

[5] *Perspectives on Contemporary Theatre,* p. 112.

[6] In the Spring of 1968, the Teatro Campesino was awarded an Obie.

[7] Luis Valdez became interested in drama at a very early age. He recalls that as early as the first grade he organized his own plays at school and at home. While in high school, he became very active in the Speech and Drama Department, and his talents won him a scholarship to San José State University where he first majored in science and then switched to English. During his sophomore year he wrote a one-act play entitled *The Theft* which was awarded first prize in a contest sponsored by the San José Theatre Guild. In October of 1968, he produced *The Shrunken Head of Pancho Villa,* a full-length play he wrote for the Northwest Drama Conference at San José State University.

[8] "El Teatro Campesino: Interviews with Luis Valdez," *Tulane Drama Review,* II (Summer 1967), 79.

[9] *Program for Radical Theatre Fetival,* p. 19. Eric Bentley in *the Theatre of Commitment* (New York: Atheneum, 1967), pp. 124-125, remarks that people attribute the slogans "art is a weapon" and "all art is propaganda" to the influence of Marxism. He points out, however, that such phrases have their "utility in reminding us that even classic writers of wide academic acceptance had some axe to grind."

130

[10]*Actos: El Teatro Campesino* (La Cucaracha Press, 1971), p. 2.

[11]The founding of the Teatro Campesino in 1965, however, does not mean that Chicanos did not have a dramatic tradition prior to that year. On the contrary, Chicano theatre has its roots in the ancient culture of the Mayans and Aztecs as well as in the Spanish heritage of the Americas (See Jorge A. Huerta, "Chicano Teatro: a Background," *Aztlán,* II [Fall 1971], 63-71).

The Spanish conquistadores and active missionaries brought the religious and popular Spanish drama of the Golden Age to this continent. The Church aptly utilized religious drama to convert the Indians to Catholicism, making liturgical theatre the most popular in the southwest (See M.R. Cole, "Los Pastores," *Memoirs of the American Folklore Society,* IX, [1907]; Edwin B. Place, "A Group of Mystery Plays Found in a Spanish Speaking Region of Southern Colorado," *University of Colorado Studies,* XVIII [August, 1930]; Willis Knapp Jones, *Behind Spanish American Footlights* [Austin: University of Texas Press, 1966]).

The tradition of performing liturgical plays in the southwest continues to this day. As Philip Ortego states: "Mexican Americans. . .annually stage the old plays in much the same fashion as the early English folk dramatists staged their plays in town squares, churches and courtyards" (*We are Chicanos: An Anthology of Mexican American Literature,* edited by Philip Ortego [New York: Washington Square Press, 1973], p. 222).

It is also interesting to note that the first Spanish language play performed in the United States was on April 30, 1598, 67 years before the first English play was performed in this country (Herbert E. Bolton, *The Spanish Borderlands* [Yale University Press, 1921], p. 127).

[12]"History of the Teatro Campesino," *La Raza,* I, 6 [?], p. 19.

[13]*Actos: El Teatro Campesino,* p. 3. Although Luis Valdez believes in awakening social consciousness, he is cautious not to obliterate individuality in the process. He holds that every individual, regardless of origin, is sacred and unique. He therefore categorically rejects the melting pot theory of this country. He states metaphorically: "Every man has his own heart. Who gives you the right to cut out a man's heart and put it in a melting pot?" (as quoted by Stan Steiner, *La Raza: The Mexican Americans* [New York: Harper & Row, 1968], p. 337).

[14]*Actos. . .* , p. 3.

[15]For a brief discussion of this play see Francisco Jiménez, "Chicano Literature: Sources and Themes," *The Bilingual Review/La revista bilingüe,* I (January-April, 1974), 14.

[16]Bagby, p. 77.

[17]*Actos,* p. 4.

[18]Bagby, p. 77.

[19]*Actos,* pp. 40-45.

[20]*Actos,* p. 5.

[21]Ibid.

[22]*Actos,* p. 6.

[23]*Program for Radical Theatre Festival,* p. 20.

[24]*Actos,* p. 6.

[25]"Notes on Chicano Theatre," *Chicano Theatre,* I (Spring, 1973), p. 7. According to Luis Valdez, religion is Chicano theatre at its highest point (*Actos,* p.1).

[26]*Actos,* p. 6.

Francisco Jiménez

[27]Ibid., p. 5.

[28]Bagby, p. 74.

[29]Ibid., p. 73.

[30]Bagby, p. 77.

[31]Ibid.

[32]This distinctive characteristic of the Teatro Campesino, however, does not detract from its effectiveness. As Dan Sullivan, dramatic critic for *Los Angeles Times* observed: "Is there anywhere a group of actors more in touch with themselves and the basic realities of life than these? A board and a passion is almost literally all they have to offer, yet the results make most big-city theatre seem skimpy" (El Teatro Campesino in Halloween Program," November 1, 1970).

[33]As quoted by Steiner, p. 329.

[34]For a detailed description of mime, see Richard Shepard, *Mime: The Technique of Silence* (New York: Drama Book Specialists, 1971).

[35]Bagby, pp. 77-78.

[36]"El Teatro Campesino—Its Beginnings," *The Chicanos: Mexican American Voices,* edited by Ed Ludwig and James Santibañez (Baltimore: Penguin Books, Inc., 1971), p. 115.

[37]For a discussion on Chicano language see Stan Steiner, "Brown Studies: The Language of La Raza," *The Center Forum,* IV (September, 1969), 4-5; George R. Alvarez, "Caló: The 'Other' Spanish," *A Review of General Semantics,* XXXIV (March, 1967), 7-13; Rafael Jesús González, "Pachuco: Birth of a Creole Language," *Arizona Quarterly,* XXIII (Winter, 1967), 343-56; Anthony Girard Lozano, "Grammatical Notes on Chicano Spanish," *The Bilingual Review/La revista bilingüe,* I (May-August, 1974), 147-151.

[38]As quoted by Steiner, p. 328.

[39]*The Chicanos: Mexican American Voices,* p. 116.

[40]*Actos,* p. 1.

[41]See *La Gran Carpa de los Rasquachis,* unpublished. A videotape of this play, property of El Teatro Campesino, is in the possession of Dr. E. Glass, professor in the Department of Classic and Modern Languages, Queensborough Community College.

[42]Bagby, p. 78.

[43]This year (1974), the festival was held in Mexico City on June 26.

[44]Leaflet dated 24 of June, 1973.

[45]Anonymous member of Los Topos speaking at "Sexto Sol Conference" at Stanford University on March 30, 1974.

III. Critical Trends:
An Overview

Situations differ, opportunities vary, I know, but it will always be necessary to insist (and in a more than theoretical way) that criticism is a collaborative and creative interplay. It creates a community and is inseparable from the process that creates and keeps alive a living culture; that creates a civilization, insofar as a civilization is something more than a matter of material conditions and externalities of social behaviour. If you believe that literature matters, you are committed to believing that.

F. R. Leavis

CURRENT TRENDS IN
CHICANO LITERARY CRITICISM

Carmen Salazar Parr

The recent increase in Chicano publications has produced a large body of critical works which examines and evaluates the various attitudes, issues, and problems generated through the creative process of literature. This body of literary criticism encompasses a variety of theoretical formulations which, for the most part, attempt to define critical approaches that will interpret the essence of Chicano literature as socio-historico-political documents *and* as works of art.

I propose, in this essay, to summarize a number of recent studies which reveal a variety of approaches suggested by Chicano critics: ethno-generic, comparative, Marxist, archetypal, thematic. It is by no means an exhaustive survey, nor is it a defense of any one method, but an attempt to show the direction which Chicano criticism is taking. Certainly our critics are very much at work. More importantly, like Chicano artists, they are reflecting a continuing battle against oppression, precisely by freeing themselves from any one restrictive dogma. They are claiming the same freedom of expression, recognizing that to assimilate a certain critical posture does not by any means make them less Chicano.

What characterizes Chicano literary criticism is a formalist type of approach, but one which complements sociological and historical analysis. In general, it seems to me, Chicano critics have been polarized into two groups: those who see Chicano literature as reflecting the socio-historical and cultural reality of the Chicano and those who defend it in terms of its universal, transcendental values.

A defense of universality is undertaken by Guadalupe Valdés Fallis, Sylvia González, and Juan Bruce-Novoa. Contradicting the judgment by Rafael Jesús González, and by extension, all those who are of the opinion that Chicano literature is for the most part polemical, propagandistic, and political, Valdés Fallis studies the metaphysical anxiety and the existence of God in three works: . . .*y no se lo tragó la tierra*, *Bless Me, Ultima*, and *Pocho*.[1] Far from being merely a vehicle for the exploration of the Chicano political consciousness, she maintains, the Chicano novel is deeply rooted in man and his predicament in the inhospitable universe of our times. Such transcendental values reveal that Chicano literature is in the mainstream of contemporary thought and culture.

Somewhat more detailed is the essay by Sylvia González in which she posits the notion that national traditions are adaptations of universal styles and that national character is but a step toward universality.[2] In order to attain this universality, one must take a step back into history, establish a sense of national identity, and finally transcend this nationality in search of universal values. Sylvia González compares the Chicano literary tradition with the Anglo-American one. In the beginning Anglo-American literature was rooted in English traditions. Similarly, Chicanos looked back to their Mexican heritage. In both traditions, the period of searching is followed by a political and nationalistic one. This, in turn, must evolve, according to González, into a universal expression. Supporting wholeheartedly Vasconcelos' concept of "the cosmic race," González sees the Chicano as the prototype of *la raza cósmica*, as inheritors of East and West who must maintain a harmonious combination of the two.

Bruce-Novoa, like Valdés Fallis and González, approaches literature from a universal perspective by proposing a theory of literary space.[3] Drawing on the theoretical formulations of Mircea Eliade, Georges Bataille, and the Mexican authors Juan García Ponce and Octavio Paz, Bruce-Novoa concerns himself with the space of continuity, specifically literature as a form of art. The space of art is related to the definition of Chicano national character. He therefore suggests that the Chicano, finding himself victimized by the chaos of his surroundings, that is, his Mexican and American influences, pushes the two apart and builds his own reality. At the same time, he must create bonds of interlocking tension that hold the two components in relationship. The Chicano, then, is the space, not the hyphen, between the two. And Chicano art, likewise, is "the nothing of that continuous space where all possibilities are simultaneously possible and all achieved products are simultaneously in relationship, creating one unit."[4] As continuous space, Chicano art, according to Bruce-Novoa, defies any attempt at classification or definition of its characteristics.

Bruce-Novoa applied the theory of literary space to a few Chicano works in order to show in them the following progression:

chaotic discontinuity ⟶ image retrieving ⟶
union ⟶ continuous literary space.

He concluded by defining the role of the critic within that literary space, and that role, he says, is to help expand the space of Chicano criticism "in which all theories act as interrelated tensions to in turn create the central sum of the Chicano perspective."[5]

Gustavo Segade sees Chicano literature as a historical, cultural, and mythic dialectic of the Chicano people: both unique and universal.[6] The literary dialectic of Chicano writers, he says, is based on a historical dialectic and their relationship with Mexican and North American realities. For Segade, this is not a simple relationship, but a rather complex one. The artistic process points out the real contradictions which human beings find around them. This process, he insists, does not imitate reality; it creates it.

Through Chicano literature we participate in a dialectics of reality. The artistic process begins with the artist and is completed with the reader and the critic "to carry it on to the infinite number of times that the work of art can begin the process of creating mythic time-space."[7]

Segade concludes that the discovery of universal meaning occurs when we are most ourselves. That experience is turned into literature, and in that way we come into communion with the rest of humanity, be they Russians, Native Americans, Asians, Africans, or others.

One danger with the whole question of universality, it seems to me, is that too often it emerges as a means of defending a literature which would otherwise not be accepted by "others." Black literature has gone through a similar phase, as George E. Kent observes: "Often, universalism, to the degree that it is being genuinely recognized, is simply an acknowledgement that 'others' now have achieved the psychological readiness necessary for entrance into the work. Thus people who would earlier have called Wright's fiction simply 'protest' are now beginning to see him as 'universal.' The blues, which at one time was a form completely addressed to Blacks and, when recognized at all, was seen largely as something quaint, is now universal."[8] To be valid, universalism must not fall into vague abstractions, but must probe instead the complexity of a people's experience.

Another approach suggested for the study of Chicano literature is the ethno-generic approach.[9] In his analysis, Donald Castro studies three novels: *Pocho, The Plum, Plum Pickers,* and *Chicano.* He maintains that genre ought to be viewed as something other than definition, that is, it ought to be descriptive. It becomes an analogical concept rather than abstracted definition. Since analogy is concerned with patterns and similarities, the task of the critic becomes the identifying of those patterns. Hence, a statement such as "It is a Chicano novel," when viewed as description rather than definition, eliminates evaluation and explanation of the work. Instead, it juxtaposes the work among other works yielding the same pattern. Of course, says Castro, juxtaposition is not an end in itself, but a means to an end: the acquisition of a new perspective. Consequently, this is more meaningful than the defenses or denials of whether a work is Chicano or not based on definitions which equate kind with essence. From the point of view of the artist, says Castro, genre can be a perspective and a strategy by which he organizes his work among other works, and, more importantly, the phenomena of the world. The *gestalt*, the *weltanschauung,* becomes the chief point of analogy among works in the same genre.

Treating the Chicano novel as an ethno-genre, Castro demonstrates how it presents the Chicano as viewing the world in flux, in transition, as time-historical. Thus, Mexico is seen as time-past, the United States as time-future, while time-present is the transition, the life of flux, chaos, and struggle of the Chicano. Ultimately, Castro maintains that the structure or form of the Chicano novel is determined not only by a *weltanschauung,* but by a *kunstwollen,* an esthetic intent. This *kunstwollen* mirrors time-present in such a way as to invoke the emotions: nemesis and aidos (anger and conscience). For this reason, a common metaphor in Chicano literature, that of *el espejo*, the mirror, is more accurate if it is thought of in the Renaissance sense of *ejemplar,* rather than in the modern sense of a "slice of life."

In a very suggestive essay, analyzing specifically the function of *el espejo,* Juan Rodríguez studies the theme of the search for identity in Chicano literature.[10] He rejects the idea that this theme should be considered in its universal aspects. Rather it must be seen specifically within the particular context of Chicano literature. Thus, Rodríguez cites as examples *I am Joaquín, Peregrinos de Aztlán,* and "El año perdido." In addition, there is the mirror of time, as reflected in *Bless Me, Ultima, Peregrinos de Aztlán, . . .y no se lo tragó la tierra, The Autobiography of a Brown Buffalo,* and parts of *Estampas del Valle.*

Rodríguez discusses the image reflected in the mirror as one which accentuates the alienation, the *condición enajenada* of the Chicano. Once the Chicano sees a horrible reflection of himself, he tries to avoid that reality by identifying with other characters, those who are less vulnerable to the concrete conditions of reality. Thus, he takes on multiple personalities. For example, the narrator of Zeta Acosta's novel assumes the roles of Humphrey Bogart and Charles Atlas. But, according to Rodríguez, this role-playing only alienates him more and eventually brings about a desire to know the total image, the *imagen no-enajenada* of the Chicano; thus, the incentive for a return to the past, to the lost paradise. But, the return to the past does not discover any paradise as expected. On the contrary, it makes the Chicano realize that things have not changed, that his has been an eternal existence for satisfying the needs of the privileged classes. The end of the journey comes with an awareness of his Chicano circumstance, and *this*, says Rodríguez, is the identity searched for. Rather than a cultural/racial search for identity which inquires "What am I?", the search or *búsqueda* is a political, historical, and economic one which inquires "How do we live?" and "How do we work?"

Juan Rodríguez opts for an approach which concentrates on the content of the work and especially on the conditions which produce that work. He rejects the whole concept of universality in favor of a Marxist perspective stressing the relevance of economic and historical forces in the formation of social views. Marxism offers him a framework in which to contemplate the social sources of alienation and to explain the material conditions which determine the authors' ideological biases. From a Marxist perspective, too, he offers an in-depth analysis of four short stories[11] from Rivera's *. . .y no se lo tragó la tierra* which best illustrate the author's intent: questioning certain set values such as those imposed by religion in order to become aware of the power structures that control the lives of the Chicano.

Alienation is also the subject of a study by Frank Pino, Jr.[12] Viewing the image of the "outsider" in an existential sense, as a symbol for the Mexican American experience, Pino concentrates on *el otro* in Rivera's *. . .y no se lo tragó la tierra* as an archetype which not only contains sociological import but is also endowed with epistemological, ontological, and phenomenological values. Pino maintains that the outsider image transcends any single level of meaning and effects a unity of philosophical, sociological, and psychological perspectives. These are reflected in the narrative technique whereby the protagonist, the narrator, and the center of consciousness are one and the same.

Pino discusses not only the insider-outsider roles of the characters but also the problem of distance between the reader and the experiences narrated. He therefore focuses on the artistic process in relation to the thematic aspects which he reveals as a combination of (1) the themes of remembrance, discovery, and will, (2) accounts of discrimination, alienation, and cultural conflict, and (3) the concepts of *ensimismamiento*, otherness, and unity.

In an in-depth study of the oneiric structure in *Bless Me, Ultima*, Roberto Cantú analyzes the relationship between the structure, the plot, and the thematic meaning of the work.[13] The ten dreams which the young Antonio has, thematically cover three basic aspects: (1) conflict in which the *curandera* Ultima intervenes as a reconciliator; (2) the destiny of the Marez-Luna family, especially that of Antonio; and (3) prophecy and revelation. More than offering a mere classification of dreams, Cantú draws on Mexican folklore, Nahuatl thought, and Jungian myth in order to explain the symbolism which is so much a part of the novel.

A comparative approach is used in the critical works of Charles Tatum and Guillermo Rojas. Charles Tatum,[14] in studying Chicano prose fiction and its ties to Mexican literature, rejects Wellek and Warren's warning that "the problem of 'nationality' and of distinct contributions of the individual nations, instead of being studied with theoretical clarity, has been blurred by nationalistic sentiment and racial theories."[15] Tatum points to a clear precedent for the comparative approach in Hispanic literature and proceeds to outline the similarities between contemporary works such as *Pocho, Chicano, The Plum, Plum Pickers, Estampas del Valle, . . .y no se lo tragó la tierra, Peregrinos de Aztlán* and the writings of the Mexican authors Azuela, Rulfo, and López y Fuentes.

The same comparative approach is used by Guillermo Rojas as he traces the influence of the novelists of the Mexican Revolution in *Estampas del Valle, . . .y no se lo tragó la tierra,* and *Peregrinos de Aztlán.*[16] By studying the characterization process, the style, structure, and language, Rojas concludes that these three works follow essentially the techniques of the Mexican novelists and that these techniques function to give the works a social realism in order to attack the political, social, and economic problems of the Chicano.

In this brief summary of a few representative studies of Chicano literature, I have attempted to indicate the present trends in Chicano criticism. There are some general observations to be made. First, Chicano literary criticism is still very much in the developing stages. What passes for criticism in many cases is, at best, a list of plot summaries and panoramic views. We need more in-depth studies of single works or single aspects of works as exemplified by Cantú's "Estructura y sentido onírico en *Bless Me, Ultima*," and Rodríguez's "Acercamiento a cuatro relatos de . . .*y no se lo tragó la tierra.*" Too often, in an effort to exhaust a theme, the critic will select four, five, or more works and yield a superficial analysis.

Second, we need more studies on poetry and theatre. Chicano poetry has been neglected in spite of the fact that it constitutes an important form of expression. Few works deal with specific poets. Tino Villanueva with his study of "Más allá del grito: poesía engagée Chicana"[17] and Daniel Testa with his analysis of "Alurista: Three Attitudes Toward Love in His Poetry"[18] are setting the pace in this area.

One works which merits study is Ron Arias' *The Road to Tamazunchale.* It is a work which moves away from social realism to join the ranks of the so-called "new novel." In a forthcoming article, Eliud Martínez examines the esthetic qualities of the work and shows how art does not necessarily preclude social commentary.[19] Both the novel and the analysis of it are indicative of the freedom of expression which artists and critics demand in the creative process.

Finally, it seems to me that the Chicano today is aspiring toward a synthesis of his being, toward an expression of universality derived from a desire to fuse all that is human, and that this universality is perhaps best expressed in the Chicano arts emerging today. Though there are elements that stem from a nationalistic viewpoint, artists, poets, and critics are not only creating new forms but are incorporating the methods, approaches, and philosophies of other cultures to achieve a synthesis of tensions.

The answer lies in assimilating without being assimilated, *asimilar sin ser asimilado*. In the words of the Mexican philosopher Leopoldo Zea:

> Se trata, no de ser incorporado, asimilado, sino de incorporar y asimilar. Es en esta preocupación que coinciden negritud y mestizaje latinoamericano. El negro no quiere dejar de ser negro para ser blan-

co, como tampoco el latinoamericano dejar de ser mestizo para ser europeo o anglo-sajón. De lo que se trata es de comulgar la cultura del blanco, la cultura europea u occidental, así como toda expresión cultural del hombre sin que por ello se deje de ser hombre concreto, negro o latinoamericano. El ser negro o ser latinoamericano, debe ser enriquecido, ampliado, nunca negado. A su vez, el otro, el blanco, el occidental, cualquier hombre, puede enriquecerse con la experiencia cultural del negro y del latinoamericano.[20]

The key word in this process of assimilation as described by Zea is the word *comulgar*—that is, to bring to communion, to blend, to synthesize the different cultures. Current trends in Chicano literary criticism indicate that we are moving toward that process of synthesis. We are expanding that literary space of which Bruce-Novoa writes.

LOS ANGELES VALLEY COLLEGE

Notes

[1]Guadalupe Valdés Fallis, "Metaphysical Anxiety and the Existence of God in Contemporary Chicano Fiction," *Revista Chicano-Riqueña,* III, 1 (Winter 1975), 26-33.

[2]Sylvia A. González, "National Character vs. Universality in Chicano Poetry," *De Colores,* I, 4 (1975), 10-21.

[3]Juan Bruce-Novoa, "The Space of Chicano Literature," *De Colores,* I, 4 (1975), 22-42.

[4]Ibid., p. 28.

[5]Ibid., p. 40.

[6]Gustavo Segade, "Toward a Dialectic of Chicano Literature," *Mester,* IV, 1 (Nov. 1973), 4-5.

[7]Ibid., p. 5

[8]George E. Kent, *Blackness and the Adventure of Western Culture* (Chicago: Third World Press, 1972), p. 28. Kent discusses the problem of Universalism: "And the problem with universalism is that its current use misdirects the writer and the critic, and leads to vague abstractions (Man, the Human Condition) and packs concealed cultural referents. Any universalism worthy of recognition derives from its depths of exploration of the density, complexity, and variety of a people's experience—or a person's. It is achieved by going down—not by transcending."

[9]Donald Castro, "The Chicano Novel: An Ethno-Generic Study." *La Luz* (April 1973), 50-52.

[10]Juan Rodríguez, "Temas y motivos de la literatura chicana," manuscript.

[11]Juan Rodríguez, "Acercamiento a cuatro relatos de . . . *y no se lo tragó la tierra,*" *Mester,* V, 1 (Nov. 1974), 16-23.

[12]Frank Pino, Jr., "The Outsider and 'el otro' in Tomás Rivera's . . . *y no se lo tragó*

Carmen Salazar Parr

la tierra," *Books Abroad,* XLIX, 3 (Summer, 1975), 453-458.

[13]Roberto Cantú, "Estructura y sentido de lo onírico en *Bless Me, Ultima,"* *Mester,* V, 1 (Nov. 1974), 27-41.

[14]Charles Tatum, "Contemporary Chicano Prose Fiction: Its Ties to Mexican Literature," *Books Abroad,* XLIX, 3 (Summer 1975), 431-438.

[15]Quoted in Tatum's article.

[16]Guillermo Rojas, "La prosa chicana: Tres epígonos de la novela mexicana de la Revolución," *De Colores,* I, 4 (1975), 43-57.

[17]Tino Villanueva, "Más allá del grito: Poesía engagée chicana," *De Colores,* II, 2 (1975), 27-46.

[18]Daniel Testa, "Alurista: Three Attitudes Toward Love in His Poetry," *Revista Chicano-Riqueña,* IV, 1 (Winter 1976), 46-55.

[19]Eliud Martínez, "Ron Arias' *The Road to Tamazunchale:* A Chicano Novel of the New Reality," to be published in *Latin American Literary Review.*

[20]Leopoldo Zea, "Negritud e indigenismo,"*Cuadernos americanos,* CXVI, 5 (Sept.-Oct. 1974), 26-27.

CRITICAL APPROACHES
TO CHICANO LITERATURE

Joseph Sommers

Introduction

The ideas which follow are part of a longer study in progress, tentatively entitled, "From the Critical Premise to the Product: Critical Modes and their Applications to Chicano Literature." It is a study in three parts. The first attempts to gauge the social and cultural context of Chicano literature and literary study at the present moment. The second part, from which the ideas below are abstracted, tries to single out three critical approaches to Chicano literature, examining them in terms of assumptions, methods, and consequences. The approaches are termed formalist, culturalist, and historical-dialectical. Part three is in many ways an acid test, since it represents an effort to demonstrate how each approach functions when applied to a specific literary work. I have chosen the narrative text by Tomás Rivera, *. . .y no se lo tragó la tierra*,[1] which is rich and complex in both form and meaning, thereby providing a formidable challenge to any critic.

The aim here is to avoid twin dangers which might undermine the arguments presented. One danger might be termed pluralism, a tendency to assume a neutral posture and to infer that all approaches are equally valid, perhaps leading to the same objective. The other danger is to be prescriptive, assuming that one approach is totally correct and that other views must be totally rejected. My intention is to demonstrate the possibilities and the shortcomings of the first two critical approaches and to make clear why I advocate the third. I assume that to disagree is not to censure, that disagreement can be based upon respect, and that the process of testing and contrasting ideas can be productive.

A brief summary of the first section of the longer study will help to frame the ideas from the second part of that study presented below. The need to define critical strategies when analyzing and interpreting Chicano literature is greater than ever, because the social and cultural atmosphere in which this literature exists at present is more difficult and hostile than was the case a decade ago. In the first place there has been a withdrawal from academic commitments of the 1960s: to recruit minority students and faculty on all levels; to promote actively the study of minority literatures; to question and reform hardbound educational norms and traditional academic standards; to amplify accepted views of what constitutes our national ("American") literary tradition.

In the second place, what legitimation has been accorded to Chicano literature and to related teaching and research in this field has been limited and ambiguous. The tendency has been to favor either the assimilation of the literature into an engulfing Anglo-American literary mainstream, or the dilution of critical perspective by means of newly validated formulae such as "cultural pluralism" or "ethnopoetics."

The Formalist Approach

Of the three main lines of critical approach to Chicano literature, the most prominent in academic publications is that which attempts to apply the norms and categories of formalist criticism, seeking to validate Chicano texts, for both Chicano and Anglo readers, as authentic modern literature.

The methodology varies, but the two most common features are reliance on comparative criteria and stress on textual analysis. Some comparatists focus on identifying literary influences (for example, Juan Rulfo on Tomás Rivera), tending to base their claims for the validity of the Chicano text on its derivation from sources of recognized excellence. Others refer to established definitions such as "modernism" to call attention to what for them is a "newly emerged" literature. Textual critics try to show that the criteria of stylistics and more recently of structuralist criticism can reveal in a Chicano poem or narrative the types of complexity and levels of formal coherence identified with the exemplary texts of modern literature. Other critics such as Juan Bruce-Novoa retain the formalist insistence on separating the text from its social context but, nonetheless, seek to account for "meaning." This approach to "meaning" limits it to the realm of the imaginary, postulating the text as occupying "imaginary space,"[2] as being mental experience which provides an alternative to lived experience, to the chaos, injustice, and temporality of the real world. Meaning, rather than reference to reality, becomes yet another index of the literariness of the work.

What underlying assumptions characterize this approach to a given text? For one, emphasis on accepted major works as models carries the assumption that literature is a phenomenon of print, with the most respected exemplars being those consumed by the educated middle class. A concomitant assumption attaches relatively low value to oral literature, which introduces collective themes based on concrete experience, which relies upon oral transmission, which is frequently anonymous, and which historically has provided a source of resistance to the dominant ideology.[3] A second concomitant assumption is stress on the text as individualized creation. In this view, the act of literary production is the artist's private struggle to find a personal voice and to express an individualized response. The poet is seen as arbitrarily gifted with the quality of genius, as being endowed with special intuitive insights and access to the truth.

A further assumption is that the prime feature of a literary text is its aesthetic quality, which cannot be measured by the yardstick of meaning or cognition, for these are categories which normally rest upon criteria of reason and of reference to experienced reality. Aesthetic quality, on the other hand, can be uncovered by analysis of features contained within the text, features which when taken together explain the qualities of unity and complexity.

Finally there is a widespread tendency to value the quality of "universality." This quality is rarely defined, except by implication or by negation. Some critics seem to state that to be universal is somehow to transcend "social protest" (presumably they would strike Galdós, Neruda, and the entire picaresque novel from the "universal" list). Others seem to suggest that literature achieves universality by avoiding the regional or the immediately historical in favor of the abstract, the metaphysical, the imaginary, or the timeless themes and myths of world culture (this would eliminate Balzac, Tolstoy, Malraux and the corpus of Spanish epic poetry). What seems involved beneath the surface of these notions is a fragmentation of categories which might otherwise be seen as interconnected, such as the artistic and the social, or the imaginary and the historical. Certainly one can infer from this view of universality a conception of literature as distraction, or as aesthetic object, or as a distinct mode of mental activity from other disciplines, or as being embodied by a succession of masterpieces insulated against the ravages of time by protective jackets of brilliant thematic colors.

What are the consequences in terms of produced literary criticism when these assumptions constitute the critic's point of departure? On the positive side is a healthy stress on intensive analysis of the formal qualities of given texts. On the other hand, reliance on the printed text has implied accepting the notion of either a dearth or a poverty of literary history. Thus the bulk of this type of criticism tends to be ahistorical, concentrating on contemporary texts and their modernism. By extension this has meant a thrust toward the assimilation of Chicano literature, or more precisely a select number of Chicano texts, into the standard reading list of the educated reader, primarily in academe. The critic's role, when these assumptions are primary, is, as Bruce-Novoa phrased it, "to lead the reader back to the literary work itself,"[4] for literature in this view constitutes a separate, non-referential, transcendental reality.

The Culturalist Approach

The second line of critical approach, prominent during the 1960s, is based on the notion of *cultural uniqueness*. It aims to value Chicano literature precisely because in it one finds expression of the distinctive features of Chicano culture. An earlier philologically oriented but, nonetheless, culturalist variant, practiced by Aurelio Espinosa half a century ago, stressed the survival of authentic Spanish forms in the Southwest.

The critical methodology tends toward the descriptive, identifying cultural features: family structures, linguistic and thematic survivals, anti-gringo attitudes, pre-Hispanic symbology, notions of a mythic past, and folk beliefs ranging from *la llorona* to the Virgin of Guadalupe. Some culturalist critics, waging a necessary struggle against the elitism which characterizes purist notions of literary Spanish, stress the distinguishing presence in Chicano literature of what has been called the binary phenomenon—a process by which linguistic symbols and syntactic structures of two languages interact in the same text. Others stress the presence of Aztec symbols or myths. Thus Herminio Ríos and Octavio Romano find special value in *Bless*

Me, Ultima, the novel by Rudolfo Anaya, because, "It is from our collective memory that he draws myths such as that of Cihuacoatl. . . . And it is from our collective subconscious that the myth of the Golden Carp arises. . . .Anaya takes us from the subconscious to the conscious, from the past to the present. . .in so doing, he has helped us to know ourselves."[5]

What assumptions underlie culturalist criticism? One important concept is evident in the above quotation. Stated in bare terms, it is that present-day Chicano mental structures, by dint of a sort of Jungian operation of the collective unconscious, retain continuity with the thought patterns and the cosmology of the Aztec past. Also implied is the notion that rediscovery of cultural origins, of original myths, will impart a healthy consciousness of uniqueness to the generations of the present. This notion that the distant past—and here I refer to a mythic, magical past rather than a past seen as a point in a historic process of change—shapes and controls the present, regardless of social and historical change, is by no means original. Mexican examples embodying the same anti-historical view are the essay by Octavio Paz, *Posdata*,[6] and *Tiempo Mexicano*[7] by Carlos Fuentes. It was this ingredient in Chicano thought which led Philip Ortego to state in 1971: "Perhaps the principal significance of the Chicano Renaissance lies in the identification of Chicanos with their Indian past."[8]

There are other related assumptions which form part of the matrix of culturalist thought. One is the positive value attached to traditional culture, regardless of its social content. For example, the traditional role of the church, whether in its mystical or its adaptive manifestations, is seen as integral to Chicano culture. A further tendency is to criticize the materialism, racism, and dehumanization of contemporary capitalist society by counterposing idealistically the values of traditional culture, presenting these values as flawless and recoverable in unchanged form. Needless to say this construes culture as static and separable from the historic process, rather than dynamic, creative and responsive to experience.

Another notion of culturalist thought, embedded in the Plan de Aztlán, places primacy on the distinctive ethnic origins of Chicano culture, setting it apart from other cultures and indeed from other nations. Here the stress is on racial fusion, on Indian and Mexican constituent elements, with occasional references to a Hispano component. There is frequent harking back to José Vasconcelos' slogan, "la raza cósmica," and to *mestizaje* as being the distinctive feature characterizing the Chicano experience. The key assumptions here not only incorporate a view of culture as static, but also construe race (and ultimately nature and the biological process) as the controlling element in culture, while positing culture as the central determinant of a people's experience. This line of thought tends to subordinate the idea that culture might be connected to the social condition of class, as well as the view that cultural forms evolve in response to the specifics of the historical process.

In terms of critical strategies, the above assumptions clearly point toward the adoption of one of the several variants of "myth criticism" which have been in vogue in academe recently, centered on the concepts of archetypal qualities in human nature and archetypal patterns in human relations.

A further implicit assumption in some culturalist criticism, not in consonance with reliance on myth criticism, is that Chicano literature can be understood only by Chicanos and interpreted only by Chicanos. In this view, Chicano critics writing from a Chicano perspective and publishing in Chicano periodicals are the only reliable sources of understanding of Chicano literature. Accompanying this assumption is the idea that all literary expression by Chicanos constitutes a contribution to the body of Chicano culture. This assumes that *lo chicano* is good by definition, thus subordinating the critical function of literary criticism.

The consequences of this approach to literary analysis are multiple. One is to conceive of Chicano literature as ethnic, designed for and limited to an ethnic readership, to be isolated academically within ethnic studies programs. Related is the notion that Chicano literature is separable from other literatures which in fact may have comparable structural features (such as an oral tradition or the bilingual mode or historical trajectories involving the confrontation with class exploitation and institutionalized racism). A further consequence is to reject the struggle to critically redefine standard exclusivist views of American literature. Finally, whereas formalism tends to ignore the past, focusing on modernism and its virtues, culturalism tends to ignore the present, stressing in nostalgic and idealized terms the predominance of the past.

The Historical-Dialectical Approach

The third line of critical approach, best characterized as historically based and dialectically formulated, and espoused by this critic, rejects the classic distinction sanctified by René Wellek and Austin Warren between the "intrinsic" and the "extrinsic."[9] It includes the work of Marxists but is not practiced exclusively by Marxist critics.

This approach begins by explaining the singular formal qualities of a text which distinguish it from alternate modes of verbal expression. It must also account for the manner in which a given text rejects, modifies, and incorporates features of other texts which have preceded it. Analysis, then, includes the notion of intertextuality, the response to literary tradition. Since the critic sees literature as a cultural product, the text is also studied in relation to its cultural ambiance, which process in turn means understanding societal structures.

Finally the critic assumes that to consume literary texts, even in their most fantastic and abstract variants, is a form of cognition, for the text comments upon, refers to, and interprets human experience. Seeing this experience across time, the critic incorporates reference to the dynamics of the historical process into the content and the context of the work.

One aspect of the dialectics of this approach, combining formal, cultural, and historical analysis, is the need to identify an internal Chicano literary dynamic and simultaneously to account for interactions with both Mexican and North American middle-class and popular literary traditions. Treating critical approaches dialectically, the critic does not reject formalist or culturalist analysis out of hand, but tries to incorporate their positive features into a system which transcends their self-imposed limitations.

While no one critic has worked exclusively along these lines, three examples come to mind of differing but important degrees and kinds of compatibility: Américo Paredes, in his intense study *With a Pistol in His Hand: A Border Ballad and its Hero*,[10] which examines a particular corrido and shows how this popular literary form creatively blends myth and history to forge a tradition of cultural response to repression on the Texas-Mexican border; Luis Leal, in his rigorously researched article "Mexican American Literature: A Historical Perspective,"[11] which explores the problems of historical periods and of literary development within different genres, providing valuable pointers toward future research in literary history; and Carlos Monsiváis, in his comparatist study published in 1974,[12] which sets out parallels and divergences between Mexican and Chicano literatures, examines in each the consequences of cultural imperialism, and goes on to show the ideologically contradictory ways in which Mexican literature has responded to its historical reality, ranging from internalization of the dominant ideology, on the one hand, to struggling for a critical perspective on the other.

Perhaps three assumptions of this critical approach can be identified. One stems from the understanding that Chicano literary expression is bound up with the historic pattern of economic and social oppression prevailing since 1848. In economic terms this oppression has eliminated upward class mobility, consigning Mexican-descended Americans almost uniformly to working class status, whether urban or rural. This fact, compounded enormously by the racism of linguistic discrimination, has historically limited access to education, to literacy, to the print media including journals, libraries, and publishing houses, and to the related distribution systems which shape the growth of a literary market. Logically, then, the trajectory of Chicano literature differs crucially from the mainstream models of both Mexico and the United States. The mapping of this literary tradition will have to account for an important popular stratum, only rarely available in print, which includes corridos, folk tales, historical narrations, and *teatro de carpa y de revista*.[13] It must search out the work of artists whose impact was local or regional, and expect thematic emphases more centered on the social, cultural, and historical than the personal, individualized, and psychologically introspective.

A second assumption incorporates ideology into literary evaluation. The defining of literary history can be seen as part of the struggle for cultural expression in the face of oppression. Thus a text by a Mexican American celebrating the patriotism of New Mexicans fighting with Theodore Roosevelt in 1898 to suppress Cuban independence would certainly merit serious study stressing ideological contradictions. But it might well be seen as less central or progressive than, say, the corrido tradition. Similarly, the critic would analyze the view of culture embedded in the literary makeup of a text with these questions in mind: Is this view of culture static or dynamic? Is the substance of Chicano culture, as interpreted in the text, its capacity to provide the forms and encourage the spirit of resistance, or is it the harking back nostalgically to a forgotten, idealized, and unrepeatable past?

The third assumption is that literature, rather than merely reflecting historical experience, in its very form and structures interprets this experience and is capable of impact upon the reader's consciousness. By this logic the writer is neither omniscient *vate*, seer, nor self-annointed revolutionary, but rather a creative interpreter, one who is part of a group and must assume the contradictions of this social condition and struggle to resolve them.

Different consequences derive from this approach to Chicano literature. For one, emphasis falls upon a *critical* criticism. The role of the critic is to challenge both writer and reader to question the text for meaning and values, which needless to say are inseparable from its formal disposition, and to situate this meaning and these values in a broad cultural framework of social and historical analysis.

Further, there is concern for comparative study. For example, there might well be interest in research contrasting the roots and development patterns of the corrido and Chicano narrative, or of the corrido and the blues.

Another consequence is insistence on multiple responses to the hostile cultural environment which now prevails, responses transcending the double trap of ghettoization or assimilation. On the one hand, there is the need to define, study, and teach Chicano literature in all academic settings, to devote scholarly meetings to it, to encourage historians and critics of Chicano literature by means of grants and other positive recognition. On the other, there is the simultaneous need to see Chicano literature incorporated into the purview of both Spanish and English departments. Chicano literature can be seen as nourished by Latin American literature, especially that of Mexico, and as contributor to these traditions. But this Latin Americanizing of perspective need not contradict an analogous North Americanizing process in teaching, rendering Chicano literature integral to the "American" literary tradition. Specialists in American literature should be expected to know Spanish in order to command a full understanding of their field.

But perhaps the most urgent priority, and the note to underline in ending this paper, is the need for work, interchange, and dialogue centering on what might be seen in national terms as a metaproject: the elaborating of a Chicano literary history.

UNIVERSITY OF CALIFORNIA, SAN DIEGO

Joseph Sommers

Notes

[1](Berkeley: Quinto Sol, 1971).

[2]This is a central notion in his "The Space of Chicano Literature," *De colores* (Albuquerque), I, 4 (Winter, 1975), pp. 22-42.

[3]Arturo Islas seems to imply this assumption of low value in "Writing from a Dual Perspective," *Miquiztli* (Stanford University), II, 1 (Winter, 1974), p. 2: "More often than not, much of the fiction we do have is document, and sometimes not very well written document. Much of what is passed off as literature is a compendium of folklore, religious superstition, and recipes for tortillas. All well and good, but it is not literature."

[4]Bruce-Novoa, "The Space of Chicano Literature," p. 39.

[5]"Introduction," *Bless Me, Ultima* (Berkeley: Quinto Sol, 1972), p. ix.

[6](México: Siglo XXI, 1970).

[7](México: Joaquín Mortiz, 1971).

[8]"Chicano Poetry: Roots and Writers," in *New Voices in Literature: The Mexican American. A Symposium.* (Edinburg, Texas: Dept. of English, 1971), p. 11.

[9]This distinction underlies the entire structure of their important volume, *Theory of Literature* (New York: Harcourt Brace, 2nd ed., 1965).

[10](Austin: University of Texas Press, 1958).

[11]*Revista Chicano-Riqueña* (Gary, Indiana), I, 1 (Spring, 1973), pp. 32-44.

[12]"Literatura Comparada: Literatura Chicana," *Fomento Literario* (Congreso Nacional de Asuntos Colegiales), I, 3 (Invierno, 1973), pp. 42-49.

[13]Tomás Rivera stresses the importance of the corrido and other popular literary forms, and calls for study of Mexican American newspapers of the nineteenth century in "Into the Labyrinth: The Chicano in Literature," in *New Voices in American Literature: The Mexican American. A Symposium.* A point of departure for periodical research is the article by Herminio Ríos and Lupe Castillo, "Toward a True Chicano Bibliography: Mexican American Newspapers, 1848-1942," *El Grito*, III, 4 (Summer, 1970), pp. 17-24. Examples of recent research which has uncovered valuable material are two articles by Doris L. Meyer, "Anonymous Poetry in Spanish-language New Mexico Newspapers, 1880-1900," *The Bilingual Review/La revista bilingüe*, I, 2 (Sept.-Dec., 1975), pp. 259-275; and "Banditry and Poetry: Verses by Two Outlaws of Old Las Vegas," *New Mexico Historical Review* (Oct., 1975), pp. 277-290.

LA NOVELA CHICANA DE LOS SETENTA COMENTADA POR SUS ESCRITORES Y CRITICOS

Salvador Rodríguez del Pino

Durante la primavera de 1977,[1] se empleó por primera vez el medio de la televisión para entrevistar a novelistas y críticos chicanos sobre "la novela chicana de los setenta". Esta serie de entrevistas se llevó a cabo en la Universidad de California en Santa Bárbara con el nombre de *Encuentro*. El propósito de las entrevistas fue dar a conocer, audiovisualmente, a los creadores y comentaristas de la ahora madura novelística chicana. El formato fue de carácter informal para resaltar la espontaneidad de los entrevistados que aunque expertos en su campo, estaban convencidos de que era la mejor manera de evitar una forma estática que reflejara clichés y repeticiones de previas entrevistas o estudios literarios. El medio escogido permitió crear un documento histórico-literario que ofrece la oportunidad de ver y escuchar a los propios autores hablando y comentando su vida, obra e ideología, y proporciona al estudiante de la literatura chicana un acercamiento más íntimo a las obras y sus autores.

Esta perspectiva no es novedosa en el campo literario actual puesto que la televisión ya se ha empleado con varios autores de la literatura universal; pero el valor verdadero de las entrevistas radica en el concepto de la serie, que por primera vez junta a la mayoría de los autores y críticos chicanos para que expongan una visión a la vez amplia y sintetizada de la novelística chicana. Por esta razón, no solamente se entrevistaron a los autores de las obras chicanas, sino que también se incluyó un contrapunto de perspectivas provenientes de los críticos que comentaron a su vez sobre estos autores y sus obras. Los autores entrevistados fueron: Alejandro Morales, autor de *Caras viejas y vino nuevo*; Tomás Rivera, autor de *...y no se lo tragó la tierra*; Aristeo Brito, autor de *El diablo en Texas*; Miguel Méndez, autor de *Peregrinos de Aztlán*; Rudolfo Anaya, autor de *Bless Me, Ultima* y *Heart of Aztlán*; y finalmente Ron Arias, autor de *The Road to Tamazunchale*. Los críticos entrevistados fueron: Tomás Ybarra-Frausto, Juan Bruce-Novoa, Juan Rodríguez y Luis Leal, todos ellos conocidos en el campo de la crítica chicana y latinoamericana. Las entrevistas se realizaron en inglés, excepto la de Miguel Méndez que se hizo en español. El entrevistador y organizador de *Encuentro* fue el profesor Salvador Rodríguez del Pino, quien actualmente enseña literatura chicana en el Departamento de Estudios Chicanos de la Universidad de California en Santa Bárbara. La serie fue auspiciada por el Departamento de Estudios Chicanos, el Centro de Estudios Chicanos y el Centro de Recursos de Instrucción de dicha universidad.

El alcance de este documento literario tal vez no se llegará a conocer hasta que haya sido completamente evaluado por la siguiente generación de escritores y críticos chicanos, cuyas influencias y direcciones puedan ser trazadas sobre la producción de la generación actual. Sin embargo, en forma de comentario y descripción, haré una sinopsis de los temas, influencias e ideologías que evidentemente surgieron en la serie de entrevistas. Me será un poco difícil organizar adecuadamente todos los enfoques y puntos de vista expresados por los participantes ya que algunos de ellos hicieron comentarios divergentes y aun contradictorios a las opiniones de los demás. Estas notas estarán basadas no solamente en las entrevistas, sino que también agregaré mis propios puntos de vista extraídos de las conferencias previamente presentadas a los estudiantes del curso sobre "La novela chicana contemporánea", en el cual participaron todos los escritores y críticos, incluyendo también a John Rechy, quien no pudo ser entrevistado. Los temas que se comentaron durante las entrevistas fueron los siguientes: la literatura chicana en general; la novela chicana y sus autores; temática, forma y estructura de la novela chicana y la expresión lingüística del escritor chicano. Mencionaré lo que se dijo acerca de estos temas y me referiré, cuando haya menester, a la persona o personas cuyos nombres sean de importancia para los comentarios citados.

Sobre la literatura chicana en general

Todos los participantes convinieron en que sí existe una "literatura chicana" nacional en relación con lo que se denomina "literatura mexicana", rusa, francesa, etc. Estas literaturas nacionales expresan la experiencia propia de su cultura, herencia y valores nacionales y tienen rasgos distintivos que las caracterizan en relación a las demás literaturas. A veces puede haber una ofuscación relativa entre la literatura chicana y la mexicana en cuanto a valores y fuentes de experiencia que provienen de las mismas raíces socioculturales e históricas, como en el caso de *Peregrinos de Aztlán*. Esta obra podría ser clasificada dentro de la literatura mexicana, nos dice Luis Leal, pero al leerla detenidamente vemos que existen ciertos elementos como la experiencia del emigrado, el enajenamiento causado por el choque de culturas y la visión del hombre que no encuentra arraigo, que sirven como indicios para situar a la obra al margen de la literatura mexicana. El mundo de estos escritores, al novelar el universo chicano variado y diverso, proviene de la experiencia personal y la perspectiva de cada autor. Así tenemos a Rivera que expone un mundo chicano donde la impotencia de los personajes oprimidos por el sistema social se enfoca desde una perspectiva histórica. Dentro de esta perspectiva, la conciencia del chicano campesino, que sigue como nómada las cosechas de trabajo, todavía no se rebela en contra del sistema social y político que lo oprime, sino que solamente se alza contra la opresión divina y la fatalidad. Durante los años descritos por Rivera, los cuarenta y los cincuenta, apenas existía la noción de que uno se podía rebelar en contra de los sistemas del hombre y sólo se tenía conciencia de una opresión superhumana, ya sea la divina o la diabólica. Sin embargo, la semilla de la identidad o de su búsqueda germina a través de los relatos terminando en la sospecha de una identidad y conciencia chicanas. Rivera describe a sus personajes tales como eran en ese tiempo y no como serían si los presentara con un enfoque contemporáneo. Si Juan Rodríguez dice que hay una "problemática en el libro de Rivera",[2] es que el problema es suyo y no del libro. En contraste con Rivera están los libros de Oscar Zeta Acosta, cuyo protagonista está consciente de su identidad pero no quiere aceptarla. No la acepta porque la encuentra estereotipada, y trata de adoptar, o mejor dicho crear, una identidad personal a su hechura y conveniencia. Por esta razón empieza una odisea no de búsqueda sino de encuentro, que elimine esa identidad heredada e impuesta para encontrar una que él supone verdadera, que realmente represente lo que él supone ser.

Salvador Rodríguez del Pino

Nunca se sabe si la encuentra. Nos damos cuenta que al protagonista le importa poco quién es; lo que más le importa es lo que quiere ser y hacer. Los libros de Anaya nos descubren los mitos, tradiciones, supersticiones y valores de un universo chicano donde las tradiciones hispánicas y mexicanas se preservan, primero dentro de un ambiente bucólico y después en el barrio, en que las fuerzas del bien y del mal universalizan la experiencia chicana, cuyo mundo queda expuesto a las mismas preocupaciones humanas de todos los pueblos en condición similar. En conclusión, la novela chicana representa y describe un mundo o *weltanschauung* compuesto de elementos y experiencias inconfundiblemente diferentes del mundo mexicano y americano, sin negar la génesis que le dio vida o la realidad de su mestizaje que lo aparta de los dos.

La novela chicana y sus autores

La mayoría de los escritores que tratamos son académicos que se han instruido bajo las normas literarias hispánicas o americanas y que dominan los dos idiomas que integran su dualidad cultural. Estos autores no son producto del pueblo autodidáctico, popular y espontáneo; su arte ha sido aprendido bajo la estricta disciplina académica de los departamentos de literatura hispánica o americana. Todos los autores entrevistados son profesores en universidades donde enseñan literatura chicana, hispanoamericana o mexicana. Todos tienen algo que contarnos sobre las experiencias que ellos mismos identifican como chicanas, y su necesidad de comunicar un mundo de experiencias análogas aunque diferentes en impresiones vitales es la energía motivadora que los impulsa como escritores. Miguel Méndez, el único autodidacta del grupo, es ahora profesor de literatura y del idioma español en el Colegio Pima del Estado de Arizona. Méndez relató en la entrevista la vida de albañil que ejercía hasta hace poco. Un ávido lector de toda clase de libros, empezó desde muy joven a escribir cuentos y poemas, los cuales se publicaron en revistas y periódicos; de esta manera alcanzó cierta fama de escritor fuera de su profesión de albañil aunque sus compañeros obreros ignoraban su pasatiempo y ambición. Había ocasiones en que se anunciaba enfermo para poder ir a dar una conferencia en la universidad y regresar a tiempo al trabajo que le daba el sustento.

Casi todos nuestros escritores tienen sus raíces en la clase campesina y trabajadora y de ella sacan sus más interesantes experiencias. Les es preciso rescatarlas y documentarlas para que las siguientes generaciones de chicanos no se olviden de esas raíces. También es interesante saber que todos ellos lucharon para conseguir que se publicaran sus libros; a veces tuvieron que establecer sus propias editoriales, como en el caso de la *Editorial Peregrinos*, o como Alejandro Morales, ir a México para que sus libros fueran publicados en español. Para todos la mayor ambición es tener el tiempo y la libertad de seguir creando y escribiendo, ya que al pasar a las filas académicas tienen que dedicarse a la investigación literaria o funcionar como administradores, tareas que les impiden continuar su trayectoria de escritores. Sin embargo, ninguno de ellos se mantiene de sus libros porque la literatura chicana no ha trascendido todavía los límites de las clases de literatura chicana o del pueblo chicano lector. Una excepción es el caso de Rolando Hinojosa; su libro fue premiado en Cuba y puede que represente la apertura esperada para que la literatura chicana penetre en el público lector hispanoamericano.

Temática, forma y estructura de la novela chicana

Los novelistas chicanos son tan diversos en su temática como lo son en su ideología. Es evidente que una de sus preocupaciones es la identidad de lo chicano y del chicano. Sin embargo, con la publicación de *The Road to Tamazunchale*, la temática de la novela chicana entra en una nueva etapa que es más creación que recreación. Tomás Rivera ha dividido la temática de la novelística chicana en tres etapas: conservación, lucha e invención.[3] La etapa de conservación consiste en recrear la historia pasada del pueblo chicano para preservar las tradiciones y los valores culturales que lo identifican por medio de los hechos, anécdotas y relatos que oyeron los novelistas de sus padres y abuelos o los que se basan en sus propias experiencias de la infancia. Entre las novelas de este tipo se hallan: *. . .y no se lo tragó la tierra*, *Bless Me, Ultima*, *Chicano* y *Peregrinos de Aztlán*. En estas obras se cuentan las historias oídas o vividas de un pasado que, aunque no lejano, está preñado de luchas por sobrevivir en un ambiente hostil y extraño en cuanto a cultura y a valores morales y sociales. Aquellas vidas hicieron posible la perpetuación de la raza por medio de su presencia imponente y por la resolución de no permitir la extinción de su herencia.

La segunda etapa es la lucha, las novelas que hacen una llamada a la acción social o dan posibles soluciones para continuar la batalla hacia una reconciliación de iguales pero diferentes, hacia la aceptación de igualdad para los chicanos: el reconocimiento a la vez de sus derechos humanos y políticos y de su derecho a preservar la herencia y cultura chicanas. Las novelas que pueden representar esta etapa son: *The Autobiography of a Brown Buffalo, Heart of Aztlán, El diablo en Texas, Caras viejas y vino nuevo* y *The Revolt of the Cockroach People.*

La tercera etapa, la invención, es la que apenas comienza con *The Road to Tamazunchale.* El tema de esta novela breve es la muerte, universal y omnipresente en todas las literaturas nacionales pero diferente en su interpretación cultural. La perspectiva chicana sobre la muerte puede venir de la interpretación mexicana en cuya temática se encuentra enraizada; no obstante, tratado por Arias el tema se vuelve un gozo al vivir el protagonista moribundo la vida que jamás disfrutó. ¿Influencias de García Márquez? Indudablemente. Luis Leal le encuentra un parecido a *El coronel no tiene quien le escriba* de García Márquez, pero las influencias son tan importantes e inevitables para un escritor como lo es la historia para el ser humano. Sin embargo, la importancia de esta obra radica en la invención o creatividad de la imaginación chicana que vira del rescate a lo irrescatable. En *Tamazunchale* la creatividad chicana se libera de un dogmatismo jamás admitido que encerraba a la narrativa chicana dentro de los límites del "Movimiento" de los sesenta (ejemplo de lo cual fue el negar a Tomás Rivera la publicación de su cuento *El Pete Fonseca* por no seguir la filosofía literaria que imperaba en ese tiempo).

La experiencia del pueblo chicano no es única en el concierto de las culturas mundiales, sino que es meramente una perspectiva dentro de la realidad universal. La temática chicana sigue su curso dinámico y aunque el sueño de un Cervantes chicano sea una quimera, lo seductor de ese sueño sigue siendo una motivación poderosa para el escritor chicano.

La expresión lingüística del escritor chicano

La expresión lingüística del chicano, más que otro factor, es uno de los elementos claves para la clasificación de la literatura chicana. Durante las entrevistas se intentó clasificar a la novela chicana según el criterio del lenguaje empleado, pero surgieron discrepancias ya que la novela chicana se vale de varias formas lingüísticas: el inglés, el español, la expresión bilingüe y el vernáculo chicano, todos empleados en diversos contextos. Los novelistas que escriben en inglés son: Rudolfo Anaya, Ron Arias, Oscar Zeta Acosta, Edmundo Villaseñor, John Rechy, Richard Vásquez y Orlando Romero. Los que escriben en español son: Tomás Rivera, Rolando Hinojosa, Alejandro Morales, Miguel Méndez y Aristeo Brito. Hasta la fecha no existe una novela chicana que use totalmente lo chicano como sí lo hay en la poesía. En la mayoría de estas obras las locuciones bilingües se yuxtaponen a las chicanas ya sea en forma de diálogo o para dar realce al mundo novelado. Un caso excepcional es la novela de Alejandro Morales; a pesar de estar completamente escrita en español, al leerse parece expresarse en una forma distinta al español genérico. Llegamos al punto de perturbarnos por la infusión de una sintaxis o estructura que denota "un raro modo de expresión". Esta infusión de un elemento estructural ajeno perturbará quizá al lector latinoamericano, pero para el bilingüe chicano es tan natural como si se oyera hablar a sí mismo. En el caso de Miguel Méndez este elemento no perturba puesto que dentro del lenguaje empleado, el español, hay una superposición de varios niveles de expresión y de estilo. Forman un mosaico de versatilidad lingüística que impone al lector un profundo conocimiento de todas las posibles variaciones a que puede llegar un lenguaje nacional.

Los que escriben en inglés también emplean varias expresiones dialectales dentro de ese idioma como el *Black English*, el *American slang*, y trazos inconscientes de lo que algún día se llegará a denominar el *Chicano English*. Estos escritores también usan expresiones chicanas en español, a veces en bastardilla, pero frecuentemente éstas serían incomprensibles para el público lector de habla inglesa. Las locuciones chicanas intercaladas se vuelven clichés muy pronto y sólo sirven para subrayar que la novela fue escrita por un chicano. Después de haber dicho todo lo comentado acerca de la expresión, volvemos a la médula: que la expresión chicana contiene tres formas: la inglesa, la bilingüe-biconceptual, y la española. Sea cual fuere el lenguaje, el dialecto o la variedad lingüística empleados, el chicano lo moldeará a su propia imagen.

Conclusión

He comentado la novela chicana partiendo de las opiniones presentadas por los escritores y críticos chicanos que fueron entrevistados. Mis propias opiniones están entrelazadas a lo que se dijo en cuanto a autores, temática y expresión; pero ¿cuál es la conclusión, el verdadero valor de estas observaciones? Como dije anteriormente, no se sabrá del todo hasta la próxima generación; sin embargo, sí se puede llegar a algunas conclusiones tentativas. Todos los entrevista-

Salvador Rodríguez del Pino

dos estuvieron de acuerdo de que sí existe una "novela chicana" puesto que ésta contiene todos los elementos literarios necesarios para describir una experiencia sociocultural en términos vitales y auténticamente propios. Hubo algunas discrepancias sobre si lo escrito en español pertenece a la literatura mexicana y si lo escrito en inglés pertenece a la literatura americana. Algunos se abstuvieron de comentar; otros, dudando la verdadera existencia de una nación chicana, alegaron que la diversidad lingüística refleja la situación actual. Uno de los puntos que casi todos mencionaron fue la ausencia de novelistas chicanas. La mujer chicana brilla por su ausencia en este género a pesar de que existen buenas cuentistas como Estela Portillo, autora de *Rain of Scorpions and Other Writings*.

Siendo éste el primer intento de sondear a los escritores que actualmente están creando la literatura chicana, me permito concluir que la cooperación por parte de todos los contribuyentes ya sean escritores, organizadores, patrocinadores y técnicos queda todavía incompletamente reconocida. Todos creemos que valió el esfuerzo simplemente por la visión y fe que tenemos en la literatura del futuro.

UNIVERSITY OF CALIFORNIA, SANTA BARBARA

Notas

[1] Este comentario está basado en la serie *Encuentro*, donde se entrevistaron seis novelistas y cuatro críticos de la literatura chicana (Universidad de California, Santa Bárbara, 1977).

[2] Juan Rodríguez, "La problemática de . . .*y no se lo tragó la tierra*", conferencia presentada en el Centro de Estudios Chicanos (Santa Bárbara, 7 de abril de 1977).

[3] Tomás Rivera, "La novela chicana: forma en busca de vida", conferencia presentada en la clase "The Chicano Novel" (Santa Bárbara, 31 de mayo de 1977).

CHICANO LITERATURE:
ART AND POLITICS FROM THE
PERSPECTIVE OF THE ARTIST

José Antonio Villarreal R.

As is so often necessary, before we can discuss Chicano Literature in any context, there is need to define the term. We must consider, if only briefly, the genesis of the phenomenon, its development, its causes and effects. We cannot begin to define the word "Chicano" in other than a generic sense. The word means many things to most of us—those of us so categorized, as well as those outside the sphere of its influence. Certainly, the current definition is one that was not true in my day, in my father's day, in my grandfather's day. Yet, it is a word that has been used for generations, very much as the word *raza* has been used, meaning not a race, but a people—*el pueblo mexicano,* not necessarily mestizo, but Mexican, no matter where born, no matter where reared. Today, of course, it has become a slogan, a political term of utmost validity. And it has come to mean "el pueblo mexicano en el extranjero, inclusive en Norteamérica." Whatever we choose to call ourselves—Mexican-American, Latin-American, sometimes even Spanish American—we *are* Chicanos because we were born in America or came here at an early age. Yet it must be understood that for the majority of our people, our people here being those of our ethnic and cultural background, the term can never mean other than what it meant to us when we were growing up as second- or third-generation Americans. To us it was a term of endearment, very much like the word *pocho,* a term our parents used in those days when we were alone in a new country—alien, striving, expending our every energy merely to keep ourselves alive. This means, of course, that we who call ourselves Chicanos are a minority within a minority, and we as writers or scholars form an even smaller minority which pretends to speak for all our people. Nevertheless, the word "Chicano," because it has become a term implying freedom and equality, a symbol for an end to inequities against *all* our people, whether they are with us or not, is dynamic and important.

As for the word "Literature," definition should not be necessary. Suffice it to say that we have several distinctions in the meaning of the term in its purest sense. We can mention the theory of art-for-art's sake. In fact, we have seen it in the literary movement called Aestheticism in the latter half of the nineteenth century. That movement, which spanned a half century stemming from the advent of the pre-Raphaelite brotherhood of painters headed by Dante Gabriel Rossetti in 1848, rejected Renaissance and post-Renaissance art. Its culmination was brought to the point of absurdity by Oscar Wilde who insisted that aesthetic considerations were absolutely independent of morality. We can also mention the Platonian idea of literature and politics to show that the argument between the two is as old as art itself.

In the course of my dissertation, I speak of literature as art, and as a novelist I speak of the novel. In his preface to *Mexico in its Novel,* John S. Brushwood states: "The novel is particularly capable of expressing the reality of a nation, because of its ability to encompass both visible reality and the elements of reality not seen."[1] For the moment we can accept the fact that art expresses the reality of an individual or individuals and, hence, of a people. We can apply this to Chicano Literature because regardless of definition, we are a people, a very singular people even though most of us are American, live in the United States, and live according to the customs, mores, and traditions of America. We can, in fact, be called a nation within a nation. Our external or visual reality can be expressed by craftsmen, but our innermost reality, the nuances of human life, human situations, human circumstances—our *corazón*—can be exposed only by the artist. Because this is the ideal function of art, the ideal role of the artist is to perform this function. Whether the artist succeeds or not is to a great extent dependent upon his talents and his perception, his awareness and his sensibilities, but most importantly his susceptibility to outside pressures and traditions that would inhibit him from attaining his goal. The question here is: *¿O somos fieles a nuestra dedicación como artistas, o nos convertimos en títeres?* Either we maintain our commitment to art, or dance to whatever tune is prepared for us. I speak now of the artist, or one whose intent is to create in any particular form.

We often speak of gifted writers, painters, composers, or perhaps sometimes we speak of particular gifts, yet what I have just mentioned is the most singular gift of all. I use the term "intent," which we can substitute for "goal," but the fact remains that the greatest gift is the opportunity to make a decision as to whether one should pursue art or be content with something less. Very few people ever have the opportunity to make such a decision and, unfortunately, some of our young people are not allowed to make it.

Not long before he died, Pablo Neruda said: "The poet who does not share in the struggles of the oppressed and humiliated is not a poet but merely a manniken for the shop window of elegant stores for the rich." Neruda's view may seem similar to Plato's when considered in a literal sense, but a close look reveals that Neruda does not speak specifically of the work, nor does he, even by implication, state how the work should be created. Yet statements such as Neruda's are used by influential spokesmen on our literature within the political community of our movement to impose restrictions and dictate subject matter to our work. They forget that Neruda has also said that he does not encourage young writers to work with political themes until they learn to write. This last point can also be construed in a number of ways.

At the time it was formulating, we knew that Chicano Literature was evolving because of a need for expression, a need for a means to teach our young people that we, not unlike other forgotten Americans, also had a fight on our hands. We had a frantic need to tell our story, a need to produce so desperate that we were willing to settle for anything. We did not stop to think that the gestation period of a literature could perhaps be measured in decades. Moreover, only a few of us recognized the fact that we had to teach not only our people but also the dominant peoples in America that we too had a heritage, that we too had dignity. And very few of us knew that if we were to use such a term as "literature," we should strive to live up to its artistic implications, that we should strive to create *literature.* What resulted then is that an unwritten set of standards began to take form. Codes for Chicano Literature were explicit. First and foremost was the fact that we could never criticize ourselves as long as we followed the developing pattern. Whatever was Chicano was good; what was for the Movement was good because the Movement was for all Chicanos.

José Antonio Villarreal R.

Another characteristic of this new literature was that it must perpetuate the idea that the Chicano was the most impoverished person in America, that our plight was the direct result of racism, and that we, like the demagogues in our political forefront, must expound our answers to this situation. We should fight racism with racism, hatred with hatred. Political rhetoric no different from harangue, appealing to emotion at the expense of reason, was expected from us. The fact that those of us with artistic temperament could not interpret the function of art in this manner was not considered. Our Spanish or European heritage was repudiated out of hand; our indigenous beginnings were heralded. And in reviving ancient Indian myths, we created a new mythology which gave a picture of an Aztec Arcadia, which spoke of a civilization so advanced that the Spaniard—the White European—was forced to destroy it. According to this new legend, tens of thousands of volumes representing indigenous literature and, thus, the Chicano literary heritage were burned by the Church. The facts that the Aztec Confederation was comprised of slave states, that society was dominated by a small elite group, that the State and Religion were one, dedicated to the task of keeping the masses subjugated exactly as they were before the Mexican Revolution, were not mentioned. This attitude became so widespread that it is surprising that we did not begin to take on Indian names, build temples, and search for virgins to sacrifice.

This development had a number of harmful effects. The first was, of course, that it made for a confusion between the work and its results. By making what the work *did* more important than what it *was*, the work itself lost its identity as an artistic object.[2] This meant also that the artist allowed himself to be pressured into discarding his most important characteristics—integrity, honesty, fidelity. And with this, there now appeared a number of persons, committed to the movement and even sincere, who criticized us on these very terms. Until recently, perhaps two years, almost every critic of our work came from the field of sociology, political science, history, anthropology, or related sciences. With rare exceptions, most were totally lacking in sensibility, never having developed an emotional and intellectual apprehension or responsiveness to aesthetic phenomena. In short, we reversed Wilde's posture in an equally absurd manner by insisting that ideological and political considerations were totally independent from aesthetic values. And the term "Chicano Literature" was fast becoming valid only within a political context.

The result, then, was that we now wrote specifically for the Chicano. We had a captive audience which already believed and knew our situation well. And he who might perhaps want to know of us, of our social and economic conditions, our aspirations, our dreams, our humanness was driven off by the outright propagandistic elements or by the third rate quality of most of our literature. For by now there was a proliferation of writings called Chicano Literature and, as long as a work fit the mold created by the activists, it was not only considered good but was exorbitantly lauded. This led to statements by people who knew better such as, "*The Plum, Plum Pickers* is the greatest Chicano novel," or to favorable comparisons of *I Am Joaquín* to *Martín Fierro*. In the former case, such criticism precluded a statement of the real worth of Raymond Barrio's work—the author's experimentation with form and structure in an effort to create an artistic entity. In this way, we performed a great disservice to the Movement as well as to the idea of literature. It came about because we refused or could not understand that we could be didactic without sacrificing our artistic qualities, that even though the primary aim or intent of our work might be to propound an ideology, a political teaching, or a moral truth, we need not rule out an aesthetic presence. We know of the many literary works that have been didactic, from *The Inferno* to the *Faerie Queen, Gulliver,* and *Quijote*; in recent years the works of Orwell have been prime examples. Then there are the Mexicans such as Rulfo, Yáñez, Fuentes, and even Spota, and the contemporary South and Central Americans. I mention the Mexicans specifically because they are visual evidence of our potential, since we not only share a similar experience, but carry the identical blood line. In every case here, however, the didactic elements do not dominate, but form a part of the artistic experience.

Despite my anger, all this has had little adverse effect on my writing primarily because I began writing long before the emergence of the current wave of social protest. The movement, in fact, helped me tremendously if only by the fact that it gave new life to my published work. Yet, the very people who forced the renascence of my work immediately criticized me because I had not written a militant book. Such criticism is disturbing, whether it is about my work or someone else's. It is disturbing mainly because I know what it can do to our young, potentially unfulfilled writers. And all writers who have a Spanish surname will carry the ethnic label, whether by design or not, and will be subject to Movement criticism. It is, unfortunately, the nature of that particular criticism to subvert rather than to encourage the artist. A case in point is John Rechy, who not only because his name does not sound Chicano but also because he does not write exclusively of the Chicano experience—a term which needs definition also—has gradually been excluded from the ranks of Chicano writers. Another is the late Amado Muro, more Mexican than many of us, who lived the Chicano experience, but has been repudiated by the pundits because his name was really Charles Seltzer.

To me the ethnic label has been detrimental only in that it retarded the development of my writing skills. The fact that Chicano criticism has dealt chiefly in sociopolitical terms has precluded critical activity with respect to our work from outside the Chicano sphere. Contrary to common belief, artists need qualified criticism. It is necessary so that we can improve. More importantly, it is necessary because we have an embryonic genre on our hands, and it is only the competent critic who will define it. It has been only recently with the advent of the Chicano scholar, usually from the field of Latin American literature or even classic Spanish literature, that we are receiving the type of assessment needed for so long. Outside of the aforementioned John Rechy, who is now considered to be outside our circle, we are not compared with first rate American or British contemporary writers. We need a National Book Award or even a Pulitzer, someday perhaps even a Nobel. Not because we want to be *güeros*, nor for false status, but as an indication that we are taken seriously. The criticism we have had up until now has prohibited the development of form, of structure, and of a style we can call our own. We are traditional to the extreme. We write in English most of the time and, even when we do not, we are obliged to translate. Some of us read Spanish, Mexican, and Latin American writers in the original, but the majority of us know this literature only in translation. And although we do not want to accept this fact, much of our influence comes primarily from English letters, British and American.

Although Mexico is a relatively new nation, our roots are very old both in America and in Europe. Our people in this country have been a lonely and isolated people. True, we have also been an abused and exploited people. And a part of our emergence has been through our art. To date it has been apparent that our heritage and our social and economic condition are the only characteristics that bind our literature into some form. This is what Philip Ortego calls our commonality of experience. This aspect is evident in much of our most serious work. Yet it is not enough. We have had but little time in which to create a literature. In his essay, "Chicano Literature: Sources and Themes," Francisco Jiménez quotes Eliú Carranza who in turn uses Octavio Paz' terminology to describe the phenomenon of Chicano writing in this fashion:

> . . .the essence of the Chicano Cultural revolution. A confrontation and a realization of worth and value through a brutally honest self-examination has occurred and has revealed to Chicanos a link with the past and a leap into the future. . . .This is self-determination. . .for the Chicano has shown his face at last! He has removed the mask and seen himself for what he is: a human being! He dares now to show himself as he really is—publicly.[3]

This is sheer bombast, of course, and in keeping with the accepted language of Chicano criticism and political rhetoric. Yet it is not difficult to relate such a statement to our literature, despite the fact that the right to examine ourselves in a brutally honest fashion has been denied us and because the very realization that we are human is what has enabled us to produce the few pieces of literature we can call our own. The essence of the statement is true, however, for there is no doubt that our literature is an intrinsic part of our Movement. And although we have not yet produced a writer that is artistically great in the universal sense, we must accept the fact that our potential is now in evidence. Eventually men of letters will see our work, because eventually we will not be denied.

Recently I was told by an old friend, a scholar, a sincere man intensely involved in the Cause, that we cannot afford the luxury of attempting to create art. It is not a luxury, of course. It is an obligation, a responsibility we dare not shirk. As artists we must, through our pride and arrogance, and perhaps even insolence, ignore the warnings from the gods and, although it be a grievous sin, transcend the codes of the Movement as we create. Then, and only then, will we have a literature. Then, we will truly contribute to the Cause. What we create may not be called Chicano Literature—most probably it will be a sub-genre of American literature because it is in English, no matter how many *pochismos* we use—but it will belong to us and it will express our singular experience and lay bare, for the world to see, the soul of our people.

UNIVERSITY OF SANTA CLARA

José Antonio Villarreal R.

Notes

[1] John S. Brushwood, *Mexico in its Novel* (Austin and London: University of Texas Press, 1966), p. ix.

[2] Wimsatt & Beardsley, "The Affective Fallacy," *The Sewanee Review,* Vol. 57 (1949), p. 31.

[3] Francisco Jiménez, "Chicano Literature: Sources and Themes," *The Bilingual Review/La revista bilingüe,* I, 1 (Jan.-April 1974), p. 5.

IV. Critical Applications

After all, I believe that criticism is a personal affair, and that the less we critics try to disguise this from ourselves, the better. On what excites and attracts and fascinates us in pursuit of our own completion, in obedience, if you like, to our own secret rhythm which we also must have if our work is to be vital at all—on that alone we shall have something to say worth hearing.

John Middleton Murry, *Discoveries*

LA BUSQUEDA DE IDENTIDAD Y SUS MOTIVOS EN LA LITERATURA CHICANA

Juan Rodríguez

Afirmar que uno de los temas principales de la literatura chicana es la búsqueda de identidad, sería repetir una de las perogrulladas predilectas de quienes tanto vociferan sobre el asunto, a pesar de aún no haber dominado siquiera los conocimientos básicos de la materia, tanto humana como literaria,[1] que les otorgarían una percepción realmente crítica, cuya mayor virtud se manifestaría en la eliminación de gran parte de los juicios gratuitos y las más veces equivocados que siguen apareciendo en torno a esta literatura. Nos referimos, pues, a la plaga de falsos comentaristas quienes, junto con sus cómplices, los ya delatados falsos cronistas de la vida chicana,[2] pululan por todas partes con ínfulas y pergaminos vistosos que sometidos a honesto y riguroso análisis, revelan su refinado talento para escribir mucho y contribuir nada o muy poco a la crítica literaria chicana.[3]

Eso aparte, la búsqueda de identidad sí se plantea en la literatura chicana;[4] así como se plantea en el fondo de todas las literaturas occidentales desde que la Primera Revolución Industrial y su aparato político, social y económico minaron la integridad del hombre, momento en que los productos de la actividad humana, al igual que las propiedades y capacidades del hombre, se convirtieron en algo independiente y ajeno a éste. Por lo tanto, lo realmente importante no está en el afirmar lo universal del caso, ni tampoco en el señalar los motivos con los cuales se presenta el tema—motivos que también se dan en todas las otras literaturas—, sino en el indicar y a la vez valorar las consecuencias de esa búsqueda y esos motivos, tal como se presentan en la literatura chicana y, por extensión, en toda la literatura burguesa occidental. Para realizar eso es menester ver, aunque sea someramente y con visión panorámica, algunas de las obras chicanas más importantes en que el tema de la búsqueda de identidad y sus motivos aparecen en primer plano.

Darse cuenta de que se carece de algo, de que algo que antes se tenía ya no se tiene, es, por supuesto, la raíz de la cual brota toda búsqueda. Consecuentemente, un *awareness*, un estar consciente de sí mismo, de su circunstancia respecto a la de los otros, un reconocimiento de su otredad, son el *sine qua non* de la búsqueda de identidad del chicano en la literatura. Difícil sería encontrar dos mejores ejemplos (aunque ideológicamente opuestos, como veremos después) de este punto de partida, que el protagonista de "El año perdido", cuento introductorio de la novela de Tomás Rivera, . . .*y no se lo tragó la tierra,*[5] y Adán, protagonista del espléndido cuento de Genaro González, "Un hijo del sol".[6] (Para ver claramente este punto de partida, véanse las citas que de estas dos obras presentamos más abajo.)

Esta condición fundamental, la de "verse a sí mismo", explica la omnipresencia del espejo como motivo en las obras chicanas, motivo tempranamente—a principios del renacimiento de la literatura chicana[7]—reconocido en el Prefacio a una de las obras señeras de esta literatura, y cuyo título ya en 1969, fecha de su primera edición, se convierte en símbolo y meta de esa misma literatura. "Para conocerse, para saber quiénes son, a algunos les basta con ver su reflejo. Por eso. . .*El Espejo-The Mirror.* Que este libro sirva de espejo para los muchos que aquí se ven."[8]

Para conocerse, para saber quién es, Rodolfo Gonzales, en su *I Am Joaquín,* acude al espejo—así sea por alusión—y exclama: "I look at myself".[9] El bisonte pardo, o sea Oscar Zeta Acosta, inicia su autobiografía con "I stand naked before the mirror",[10] pose que llega a caracterizar su patética e hipócrita historia personal. En otra realidad, más concreta y menos inflada, el viejo yaqui, Loreto Maldonado, triste y venerable protagonista de *Peregrinos de Aztlán,* novela de la pluma del trascendido Miguel Méndez, también ve el reflejo de su condición decrépita en las vidrieras de los almacenes de Tijuana: "Frente a los mismos ventanales, muros de tentaciones, volvía a mirarse Loreto. . .desde su elástica juventud la mirada remota de muchas ancianidades".[11]

En "El año perdido" se da otro tipo de espejo. Allí Rivera magistralmente utiliza un espejo metafórico en el cual el reflejo es capaz de llamar al reflejado. En virtud de ello el protagonista "se dio cuenta de que él mismo se había llamado".[12] Con Rivera el espejo significativamente deja de ser objeto inanimado y alcanza matices

Juan Rodríguez

inesperados, repletos de posibilidades.[13]

El uso del espejo en "Un hijo del sol" es más elaborado:

> A large wall mirror faces him. He tries to look at the mirror with detached inspection, but his gaze immediately locks him *into* the mirror. . .In doing so, his eyes alternately become beholder and beheld, beheld and beholder. As if they can only see and know themselves by being *other* eyes, outside eyes which likewise must be seen by what they see. Adán stared. . .Stared back. . .Stared back. Two pairs of eyes—those of himself and of his reflection—mesmerized each other and met at some *distance between* the mirror and Adán. He felt himself as being some place *outside* of his body. Where am I? he thought. Space. Spaced out. Estoy afuera. Yo soy. . .Adán nadA. Adán nadA. adán nada. . . .[14]

Con todo, el "mirarse al espejo" no resuelve el problema de la identidad, sólo lo plantea. En general la imagen en el espejo pone en relieve la condición enajenada del chicano, condición en que las relaciones humanas se establecen de modo espontáneo y fuera del control humano. En algunos casos la enajenación se manifiesta a través de una vida sórdida (*Peregrinos de Aztlán*); en otros aparece como decadencia (*The Autobiography of a Brown Buffalo*); en la mayoría, empero, se presenta como una separación, una confusión, un aislamiento marcado por la introspección, casi una angustia existencialista. Es el caso de los protagonistas de "Un hijo del sol" y "El año perdido", entre otras muchas obras chicanas.

Ante la imagen de su condición enajenada, el chicano en la literatura trata de evadir esa realidad de varias maneras, y esto ya significa una búsqueda de identidad. Una de las favoritas es la máscara, la identificación con otros personajes, menos susceptibles a las condiciones concretas de la realidad. Decididamente el chicano se convierte en otro, toma la identidad de otro y de otros, empieza a funcionar con múltiples personalidades; comienza a desarrollar papeles de personajes ajenos, inauténticos a su ser, pero a los cuales acude por creerlos—y esto se le inculca desde niño—inviolables, indomables, los super-machos de un sistema absurdo.

Expliquemos: Zeta Acosta, al verse al espejo, se duele de su estado enajenado e inmediatamente toma (consume, sería más preciso decir) el *role* de Humphrey Bogart, de Charles Atlas, de James Cagney y de otros muchos, todos ellos héroes "populares" creados para mistificar la realidad y para adormecer al pueblo. A fin de cuentas lo mismo sucede con el despistado Joaquín de Rodolfo Gonzales. Si bien los héroes (Moctezuma, Hidalgo, Madero, Villa, Zapata, etc.) con quienes se pretende establecer cierta identidad chicana, se sitúan más cerca del chicano en términos culturales e históricos, no dejan de ser una serie de paladines históricos que por haber sufrido la mistificación y confusión consecuentes, resultan tan "irreales" como los héroes comercializados por las revistas populares, por los *comics*, por la radio, por la televisión y por las películas de ambos lados de la frontera.[15]

Todo este juego con la identidad de otros, sin embargo, por realizarse de manera acrítica, redunda, como es de esperar, en nada eficaz. Y aquí como contraste positivo a lo arriba dicho, se debe mencionar el procedimiento que siguió el Teatro Campesino en su primera etapa, la etapa de los *Actos*. En *Las dos caras del patroncito*,[16] por ejemplo, los actores toman la identidad de otros: el patrón, el esquirol, etc.; pero todo esto se realiza precisamente para destruir el mito, para exponer su realidad. Ahora bien, compárese este uso positivo de la máscara con el uso negativo que después distanciaría al Teatro Campesino del pueblo chicano.[17] Nos referimos a su etapa de *Mitos*, etapa en que la función de la máscara es muy distinta porque se utiliza para mistificar la realidad. La obra más representativa de esto es *El fin del mundo*.[18] Salvo la excepción que nos da el Teatro Campesino en su primera etapa, el *role-playing* sirve sólo para enajenar al chicano aún más; de suerte que se acentúa la búsqueda de identidad.

Este nuevo afán nos lleva a otra manifestación de la búsqueda: el volver al pasado en busca del *ubi sunt*, del *là-bas*, del paraíso perdido en el que el chicano, se supone, gozaba de su ser completo, poseía una identidad. En algunas obras este afán se resuelve en empeño completamente utópico. La máxima y más desarrollada realización de esto se da en el mito de Aztlán, que si bien fue ingeniosa y oportunamente rescatado del olvido por el vate Alurista (*Floricanto en Aztlán*[19]), en nuestros días ya se ha convertido en bagaje demasiado pesado para el movimiento chicano. De hecho, el viaje al pasado, viaje realizado en el tiempo, es tan común que no valdría citar ejemplos; sólo hace falta pensar en todas las obras chicanas en que aparece la nostalgia. Asimismo los viajes al pasado, realizados en el espacio, estrían la literatura chicana; citamos sólo dos ejemplos: *The Autobiography of a Brown Buffalo* y "Un hijo del sol".

Pero el viaje al pasado resulta igualmente inútil. Por un lado termina en mitos indígenas tan remotos que pierden su sentido benéfico original; sólo otorgan una identidad hollywoodesca o libresca, en todo caso ajena a la realidad concreta del chicano (*Floricanto en Aztlán*). Por otro lado da a un mundo místico, cerrado, fabricado

Juan Rodríguez

en torno a la superstición (*Bless Me, Ultima*[20]). En otros casos, y son los más, no se encuentra, por supuesto, ningún paraíso perdido, ni siquiera "la falla que en algún percance hubiera trastocado las cosas, convirtiendo lo que pudo ser sublime en algo disparatado, absurdo",[21] sino que se da con la misma enajenación de siempre (*Peregrinos de Aztlán*).

Consecuentemente el viaje termina como tiene que terminar: en la frustración; pues únicamente así puede terminar un viaje a ciegas en el cual es imposible reconocer el fin, en el cual jamás se está consciente de haber llegado porque en realidad no hay adónde llegar, es decir, no hay paraíso perdido. Por lo tanto, no nos sorprende el pensamiento desapacible de uno de los personajes del penúltimo cuento de . . .*y no se lo tragó la tierra,* "Cuando lleguemos":

> —Cuando lleguemos, cuando lleguemos, ya la mera verdad estoy cansado de llegar. Es la misma cosa llegar que partir porque apenas llegamos y. . .la mera verdad estoy cansado de llegar. Mejor debería decir, cuando no lleguemos porque ésa es la mera verdad. Nunca llegamos (pág. 114).

Así y todo, algunos chicanos en la literatura sí encuentran la identidad. Por ello vale la pena ver la manera en que llegan a tan feliz hallazgo. Aunque varios ejemplos se pudieran estudiar,[22] ciñámonos a los dos que al principio de este ensayo mencionamos como las dos obras en las cuales mejor se presentaba el tema de la identidad, "El año perdido" y "Un hijo del sol". En aquél el protagonista descubre el poder de la palabra, la capacidad de crear su propia realidad ("Se dio cuenta de que él mismo se había llamado"), grata realidad en la cual él puede "por primera vez. . .hacer y deshacer cualquier cosa que él quisiera".[23] No obstante, esta manera de encontrar la realidad tampoco da resultado porque la identidad que se encontró fue íntima, cerrada en sí misma, una identidad mental y nada más. (Nótese que el protagonista a través de la novela nunca le dice a nadie de su hallazgo, nunca comunica su nueva visión de la realidad.[24]) Las consecuencias pésimas de esta manera de "encontrar" la realidad nos dan obras como *The Road to Tamazunchale*,[25] *Nambé Year One*,[26] *Bless Me, Ultima, Estampas del Valle y otras obras* (sólo de manera parcial[27]), obras en que los problemas reales del chicano se ignoran, se callan, se distorsionan o se dan por resueltos, hecho que se debe a que estas obras parten de una identidad mental ya recuperada, es de imaginarse, de la manera planteada en "El año perdido".

"Un hijo del sol" resuelve el problema de modo más positivo, aunque no sin sus limitaciones.[28] Allí el protagonista, Adán, afirma su liberación (es decir, su hallazgo de la identidad) mental en la esfera de la acción física, la esfera social. Después de haber conocido su otredad, de haber pasado por la etapa mental (véase el párrafo de esta obra anteriormente citado), se dirige a un baile donde surge un conflicto racial entre chicanos y anglos; es allí donde comunica su identidad:

> More people, fighting, pushing, running away. Adán looks at the Chicano on the floor; a hard fist is thumped onto his kidneys. Adán moves away, reaches for his knife, turns back to see a shock of blond hair and eyes crying. . .Adán suspends the knife in final decision, weighing the victim versus the act. . .An obsidian blade traces a quick arc of instinct—somewhere in time an angry comet flares, a sleeping mountain erupts, an Aztec sun explodes in birth*** (pág. 316).

Este cuento, a nuestro parecer el mejor de todos hasta ahora, es el único en toda la literatura chicana que ofrece una búsqueda y un encuentro de la identidad en términos positivos y viables. Preciso: toda la cuestión de la búsqueda de identidad se presenta tanto en su proceso mental, el cual es imprescindible, como en su manifestación social, aunque el dónde y por qué surgió sean discutibles.

El hecho de que sea ésta la única obra chicana en que la búsqueda de identidad se plantee en forma progresista, nos lleva al punto más endeble de nuestra literatura, a saber, la aparente inabilidad de nuestros escritores de reconocer que, querámoslo o no, hemos incorporado—unos más, otros menos—la visión del mundo de las clases dominantes, y que concomitantemente nuestra acción en la historia—inclusive en la creación literaria—estará mediatizada por esta circunstancia. Que toda nuestra literatura surja de esta condición de dominado significa que desde un principio se abre una distancia entre el escritor chicano y su pueblo, distancia que hay que reconocer honestamente para minimizarla con pleno conocimiento de causa.

Si el escritor chicano no se enfrenta a esta realidad, nuestra literatura seguirá presentando obras debilitadas por (a) un yoísmo pernicioso que da cabida a héroes románticos (héroes narcisistas que se colocan sobre el pueblo) o héroes existencialistas (héroes masoquistas autodesterrados del mundo) cuya exagerada individualidad se vuelca en escapismo o ensimismamiento autocomplaciente; (b) referencias acríticas al pasado tanto mítico como histórico; (c) la presentación de temas y causas materiales que implícita o explícitamente dan por solucionados o niegan por completo los problemas del chicano; (d) el no surgir de estar inmiscuidos en nuestra realidad histórica y social—lo cual, dígase de paso, no significa ninguna limitación

Juan Rodríguez

artística, a despecho de lo que las clases determinantes nos quisieran hacer creer. En definitiva, mientras no se reconozca que ninguna individualidad (identidad recuperada) es posible sin personalidad, sin su constante e imprescindible punto de referencia—el grupo social—la brecha que cada día más se patentiza entre el escritor y el pueblo chicanos se ensanchará. Por consiguiente, los nuestros rayarán muy alto en la literatura burguesa, ésa que por chauvinismo clasista se llama a sí misma universal (como si todo el universo fuera burgués), pero a la vez sus esfuerzos representarán un engaño más del pueblo trabajador chicano, por tantos años sediento de voz, de justicia, de paz.

UNIVERSITY OF CALIFORNIA, BERKELEY

Notes

[1]Desde el "renacimiento de las literaturas de minoría", fenómeno de las dos últimas décadas de este siglo, se viene acudiendo al corolario de la idea reaccionaria del "arte por el arte" [Cf. Gyorgii Plekhanov, "On Art for Art's Sake", *Marxism and Art: Writings in Aesthetics and Criticism,* ed. Berel Lang and Forrest Williams (New York: David McKay Company, Inc., 1972), págs. 88-99] para justificar y defender esta falta de conocimiento fundamental. El corolario aboga por un acercamiento "crítico" *formal,* cuyo lema se resuelve en "it should be recognized that the only standard to apply to imaginative literature written in English yet tied closely to a non-Anglo culture is that artistic standard applied to a work by Ernest Hemingway or Joyce Carol Oates," y que además, afirma: "Anyone capable of sensitive reading and teaching of English and Anglo-American literatures is eminently qualified to deal with American minorities literature from the *artistic* standpoint [Lester A. Staniford, "Up Against the Art in Minorities Literature", *Bulletin of The Cross-Cultural Southwest Ethnic Studies Center,* III, 1 (May 1975), 1; subrayado nuestro].

Este procedimiento obviamente ofusca y/o ignora los factores históricos, económicos, sociales y culturales de cada grupo minoritario, factores que si bien se generalizan por tratarse del mismo opresor, a la vez se particularizan—más allá de los evidentes orígenes distintos de cada grupo—por el grado y los medios de resistencia a esa opresión. En verdad este acercamiento "crítico", que se complace en disecar (¿por fácil y conveniente?) el esqueleto, la forma, e ignorar el fondo (¿por ser tarea más ardua e iconoclasta?) de no sólo la obra misma sino el de las condiciones que producen la obra, repite fielmente en el campo de la crítica literaria la situación socio-económica de las minorías: a la literatura de éstas se le medirá/juzgará por el *patrón* vigente, esto es, por los valores y los gustos de las clases dirigentes.

[2]Remito al lector a nuestro trabajo sobre "El desarrollo del cuento chicano", que aparece en este volumen.

[3]De los muchos ejemplos que se podrían traer a colación, sólo apuntamos estos: Charles M. Tatum, "Contemporary Chicano Prose Fiction: A Chronicle of Misery", *Latin American Literary Review*, I, 2 (1973), 7-17, e incluido en este volumen; Lino Landy y Ricardo L. Landy, "Literatura chicana", *Grito del Sol*, I, 1 (January-March 1976), 25-38.

[4]La prueba está en que muchísimas obras chicanas relatan historias de iniciación en las cuales el héroe pasa de un estado confuso a uno "liberado". Ejemplos son las obras que aquí se estudian.

[5]Tomás Rivera, *. . .y no se lo tragó la tierra* (Berkeley: Justa Publications, 1976), pág. 1.

[6]Genaro González, "Un hijo del sol", *The Chicano: From Caricature to Self-Portrait*, ed. Edward Simmen (New York: New American Library, 1971), págs. 308-316.

[7]Fue Phillip Ortego quien primero adelantó la idea de que el florecimiento de la literatura chicana durante los 60 era en efecto renacimiento. Véase su artículo "The Chicano Renaissance", *Social Casework*, 52 (May 1971), págs. 294-307.

[8]*El Espejo-The Mirror: Selected Mexican-American Literature*, ed. Octavio I. Romano-V., primera edición (Berkeley: Quinto Sol Publications, 1969), pág. v.

[9]Rodolfo Gonzales, *I Am Joaquín* (Denver, Colorado: Crusade for Justice, 1967), pág. 3.

[10]Oscar Zeta Acosta, *The Autobiography of a Brown Buffalo* (San Francisco: Straight Arrow Books, 1972), pág. 11.

[11]Miguel Méndez, *Peregrinos de Aztlán* (Tucson, Arizona: Editorial Peregrinos, 1974), pág. 33.

[12]*. . .y no se lo tragó la tierra*, pág. 1.

[13]Una de estas posibilidades sería llevar al extremo el "verse a sí mismo". Que Rivera haga precisamente esto en uno de los relatos de su novela aún inédita, *La casa grande del pueblo*, queda muy en acorde con su elaboración del tema de la búsqueda de identidad en términos en los cuales lo que más importa es el encontrar un sentido *personal* a la vida íntima; por lo tanto, más que una búsqueda de identidad se da en él la búsqueda del sentido del vivir, así a ese nivel abstracto y trascendental. La anécdota de "La cara en el espejo" va más allá de un mero verse al espejo (primer paso); supera un "llamarse a sí mismo", simple comunicación entre reflejo y reflejado (segundo paso) y entra en pleno terreno de la metamorfosis. El reflejado se convierte en reflejo, esto es, el espejo trastoca la realidad: el que estaba fuera del espejo queda dentro y viceversa. Pero hay más: el reflejo no corresponde a la persona que se veía al espejo; el reflejo es otra persona (paso máximo).

[14]*The Chicano: From Caricature to Self-Portrait*, pág. 315.

[15]Por supuesto, el uso de la máscara tiene sus matices. Frankie Pérez, por ejemplo, personaje de *Peregrinos de Aztlán*, encontrándose ante el peligro del "enemigo" vietnamita, no toma la identidad de héroes del cine o de la historia, pero sí:

> Invocaba a los ídolos legendarios que habitan en el corazón de sus coterráneos. "Superman" destruyendo aviones en el aire a puros escupitajos, levantando convoyes con el dedo meñique, ganando la guerra en un abrir y cerrar ojos. "Batman" con su genio y fuerza dominando a los tontos asiáticos que no saben pelear, porque son miedosos y cortos de entendederas. Y si estos seres ultra-potentes no dominaban al injusto enemigo. ¡Ah! Ahí estaba el grande, el sublime, el invencible y además, exquisitamente bello. ¡El Gran Cowboy! El más grandioso héroe legendario de su patria (pág. 174).

Juan Rodríguez

Otro matiz aparece en "Pachuco Remembered", poema de Tino Villanueva, *Hay Otra Voz Poems* (Staten Island, New York: Editorial Mensaje, 1972), pág. 40-41. Al verse castigado físicamente por sus maestros anglos, el pachuco paradójicamente alberga deseos de convertirse en el tipo de *All-American boy:* "Emotion surging silent on your stoic tongue; machismo-ego punished, feeling your fearful eyes turn blue in their distant stare" (pág. 41).

[16]Luis Valdez y El Teatro Campesino, *Actos* (Fresno, California: Cucaracha Press, 1971), págs. 7-19.

[17]Para la mejor presentación del "ensimismamiento" del Teatro Campesino, véase el excelente ensayo de Enrique Buenaventura, "La búsqueda de la identidad: Carta abierta a Luis Valdez", *Sí se puede,* II, 1 (August 15, 1975), pág. 9.

[18]Desgraciadamente los *Mitos* todavía no han sido publicados; quizás porque aún se estén elaborando a base de la reacción del público. Ojalá que en la obra final no se perpetúen mitos sino que se cuestionen con honestidad y coraje.

[19]Alurista, *Floricanto en Aztlán* (Los Angeles: Chicano Studies Center at UCLA, 1971).

[20]Rudolfo Anaya, *Bless Me, Ultima* (Berkeley: Quinto Sol Publications, 1972).

[21]*Peregrinos de Aztlán,* pág. 33.

[22]El mejor estudio de este aspecto en la novela *Pocho*—y, en efecto el mejor análisis de toda la obra—es el lúcido trabajo de Rafael Francisco Grajeda, "The Figure of the Pocho in Contemporary Chicano Fiction", Tesis doctoral, The University of Nebraska-Lincoln, 1974, págs. 30-40.

[23]*. . .y no se lo tragó la tierra,* pág. 54.

[24]Este aspecto problemático lo estudiamos detalladamente en un ensayo de próxima aparición, "The Problematic in Tomás Rivera's *. . .y no se lo tragó la tierra*".

[25]Ron Arias, *The Road to Tamazunchale* (Reno, Nevada: West Coast Poetry Review, 1975). Mariana Marín en su ensayo *"The Road to Tamazunchale:* Fantasy or Reality", de próxima publicación en el número especial que *De Colores* dedicará a la crítica literaria chicana, expone el problema al cual aludimos.

[26]Orlando Romero, *Nambé Year One* (Berkeley: Tonatiuh International, 1976).

[27]Rolando Hinojosa, *Estampas del Valle y otras obras* (Berkeley: Quinto Sol Publications, 1973). Para una explicación esclarecedora tocante a este elemento en la obra de Hinojosa, remito al lector al agudo análisis de Luis María Brox, "Los límites del costumbrismo en *Estampas del Valle y otras obras",* *Mester,* V, 2 (Abril 1975), 101-104.

[28]En nuestro análisis "La búsqueda de identidad en tres cuentos chicanos", ensayo aún inédito en el cual estudiamos de cerca "El año perdido", "El don" (cuento de Sylvia Lizárraga que desafortunadamente todavía no se publica) y "Un hijo del sol", se señalan estas limitaciones.

SIMBOLOS Y MOTIVOS NAHUAS EN LA LITERATURA CHICANA

Egla Morales Blouin

La nueva y vigorosa literatura chicana es literatura de protesta social, de queja humana, de lirismo vital. Comunica un contenido psíquico de angustia y soledad en un medio hostil y la esperanza de un futuro mejor. Como portavoz de un pueblo que necesita afirmar su valor y anclar sus raíces, esta literatura refleja un intento deliberado de identificación con el pasado prehispánico en que el hombre vivía donde pertenecía y era parte armónica de su ambiente. Como realidad chicana, convive en ella lo mexicano-español con lo 'anglo'. Al mismo tiempo, hay una superposición temporal del pasado indio sobre la experiencia actual, según el autor chicano interpreta y utiliza elementos culturales y literarios de los pueblos nahuas, en los cuales encuentra un paralelo existencial y simbólico.

Como los aztecas, los chicanos han sufrido los rigores de la vida migratoria. La leyenda cuenta que la tribu azteca, guiada por su dios tutelar Huitzilopochtli, emigró hacia el sur desde su antigua patria de Aztlán para hallar la tierra prometida en el Valle de Anáhuac. Aztlán, 'tierra blanca' del norte, es ahora símbolo de la tierra que ocupan los chicanos y que consideran suya. En la Fiesta of the Chicano Youth Liberation Conference convocada por el líder 'Corky' Gonzales en Denver, en marzo de 1969, se leyó el manifiesto titulado "El plan espiritual de Aztlán", donde se identificó a los chicanos como "habitantes y civilizadores de la tierra norteña de Aztlán, de donde provinieron nuestros abuelos".[1] Aztlán, sin embargo, más que lugar geográfico, es símbolo espiritual de una patria interior donde se refugian buscando unión y amor las gentes de la Raza. Así, el poema "Los caudillos" de Raúl Salinas, escrito en prisión, está ano-

tado: "written from Aztlan de Leavenworth".[2] Es decir, que donde-
quiera que haya un chicano, allí está Aztlán. Es esta misma autoc-
tonía la que canta Sergio Elizondo con ironía lírica: "Tierra perdida,
llama de amor; / Tierra de basura, estoy lleno de amor". Por ella se
singulariza el joven chicano que "trabaja, pisa la tierra, / es de aquí,
de Aztlán". Allí vive y crece el recuerdo de los adalides del movimiento chicano, según Joaquín Murrieta: "Estoy, en el aire y a todas
partes / de la creciente Aztlán voy".[3]

Como contraste a las repetidas humillaciones que brinda la realidad socio-económica, el constante recuerdo de una orgullosa ascendencia azteca sostiene al chicano. Y si la "Oda al molcajete" de Jesús
Maldonado (el flaco) aprecia el encanto de un humilde utensilio de
cocina azteca, "Allí naces otra vez. . .magia de Aztlán" (*Lit. Chic.*
119), otro poeta, Alurista, insta a no olvidar "la magia de Durango /
y la de Moctezuma / el Huiclamina".[4] Rey y guerrero por excelencia,
Moctezuma el Huiclamina, durante el más alto poderío azteca envió
expediciones en busca del mítico Aztlán en un esfuerzo por encontrar
y exaltar sus propias raíces históricas.[5] Enumerando las presentes
desventuras del chicano, Rodolfo 'Corky' Gonzales resume su poema
"I am Joaquin" (*Lit. Chic.* 89): "These then / are the rewards / this
society has / For sons of Chiefs / and Kings", y exclama: "I am Aztec
Prince and Christian Christ / I shall ENDURE!". Luis Omar Salinas
proclama: "I am an Aztec Angel" (*Lit. Chic.* 36), y Alurista suaviza
una humillación: "the man / he doesn't know my raza is old / on the
streets he frisks me" (*Espejo* '69, 173).

En su anhelo de crear una identidad propia al igual que para su
pueblo, el autor chicano proyecta su yo dinámicamente hacia el lector
chicano, como espejo y ejemplo. Su yo rompe las barreras temporales,
apareciendo como hombre del presente, del pasado y del futuro. El
hombre del presente afirma su presencia física, desarrollando insis-
tentemente el tema de su raza, que es en carne y sangre una herencia
del pasado y que apunta hacia un hombre del futuro que se reconoce
y que acepta quién es y cómo es. De este modo, el color de la piel y
los atributos físicos que por prejuicios raciales han separado al chicano del 'anglo', se convierten en elemento estético de su obra. Elizondo describe a sus antepasados: "Mis abuelos barbas de olor a tortilla / piel de sol en la tierra, / y lengua que mece las ramas" (*Perros*,
6). Se describe a sí mismo: "Moreno por las alas de la pasión de mis
padres" (*Perros*, 16). Admira la belleza de la mujer chicana: "En su
morena piel / el sol fundió la miel" (*Ibid.*). El típico 'macho' del barrio tiene "Pelo negro cola de caballo" (*Perros*, 38), motivo que repite

Jesús González: "cuelga tu melena / pavorosa y negra / sobre el mirasol!"[6]

El bronce, asociado por su color amarillo rojizo con la piel del indio, se convierte en imagen frecuentemente elaborada en esta literatura.[7] "Ay Raza Vieja / Raza nueva y orgullosa / Sun bronzed and arrogant" afirma Roberto Vargas (*Lit. Chic.* 55). El matiz bronce se extiende subjetivamente a objetos como el molcajete, "tu vientre bronceado"; a la mezcla que se hace en su interior, "la Bronce Boda alcaweta (sic)"; a la voz del poeta, "y canto hoy mis versos bronces" (Maldonado, "Oda", *Ibid.*), donde al color se añade la dimensión de sonido implícito en el metal; y hasta a las lágrimas: "Mis ojos hinchados / flooded with lágrimas / de bronce" (Alurista, *Espejo* '72, 268). Pasando más allá del concepto sensorial del hombre color de bronce, el tema de la raza se profundiza en imágenes que hermanan al hombre con las mismas sustancias de la tierra. "Eres barro / -Ometéotl te moldeó / de pómulos gatunos / . . .de bronce calor fundido / . . .-naciste y eres / barro / bronce barro en tu perfil" (Alurista, *Espejo* '72, 270). Se interroga a la mujer, quizás como portadora de los secretos del origen de la raza: "are you soil's red-yellow ochre / are you lava's brownish umber / or the gray-brown bark of cottonwood?" (Octavio Romano, *Espejo* '72, 54).

Los cuentos alegóricos de Rudy Espinosa exaltan esperanzadamente la raza obscura: "Rosalia put her lovely brown body, clean and bronze, against the face of the moon. . .her dark eyes that reflected alma. . .our bronzed faces are but a coloring of volcanic ash", en contraste con "Captain White Eyes y su gente 'the White Eyes' que no son de la Raza" (*Espejo* '72, 195). Estas imágenes a veces culminan en una fusión total del hombre con la tierra, como en el cuento de sabor indígena "Tata Casehua", de Miguel Méndez:

> el muchacho estático parecía de barro muerto. . .Juan Manuel Casehua. . .hoy parece piedra, es una piedra. . .su rostro de barro viejo semeja la piedra mal labrada. . .Juan Manuel Casehua. . .marchaba la tarde volviéndose de arena, trocando a saliva por tierra, inhalando y exhalando polvo. . .¿No ves que mis manos son de tierra? Y mis pies que son de tierra vienen pisando sobre la tierra (*Espejo* '69, 30-43).

La tierra constituye una constelación de símbolos, de gran potencia anímica, extraídos de la mitología y las leyendas nahuas. La visión del hombre como producto de la tierra que es fuente de sustento material y espiritual a la vez, no es novedosa; pero el énfasis y enfoque de esta visión tienen rasgos particulares en cada cultura. El enfoque mitológico de Mesoamérica sobre la creación, y en particular el de los pueblos nahuas, es el que prevalece en la literatura chicana. Un ensayo de Enriqueta Vásquez, "La santa tierra", trasluce la voluntad de conservar esa herencia cultural.

> I remember well the things that my father taught in regard to the earth, land and people. . .For in the wisdom of our viejitos we learned about human beings and the universe; we learned about the earth, the land, and we called it: la madre tierra, la santa tierra, la tierra sagrada (*Lit. Chic.* 276).

La metáfora del hombre como germinación de la tierra es característica de la literatura náhuatl y aparece desde los más antiguos códices que tratan de recordar a "quienes aquí vinieron a sembrar / a los abuelos, a las abuelas" (León-Portilla, *Los antiguos*, 22). Esta percepción vegetal del hombre se repetía en la poesía: "sólo por breve tiempo / sólo como la flor del elote, / así hemos venido a abrirnos. . . sobre la tierra" (*Ibid.*, 173). "Como yerba en primavera / es nuestro ser. / Nuestro corazón hace nacer, germinan / flores de nuestra carne."[8] Dentro de este contexto cíclico—renovación-destrucción interminable—se concilian las imágenes de Miguel Méndez: "Padre. . .te busqué para que me volvieras semilla y me resembraras lejos de las plantaciones de cuchillos. . .Ha nacido un niño como nace una planta" (*Espejo* '69, 65).

La mitología azteca asociaba la potencia destructora de la tierra con el símbolo de un reptil monstruoso, una parte tiburón y otra parte lagarto, o una rana fantástica con garras y con la boca armada de grandes colmillos.[9] La tierra traga a los hombres y se nutre de ellos y también traga los astros cuando se ocultan por el poniente. La lejana resonancia de estos misterios nahuas presta una doble profundidad a ciertas imágenes ctónicas de la literatura chicana: "la tierra rajándose en trompas hambrientas cual vagina gigante que se abre, engulléndose la carroña de los mismos seres que pare" (Miguel Méndez, *Espejo* '69, 61); "he traversed the reptilian earth" (Miguel Ponce, *Espejo* '69, 162). El cuento ". . .y no se lo tragó la tierra" de Tomás Rivera, en la colección de cuentos del mismo nombre, narra la emancipación de un adolescente del miedo ancestral a la deidad y su asociación con el poder destructor de la tierra.[10]

Otra potente constelación de símbolos, quizás la más importante, es la del sol. Al identificarse con el pueblo azteca, elegido del dios Sol, el pueblo chicano también se considera pueblo del Sol. Así se denomina en el "Plan espiritual de Aztlán" arriba mencionado. La editorial Quinto Sol, difundidora de literatura chicana, ha plasmado en su rúbrica la tradición náhuatl de que el mundo ha sido creado y destruido cuatro veces consecutivas. Cada época es un sol, y estamos en la quinta edad del hombre, o quinto sol. Roberto Vargas levanta su canto revolucionario "EN ESTE DIA DOMINGO / BAJO TODOS LOS SOLES / QUE SIGUEN", estableciendo así su afán de eternidad (*Lit. Chic. 55*). Este mito de las edades del hombre se halla representado en la fabulosa Piedra del Sol, que muchos interpretan como calendario azteca. En medio del disco monolítico está modelado el rostro de Tonatiuh, dios solar por excelencia, de cuya boca emerge la lengua como cuchillo de pedernal figurando la luz solar.[11] Alurista invoca esta visión: "en su tributo el solar Tonatiuh / Emanando rayos de obsidiana;. . .Tonatiuh rajo grietas / -brotafuego". Al sentirse abatido por el asesinato cultural de su pueblo, el poeta busca refugio en este dios, dador de la vida. "Y corrí hacia el sol / el de mis padres" (*Espejo* '72, 269-271). Por otra parte, José Montoya sintetiza esa atracción del sol en una visión en que coexisten cristianismo, budismo y culto azteca. En uno de sus poemas, tres *bothisattvas* galopan como figuras del Apocalipsis "Running, running, toward the setting sun / Shouting, Jesus saves!" (*Espejo* '69, 183). Otro sincretismo del sol con la deidad cristiana se nota en un cuento de Carlos G. Vélez: "The sun shone brightly overhead—a thin, yellow eucharistic host suspended by invincible wires". La metáfora se amplía con la imagen de rayos convertidos en "golden spokes" como en las representaciones iconográficas indígenas (*Espejo* '69, 128).

La encarnación del sol más venerada por los aztecas fue Huitzilopochtli, concebido como joven guerrero que nace todas las mañanas del vientre de la vieja diosa de la tierra y que muere todas las tardes (A. Caso, 23). Su contienda diaria contra sus hermanos la luna y las estrellas, significaba un nuevo día de vida para los hombres. Alimentándolo con la sustancia mágica de la vida contenida en la sangre humana, el hombre se convertía en colaborador de los dioses por medio del sacrificio. Esta era la misión primordial del pueblo elegido del sol. Eduardo Noguera explica que a Huitzilopochtli también "se le representaba en forma de un pájaro colibrí, ave que chupa la tierra y que alegóricamente chupa los pechos de la madre, es decir, extrae el sustento de la tierra, la madre dadora, representada por Cihuacóatl".[12] El poema "México" de Rafael Jesús González, que personifica la fiera naturaleza mexicana en su totalidad, contiene una imagen similar: "Muerde el sol los pechos de tus grises colinas" (*Espejo* '72, 273). Elizondo también ve los cerros como pechos de la madre tierra: "iba montado por los cerros redondos / chichis de Califas" (*Perros*, 68).

Egla Morales Blouin

Don José María Vigil, en su *Historia de la literatura mexicana,* comenta la literatura prehispánica, que "abunda en imágenes atrevidas que llegan a veces a lo terrible, en giros de extraña elocuencia que caracterizan las oraciones de pueblos acostumbrados a vivir en comunión íntima con una naturaleza de exuberancia monstruosa".[13] Las contundentes imágenes de humanización de la naturaleza que aparecen en la literatura chicana demuestran la continuación de esa tradición prehispánica. Méndez, por ejemplo, ofrece: "En el centro de la barriga hinchada del cielo está hundido el sol como ombligo de fuego" (*Espejo* '69, 38). La crueldad inherente en un sol que exige la destrucción de los humanos se recuerda en frecuentes imágenes logradas por alusiones a las ideas de cortar o herir. "Amaneciendo resurgirá la fogata calentando sus machetes al rojo vivo, para hundirlos sin lástima en la entraña de esta tierra" (Méndez, *Espejo* '69, 43). Del mismo autor: "Mira ese ser, el que dijo ser sol, y tuvo para su antojo sus propias tijeras" (*Ibid.,* 65). Del poemario de Elizondo: "En las horas redondas de cigarras, / punza el sol con güeros hilos" (*Perros*, 22).

En la realidad cotidiana del campesino chicano, el sol es todavía un ser cruel, que aun sin cuchillo ritual, continúa sacrificando al hombre: "Y mi espalda arde / under hot Azteca sun / ...algodón piscando / y al sol la cara dando / como si rezando / a un Dios Todopoderoso" (Maldonado, *Lit. Chic.,* 34). Romano dedica toda una desafiante plegaria al sol: "En lugar de los niños que nada te han hecho / quémame a mí / ...sol que quema / quémame a mí" (*Espejo* '72, 280). Tomás Rivera, cuyo citado libro de cuentos *"...y no se lo tragó la tierra"* está dividido en doce narraciones a manera de calendario, y que por nuestro contexto nos hace pensar en la Piedra del Sol, utiliza el tema del sacrificio humano de modo no declarado, es decir, como substrato de memoria racial. El sol no es sólo un estorbo físico, sino que se percibe como poder sobrenatural en el diálogo de sus personajes: "ya aplanándose el sol ni una nubita se le aparece de puro miedo. . .El sol se lo puede comer a uno" (pág. 15).

En el cuento "Un rezo" del mismo autor, por medio de la plegaria de una madre que ruega por el hijo que peligra en Corea, se realiza la sutil fusión de Jesucristo y los santos cristianos con aquellos dioses prehispánicos que aceptaban la dádiva del corazón humano. La madre pide desesperadamente: "tápale su corazón con tu mano. . .regrésenme su corazón. . .Aquí está mi corazón por el de él. . .Aquí está mi pecho palpitante, arránquenmelo si quieren sangre" (pág. 15). El sacrificio humano aparece repetidamente en esta literatura, y en algunos autores se evidencia el deseo de explicar y revalorizar el sentido trascendental del sacrificio. Alfonso Caso ha hecho notar el orgullo del tenochca en mantener el orden del mundo por medio del sacrificio. "La misión del tenochca es estar al lado del Sol, que representa el bien, en contra de los dioses espantables de la noche, símbolos del mal" (pág. 122). Así, en una corta narración poética, Juan García revive el sentimiento de dedicación salvadora del mismo inmolado: "My mortal body lying there, bathed in blood, as I, my soul immortal, assumed a new person. That of God. The Sun God" (*Espejo* '69, 236). Como símbolo y complemento del tema del sacrificio ritual, se continúa en la literatura chicana el motivo de las plumas, que es uno de los motivos más característicos en los antiguos escritos nahuas. Consideradas por el pueblo náhuatl como una de las cosas más preciosas de la tierra, las plumas de pájaro servían de adorno para trajes ceremoniales, cascos, escudos y estandartes guerreros. Las más apreciadas eran las plumas del quetzal, símbolo de adorno precioso o atavío, y eran cotizadas con igual valor al de las joyas primorosas. De alto valor también eran las plumas de águila, garza, colibrí, papagayos y otras que adornan los tocados de los dioses en sus representaciones plásticas. Las víctimas de los sacrificios rituales, en honor a la alta misión que desempeñaban, llegaban al altar ataviados con plumas o las llevaban en la mano como obsequio al dios que los esperaba.

En la antigua poesía náhuatl las plumas simbolizaban belleza, riqueza, nobleza y valor: "Como esmeraldas y plumas finas / llueven tus palabras" (*Trece poetas*, 203). "Invitas al placer / Sobre la estera de plumas amarillas y azules" (*Trece poetas*, 49). "Anda volando el ave de las plumas finas, / Tlacahuepazin...Se embriagan,...los príncipes que parecen aves preciosas, ...los posesores de los escudos de plumas" (*Ibid.*, 118). En la poesía chicana la imagen de las plumas aporta no sólo su belleza innata, sino que invoca el uso ritual. De este modo, Alurista, recordándole a su raza el origen de barro de la segunda creación del hombre, también recuerda el honor del sacrificio en conjunción con las plumas: "en tus venas crecen plumas / y Quetzalcóatl se embellece" (*Espejo* '72, 270). Otro de sus poemas destaca el honor del sacrificio en su función de dar vida: "at the sacrificial Teocatl / my fathers wore their plumage / ...and soplaron vida con sus solares rayos / en mi raza" (*Ibid.*, 271). En los versos de Rafael Jesús González se unen de nuevo las ideas de venas y sangre con el emplumado, el que se sacrifica: "Al caer el sol que has emplumado /

tienen tus cerros filigrana de venas en sus frentes". En este caso, la alusión es a la creencia que el dios solar, vencido al final del día, cae en las fauces de la tierra. De este modo, el sol alimenta a la tierra igual que el humano sacrificado alimentaba a la deidad. Otro poema del mismo autor enhebra "quejidos de plumas" en que el dolor implícito en "quejido", unido a la presencia de "plumas", de nuevo evoca el sacrificio (*Espejo* '72, 273-274).

Cuando el motivo de las plumas aparece adjetivado, la imagen sensorial toma con mayor fuerza el primer nivel interpretativo. En el verso "fogoso ritmo de plumas danzantes" (Alurista, *Espejo* '72, 269), el movimiento sugerido es lo primero que cautiva la imaginación del lector. Sin embargo, se impone inmediatamente la idea de algún rito o celebración en que los participantes bailan, adornados de plumas. De igual manera, el irisado calidoscopio que sugieren los versos "ya yo sueño / de pavos magníficos / con / plumas azules / . . .plumas rojas; / que se hacen anaranjosas", se transforma en metáfora del sol, dios guerrero que cruza los cielos, con la próxima alusión: "como en la tarde / . . .el sol tira para todo / el cielo rayos / anaranjándose / con tiempo" (Ernie Padilla, *Espejo* '72, 255).

Otro motivo azteca convertido en símbolo chicano es el de la obsidiana, que también se relaciona con el sacrificio humano por ser de obsidiana los cuchillos que usaban los sacerdotes para inmolar a las víctimas. La obsidiana se usaba también para espejos, para incrustación en mosaicos y para adorno de instrumentos y joyas. Además se trabajaba en hojas delgadísimas a modo de escalpelo para diversos usos quirúrjicos.[14] Lewis Spence ha denominado la fe azteca "religión de obsidiana", aduciendo sus orígenes de pueblo cazador.[15] Los siguientes ejemplos de este motivo son de la literatura náhuatl. De la prosa: "Un viento como de obsidianas sopla y se desliza sobre nosotros" (*Antiguos mexicanos,* 149). De la poesía: "su cuerpo tatuado con navajillas de obsidiana" (*Ibid.,* 163); "Mi corazón quiere / la muerte a filo de obsidiana" (*Trece poetas,* 35). En la poesía chicana se notan ejemplos como éstos: "i crawl / . . .to the temple of mud and blood / ready to be struck / by the obsidian knife of recollection" (Miguel Ponce, *Espejo* '69, 163); "el solar Tonatiuh / Emanando rayos de obsidiana" (Alurista, *Espejo* '72, 269); "¡llora, hijo, llora! / . . .Que aquí no hay obsidiana" (Rafael Jesús González, *Espejo* '72, 276).

Rechazando la pasividad tradicional del inmigrante mexicano, el nuevo chicano asume algo de la actitud agresiva que caracterizaba la psicología místico-guerrera del azteca. Este tono aguerrido se transparenta en el uso de símbolos como águila y tigre (en realidad, jaguar) que daban nombre a los dos grupos más selectos de guerreros aztecas. Dentro de la copiosa simbología zoológica de los tenochcas, águilas y tigres encarnaban el eterno combate de las potencias de la luz contra las tinieblas. El águila se identificaba con Tonatiuh y Huitzilopochtli, deidades del sol, del cielo azul y de la luz en general. Huitzilopochtli, como águila blanca, guió a la tribu azteca al lugar donde encontraron el signo sagrado del águila comiendo una serpiente, y allí se fundó Tenochtitlán (Caso, 53, 119).

El tigre se asociaba con Tezcatlipoca, dios del cielo, de la noche y de las potencias de la oscuridad. La mención de águilas y de tigres en la literatura náhuatl es constante. Nezahualpilli, por ejemplo, describe la acción guerrera: "El águila grita, / el jaguar da gemidos, / . . .rectamente los mexicanos / hacen la guerra" (*Trece poetas,* 116-117). Temilotzón, famoso capitán, es loado como "Jefe de águilas / . . .Gran águila y gran tigre / águila de amarillas garras / y poderosas alas, / rapaz, / operario de la muerte" (*Ibid.,* 183). Para los chicanos, de nuevo, las águilas y los tigres representan valor y empuje, ahora en pro de una causa social. La bandera diseñada por César Chávez "Tiene un águila negra, / alas iguales / hecha de puro algodón" (*Perros,* 30). (Este verso también nos hace recordar que el algodón era algo especial entre los aztecas y sólo los nobles, sacerdotes y guerreros llevaban ropas de este material.) La rabia reprimida estalla en el mismo poeta, Elizondo, que exclama: "en casa alta vivo y rujo / como tigre enjaulado" y se siente "águila cuando brinco" (*Ibid.,* 28, 18).

De ambiente idealista y edénico, algunos cuentos de Espinosa tienen como lema la frase de Chávez "Within each grape there is a little eagle". El protagonista de sus cuentos es un niño, Aguilita, o 'Little Eagle', símbolo de la potencia de libertad, progreso y bienestar futuro de la raza. Aguilita sueña "en vuelos a estrellas lejanas en los que llevaba. . .poderosas alas de dos águilas en sus brazos y piernas". Cuando muere la madre, el niño consuela a su hermana: "Mama held us beneath the hearts of stars and spears of Eagle Knights tightened with feathered ornaments, and sitting down before a ray of light" (*Espejo* '72, 198, 202). Alurista recuerda los antepasados "de firmeza y decisión / of our caballeros tigres" (*Lit. Chic.,* 31). La dialéctica entre luz y tinieblas simbolizada por ave y felino se recoge en el poema "Angola" de Ponce: "Gutterals (sic) of panther night, screeches of avian day" (*Espejo* '69, 170).

Otro símbolo fascinante por su antigüedad es el de la serpiente,

187

heredado quizás no tanto de la literatura náhuatl como de la imaginería religiosa prehispánica. La deidad principal de los antiguos nahuas era Quetzalcóatl, 'serpiente emplumada', padre creador de la quinta humanidad. Eran serpientes de fuego las que transportaban al dios Sol en su camino diario por el cielo. La serpiente cascabel representaba a Chicomecóatl, diosa de la vegetación. Avatares de la diosa de la tierra eran Cihuacóatl y Coatlicue, 'mujer serpiente' y 'falda de serpientes' respectivamente. Casi todos los dioses en sus representaciones llevan algún fetiche relacionado con la serpiente. Aunque el significado original permanece hermético y probablemente debe buscarse en un arquetipo universal, los dioses nahuas que más obviamente ostentan atributos de serpiente son aquellos que se asocian con el agua, el origen y la fertilidad, especialmente deidades femeninas como Chalchiuhtlicue, que se identifica con el agua, la luna y los partos, entre otras cosas. La asociación de luna con serpiente se halla en un poema de Estupinián, que busca "una luna de plata. . .española, mexicana / (pero quise decir chicana) / donde meteré la serpiente / que me muerde las entrañas" (*Espejo* '69, 194). Aunque el dolor comprendido en estos versos no es físico, la imagen es interesante considerando que los curanderos aztecas, en su vocabulario secreto, llamaban a los dolores 'serpientes' (Caso, 111). Octavio Romano, en su "Mosaico mexicano", desarrolla el símbolo de la serpiente-río, remitiéndose al sentido autóctono del origen: "a serpent's in the river"; "Seed serpent and seed-lance / bedded down with brown river" (*Espejo* '72, 54-74). En el cuento "Tata Casehua", de Miguel Méndez, el niño narrador experimenta una especie de transubstanciación con el río y su espíritu serpiente: "le animó una ternura sublime brotada de un principio ignorado; lo acarició devoto tocando su cuerpo líquido. . .emergió moteado. . .Retrocedió. . .curvándose en ese, vibrante, vuelto todo él índice acusativo" (*Espejo* '69, 37).

A menudo el título de la composición enfoca inmediatamente al lector hacia el mundo indígena: "El sonido del Teponaztle", "Tenochtitlán", "En defensa de un hijo de Nezahualcóyotl", son títulos de poemas que nos encauzan hacia la interpretación deseada por el autor. Otras veces la composición entra completamente en el ámbito arcaico y misterioso del pasado indio. El poema "cantos de ranas viejas" de Alurista reúne una pluralidad de elementos mayas y aztecas relacionados con el dios de la lluvia, Tlaloc, cuya representación es la rana. Diversos niveles poéticos se interpenetran en una variedad de reiteraciones del motivo lluvia: lagunas, perlas de mejillas, pantano, cenote, lamosa tumba, esmeraldas lágrimas, tempestuoso lamento, la sabia (sic) del sol, ojos de sapo, todas imágenes líquidas o lluviosas que se aúnan al dolor y su manifestación líquida: las lágrimas (*Espejo* '72, 269).

Alusiones oscuras a elementos menos conocidos se pueden detectar en alguna composición que otra. El poema de Estupinián que comienza "Haré de mis versos / dos bellas zapatillas de oro / para los pies divinos, humillados" seguramente se refiere a las zapatillas de oro que, según la leyenda, llevaba Moctezuma Xocoyotzín en ese día de humillación en que se enfrentó a Cortés. También es posible que los paradójicos versos de Elizondo "allá otros que buscan consuelo / en esposas violadas por ellos mismos" se refieran a los ritos aztecas del *jus primae noctis*. Según el libro de Victor W. Von Hagen, *The Aztec: Man and Tribe* (New York: 1958), la defloración de la novia se llevaba a cabo por los tíos, hermanos o el mismo padre de la doncella, lo cual libraba a la pareja de malignas influencias sobrenaturales (64-65).

El tema sobresaliente de la literatura chicana estudiada es la afirmación de identidad de este pueblo. Esto se realiza proyectando una especie de 'individualismo en masa', encarnado en la voz del escritor que habla por y para su gente. Indagando en sus orígenes, el chicano parece encontrar que lo que más exactamente caracteriza su actitud subjetiva hacia la vida, halla eco y fuente de símbolos en su pasado prehispánico. Este legado pertenece por igual al mexicano de México, pero el chicano vive otra realidad que lo separa de aquél, y que lo sitúa en la confluencia de dos vertientes culturales. El pueblo chicano opta por hacer su patria de un mundo espiritual que lleva a cuestas.

Para resumir: por la influencia de elementos mitológicos indígenas, la literatura chicana se carga de un fuerte sabor telúrico. La violenta personificación de la naturaleza es uno de sus recursos principales. Alusiones a un mundo arcaico cuya elaboración de metáforas y símbolos procede de una larga tradición de signos esotéricos, añade la belleza del misterio a su expresión. Al mismo tiempo se establece una doble visión en las imágenes: las asociaciones del autor en el momento de la creación, más las 'arborescencias subterráneas', como diría Bousoño, que independientemente se ramifican por la tradicionalidad de los símbolos. La expresión chicana en modalidades del inglés y del español más la combinación de ambos idiomas, expresa su vivencia, y junto a la superposición del pretérito, implícita en los motivos antiguos, produce una curiosa simultaneidad de

Egla Morales Blouin

tiempos. De este modo la experiencia chicana se expande, rompiendo barreras lingüísticas, nacionales y temporales.

GEORGETOWN UNIVERSITY

Notas

[1]Ernie Barrios, ed., *Bibliografía de Aztlán: An Annotated Chicano Bibliography* (San Diego State College: Centro de Estudios Chicanos Publications, 1971), vi.

[2]Antonia Castaneda Shular, Tomás Ybarra-Frausto, and Joseph Sommers, eds., *Literatura Chicana: texto y contexto* (New Jersey: Prentice-Hall, Inc., 1972), 73.

[3]Sergio Elizondo, *Perros y antiperros: Una épica chicana* (California: Quinto Sol, 1972), 4, 36, 66.

[4]Alurista, "must be the season of the witch", *El Espejo*, 3rd pr., Octavio I. Romano-V., ed. (California: Quinto Sol, 1969), 176.

[5]Miguel León-Portilla, *Los antiguos mexicanos* (México: FCE, 1961), 97.

[6]Rafael Jesús González, "Sur El Paso", *El Espejo*, 5th pr., Octavio I. Romano-V., Herminio Ríos C., eds. (California: Quinto Sol, 1972), 276.

[7]El bronce fue desconocido por los aztecas, aunque el cobre sí se llegó a usar generalmente en el imperio azteca poco antes de la Conquista. Ver: *Ancient America*, Jonathan Norton Leonard and The Editors of Time-Life Books (New York: Time, Inc., 1967), 122-123.

[8]Miguel León-Portilla, *Trece poetas del mundo azteca* (México: Sep/Setentas, 1972, ed. orig. UNAM, 1967), 145.

[9]Alfonso Caso, *El pueblo del sol*, segunda edición (México, FCE, 1962), 72-73.

[10]Tomás Rivera, *". . .y no se lo tragó la tierra"* (California: Quinto Sol, 1971), 66-70.

[11]Eduardo Noguera, "La escultura", *México Prehispánico, Antología de Esta Semana, 1935-1946* (México: Ed. Emma Hurtado, 1946), 586.

[12]Eduardo Noguera, "Coatlicue", *op. cit.,* 473-474.

[13]José María Vigil, "Historia de la literatura mexicana", en Luis Castillo Ledón, "La literatura", *México Prehispánico*, 666.

[14]George C. Vaillant, "Ornamentos" y "Las artes menores", *México Prehispánico*, 614-636.

[15]Lewis Spence, en Erich Neumann, *The Great Mother,* 2nd. ed. (New Jersey: Princeton University Press, 1972), 190.

THE ROLE OF WOMEN
IN CHICANO LITERATURE

Judy Salinas

From the *First Book of Enoch, XVIII, 11* and *XIX, Vs. 1,2,* and *3*:

And I saw a deep abyss and columns of heavenly fire, and among them I saw columns of fire falling, which were beyond measure alike upwards and downwards. . . And Uriel said to me: 'Here shall stand the angels who have lain with women and whose spirits, assuming many different forms, defile mankind and lead them astray into demonolatry and sacrificing to demons: here shall they stand until the Day of Judgement. . . . And the women whom they seduced shall become Sirens.'

> Robert Graves, *The White Goddess* (New York: Farrar, Straus and Giroux, 1966), pp. 83-84.

From over the temple of Neith (Lamia— Libyan Serpent-Goddess):

> I am all that has been,
> that is,
> that will be.
> No mortal has yet lifted
> the veil from my face.

> Robert Graves, *The White Goddess*

The cultural and traditional roles and stereotypes of woman and the Hispanic woman in particular as depicted in literatures have been perpetuated through the centuries by authors reflecting their societies' majority views—male and female alike. There are two main categories or images of woman with variations and generalizations of these two. First, there is the "good" woman, symbolized by the Virgin Mary, who can think no evil, do no evil, is pure, innocent, understanding, kind, weak, passive, needs to be protected but yet has an inner strength which God granted her, a capacity for enduring and suffering, an inner strength which she passes on to her children, the procreation of which is her task in this world, or ought to be, along with that of making her man happy and satisfied with a minimum of nagging and complaints. In toto, she is frequently an absurd idealization that neither can be achieved nor sustained by a human being. Second, there is the "bad" woman, symbolized by Eve, who is a temptress and seductress, representing evil through love and the perversion and excesses of its passions. It was Eve who caused the downfall of man and mankind and the "bad" woman will do the same because her sole purpose is to entrap, confuse, entice, manipulate, and weaken man by means of all her magical and mysterious powers. She is the one against whom man and mankind have been warned throughout literary history. Her treachery and alliance with the Devil and his cohorts make of her the dreaded tool for the future downfall of individual men in all societies. She is morally judged and condemned by all and must suffer a severe punishment for her evil actions, usually death by murder or suicide.

A third gray-area category blending these two principal images occurs when they overlap and are synthesized into a duality presented in varying degrees of realism in individual female characters, although one image consistently dominates the other. The emphasis in most literature is on some evil or bad action of the woman—be it a spiritual black thought or a blatant example of malice toward another. In other words, all women who use evil in any form or who do anything contrary to the accepted customs and mores of their society are punished. If they are not absolutely pure, good women—good mothers and faithful wives—or they are not Virgin Marys, they pay for it, sometimes in a way as severe as the totally "bad" woman stereotype must. It is clear that an evil, selfish, dominating female character provides far more interesting and intriguing development in a literary work than does a kind-hearted, idealized "good" woman.

These two principal concepts of woman have persisted in Spanish, Spanish American, Anglo-American, as well as in almost every other literature, from their respective beginnings to contemporary examples. In an examination of Chicano literature, a direct product of these, the same categories do continue to persist in varying degrees. But there are two new elements of presentation which make the portrayal of woman in Chicano literature unique and totally distinct from the traditional symbolistic and stereotypic influences of its parent literatures. First, Chicano publishing houses not only encourage women to write by soliciting works expressing their views and perspectives of life, but also publish their finished products, which gives to the development of Chicano literature a breadth and strength which can only serve as an advantage to its growing importance. Second, and most important, is the presentation of woman as a human being. She is accepted as such and far more consistently presented as a duality of good and bad in several Chicano works, or as a healthy blending of all that lies between the extremist dualities. She is neither morally judged nor condemned for what would traditionally be termed "bad" thoughts or actions, nor is she absurdly idealized and put on a pedestal as is a statue of the Virgin Mary or the Virgen de Guadalupe. These distinctive treatments occur in the works of four principal Chicano writers. In Carlos Morton's dramatic parody of the fall of man, "El Jardín," we see the transition of the stereotype classic Eve to a human character, a synthesis of bad and good living in contemporary South Chicago and contending with the problem of ethnic oppression and discrimination. From Eve who causes the expulsion of the human race from the Garden of Eden because of her selfishness, coquettishness, and evil, she becomes the Chicana Eve who symbolically represents hope and faith for the future of La Raza. In Rolando Hinojosa's work *Estampas del valle y otras obras*, and to some extent in Estela Portillo's play "The Day of the Swallows" and completely in her short story "The Paris Gown," we see the "bad" of woman deemphasized and the humanness emphasized through an understanding of her role in Chicano society and in all of society and how it restricts or frees her. In selected poems of Bruce-Novoa, we see woman accepted, respected, and loved for the humanness of her powers of good and evil and for her blended duality itself—without judgment, but with a treatment of admiration and acceptance as in Hinojosa's work.

The Good Woman

The Virgin Mary image is exemplified in Spanish American literature in the nineteenth-century romantic novel by Jorge Isaacs, *Ma-*

Judy Salinas

ría. In the title and in the characteristics of the heroine herself, we perceive the obvious cultural and historical reference and immediately think of variations of this name in other literary works and female images. María herself is a virgin, a pure, young, typical romantic heroine who is weak, suffering, passive in her role in life and totally incapable of an evil thought or act. All she wants is to do good, help others, and love and serve her man in marriage. Her perfection and purity are symbolized by the paled whiteness of her skin and her thoughts. She is the totally "good" woman just as is Tía María from *La gaviota*, a nineteenth-century Spanish novel by Fernán Caballero. Tía María is the stereotyped good mother. Throughout the novel she persists in her total goodness and kindness to others and in her understanding of everything, with never a flaw in her perfection. In many Chicano works, we see this same image presented primarily in mothers and wives who are portrayed with great respect, admiration, and love; yet, they are still often idealized in an exaggerated and unrealistic manner. They are shown as hardworking, suffering, tired, enduring all hardships, and making all sacrifices for their families with little complaining. The Chicano wife and mother is presented in this traditional and idealized style in the poem "La jefita" by José Montoya.

La jefita

When I remember the campos
    Y las noches and the sounds
Of those nights en carpas o
Vagones I remember my jefita's
    Palote
    Clik-clok; clik-clak-clok
    Y su tocesita.
(I swear, she never slept!)
Reluctant awakenings a la media
Noche y la luz prendida.
    PRRRRRRINNNNGGGGGG!
A noisy chorro missing the
    Basín.
¿Qué horas son, 'ama?
Es tarde mi hijito. Cover up
Your little brothers.
Y yo con pena but too sleepy,
    Go to bed little mother!
A maternal reply mingled with
The hissing of hot planchas

Y los frijoles de la hoya
boiling musically dando segunda
a los ruidos nocturnos and
The snores of the old man
      Lulling sounds y los perros
Ladrando—then the familiar
Hallucinations just before sleep.
      And my jefita was no more.
But by then it was time to get Up!
My old man had a chiflidito
That irritated the world to
Wakefulness.
      Wheeeeeeet! Wheeeeeeet!
¡Arriba, cabrones chavalos,
Huevones!
      Y todavía la pinche
      Noche oscura
Y la jefita slapping tortillas.
      ¡Prieta! Help with the lonches!
      ¡Caliéntale agua a tu 'apa!
(¡Me la rayo ese! My jefita never slept!)
Y en el fil, pulling her cien
Libras de algoda se sonreía
Mi jefe y decía,
      That woman—she only complains
      in her sleep.[1]

La jefita, like most mothers and wives in prose fiction, is not a multi-dimensional human character—she is a stereotype. She is a very good woman and we see through her that the stereotype perpetuation continues, partially due to the Hispanic cultural and societal influence and tradition in Chicano life.

This same stereotype of the hard-working, self-sacrificing, and long-suffering Chicana mother and wife appears as well in Raymond Barrio's *The Plum, Plum Pickers*. The novel centers principally around the life of the Gutiérrez family as representatives of other migrant worker families who have come from Texas temporarily to settle at the Western Grande Fruit Company Compound in Santa Clara County, Califas. The company is owned by Fred and Jean Turner and run by the foreman, Morton J. Quill. Amid the squalor and the sickening and less than humane or human conditions of the camp, Guadalupe Gutiérrez, her husband Manuel, and their three children, Manuelito, Mariquita and baby Cati, somehow manage to better their lives by eventually getting to work on a permanent basis for another, yet more humane, fruit-grower who is less a slave exploiter than Fred Turner, Mr. Schroeder. Throughout the novel, Guadalupe, referred to as Lupe, dominates the character development and attracts the reader, as Barrio apparently intended, although at times with inconsistent and perhaps unintended emphasis and influence. Like "La jefita," Lupe suffers and endures unbelievably intolerable, unfit and inhuman conditions in the camp, but she does not merely have to exist through the constant work, sacrificing, and nothingness, helped as is "La jefita" by the sustaining love of her children and her husband and by the reward that she and they gain at the end of the work with a better and more permanent life working for the Schroeders. Because this is a propagandistic and socialistically oriented novel, Barrio does not intend that their lot be terribly improved, but rather that they have some chance for stability and a chance for success with living and not just existing, as shown in the outcome of the novel with their change of status from migrant to permanent workers.

Lupe is not as idealized a stereotype as is "La jefita," for she is treated in a longer prose work affording a better chance to know her as a person. Also, Barrio presents her stylistically in such a way that we come to know her intimately. We live within her thoughts, her hopes, her fears, her doubts, dreams, and disappointments.

The tone is set at the beginning of the work with the following descriptions of the Western Grande Compound and its foreman. That the Company's title merely indicates it to be a "western branch" symbolically of Rio Grande City is evident.

> The Western Grande Compound, the pickers' paradise, the migrants' home away from home, his own proven domain, was also Mr. Quill's own private gravy land train. He was trying to learn, and perfectly willing to let it be his undoing. Mr. Turner's guidance was truly a godsend. Right at this moment, however; right now, with the weather piling up, he found he couldn't prognosticate right. Would they or would they not pick prunes, all the prunes, and nothing but the prunes, those pious and pretentious prune pickers?[2]

Mr. Quill further ponders and accepts the emptiness of his own life and the path of least resistance about the conditions of the camp with which the migrants must live.

> . . .Weren't these migrants much better off precisely because of Mr. Turner's limitless benevolence. The Western Grande was only slightly weathered. House. Lean-to. Walls. Roof. A place to roost and cook and slap their tortillas around in was a godsend to most of the riffraff

coming by here from Texas. And after all, thought Mr. Quill, inno-
cently reversing himself every time the logic of the matter got too
much for him, weren't these workers human beings too. Mr. Turner
often said, and he was often absolutely right, that do-gooders did all
the world's total harm. (pp. 4-5)

Through Quill's thoughts we meet Manuel and Lupe, only too obviously named after the Virgin to whom and from whom she seeks
solace and hope.

> . . .Manuel Gutiérrez in Cabin No. 9 was a good one; slow but effi-
> cient; never complained; always hungry; never caused trouble, his
> wife Lupe helped out too, although their tots often got in the way. Too
> many kids. Wasn't that the poor for you though. And wasn't it good
> for them to go out into all that fresh natural air and free sunshine,
> though. (p. 5)

Lupe starts a typical day awakening Manuel to a day of inexorably
demanding work and we see our first glimpse of Barrio's stylistic
ability in developing Lupe so that we know more of her as a human
than as a mere stereotype or a foil for the author to develop the male
protagonist, as is done in so many other Chicano prose works, the
best example being that of Esperanza in Edmund Villaseñor's novel
Macho. Lupe, along with a younger and more modern and settled
Chicana of the Santa Clara community, Margarita, Jean Turner, and
Phyllis Ferguson, the Compound prostitute, are the best-developed
and well-presented characters in the entire novel. Barrio's understanding of and insight into their inner emotions and souls make this
novel one of the best stylistic presentations of the thoughts and feelings of female characters in Chicano literature, though the stereotypes certainly do not change. He writes of Lupe:

> She saw a dark hulk standing in Mr. Quill's doorway, and then
> another. She recognized Pepe Delgado talking to Mr. Quill. They
> were probably discussing plans to tear down the shacks after all. Their
> homes. That was it. They were already starting. She was ready to start
> crying. After all this time. Moving, always moving. From Guadala-
> jara to Monterrey to Reynosa, then across the border to Laredo and
> then that hijo de a maldito malcriado hijo de la gran puta Texas Rang-
> er in Rio Grande City—and now here, Santa Clara. Moving, moving,
> always moving. A big jump. She'd heard that's what gypsies were like,
> and she didn't like it, not one bit. She? A gypsy? (p. 8)

Through pressure from benevolently inclined forces, there are those
who want the squalid conditions of the camp destroyed, if not improved, and the furor rages in the local radio newscasts and newspaper accounts scattered throughout the novel for effect. Lupe her-

self constantly doubts and questions the reasons for her life, her culture, her familial existence, her future and that of her race and her family, but also struggles within herself to understand not only her small part of the world but the whole world and the universe in general. Uneven in his character development and presentation and its literary sophistication, Barrio's presentation of Lupe is inconsistent—painfully naive and ignorant at times, at other points in the work she is shown wise beyond her years and experience and sophisticated in the realities of life and its hardships. Fitting into the stereotype of Mother and Wife first, we experience with her the fear that she felt when during the celery-pickers strike in Rio Grande City and The Valley, the Ranger Captain McAllee threatened to take her children, thereby her life, from her.

> . . .Manuel, silent most of the time anyway, was by nature of quiet disposition, which was just fine for Lupe as she liked so to rant on and on. Except now. Now she wanted to be quiet too. So many things were bothering her all at once. The time the Texas Rangers arrested Manuel for walking with the pickets, when she was too speechless to talk, when the Ranger threatened to arrest her and take her children from her, still frightened her, like a living nightmare. Afterwards, Manuel planned their move away from Texas, anywhere, when he saw the children hungry. To try to find a little better way, a less bitter way to live and to work and to find a little joy. Lupe didn't want that to ever happen again. She prayed it would never happen again. She would be good, she would be quiet, please, dear dios she would complain no more; at least she didn't have the police to worry about here in Santa Clara; she felt confident with them, and was confident they were at least impartial, and for that alone she was grateful. (p. 10)

Like so many other nameless Hispanic women, at least as presented in literature, her prime importance and role in life centers around the protection of her children and the care of her husband. Fortunately, Manuel is not the typical "macho" who abuses his wife both physically and verbally and demands from her inhuman feats for his personal caprice. But he too falls into the stereotype of the man squandering his meager earning on liquor only after having slaved all day to make his family's life better.

> . . .The one thing they did which as a woman she did not like she could do little about: she didn't like their dragging Manuel to the Golden Cork cantina across the boulevard on El Camino Real for their Saturday night hijinks. To dine on beer. Manuel could drink up a whole day's pay in one night. Though most of their big debts were once again nearly paid up, they were still in debt to Mr. Quill and Mr. Turner for the unpaid part of last winter's food and lodging.

Manuel, he worked very hard and he could find work where others gave up. He certainly did work hard. Certainly he had a right to a little distraction. But didn't she also? Of course she did. Fighting to keep a tear from spurting out, Lupe squashed the sponge in her dripping fist. The dishes took an unmerciful beating that morning. (p. 14)

Here she is thinking of the revelry of Manuel's four compañeros from Rio Grande City with whom they have traveled from state to state and of whom she is fond. Yet, their friendship and common feudal bonds have not changed her own personal life and its dismal and futile outlook. However, she does not frequently complain aloud to Manuel—she keeps it within herself, locked in her emotions and her thoughts and her soul. For Manuel and Lupe and their children there is little hope of surmounting the trying difficulties of their limited world—they are exploited and in a kind of serfdom to the rich, the owners, nature and its abundant crops and the law of supply and demand.

One of Lupe's worries that morning of the beginning of the work, is that she is pregnant again. She is dizzy and frighteningly ponders the consequences of what that would mean to their lives. In her dizziness, she wants to strike out at something, anything. As she thinks, a symbol of the downtrodden, the exploited of the world and many minority groups appears, reminiscent of Brown Buffalo, Oscar Zeta Acosta's *The Revolt of the Cockroach People.*

. . .she found the only thing she really felt like doing was kicking their only broken chair. A thick, shiny, dark brown cockroach the size of a small mouse scudded past her toe with great confidence. She almost threw up. She had to get a good grip on herself. What in God's name was one more cockroach? It looked so much like a big ambulating red kidney bean. She couldn't help herself. She couldn't be pregnant. She just couldn't be. No, no, dear God, dios mío. She looked up through the smudge in the window at the gray sky, at all those giant silent plum trees outside, and prayed silently to herself. She couldn't help pitying herself. The world seemed like a fury and all the gringos therein intent on lying and stealing and having their special fun and everything they wanted in huge carload lots, wholesale, special. And and and here and she couldn't even get herself a new dress. Not even a cheap dress. She wouldn't even be able to make one, with baby Cati taking all her time. *She was trapped.* (Emphasis mine) Would she rob a stage? She didn't know what she'd do. Maybe they wanted her to become a cheap prostitute, like Phyllis Ferguson, who seemed so happy at her profession, making so many men happy, and so much easy money. Well, if she did it, she'd be a good one. She knew how.
But—she couldn't. (p. 11)

Judy Salinas

The symbolism of that one more cockroach and its comparison to the kidney bean suggestively intimates that should Lupe be pregnant, that would be all that she would be bringing into the world—her world—another cockroach, another "kidney bean"—to use the derogatory and all too often used terms with which many refer to Chicanos and those of Mexican descent. Also, for Lupe to rob a stage—illogical and ludicrous—shows her at this point to be painfully naive and desperate, forgetting her space and time. And, no, definitely no, Lupe wouldn't and couldn't become a prostitute, but she contemplates what the mysterious "they" would want her to do. Who is this "they"? Perhaps her people, her family, her husband? Perhaps all the world and its traditions? She is trapped, like so many women, into a role without exit—she is like the "araña negra" in the poem of the same title by Bruce-Novoa; or like "Woman" in Jorge Alvarez's poem, who is a changeable lizard; or she is a "Serpentina" as in Delmira Agustini's poem; or perhaps she is after all the "Enigma" of Octavio Paz's "Hijos de la Malinche" from his *El laberinto de la soledad*:, all to be discussed later. She is all of these and none of them—she is the victim of darkness and caught in a web of social and psychological structure that has made her become her own victim. Lupe is good, faithful to her husband, her family, and her traditional cultural roles; she is an excellent and loving mother and wife and, yet, still somewhat empty as a person—unfulfilled in modern terms. Also, she realizes only too clearly her roles in society. She re-echoes the call to "prostitution" of herself again on the same page, reminding the reader of the choices open to women of Hispanic and also Chicano society, at least as portrayed in Chicano and most Hispanic literature.

> She kept on dressing. Would any of her dreams ever come true? No? Would she get a new dress? No? Ever? Never? When hair grew on trees, perhaps. When would that be, Manuel, dear God, ay dios mio, Manuel out there, dios, dios, dios, picking all those tender cots, everybody and Roberto's crew, picking like filching idiots in the hot maniacal sun to the limit all summer long, storing away like squirrels for the hungry fall hunger and the starving winter, those long cold days, and for the nice rich people like the Turners . . . .Maybe they really did want her to become a prostitute. Maybe that was all there was to it. Mother, prostitute, and wife. Ay dios. (p. 11)

Most revealingly, Lupe summarizes the stereotyped roles and images of the Chicana and woman in general in those three words: "Mother, prostitute, wife." She does not include lover, nor person, nor human being, nor any other word which makes of her a human not playing

The Role of Women

or fulfilling a predestined stereotyped and socially accepted role because of her sex. She is like "La jefita," though certainly not as idealized, not as uncomplaining, not as unbelievable. Yet, she, too, plays out her roles and only too painfully realizes their limitations and restrictions upon her as a person. She does not fight the roles, however —she accepts them. But, it is in her doubts, her realization that her husband cannot and does not understand their psychical differences and never will that at least makes her less of a stereotyped character than in most Latino works and, in particular, in most Chicano prose. One of Lupe's solaces, as mentioned before, is her namesake, the Virgen de Guadalupe. We sense her stereotypic dependence upon what that symbol represents and her sincere longing for help from that representative of her faith in the following passage, just after she has contemplated the prospect of becoming the exact opposite of the "Virgen"—a prostitute.

> She sat pensive for a long time, studying her little brown ceramic statuette of la Virgen de Guadalupe, her namesake, and Mexico's greatest mother, a young, loving, smiling, peaceful, warm, life-loving madonna, so sweet and serene, so lost, so unperturbed, half in dim yellow light, half lost to subdued shadows, next to the torn window curtain casting its shadow against the rugged textured grain of the wall planks. (pp. 11-12)

The irony of Lupe's life is clearly and realistically compared without necessary explanation in the previous description. Lupe would like to be like the Virgen, unperturbed, loving, serene, sweet, and in peace —but, she must live the realities of life that the statuette must not. And, yet, in this inconsistency and that of the human being, she is more often than not as forgiving, loving, and lost in her own life as is her Virgen. In waiting for Manuel to return from picking, we see a typical afternoon for Lupe when she, too, is not picking fruits to feed the "Turners" of the world.

> Lupe listens.
> Rocking back and forth in her worn-smooth Salvation Army rocking chair, in the gloom of yet another long sunny afternoon. Trying not to wonder when Manuel would get back from the day's picking. Feeding the bottle to baby Cati. Bueno. Listening to Manuelito running his plastic car vroom vroom back and forth on the splintered floor. A lucky fever, passing so quickly. Que bueno, for they didn't have or even know a doctor. Mariquita in the corner, splashing water in an open pan, adrift in her own small sea of dreams. (p. 31)

All this thoughtful pondering occurs as the Blue Angels' pilots zoom overhead to Moffett Field and la Malpagadora, the wailing singer,

sings of "los celos me vuelven loco, y poco a poco. . . .(p. 32) Lupe
thinks:

> . . .ah, the greatest shame in the world. Sí, sí. Lupe, pushing a fork into
> the moist earth of the plastic pot sitting on her sill, recalling dimly that
> avocados (sic) were said to have originated in her homeland, in south-
> ern Mexico, and avocadoes were luxuries beyond their reach. The
> slim little plant never ceased fascinating her. The large brown egg-
> shaped stone, supported by toothpicks, had split and sent out its ten-
> der tendrils, roots down, slim stem up. Now a foot high, it had half a
> dozen long narrow leaves radiating in fan fashion, like petals on a
> flower. A small, healthy, vigorous plant. She had set it out and nour-
> ished it herself. Like herself. Another child. A child of the earth. An
> earthling. This treelet would never reach maturity. She knew that.
> She'd lost too many others. It would never bear fruit. The odds were
> too great against it. It would never shade her nor her children. But
> still—it was alive. She refused to let it sadden her. There was hope.
> And life. Esperanza y vida. It was hers. And no one else's. How she
> found the heart to keep watering it uselessly she didn't know. (pp. 32-
> 33)

She sees in this avocado some hope for a future for herself but, at one
and the same time, discounts its possibility of success, as she does
her own and that of her family—it is but one other dream that will not
come to fruition. She further wonders:

> . . .What ever happens to the almighty rich? The poor pay nothing but
> misery. I'm willing dear God, querido dios, to do anything to get my
> children to school. To feed them succulent dishes. To clothe them in
> bright orange clothing. To do anything to get us out of this endless
> trap of misery. But what? What can I do? Qué puedo hacer? (p. 33)

As befitting her role, she will not do the "anything" of becoming a
prostitute like Phyllis Ferguson—for she is a good woman. In a fore-
shadowing of a harrowing afternoon when she loses sight of her children for some time and believes them lost and devoured by a monster
of a farm machine, and as a repeat of the near loss of her children in
the encounter with the Texas Ranger McAllee in Rio Grande City,
we see the Mother and the Woman without hope, without her role;
she is totally lost and useless—just as useless socially as is Phyllis
Ferguson in her extremist dualistic role.

> In her dreams she has many nightmares. Their shack catches fire.
> The smoke chokes them to death. The flames sear their flesh horribly.
> An earthquake swallows her children. Manuel is with another wom-
> an. She wakes up in a hot damp sweat. Shaking. Trembling. A shrill
> dry cry freezes in her throat. The border patrol arrives in neatly dres-
> sed swastika uniforms. It does no good to argue that she has a legiti-

mate immigrant's card. They tear her away from her husband. They take her children. They swing their iron crosses like truncheons. Lupe runs, runs, runs. Scared. Crying. Looking everywhere for her children, her baby, Manuel. The sheriffs smash the doors down with rifle butts. The windows are nailed shut. Her potted plants are all crunched beneath their heels. They turn their rifles on her. She doesn't care. Fright turns to fury. Mr. Quill refuses to give her any more food. He makes her take her garbage back. The kids grow pale, thin, and disappear. The train crashes into their shack. The sun beats down on their nude prostrate bodies. The avocado plant wilts, shrivels, and finally becomes a thin, twisted black thread (p. 33).

Again blackness is equated with death. Her thoughts in her dreams of the border patrol either remind her of what happened or could have in the past as well as foretell for her what Jean Turner will do to her later in the novel because Lupe refuses to accept Mrs. Turner's castaway, useless clothing and Mrs. Turner seeks vengeance for a lack of gratitude on Lupe's part for her generosity.

In the Flea Market one afternoon, we clearly see the lack of understanding that exists between Manuel and Lupe—the Chicano and the Chicana—the man and the woman. Barrio includes the scene perhaps specifically to show that the culture demands that the man cannot understand the unfulfilled desires of his wife, for those desires can only be achieved through symbolic substitutions for reality.

Only at one stall did Lupe dearly want to give in: at the ceramic stand, where the garishly colored flocked bulls from Tijuana stood in tight, even rows. Not the bulls; she didn't like them; they were terrible, but behind them were some tall slim Greek maidens, heads demurely bowed in pure innocence, wrapping all the promise of an angelic world in their long glowing robes, with only the barest peep of sandaled toes peeping out. She wondered why God had been so careless as to give her such a lumpy figure. She dreamed of a paradise where she might hold herself slim and erect and virginal all over again, with thin breasts barely protruding through her silky gauze gown. But these thinlipped goddesses, these blood blond tresses caused her to wonder what kind of poison was darkening her mind. Dark was the color of blood, and dark the long silken stands (sic) of her own trensas. Dark brown, like rich coffee, were her eyes. Not light. Not pink. Not pale blue. And yet. . .she wanted to own one of these white goddesses. Why? Suddenly she felt a surge of wanting to smash them all, as a child would in full anger. . .(p. 77)

She seeks the opposite in these statuettes of the "other" society and its vision of beauty and innocence because she does not find satisfaction in that of her own statuette, though beautiful, of the Virgen de Guadalupe. She wants to smash them because she can never be one of them and they are pagan to her very essence. Yet, she continues wondering as to what it would be like to be like one of them.

> . . .She would grind them back to dust, back to marbly golden dust, turn the dust into paste with her tears. What new form could she make that would make her glad? And then the pale dress came back to her again and again. What could she, a mere woman, do? Pray? More? Pray more? Pray what? Ay dios de mi vida. Ay por dios santo. She wore out her rosaries. She kneeled. She clasped her hands in prayer. She prayed hard. All the time. Cooking. Sleeping. Walking. To all the saints. Todos los santos. To Saint Manuel. To Santa Isabel. To Santa Margarita. And to her own namesake above all, her own Virgen Guadalupe. Would she hear? This far? Outside her own land? Her own dark virgin? Ay ay ay. Virgen Guadalupe! What turmoils had been stored up for her and for her dark people and for her own dark precious children! She—when would the bright bells ring out for joy? When would they delight? When would there be light like the sun lighting the whole world with pure delight and easy laughter? (p. 77)

But, she does not ask Manuel to buy this statuette of the Greek goddess for her and ends up instead with a huge, useless pot. When they return home, he does not understand her coldness to him and her pushing him away. Only her inner frustrations could explain it, but she cannot reveal them to him—it cannot be done. Her anger at her situation in life and the futility of moving again and again brings about a fight between them and she complains and complains, driving him from the house. She knows that she has driven him out to get drunk for a day or more and to return with nothing, so she starts packing to leave him. However, Manuel returns, soothes her, tries to understand her plight, proving to her that he sincerely loves her.

> Outwardly, physically, Manuel was rough and strong. Inside he was soft and kind and even innocent. He really did see the many hurts and the many complications that constantly chipped away her reserve, her resolve, her plans, her peace of mind, her dreams. One moment angry, in the next instant she crumpled in a heap to the floor, bending over the baby moaning, sobbing, rocking back and forth. 'Why why why? God, God, God.' Sobbing over and over. 'Por que por que por que? Dios, dios, dios' (p. 90).

Manuel offers in peace and with compassion to take her out to dinner, for he has earned good money that day, but she rejects that for eating tacos, his favorite dish, at home. She thinks to herself, in finally accepting that he truly loves her and is trying his best to understand her in the only ways he knows how:

> Yes, he'd made good money that day. But what about tomorrow?

More important—what about November? And December? She held her tongue. She was tempted by the restaurant, she loved having a meal served to her at a table, but her practical nature won out. 'No. I'm much better now, Manuel.' (p. 90).

Her dreams of terror and insects, both two-legged and four-legged, cause her nightmare after nightmare. Many times Manuel has to awaken her to calm her. There is a revealing consolation in Barrio's presentation of the women in the novel in the comparison he makes: "Many times Manuel had to wake her out of her turbulent sleep when she started in moaning or screaming. Had she known that Fred Turner had to do the same for his wife Jean, Lupe might have felt better" (p. 160).

After so many trials and troubles from all sides of life, Manuel and Lupe finally do gain a little permanence and hope with the offer from Schroeder to work part-time in his nursery which will lead to full-time work in the Spring. Manuel comes home with the news to Lupe.

> . . .But now, now they had a base that would let them stay put in one place. They might even rent a house, a poor one of course, but their own house. Maybe they could even get a credit card. Lupe burst into tears.
>
> . . . .
>
> She had so much to be grateful to America for, so grateful now, so many happy tears. And maybe now, dear God, ay dios—perhaps maybe now she would also be able to plant her very own little Mexican avocado tree in a permanent spot too, her very own tree! (p. 162).

All this, only after an entire novel of having convinced herself that the "system" deserved the purest of condemnation and damnation, only after she absolutely was sure that it was rotten and could never be changed—some hope for them, yes, albeit little, but some just the same. Lupe complained, "La jefita" did not. Lupe kept struggling as probably "La jefita" did and many "jefitas" do. Yet, they both kept to their roles and traditional stereotypes. However, we come to know Lupe better, spiritually and soulfully, more so in this novel than in so many other Chicano works, all due to the literary and stylistic ability of Barrio.

The Bad Woman

Bad women or Eves are often depicted as prostitutes, mistresses, adulterous wives, or women who manipulate everyone to obtain their

Judy Salinas

own selfish desires. Many of these bad women consort with evil spirits or conjure up magical curses to hinder their rivals and more often than not, they are portrayed as presenting a false and deceptive image of goodness to the public. They appear to be everything that a "good" woman should be by traditional standards while in reality being "bad" women. In Spanish literature the classic stereotype of the truly despicable wench is Celestina in the work of the same name, a late fifteenth-century novelized drama by Fernando de Rojas. She is a former prostitute and conwoman turned go-between in love affairs. Because of her evil, cunning, and deceit she precipitates the deaths of the hero and the heroine, the latter commiting suicide, her punishment for having been involved in a socially unacceptable love tryst. Celestina is punished for her evilness, being murdered by her comrades in crime. In Chicano literature, particularly due to contemporary philosophies among Chicanos who are more openly accepting of woman's liberation or freedom from rigid images in literature and other art forms, there are few fully developed examples of a stereotypically "bad" woman like Celestina. There are, however, women who consort with the Devil through black magic and witchcraft. The witch image is presented in Spanish American literature in the 1941 novel Doña Bárbara by Venezuelan Rómulo Gallegos. Doña Bárbara symbolizes the barbarity of the dictatorial political regime of Juan Vicente Gómez during the preceding years as well as the barbarity of the forces of nature and evil in the plains and jungles. She uses all her feminine wiles and charms to entice, imprison, and destroy men. But, it is her use of magic and incantations to the supernatural forces and the Devil which make her an evil bruja to be feared by all. She suffers her punishment for evil by losing all that she had accumulated and by being forced to leave behind the vestiges of civilization, seeking refuge in the jungle from which she came. Because of the ending of the story, it is suggested that she committed suicide, but either step, death or exile, was just punishment for her indiscretions. Although she is evil, and a despicable bruja who almost murders her own daughter, Gallegos elicits some compassion and understanding from the reader for his main character, for she was fighting for survival in a world that had taken the man she loved from her, had violated her, and socially and culturally prohibited her aggressiveness and "masculine" behavior from going unpunished in the severest of manners.

Like her in their alliance with supernatural and evil forces are the three daughters of Tenorio in the novel *Bless Me, Ultima,* by the Chicano author, Rudolfo Anaya. Ultima, the "good" curandera, speaks of them to Antonio, the protagonist:

> 'They are women who are too ugly to make men happy,' she answered, 'and so they spend their time reading in the Black Book and practicing their evil deeds on poor, unsuspecting people. Instead of working, they spend their nights holding their black masses and dancing for the devil in the darkness of the river. But they are amateurs, Antonio.' Ultima shook her head slowly, 'they have no power like the power of a good curandera. In a few days they will be wishing they had never sold their souls to the devil—'[3]

Shortly after Ultima exorcises the evil curses put upon Antonio's uncle by the Tenorio sisters, they become mysteriously and suddenly ill, two of them dying. Their deaths are their traditional punishment for being evil.

Another like the Tenorio sisters in her supposed consortium with the Devil, but unlike them and more like Ultima in that she has tried to do only good for the community into which she wandered as a young girl, is Lela in "The Burning" by Estela Portillo de Trambley. Like the Tenorio sisters and Ultima, she suffers the condemnation of being destroyed as surely as they do, simply for going against the traditions of the society and the Church, although in this short story, Lela, like Ultima, meant only good for the people. The title itself reveals that she is to be sacrificed and punished for meddling with the unknown by being burned alive. She is hated by the very ones whom she has helped, for they have not understood nor tried to understand her, as she has come into their midst from another civilization and another religion. The short story begins with the council of the old women deciding Lela's fate, while all the time, Lela is dying of a fever which will find its relief in the very fire which they plan to be her "Christian" castigation. As usual, evil is associated with blackness and darkness, and in this tale there is no exception.

> The women of the barrio, the ones pock-marked by life, sat in council. Existence in dark cubicles of wounds had withered the spirit. Now, all as one, had found a hearth. One tried soul stood up to speak, 'Many times I see the light she makes of darkness, and that light is a greater blackness, still.'[4]

She is further condemned by these withered spirits:

> ...'Yes, she drinks the bitterness of good and swallows, like the devil-wolf, the red honey milk of evil.'
>
> ....
>
> The oldest one among them, one with dirty claws, stood up with arms outstretched and stood menacingly against the first lightning

bolt that cleaved the darkness. Her voice was harsh and came from
ages past, 'She must burn!'[5]

And, burn her they conspire to do, as in ages past when many
"witches" were put to death in many cultures. It is only fitting that the
council takes place on a night of thunder and lightning and storms,
for their spirits storm within them from ignorance, hate, and superstition, that which seemingly they are struggling against.

Lela had strayed from her village when young and upon crossing
through the mountains before finding this village had fallen and hurt
her leg. The shining sand where she had fallen proved to heal her
wound miraculously and with some in her apron, she had wandered
dazed into the village. Her beginning was marked with suspicion, distrust and hate.

> They took her in, but she remained a stranger the rest of her life
> in the pueblo upon which she had stumbled. At the beginning, she
> seemed but a harmless child. But, as time passed and she resisted their
> pattern of life, she was left alone. The people knew she was a Tara-
> humara from Batopilas. Part of her strangeness was the rooted depth of
> her own religion. She did not convert to Christianity. People grew
> hostile and suspicious of her.
>
> But she had also brought with her the miracle sand. It had strange
> curative powers. In no time, she began to cure those in the pueblo
> who suffered from skin disease, from sores, or open wounds.
>
> 'Is it the magic of her devil gods?' the people asked themselves.
> Still, they came for the miracle cure that was swift and clean. She be-
> came their *curandera* outside their Christian faith.
>
> The people in her new home needed her, and she loved them in
> silence and from a distance. She forgave them for not accepting her
> strangeness and learned to find adventure in the Oneness of herself.[6]

As a child, she had learned to mold clay figurines of the gods of the
rivers and the forces of nature—of life, joy, happiness. It was these
very figurines and her failure to convert to Christianity, to become
socially acceptable and not to consort with evil, that condemned her
from the beginning with the old women who sat in judgment of her
that dark and black night that has, in its blackness, meant for woman
nothingness or creativity—which, in turn, has meant total loss of
power or the acquisition of it through evil or good. Lela meant only
good, no harm, and, for that, would suffer throughout her life. Even
as these women gather wood for circling her house for the burning of
this "evil one," the parish priest himself calls upon them to forgive
her, for only they can do so, being supposedly "good Christians."
They refuse.

> And who were these women who sat in council? They were one full sweep of hate; they were one full wave of fear. Now these village women were outlined against a greyish sky where a storm refused to break. Spiderlike, apelike, toadlike was the ferocity of their deadness. These were creatures of the earth who mingled with mankind. But they were minions to torture because the twist of littleness bound them to condemn all things unknown, all things untried. The infernal army could not be stopped now. The scurrying creatures began to gather firewood in the gloom. With antlike obedience they hurried back and forth carrying wood to Lela's hut. They piled it in a circle around her house. The rhythm of their feet sang, 'We'll do! We'll do!'[7]

The irony of the situation lies, of course, in the fact that Lela is already dying of a burning fever. The parish priest makes one final attempt to stop the hordes of women who are determined to kill that dark night the very one who tried to help and comfort them in the only way she knew how.

> 'Burn! Burn! Burn!'
> The old priest reasons, 'All is forgiven, my children. She only made some figurines of clay!'
> There was a hush. The one woman with the claws approached the priest and spit out the condemnation, 'She took our holy saints, Mary, Joseph, and many others and made them obscene. How can you defend the right hand of the devil? Drinking saints! Winking saints! Who can forgive the hideous suggestions of her clay devils? Who?'
> The priest said simply 'You.'[8]

As Lela gives into her own death, she thinks of the very people who are burning her as a pagan blasphemer and as the hand of the Devil upon the earth.

> In the caves she had sadly thought of how she had failed to reach them as a friend. Her silence and her strangeness had kept them apart. But, she would find a way of communicating, a way of letting them know that she loved them. 'If I give shape and form to their beauty,' she thought. 'If I cannot tell them I love them with words. . . .'[9]

In the caves as well, she had planned the very act that would condemn her with the townspeople.

> . . . Here, in the silence of aloneness, she had looked for the little gods in the townspeople. In her mind, she had molded their smiles, their tears, their embraces, their seeking, their *just being.* Her larger self told her that the miracle of the living act was supreme, the giving, the receiving, the stumbling, and the getting up.[10]

However, the townspeole were blind to her way of expressing her love of them and to them. Like Ultima, however, Lela dies a death that has a greater justice and a significance than perhaps could have been hoped for by the reader.

> The light of the moving, mixing little gods was becoming a darkness. Her body would give in now. Yet, she still wished for Batopilas and the old ways with her last breath, 'If only. . .if only, I could be buried in the tradition of my father. . .a clean burning for new life. . . but here, here, there is a dark hole for the dead body. . . .Oh, little gods, take me back to my father. . .'
> The little gods were racing to the waterfall.[11]

In her death, she achieved the Oneness and the fulfillment that she had sought in her life. Yet, she too, like the Tenorio sisters and Ultima, is punished traditionally by being ostracized, hated, feared, and murdered, though Portillo adds this finishing, beautiful, and ironic touch to her death in an inimitable and delightfully surprising manner to the reader. It is true that the townspeople are truly the "dead ones" living in the dark hole, whereas Lela, like Ultima, has gained the Oneness of freedom and love in death.

The bad woman who appears to be good but in reality has elements of a black spirit or does something totally unacceptable to society's ideas of what a woman should be and do, is exemplified in Spanish literature in the nineteenth century novel by Pérez Galdós, *Doña Perfecta*. In Chicano literature her stereotyped image appears in two characters: Doña Marina, a cold, obsessed woman from the short story by Octavio Romano-V. entitled "A Rosary for Doña Marina,"[12] and Doña Josefa, a pious, charitable symbol of total benevolence and the paragon of virtue in the play "The Swallows" by Estela Portillo. Doña Perfecta was exactly the opposite of her name and of her public and private image. Her appearance deceived her true character—that of a cold, dominating, manipulative woman who caused the murder of her daughter's suitor which in turn drove her daughter insane. Doña Marina, like Doña Perfecta, drives away from her those who could have loved her and did. Because of her cold personality, she was deserted by her husband when still only a newlywed and that rejection by man corrupted her thoughts turning them to evil. Her niece Lina and her second cousin Pedro lived with her for some time in what seemed to be peaceful harmony. A surrogate mother, she was restrictive to Lina, but Lina never rebelled, true to the image of a good daughter—totally innocent of the ways of men and the world. But, Doña Marina becomes obsessed with the idea that Lina is carrying on a torrid love affair with a young boy who had carried her books home for her—once. Her imaginings of evil and illicit love between Lina and the boy drive her to believe that Lina has become pregnant, simply because she is ill in the morning for several days in a row. She forces Lina to go to an abortion clinic across the border, without telling her what kind of place it is. When her cousin Pedro wraps a small present to take to Lina in the clinic, Doña Marina begins to suspect that he is the father of the non-existent child. In a frenzied fit, she takes an axe and chops up the bed in Pedro's room where she believes the incestuous relationship occurred. Her twisted thoughts about innocence, love, and virtue have turned her away from those who loved her and in turn driven them from her. Pedro leaves home never to return and Lina runs away from the clinic when she discovers what is going on. Doña Marina says a rosary for them in their debauchery when in reality, she is the one who needs the rosary said for her.

Doña Josefa in "The Day of the Swallows," like Doña Marina and Doña Perfecta, appears to be the epitome of feminine virtue. She is a single woman who earns her living making the most delicate of laces, helps the poor whenever needed, is essential to all church activities, and is considered to be the kindest and most wonderful woman in the barrio. She takes into her own home a poor, innocent young girl, Alysea, after having rescued the latter from a man who was trying to force her to return to the brothel to which she had been tricked into going. When Doña Josefa's ward David has his tongue cut out by some mysterious intruder, we have the first concrete suspicion that something is very wrong in the household. It is her uncle Tomás, a drunkard and a thief, who confronts her with the possibility of being exposed for what he believes her to be—a bad, evil woman. Alysea has just left the room with her fiancé when Tomás begins to speak to Josefa:

T: (shyly) I guess she feels bad about David. . .what happened last night. . .

J: What?

T: I heard the talk in the barrio. . .someone broke into the house. . . that is. . .that is what you claim.

J: What do you mean?

T: You didn't tell me earlier. . .

J: Tell you? Why should I tell you anything.

T: The blood in the pail. . .you didn't tell me anything about that either. . .

J: So?

T: Well. . .I remember. . .all those times. . .you save the poor, innocent, helpless ones. . .you never say anything. . .it's always the barrio who puts the story together. . .you are clever. . .

J: Don't be ridiculous. . .

Judy Salinas

T: Yes. . .people have no idea how clever you really are. . .la doña
   Perfecta! You saved Alysea from the evil man. . .you saved David
   from a drunken father, the barrio tells the story of an angel. . .but
   it's funny. . .somehow. . .they never remember to tell that you
   crippled one man and the other died on the road where you left
   him. . .
J: You are pitiful. . .like those two men. . .destructive and pitiful. . .
T: Perhaps you'll get your hands on me too.
J: Hadn't you better see about that horse?
T: Now the town is busy making you out a heroine. . .an intruder?
   That's hard to believe. . .the girl looked too guilty a while ago. . .
   (he studies Josefa who is straightening up) But you. . .it's amazing!. . .such grace. . .such pious silence. . .yes. . .you are a danger-
   ous one, alright![13]

When Alysea decides to leave Doña Josefa's home to get married,
Josefa's world begins to disintegrate rapidly. It is in her confession to
Father Prado that we learn that she hates men for their crudeness and
cruelty and that *she* cut out David's tongue. But, like both Doña Marina and Doña Perfecta, she feels no sorrow for her actions nor any
guilt. Her conversation with the priest takes place the day before the
entire barrio is to honor her during the religious festival for the virgins of the parish. Father Prado praises her goodness and tremendous godly faith, calling her "a legend" among the people.[14] Unable
to withstand his praise while living with her evil actions, she is forced
to confess to the shocked and disbelieving priest that she cut David's
tongue for fear that he would reveal to the people that respected and
loved her that she was a lesbian.

P: What is wrong?
J: Forgive me, Father, for I have sinned. . . .(Father remains silent)
   I have sinned. . .I have sinned. . .
P: God forgives. . .
J: Oh, Father. . .I'm lost! I'm lost!. . . .I am guilty of grievous sins. . .
   they are beyond forgiveness. . . .people will judge them so! Father
   . . .before I tell you. . .you must know. . .I do not feel sorry. . .I
   want. . .I need. . .the calm. . .to keep things as they are. . . .David
   was hurt last night. . .I lied about the intruder. There was no in-
   truder. . .I was the one.
P: (Increduously) You. . .did that to David?
J: Yes. . .(she braces herself as if to accept the fact) I did that to
   David.
P: I can't believe it. . .you! Not you!
J: Me, Father Me!
P: It was inhuman. . .
J: Oh, Father! I. . .I don't know. . .why? why?
P: Tell me, my child, there must have been a reason. . .[15]

She continues explaining to the priest her distrust of men, and the whole ritual of love symbolized in the Bathing of the Virgins. She tells of her first sexual encounter with Alysea, a year earlier, and then relates what happened that night to David.

> J: We bathed. . .and then. . .it happened. . .(pause) Last night, after David went to bed. . .I felt the nymph magic. . .I took Alysea. . . Suddenly. . .there was David. . .In the middle of the room. The horror in his eyes. . .Why? why? There was horror in his eyes. . . Something happened to me. . .I don't know what it was. . .I ran. . . I ran into the kitchen and found a kitchen knife. . .Somehow. . . somehow I knew David would tell. . .the barrio people would look at me that way too. . .
> . . .Oh, Father. . .until last night I never knew my fears. . .I went to where Alysea was holding the frightened child. . .then. . .then I made Alysea hold him tight. . . .I took the knife and cut David's tongue. . .[16]

As Doña Josefa continues her confession, Father Prado still cannot believe nor accept that such a "good" woman with so much of God in her could have done such a thing. He says to her: "But. . .you are the most pious. . .the most constant. . .in the barrio. . .Faith shines in you. . .all the beauty you create. . . ."[17] She atones for her evil by committing suicide the next morning dressed in a white lace dress. Like most "bad" women who either consort with the Devil's agents or are socially unacceptable, she is condemned to her punishment, death by suicide. But, although Portillo punishes her in this stereotypically traditional manner, throughout the play the author elicits and maintains an understanding and compassion for Josefa and even for her lesbianism. Doña Josefa knew that neither her culture nor her peers could accept her as she really was, and thus she could not accept or forgive herself. Portillo suggests that it is wrong for women or for anyone to be so rigidly pressured into a stereotyped role, not allowing for variations. That is, she implies that Doña Josefa was not totally bad as her acts condemned her to be nor was she totally good as her false image portrayed her to be. Like Doña Bárbara, Doña Josefa must pay for flaunting social and cultural roles, but also, like Doña Bárbara, she deserves and receives some compassion and understanding from author and reader alike.

Two other women who flaunt tradition and go against customs and morés are Mariana in the novel *Chicano* by Richard Vásquez and Clotilde Romero de Traske in Estela Portillo's short story "The Paris Gown." Mariana suffers the traditional punishment, death due to a botched abortion arranged for by her Anglo boyfriend and her heroin-addicted brother, Sammy. Clotilde, on the other hand, plots and struggles to achieve a life which she herself has chosen and which can only mean banishment from her home to Paris, after having shocked her family by appearing stark naked on the night of the announcement of her engagement to a rich and lecherous old man, Don Ignacio. But, though both characters reflect some element of modern woman and a change in stereotypically presented roles, both, in their own ways, still must endure some kind of punishment from their cultures and their societies.

Mariana in *Chicano* is presented along with her twin brother Sammy after a long and sometimes tedious telling of the story of the coming to the United States of the Sandoval family from Mexico. They do emanate from an original Spanish lineage, but, in East Los Angeles in modern times, this matters little. Mariana shows herself to be the pride of her grandfather Neftalí's heart, though she decides to flaunt tradition and become involved with an Anglo boy, David Stiver. He comes to the East Los Angeles barrio on a college assignment to sociologically and psychologically determine for a term project why Sammy, like so many other statistically counted and computerized Sammies, has dropped out of school. In turn, he seemingly falls in love with Mariana. With the obvious variation of the name, María, we know only too well that she is doomed to some kind of unkindly end, probably death or an unbearable life, for in the era and the intent of the novel, she certainly could be no heroine of the classic romantic Latin American type as was *María* in Isaacs' novel. Mariana is bright, sharp, intelligent, and wise to the ways of the Anglo-Chicano community. It is she who decides to let herself become involved with David and who decides to go to bed with him. However, when she becomes pregnant, she is the wiser of the two, the more mature, the one who decides to leave David so as not to destroy his destined-to-be-prosperous life back in the Midwest and not to cause problems for him or his family. She decides to have her baby and live at home. To many, that would seem paradoxical from the often presented.images of the woman being outcast by all if she has a child illegitimately; however, she could and would be accepted by her family and still be loved, though she might indeed and most certainly would be shunned by some of her community. She would be accepted by a traditional Chicano family who loves her for not giving up her baby and for not having an abortion, which would go against a greater and more important tradition. What is so bad about the outcome of her life is that, with her potential, her wisdom, and the talented way in which Vásquez at times develops her as a character, she melts away into a stereotyped foil for Vásquez, acquiescing to David's insistence that she should have an abortion so that their love and their tacitly promised marriage could start off properly, without encumbrances or untold obligations that a baby would mean. Of course, the abortion is a botched butchery and she dies, forgiving an undeserving David to the end—an untimely death for a lovely and hopeful girl. David didn't even have the time to go see her as she lay dying in the hospital—a victim of the corruption and decadence of what tradition had become in both the Anglo and Chicano communities alike. David had to attend classes at college—they were a more important obligation to his life than was Mariana.

The author shows David as never having overcome his prejudices and never having really accepted Mariana—she was always a real curiosity to him, someone different and new with whom he could experience what he would not do with an Anglo girl. David used Mariana and in turn Vásquez uses Mariana and David to condemn the Anglo for exploitation and the Chicano for letting himself or herself be exploited by the shallowness and vacuum of Anglo "traditions" and customs. Anglo corruption of time-honored tradition and respect has reached deeply into the barrio and destroyed Sammy, many members of his family, and Mariana. However, it is not merely an Anglo destruction or an Anglo maelstrom which dictates the impersonalness of the work, as any intelligent reader of the novel will realize. Such can occur in all societies and cultures, to many, many people, particularly in such circumstances. David takes his revenge of Mariana's death out on Sammy, rather than on himself as the guilty party, by snitching to the police anonymously about a drug shipment which Sammy is bringing in from Mexico, and so David is used by Vásquez to ultimately destroy the hopes of Pete and Minnie Sandoval, well-to-do and hard-working and yet "out-of-touch" Chicanos, by destroying life in both Sammy and Mariana. However, it is the hopes of the whole culture which Vásquez warns against being destroyed as is seen in the final scene at the cemetery when Mariana is buried and her grandfather Neftalí remembers back to his idealized image of the wife he had always dreamed of having. That idealized dream had come true for him in the personage of his granddaughter Mariana, now dead, as are all his dreams.

David does at least have the decency to attend the burial but keeps at a distance as the family pays its respects, though he hadn't the guts to go to see Mariana as she lay dying in the hospital as a result of his decision and her acquiescence to it. She believed during her several days of dying that David was outside the room, waiting to be able to see and comfort her—a false hope which the doctor, Dr. Yamaguchi, had tried to console her with during her last fight for life. However, the reader realizes that Mariana must have truly known that David did not have it within him to really be just outside waiting to show his love to her. She knew him better than Vásquez had intended, for her giving into the abortion was not an action which fit into her development as a character and therein suggests a flaw in the novel.

Elizabeth Jameson, one of Mariana's best friends since childhood, calls up David to tell him of the news of Mariana's death.

> —Bueno —un respiro profundo y desigual—, ella murió.
> Una pausa larga, larga. Un suspiro profundo. Casi un murmullo.
> —¿Qué puedo decirte, Liz?
> La voz de ella mantenía un tono bajo, de enojo controlado.
> —¿Qué puedes decir? Yo te diré lo que puedes decirme. La única cosa que me haría sentirme mejor sería que dijeras que en este mismo momento estás tomando estricnina —su voz elevó el tono—. . ., pero ni diez como tú valdrían una como ella. Malvado, sucio, perverso hijo de. . .[18]

However, Mariana does die stoically almost, in forgiving David as Liz relates to him in their continued conversation.

> . . .Pero no tienes que preocuparte, David, una de las primeras cosas que aclaró desde el primer día fue que tú y ella habían terminado porque supiste que había salido con otros tipos.
> La mente de David había estado girando, pero repentinamente hizo un alto.
> —¿Qué dijiste. . .? ¿Ella dijo eso?
> —Sí, David. Ella lo dijo. Tú no la conocías muy bien, ¿o sí? De otra manera no te sorprenderías tanto. Se aseguró de que tú quedaras fuera de responsabilidades antes de que ella muriera—y la voz de Elizabeth iba aproximándose a la histeria nuevamente—. No quedaría su muerte para no causarte perjuicios, David. En efecto, toda su maldita raza es un terrible dolor en las nalgas para todos ustedes. . .[19]

David is freed from responsibilities and like the villain which the author pictures him to be, the final paragraph of the novel intimates Vásquez's hoped-for ultimate irony to the entire work.

> Finalmente se dio cuenta David de que era el último que había quedado junto a la tumba de Mariana. Como todos los demás del cortejo, empezó a alejarse lentamente y momentos después echó una mirada a su reloj y aceleró el paso. Si se apresuraba aún podría llegar a tiempo para el ensayo de su graduación.[20]

In Mariana, the traditional stereotype of punishment by death continues—in a more callous and impersonal way. No real change is seen in such a presentation of the "bad" or "evil" woman who goes against tradition. That still has not changed from pre-Columbian literature with Coatlicue's plotted death by her own children and from the *Holy Bible* when women were stoned to death for failure to follow custom, so why should one expect those roles and outcomes to change for women who do as Mariana, Ultima, Lela, the Tenorio sisters, Doña Bárbara, Doña Josefa, and others did—they certainly do not in this novel, *Chicano*.

In Portillo's story "The Paris Gown," we meet Clotilde Romero de Traske as she has a leisurely, reminiscent and most informative afternoon coffee with her granddaughter Theresa, who has come to Paris and is visiting with her grandmother. Portillo adeptly images Clotilde for us:

> . . .Somehow the word 'grandmother' did not fit Clotilde Romero de Traske, sophisticated, chic, and existentially fluent. Theresa had anticipated this after dinner *tete a tete*. In her mind there were so many things unclear about this woman who had left her home in Mexico so long ago. The traces of age in Clotilde were indistinguishable in the grace and youthful confidence exuded from her gestures, her eyes, her flexible body, and the quick discerning mind. Clotilde Romero de Traske, art dealer at the Rue Auber, was a legend back home. The stories about her numerous marriages, her travels, her artistic ventures, and the famous names that frequented her salon were many. But no one had ever discussed how she got to Paris in the first place when the women of her time had had small freedoms. Her life abroad had become scandal in epic to the clan of women in aristocratic circles back home. There was a daring in her grandmother's eyes.[21]

It is the telling of her coming to Paris that is the content of this magnificent short story, although its essence is the breaking of traditional shackles by Clo to free herself. The above description could be of the famous women of the salons of Paris during the eighteenth and nineteenth centuries in France who were oases of intellectual freedom for themselves and those who frequented their salons. In this tale, Portillo draws for the reader a human being with desires and determination and the guts to fight for them in a most provocative and inflexible manner. Clotilde was a source of bother and displeasure to her father, for she outdid her brother in each and every endeavor as they grew up. Yet, her father never acknowledged her success, her potential nor her prowess. No, he merely ignored her and resented her refusal to accept her standard of subservient, frivolous, and vacuous woman.

As Theresa and Clo are discussing history and the art treasures in Clo's room, they discuss the struggle between men and women, and Theresa thinks she understands why her grandmother never returned home.

> 'I understand now, Clo, why you never went back. In a world still archaic, women suffer the barbarism of men. An injustice.'
>
> . . . .
>
> 'I used to think so. . .when I was very young.'
>
> 'Don't you feel that way anymore?'
>
> 'No. . .I don't think so. Maybe, because I know that the instinct that respects all life, the instinct that understands equality, survives in all of us in spite of overwhelming, unfair tradition. Men know this instinct, too, although thousands of years of conditioning made them blind to the equality of all life. The violence of man against woman is a traditional blindness whose wall can be broken. Isn't that the objective of love. . .to break walls?'
>
> 'But the unfairness is still there, Clo, even today. The woman has a secondary role to that of the man, and the brutish mind accepts it. I can imagine how it must have been in your time!'
>
> Clotilde maintained the crystal of her world. 'Men have attempted fairness since the beginning of time; it's just that sometimes they are overwhelmed. . .overwhelmed.'[22]

Clo is wiser than Theresa and hopes that in the retelling of her flight from "blind tradition" as Theresa calls it, she will help her granddaughter to feel the personal and individual freedom that one gains through becoming a thinking, individual human being. It is coming a full circle in a sense, but not in the traditional sense; for even though Clo escaped the chains of servitude to roles, she still is considered by most to have been banished and thereby punished for her failure to cede to tradition. Only the reader can properly interpret whether that is punishment, sacrifice, or foolishness, based upon that reader's own values of worth and need. Clo takes us down the path of her memories along with Theresa, explaining the injustice of having been born female, or so she felt when young.

> . . .'Yes, tradition was much heavier in my time. There was but a single fate for the gentlewoman. . .one variation of a cloister or another. To marry meant to become the lonely mistress of a household where husbands took unfair freedoms, unfair only because the freedoms belonged to them and were unthinkable for women! Children were the recompense, but children should not be a recompense; they are human beings belonging to themselves; and we should not need recompense. It can turn to bitterness, then we become the bitterness itself, a patterned, strict garden of dead things, poisoned things. If

we did not marry, there was total dependency on the generosity of pitying relatives, with church and its rituals for comfort. The nunnery or running away with the stable boy offered many sacrifices and discomforts. No. . .no. . . .There must be another solution, I would tell myself!'[23]

Clo progresses with her story, relating how a wedge became driven very soon between her and her father, and subsequently, all those of her society. She tells of outdoing her brother: "I had a compulsion to compare, to outdo him, because he was a boy with born privileges and I was a girl born into a kind of slavery. I poisoned my garden early in life, but to an extent, it was my nature to want freedom. I had a mind that craved and that weighed the inequalities as a gross injustice. I found ways of justifying my opinions, my martyrdom."[24]

She continues, revealing the growing resentment between her and her father, as her mother encouraged her to be more like a woman should be and behave in her society.

'My father would say. . .A man must never allow a woman to outdo him. How typical of him! The way of the varón, and Felix was his varón. . . .I was just a daughter, an afterthought, so I thought. My mother would whisper to me. . . .Let your brother win when you race. It would please your father. . . .I did not wish to please my father with the accomplishments of my brother. To outdo him became my constant form of revenge. My father resented the fact and overlooked my ability to outdo, as if it did not exist. This was adding salt to my wounds . . . .I think I began to hate my father, poor father!'[25]

When Felix was allowed to go to Paris to paint, though he had little talent, he was permitted to do so because he was a man, but Clo was not. Her father suggested that a nunnery was perhaps the best thing for her and she knew only too well that he meant it. Finally, her father decided that she should wed a widower, extremely wealthy, and hoped that that would put an end to his daughter's unseemly and intolerable ways. However, Clo put up a mighty struggle by refusing to eat, locking herself in her room, and making everyone, especially herself, miserable. She went as far as to run away at night and when found was deathly ill with pneumonia, but, she recovered and thought that her father would at last let her be herself and have her freedom because he obviously cared for her sincerely and loved her. Yet, he threatened either a convent again or the marriage with Don Ignacio. Her remark to him as she lay convalescing was: "You simply do not unpetal a flower for your advantage. You give it the chance of life!"[26] Of course, her father refused to alter his decision. It was then that through much contemplation and the later inspiration of seeing in-

Judy Salinas

nocent young children bathing in a pond, including one little boy who had removed his clothes and joined them only to be harshly reprimanded and spanked by his horrified nurse, that Clo awakens to her solution and by all appearances accepts her forthcoming marriage to the old man. With all due expected frivolity and innaneness about the wedding preparations, she cajoles her father, with little difficulty, into sending to Paris for her wedding gown, the most beautiful and unforgettable gown to be seen in Mexico to that time. When the gown arrives, she locks herself in her room night after night and puts it on, admiring herself in it and awaiting the fruition of her plan. Then, the night of the engagement party and announcement of the wedding, she appears at the precise moment she has carefully planned for, a grand and sole appearance at the top of the staircase, and descends down it, with all eyes upon her, "stark naked." In retrospect, she reflects upon that memory:

> 'I think now it was a kind of insanity finding its own method to fight what I considered a slavery. It was simple after that. My father could not abandon an insane daughter, but he knew that my presence meant constant reminder. He let me come to Paris with sufficient funds. . .and here I made my home. . . .my home.'
> 'Do you miss the other home?'
> 'Yes, I left part of myself there and the people of my blood. . .of course there is a certain nostalgia. . .but no regrets. That's what I hope you will learn in your journeys. . .never to have regrets.'
> 'You have found. . .the freedom. . .the equality?'
> 'Yes, my child, I have known the depth of feeling in all its glorious aspects.' Both women looked out the window and caught the full colors of life.[27]

Portillo gives us two women, Doña Josefa and Clotilde, who are very different. Josefa sought refuge from her reality of never being able to be accepted by herself or by the community for being a lesbian by means of cloaking her reality in cruelty, hypocrisy, near-murder, and ultimately suicide. On the other hand, Clotilde, like a rainbow after a cool and unexpected shower, suggests the color and zest of life. However, both had to resort to subterfuge, subjugation, and to traditions, and both had to give up something to accomplish their respective essences. To be sure, Josefa is traditionally treated by committing suicide for her crime of failure to heed custom, while Clotilde has only to live with nostalgia and the knowledge that she has left a part of herself and her people behind. But, then, perhaps Portillo is suggesting to the reader that in love, and in love for freedom, there is always a loss of a part of one's self and some other way of life, for

220

freedom and equality mean openness and the absence of restrictions and limitations mean continual change and loss and new creativity. Without losing something, one cannot grow into something more fruitful and self-fulfilling.

The Duality of Woman

The duality of woman, her goodness and her potential evil by nature of being a woman, is symbolically expressed in the following poem, "Woman," by Jorge Alvarez. It is reminiscent in tone, imagery, symbolism, and content of the poem "Serpentina," by the Uruguayan Delmira Agustini.

Woman

You are the lizard I wrestle with
In the green fires of the Sunday;

You are the rose where gardeners kneel
To lick the petal flown;

You are the slippery noise I hear
With my fingers deep in the orifice
Of the early morning falcon;

You are the steps that—pat, pat, patting—
Fall asleep with warm flesh
On the nylon carpets I have known;

You are the gasp, singing in the contrail
Of a lone pigeon;

You are the oven where red-hot pistons
Bake the thousand other poems
That are never read.[28]

Woman is pleasurable, warm, soft, and good—a rose that smells sweet and gives joy, suggesting passion through its velvety beauty and red color—yet, a rose has thorns. Woman is a lizard, a cold-blooded, changeable creature that like the serpent in Agustini's poem equating woman with the viper, can bring in caresses sensual and sexual delights and ecstasy or instantaneous and painful destruction and death through poisoning.

The continued symbols of woman's evil and good or destruction and creativity out of darkness or blackness are echoed in the poems "La araña negra," "Inocencia perversa," and ". . .the more things stay the same" by Bruce-Novoa. As with "Woman" and "Serpentina," "La araña negra" in its very title suggests that woman is like a suspected and feared, loathsome creature—a devourer, a destroyer and an exigent mistress, to be served by her captive, man. Just as with Eve, Malinche, Coatlicue, and other women through the ages, she is the infinite double, never to be trusted, never to be satiated by man. She is the vessel of delight and ecstasy as well as that of inexorable pain, or, she is the vessel of nascent life and creativity. In "La araña negra," we see Bruce-Novoa's love and respect, yet a docile and passive acceptance of her demands and her role. A literary eroticist, Bruce-Novoa captures through this sensual poem the essence of what woman truly, at times, can be.

La araña negra

Me espera en la noche
la impaciente araña negra
que apenas duerme insatisfecha
aun después de haberme
picado e hinchado
y luego chupado la vida blanca,
dejándome delirante y exhausto
en el nido
de su espera insaciable.[29]

Again, woman is pictured as impatient, insatiable, unsatisfied, the real personage of control in life and in a relationship. Her power comes, as suggested in this poem, from within her psychical make-up—she can never change and never will. She does with man what she will, perhaps as the agent of the Devil, of evil, or of the promise of heights of achieving union and the quintessential element of life itself; for she is always there—she lurks, she is infinite.

This same vision or image of woman coming into the use and enjoyment of her own tremendous power as a sexual entity, but with understanding and insightful appreciation, as in Hinojosa's vignettes of "Fira the blond" and Viola Barragán, is delineated in the title poem of Bruce-Novoa's forthcoming bilingual book of poetry by the same name, *Inocencia perversa/Perverse Innocence*. In it, we see the discovery by a young girl, a "niña," of her sensual and sexual being without the author's condemning her, judging her, or punishing her in any way for exploration of her "coming to know life" through an extension of her "sueños infantiles" into reality.

Inocencia perversa

Niña,
nunca me habías contado
que de niña,
soñabas que te tocaban aquí

hasta que de tan mojada
despertabas a olerte los dedos
y seguir cálidamente acurrucada
en la vigilia de la inocencia
de tus años perversamente virginales;
como no me contaste,
sino hasta en este momento de agotamiento
que remoja las paredes
de éste, tu cuarto de juegos
                              infantiles,
donde aún nos mira tu muñeca
que se murió del susto
con los ojos de terciopelo pelados,
que cuando primero me conociste,
por aquí mismo,
las hormigas de esos sueños
te mordieron por primera vez de día,
y toda la tarde,
la voz de la maestra
se perdía
en el olor de tus sueños
de inocente,
y sólo la mirada constante
de tu súbitamente desesperante amiga
no te dejó traértelo más cerca,
untado en los dedos
como de costumbre,
pero ya sabías
que habías entrado
a la más impaciente de las vigilias,
del sueño a medio día
y la ya intolerable singularidad
de los juegos secretos,
cada vez más devastadores,
en que esa misma muñeca
se quedara triste
por ya no bastarte
y prever con sus ojos de terciopelo verde
mi presencia deseada y provocadamente violadora
en ésta, tu cama de sueños
                              infantiles;
y no me dejaste ni pensar,
aunque oscuramente lo sintiera,
que habías imaginado
las trece posibles posiciones
que querías experimentar la primera vez,
viéndonos en ellas
desde todos los rincones del cuarto
y hasta reflejados

en el espejo que inclinaste
para vernos desde allá
                desde acá,
sin saber que ya no verías
nada más que a ti misma
ahogándote en la inocencia perversa
del último de tus juegos infantiles,
el primero de tus infantiles juegos;
mas ahora me lo cuentas
todo a la vez
al darme las gracias
por haberme esperado tanto,
por durarme duro tanto,
por haberte dolido tanto
y si no puedo apurarme un tanto
para ya reempezar;
y al buscar el olor conocido,
saltan tus ojos sorprendidos al encontrar
el nuevo,
este más espeso que te traje yo,
"qué extraño" repites,
"qué extraño, pero me gusta,"
sonriendo contenta de que ahora
otros dedos te lo traen,
y los besos, porque son míos, sí,
pero también para probarte-y-nósenlos;
y después de contármelo todo,
te quedas inquietamente quieta,
mirando éste, tu cuarto de sueños
                                    infantiles,
hasta abrazarme de repente
y casi sollozando,
casi demandando,
pedirme: "ya, ¿no?"
pero, Niña, las vigilias,
las verdaderamente desesperantes,
acaban de empezar,
porque los hombres no son sueños,
ni encantados caballos de madera,
incansables en el vuelo,
y hay que esperar a que la imagen
que provocaste y devoraste
se reforme;
pero no llores,
cuéntame más de tus sueños
que te despertaban
tan mojada como ahora,
y acurrúcate en la cálida inocencia
de tus años virginalmente perversos
y espérame un poco más,

Niña,
　　un poquito más.[30]

The essence of the poem lies in the positive interpretation of the traditionally negative terms of "loss of virginal innocence" and "perversity." The girl neither loses her virginity nor her innocence in the sexual, physical act, yet she is socially and culturally perverse in traditional terms. A specifically anti-Chicano cultural poem, the irony here is in taking the negatives of traditional terms and making them positives, thereby creating tension in the field of the space of the poem that forces the traditional reader to retreat to the neutrality of the terms. In socially accepted and common terms, the girl is totally perverse; yet she has not lost her innocence at all. There has been no loss; she remains a child, innocent, and has gained in this one more fulfillment of her *sueños*. Bruce-Novoa said in an interview about his poem: "For, if anything, she expands the space of the possibilities of her innocence and virginity." She goes against all Chicano traditions in becoming a nymph, a delightful one at that, and her Chicano lover is equally as anti-Chicano culturally in that, unlike a stereotype macho, he wants to hear of her "sueños infantiles" while awaiting another erection. Both signal freedom from male and female stereotypic and traditional images for the Chicano.[31]

A woman's sexuality and sensuality have long been condemned as unbecoming, their very existence to be shunned among "good" women, because of tradition and the demands of their stereotypic roles. Bruce-Novoa states that freedom from those restrictive, culturally stifling limitations for both the Chicana and the Chicano lies in the very acceptance and total enjoyment of woman's sexuality. That the Chicana, like so many other oppressed women in all the world and among all cultures, has had to suffocate her sexual and sensual development, wants, and desires is here exposed and, by a Chicano author, shown to be a futile, perversely wrong, hypocritical, and only too powerful means of sexual subjugation. Bruce-Novoa, like Hinojosa, flaunts those traditionally stereotyped roles and images as being the exact opposite of what they have pretended to be. It is those traditional roles and images which are the perversity of the existence of the female, be she Chicana, Anglo, Puertorriqueña, Black, or whatever. In the following poem by Bruce-Novoa, "...the more things stay the same," we see woman trying only too desperately to live her life from one extreme to another—denying her very soul, her very being. It is not with impunity that she has swung

Judy Salinas

from one extreme, in her thinking, to another, sexually and personally. It must be understood by the reader that the word "whore," as is the word "virgin," is as much a stereotypic rhetorical device as any other word. In this poem and in all those of Bruce-Novoa, as well as in "Fira the Blond" by Hinojosa, the word "whore" is not used in the traditional way—it is no condemnation. It is an acceptance of what openly is contained and pulsates within all women. To *be* a "whore" does not mean that one *is* a whore. To sleep with many men or to make a living by doing so is not necessarily and should not be an immediate condemnation of that woman; she should be accepted as is any other human being—for simply being human. It is tradition and its roles for men and women, sexually and socially, which have demanded that the word have its derogatory and obviously socially unacceptable meaning, known to all. It is, however, in these works of Hinojosa, Bruce-Novoa, and to some extent in those of Morton and Portillo—all Chicanos—that a woman is no longer condemned, judged, and punished as severely for being what she is: an infinite dichotomy, a powerful, potentially creative and procreative being in all areas of life. The final lines of the following poem are no condemnation of her; it is a sad poem, not because the woman is called a "whore," but because she has not come to accept herself for being more than just *two* entities—an innocent and naive virgin or an evil and worldly-wise whore. That Bruce-Novoa concentrates upon the sexual and sensual to express himself makes his presentation of woman nonetheless valid and nonetheless important to literature, and to Chicano literature in particular; for, it points out a universal aspect of Chicano literature constantly ignored and missed by critic and author alike.

> . . .*the more things stay the same*

She came
>> to the edge
>> riding the wire
>> one hand in the orator's pledge
>> insisting she had changed.

She came
>> dressed in images
>> snipped from doggerel
>> extemporized and discarded
>> over wine and blood-tongue sausage
>> french bread or german rye
>> I never knew she swept up crumbs
>> for her scrapbook.

The Role of Women

She came
      displaying herself
      like the whore she is
      saying
            I've changed,
      aren't you shocked?
      I've loved many men
      selectively, or all at once,
      I use them at my own convenience;
      kinky sex is my latest toy,
      seducing children—22 or 64—
      teaching them to blow here behind my ears,
      while I suck or bite or masturbate;
      I've changed,
      you might not know me
      and that makes me so afraid.

She came
      with whispered stories
      of sadism—onanism—pederism—
      sodomy and other sundry glories;
      oh how I've reveled and oh how I've suffered and
      oh how I've broken the rules;
      you should have seen me!
      you really should have. . .
      It would have shocked you
      I'm sure.

She came
      then sighed,
      sometimes on the ledge I feel you
      at the tottering brink I see you
      from the indifference of not caring
      onto whose cock I'm staring
      I catch shattered fragments of you;
      I've changed so. . .
      but you said I would come
      to be what I am
      you foretold my every move
      we must have been truly in love
      for you to know me so well
      you were a genius to have seen my changes.

No.
Changed?
Foretell?
Hell
You're the same old whore
I knew as young.[32]

This same duality of character of good and evil is seen in Ultima, the "good" curandera from *Bless Me, Ultima* by Anaya, although "evil" and any of its traces are punished even though Ultima is a good person. She uses her herbs, spells, and incantations only for the good of the people, yet she is feared and shunned by many of them, even those she helps. And simply because she is involved in the "black arts," the unknown, she too, like the bad curanderas, like Doña Bárbara, Doña Marina, and Doña Josefa, must be punished for her seeming transgressions against what is natural for the role of a woman. On her deathbed, she describes herself as an avenging force which used evil against evil in an attempt to destroy it.

> 'My work was to do good, ...I was to heal the sick and show them the path of goodness. But I was not to interfere with the destiny of any man. Those who wallow in evil and brujería cannot understand this. They create a disharmony that in the end reaches out and destroys life—With the passing away of Tenorio and myself the meddling will be done with, harmony will be reconstituted. That is good. Bear him no ill will—I accept my death because I accept to work for life—'[33]

She is good, yet she too must be punished by death in a traditional way.

This duality of the female nature is accurately described by the Mexican poet Octavio Paz in his chapter on "Los hijos de La Malinche" from his essay *El laberinto de la soledad,* concentrating on the identification problems of the hybrid Mexican who can neither accept nor reject his cultural duality. Of woman, Paz says:

> La mujer, otro de los seres que viven aparte, también es figura enigmática. Mejor dicho, es el Enigma. A semejanza del hombre de raza o nacionalidad extraña, incita y repele. Es la imagen de la fecundidad, pero asimismo de la muerte. En casi todas las culturas las diosas de la creación son también deidades de destrucción. Cifra viviente de la extrañeza del universo y de su radical heterogeneidad, la mujer ¿esconde la muerte o la vida?, ¿en que piensa?, ¿piensa acaso?, ¿siente de veras?, ¿es igual a nosotros? El sadismo se inicia como venganza ante el hermetismo femenino o como tentativa desesperada para obtener una respuesta de un cuerpo que tememos insensible. Porque, como dice Luis Cernuda, 'el deseo es una pregunta cuya respuesta no existe'. A pesar de su desnudez—redonda, plena—en las formas de la mujer siempre hay algo que desvelar:
>
> > Eva y Cipris concentran el misterio
> > del corazón del mundo.
>
> Para Rubén Darío, como para todos los grandes poetas, la mujer no es solamente un instrumento de conocimiento, sino el conocimiento

mismo. El conocimiento que no poseeremos nunca, la suma de nuestra definitiva ignorancia: el misterio supremo.[34]

Paz simplifies the mystery of woman by asking whether she, in dual spirit, hides death or life behind her deceptive mask. Does she signal the continued downfall and ruin and destruction of man and mankind or does she bear the hope and solutions for a better future for man and mankind? The most logical answer, if it be an answer, is that she was and will be both and do both again and again. This enigmatic portent of her role in Chicano society is dramatically presented in the play "El Jardín" by Carlos Morton. In this drama we see the transition of the Chicana Eve from a coquettish, silly, capricious, selfish, demanding, impatient, bored, dissatisfied, vain, and "capable of anything" woman into a contemporary, thoughtful, and human Chicana Eve living in South Chicago and repaying Adam and all mankind for having caused the exile from the Garden of Eden. She does so by trying to convince him not to fight the system with guns and violence in order to right injustices and destroy oppression and discrimination, but rather to join forces with the peaceful and godlike side of his nature and go to California to fight evil with a united Raza under the leadership of César Chávez.

At the beginning of this parody of the downfall of man, Morton presents Eva as totally bad, but it is her experiences with the Serpiente/Devil and, in the conquest of Mexico by the Spanish, in particular her relationship with Hernán Cortés as his mistress La Malinche, which along with recurring dreams and destructive periods of man, give the decisive impetus to transition from evil "bad" women to "good" yet human contemporary Chicana. She embodies the spirits of both the Christian Eve and the pagan Indian Mexican Eve, Malinche, traitoress of the Aztec empire. It is through her character also that we recognize the duality of all humans, the godlike and devillike tendencies in each of us. The first description of Eva is given in the directions to the actors who are to portray the characters. "Eva: Media coquetona. Le gusta el escándalo. Desea aventura. Es caprichosa y capaz de cualquier cosa."[35] The play opens with God setting the scene as a voice from the darkness and commences with Adán and Eva discussing the Serpiente and their life in the Garden.

> Dios: (Voice) Soy la voz de Dios. I have been speaking to mis hijos since the first hombre appeared on earth. His name was Adán and he lived in El Jardín and he had a ruca named Eva who was rather coquetona. ¿Se acuerdan? (Lights)
>
> A: ¿Has estado hablando con la Serpiente, eh?

E: Sí, pues.

A: No tienes vergüenza.

E: Ahhh, he's not so bad.

A: What do you mean, tonta, he's evil!

E: He has such a nice slick body. . .he's soooooo sllliiiiiiimmmmmyy!

A: (Crossing himself) Madre mía! Mira qué ruca ésta! What difference does his body make? You should judge a man by his spirit!

E: That's your way of thinking, ése, I'm more inclined towards the flesh.

A: It turns you on, huh! Well it doesn't excite me. You are a carnal creature, Eva. . .Oh Lord. . .If I catch that snake around here again, ésa, I'm going to wring it around your neck.

E: The way he slides, slithers, on the ground. . .Uuuuummmmmm . . .He's so evil!

A: ¿Pero cómo puedes ser tan pendeja? Don't you know that he'll lead you into temptation?

E: ALL I KNOW is that he wants to teach me about life, about knowledge.

A: Eva, you're going to get us evicted from el Jardín. . .Acuérdate lo que dijo el Jefe.

E: Oh, I'm tired of all that jive the Man has been laying down on you! He's a big ranchero and we're nothing but peones. We're like playthings to him! Look, all we do is sit around all day with these tame tigers and lambs. I feel like I'm in some kinda zoo. I feel captured. Hey! I wanna little action, I wanna swing, baby. How come we never go DANCING!

A: Now you listen here! We are not his slaves and He is not our master. We have free will. He is very good to us, and under no circumstances do I want to anger him.

E: Oh, let him kick us out, I don't care. . .see if he can find two other suckers to take our place.[36]

Eva continues to reject every reason that Adán gives for wanting to stay in the Garden and for liking their existence there and complains further:

E: . . . .we're no better than WORMS to him!

A: What are you saying. . .but of course we're no better than worms . . .or whales for that matter. . .en los ojos de Dios todos somos iguales. And don't you forget it!

E: Oh, that rap you give me about equality and justice is like a tired, old psalm. Listen, brother, if we really had freedom in this here JUNGLE we'd be able to come and go as we pleased. How come we can't go visiting or touring? How come we can't fly outta here like that dumb bird over there?

A: Eva, no quiero irme del Jardín.

E: Well, I do. I'm bored. I'm stagnating. I'm depressed. I'm not satisfied!. . . .There's nothing to do here except hear the birds go

"tweet, tweet, tweet," and the sheep go "Ba, baaa, baaaaaaaa!"
Look, I want to do something with my hands, and I want to
make something. I wanna buy things. Like jewelry and clothes.[37]

Adán appeals to her vanity by saying that she needs no clothes nor
ornamentation because God made her beautiful and perfect, but her
vanity does not accept his arguments. Further, she is jealous of the
only unicorn in the Garden, wanting to make a coat for herself out of
his hide.

E: He thinks he's better than we are! You know something, I don't
like that unicorn at all, he looks at me funny. Do you know what
else, I want his hide for a coat!
A: ¿Qué te pasa? ¿Estás loca?
E: I WANT THAT DAMN UNICORN OUT OF MY LIFE![38]

God interrupts, wondering what the commotion is about and that
leads to Eva questioning who Dios is and where he comes from.

E: But where did he come from?
A: He has always been here and he will always be here.
E: Oh, yeah, that makes a lotta sense!
A: That's just the way it is.
E: Oh, brother, that's another thing that bugs the HELL OUTTA
me. . . .
A: No digas esa palabra!
E: There's no free speech en el Jardín.
A: Cállate la boca.
E: WHAAAAY CAN'T I HAVE AN AAPPPPLLLE!
A: No!
E: This diet of arroz y frijoles y tortillas is ruining my figure. Why
can't I have a nice lambchop. I'd even settle for a hotdog or unos
taquitos de pollo y lechuga y guacamole y chile—Ay qué rico!
Y un vaso de vino![39]

After Adán rejects an occasion for intimacy with Eva and leaves to
go to Bible Study class instead, Eva paces around angrily and complains aloud just before the Serpiente enters.

E: Why can't I have my way
Why do I have to stay
Here in the green Jardín
Sure it's a calm place
And larks sing, gazelles race
It hardly rains at all
Fruit from the trees does fall
Creatures both large and small
Love one and they love all
We always sleep late
Angels guard the gate

Judy Salinas

> It never gets cold here
> Nothing can be sold here
>
> But I need more than this
> More than complacency
> Or smug security
> I want to dance, I want to shout
> I want to leap, I want to fly out
> But more than just wanting to go
> Most important, I want to know

The Serpiente enters:

> E: ¡AAAyyyyyyy! Un Monster!
> S: ¿Qué monster, ni qué mi abuela!
> E: ¡Ay, qué feo eres!
> S: Hey, you just don't appreciate style and class. I'm Coco Roco.
> E: Te ves más como un coco loco que nada.
> S: ¡Baaaaah! That's the trouble with you, hyphenated Mexicans, you can't appreciate other culturas, ésa.
> E: Yo no soy "hy phenated," ése, Yo soy chicana!
> S: ¡Tu madre!
> E: La tuya que está en vinagre.
> S: Eres chicana, ¿eh? ¡A ver esta ruca![40]

After looking her over and flirting with her, he tells her that she is a "white woman living under the Gachupín Gods" and that her mind is poisoned by their treacherous white ways.[41] She protests and the Serpiente predicts her future which she also does not believe; so, to convince her, he takes her to a pyramid on earth to show her.

> S: You live here in paradise, ésa, in glory, worshipping the Gabacho God who will one day come with the soldados de España to land on our shores with promises of a new world under the domain of Jesucristo and El Rey de España. And you will be there and your name will be Malinche and you will betray the Aztec people, tu raza! You will interpret for the bearded ones and divulge all our secrets and you will even mate with their leader, Hernán Cortés, and the first of a bastard race will be born in Méjico.[42]

The Serpiente tempts her finally with the apple itself. He is standing over her atop the pyramid, holding a knife in his hands.

> S: Is not this apple red and ripe
>   Something to want to make you bite
>   Into the juices of your brain
>   Suck out creation, go insane.
> E: ¡Ay, aya, ay! ¡Qué locura!
> S: Would you not like to masticate
>   Forbidden fruit at this late date
>   Ingest your mind with this explosion

Blast off from heaven into motion
E: ¡Háblame en español!
S: Mujer chicana, mujer del sol
   Tu piel refleja la belleza de esa estrella
   Que mi cuchillo de oro
   Se case con tu cuerpo de bronce.[43]

As the Serpiente cuts into the red apple, Eva has become his pagan sacrificial victim on the altar of the pyramid, comingling the bloods and cultures of Chicano ancestry. Eva still hesitates to bite into the apple and asks if she will finally receive the material possessions, praise, tribute, worship, and devotion of all mankind for biting into the fruit. The Serpiente assures her that she will.

E: I can have a unicorn coat and a Golden Chariot to ride in?
S: Once you discover the wheel, my little quesadilla, you'll have millions of peones to serve you.
E: I'll move out of el Jardín and into a more fashionable neighborhood!
S: They'll build pyramids for you, launch thousands of ships for you!
E: Will I be worshipped?
S: Men will DIE for you!
E: Will they APPRECIATE me?
S: You will be a source of wealth and the Genesis of birth.
E: I will CREATE?
S: My little chile pepper, you will create millions of men. Just as Dios has done in his image. And some of them will go back to heaven, but MOST OF THEM WILL COME TO ME AND FUEL THE FIRES OF HELL![44]

When Eva realizes that the Serpiente is the Devil she starts to rise from the slab, but it is too late, the innocence that was hers has been replaced by the juices of the apple. The Serpiente fades away as Adán approaches and Eva easily convinces Adán to bite into the forbidden fruit.

E: Baby eat this red ripe fruit
   Swear to God it makes you shoot
   Take a bite, it tastes real good
   Eat it, honey, wish you would
A: You little fool, you've cast us out
   Of el Jardín, where we, devout
   Had lived an ageless loving life
   Without death, without cruel strife
E: Adán, cómetela si me quieres.
A: To join her in her cursed state
   A life of whim, a life of fate

> To leave all that I loved behind
> To join the wheel and low and whine
> A bigger fool is he than she
> To eat from the Forbidden Tree.[45]

But, he does join her and immediately they are faced with the responsibilities, hardships and pains of providing for themselves for the first time.

At the end of the play after the transition, Eva is not depicted by the author as an idealized "good" woman, but rather as one who kept a faith and changed from her selfishness in the Garden to become the symbol of hope and progress for the entire Chicano ethnic group. Because she learns that Adán and a friend are going to kill a gringo who has wronged them, she calls upon Dios in prayer to come to help Adán. It is God who tells her of her symbolism as the bearer of La Raza's future hope and progress.

> E: Ay, Dios Mío. ¡Tienes que ayudar a Adán! Está perdiendo la razón. I heard him and Matón talking about it. ¡Van a matar un gringo esta noche!
> D: Está perdiendo su corazón.
> E: El Diablo se lo robó.
> D: Yes, but it is man who willingly gives it up. He has the power to do evil because he is already part Diablo, just as he is part Dios. ¿No te acuerdas? You taught me.
> E: It seems so long ago, as though it were a dream. Pero, sabes, I've had many others since then. . .especially one, which left a great impression on me. . .it was about a wheel of many different colors, una rueda grandota, that was rolling down a road that went up to the sky. . .and the wheel was singing in many different languages. Isn't that strange?
> D: No, mi hija—it's prophetic. You are a seer of La Raza's futuro; that many-colored wheel is the circle of racial harmonia singing together down the road of the future and we are the people who must set an example to all of the others because we are the hub, the center of that wheel. La Raza is in the middle of black and white, ¿ves?[46]

Adán is saved and the play ends with both Eva and Adán going out to California with their baby to join César Chávez.

In blending the traditional Eve with the Mexican Eve, Malinche, Morton gives us an interpretation of the vital, symbolic role of woman and the Chicana in particular in contemporary society. His interpretation is like Paz's in *El laberinto* in the chapter on the "Hijos de la Malinche." Both Eves have been violated and are considered betrayors of their cultures; yet it is they who hold the key to the future success of those cultures and of mankind—coalition and acceptance of the openness and the harmony that being of two or more cultures should and must provide for progress to be ensured. Paz summarizes this interpretation in the following paragraph.

> . . .el pueblo mexicano no perdona su traición a la Malinche. Ella encarna lo abierto, lo chingado, frente a nuestros indios, estoicos, impasibles y cerrados. Cuauhtémoc y Doña Marina son así dos símbolos antagónicos y complementarios. Y si no es sorprendente el culto que todos profesamos al joven emperador, . . .tampoco es extraña la maldición que pesa contra la Malinche. De ahí el éxito del adjetivo despectivo "malinchista", recientemente puesto en circulación por los periódicos para denunciar a todos los contagiados por tendencias extranjerizantes. Los malinchistas son los partidarios de que México se abra al exterior: los verdaderos hijos de la Malinche, que es la Chingada en persona. De nuevo aparece lo cerrado por oposición a lo abierto. . . .Al repudiar a la Malinche—Eva mexicana, . . .el mexicano rompe sus ligas con el pasado, reniega de su origen y se adentra solo en la vida histórica.[47]

It is in certain very humorous and human vignettes of Rolando Hinojosa's work, *Estampas del valle y otras obras*, that we see the new treatment or portrayal of woman. The Chicana woman, being a participant in both Hispanic and Anglo cultures and a product of both, enjoys the advantages and disadvantages of the restrictive traditions of the Hispanic female role as well as the freer more liberated responsibilities thrust upon her by Anglo influences. In Hinojosa's work, there is little if any moral judgment, condemnation, or punishment for the woman who dabbles in superstitions or the black arts or for the prostitute or mistress who has traditionally been the "baddest" of women. In the selection "My Aunt Panchita," we see the family's "good" curandera performing her duties; however, there is no threat of an untimely death, nor is a life-death struggle against evil evident. She is a necessary, accepted, tolerated, although sometimes teased, member of the family, but she is no Ultima nor a Tenorio sister. Hinojosa vividly pictures her role in the following excerpts:

> 'Where's the patient?'. . .
> 'Okay, close the curtains. Everybody out and close the door behind you, I'm gonna begin.'
> Aunt Panchita took out a brownish egg from the grocery bag and made the sign of the cross with it over Rafa Buenrostro's face. Then she made another sign of the cross covering his entire body and began to pray:
> . . . .
> Aunt Panchita repeated the prayer, the incantation and the offer-

ing twice then broke the egg in a green plate which she placed under the bed. Rafa Buenrostro breathed deeply and fell into a sleep that lasted a day and a half.[48]

Like Ultima and Lela she is a very religious woman and only tries to do good and help people, but culturally her religiousness does not prevent her from using traditional pagan customs or superstitious rituals for dealing with maladies of the body and soul. Unlike Ultima, however, she isn't going to die for involvement with such forces.

It is primarily in Hinojosa's presentations of the prostitute and the mistress that we see a totally unreserved acceptance of such roles with a complete absence of moral condemnation and punishment. This attitude is exemplified first in the following selection, "Fira the Blond":

> Without beating around the bush: Fira the Blond is a whore. She doesn't pretend to be a whore (like maids do) nor does she whore around (like society women); no. Fira's a whore and that's that. There's more. Fira has blue eyes, short hair which she doesn't dye and a figure that would stop the hiccups of Don Pedro Zamudio, the parish priest.
>
> Fira isn't from around here. . . .but, truthfully, she certainly has to be the most beautiful woman of the Valley. . . .
>
> Fira is a serious woman who carries her whoredom like school girls carry their books: naturally. After she bathes, she smells of soap and water and when she goes to work, the curls by her temples are still wet.
>
> She works in the tavern owned by Félix Champión, an illegitimate son of my Uncle Andrés. She neither dances nor struts from table to table nor flirts nor carries on. Don Quixote used to say that being a go-between was serious business; that may be, but the occupation of being a whore in a simple tavern of a one horse town is nothing to laugh about either.
>
> The women of Klail know who she is and what she is and that's it. If they gossip, that's their business but the majority don't; the majority don't gossip. Women usually tend to be understanding when they feel like it.
>
> The only bad part of it all is that Fira won't last much longer in Klail: It's too small and, to tell the truth, money's scarce around here.[49]

Women and men can be understanding of other human beings when they want to be and it is this point that Hinojosa subtly stresses. Fira is not punished for being a prostitute, except for having a hard time financially because of the size of the town. He implies that her goodness or badness has nothing at all to do with her profession or some indiscretion she might commit against society. She is just human like anybody else; she hasn't even necessarily strayed from any righteous path; she is just trying to survive in a tough world. Hinojosa obviously respects Fira for her honesty and her naturalness. She doesn't pretend to be a Doña Marina nor a Doña Josefa, unrealistically living a life of lies. This same nonjudgmental portrayal is seen in the character Viola Barragán, a twice-widowed, fairly well-to-do Chicana who has returned to the Valley after traveling the world over. She decides to become the mistress of one Pioquinto Reyes, whom she picks out of a crowd as being a man whom she could like. Hinojosa sums up her relationship with Reyes as his mistress in the following excerpts:

> . . .Death took Pioquinto at the Holiday Inn on Highway 11 in front of what was, in its better days, the edge of the black ghetto.
> Pioquinto didn't work in the motel: he was a guest; . . .When he heard the trumpet announcing his day of judgment, Pioquinto was mounted atop Viola Barragán, a woman who, some twenty years back, was the best piece of ass around and who is still giving people something to talk about. Pioquinto kicked the bucket, so to speak, in full swing, taking up the harp like anybody else.
> . . . .
> It happened that after the burial when everyone had left, a woman. . .went over to the mound of earth where Pioquinto was resting. From her. . .purse, she took out a knotted handkerchief that she untied producing a gold ring that was neither wide nor thick. As she buried the ring at the foot of the mound, she soiled her gloves but she didn't seem to mind the mud that had formed there. . .There were no prayers nor sobs, but rather a resigned look, with her head held high, clear-eyed and without the slightest trace of emotion on her lips.[50]

Viola appears to be devoid of deep passion for Pioquinto, but her caring and love for him are evident in her gesture. In flashback form, Hinojosa gives further circumstances of Pioquinto's death:

> When Pioquinto gave up the ghost in the Holiday Inn, Viola (whom nothing could frighten anymore) dressed leisurely, left the room and elegantly went to Edgerton where she detached herself from the situation as if nothing had happened. Pioquinto was found by a janitor who notified the manager who etc., etc., . . .
> . . . .
> Viola? Doing all right, thank you. Now, at fifty some odd years she still holds up well against time. That bit about the ring, if it need to be mentioned, was a first class gesture, one of generosity worthy of instruction to those of little heart.[51]

Even though Viola flouts tradition in her relationship with a married man, she is not presented as a "bad" woman. She is not punished. As the final lines indicate, she is doing just fine. Hinojosa shows that

Judy Salinas

both Fira and Viola, who would traditionally have been depicted as "bad" women in Hispanic literatures, are just plain human.

Conclusion

Thus, we have seen that the traditional stereotypes of the "good" woman and the "bad" woman still persist in Chicano works with the softened idealization of the good mother and wife and the moral judgment and punishment of the female evil-doer. But, we have significantly pointed out that in Portillo's works "The Day of the Swallows" and "The Paris Gown" compassion and understanding for the protagonist are elicited, while in "El Jardín" by Morton the evil Eve comes to represent the symbol of hope and progress for the Chicano future. In Hinojosa's work *Estampas*, we have seen that no moral judgments occur at all; he totally rejects the idea of punishing woman for any social or moral indiscretion, thus fully discarding the traditional stereotypes of "good" and "bad" women, as does Bruce-Novoa in his works. In the latter's poems, we have seen a loved, respected, accepted, and realistic image of woman which more truly makes her human in dimension than in almost any other work, save Hinojosa's. Chicano literature offers a realistic and more acceptable image of woman than has been the case in traditional literary treatment, for she is at last depicted and accepted as a human being.

STATE UNIVERSITY OF NEW YORK, BINGHAMTON

Notes

[1]José Montoya, "La jefita," in *El Espejo - The Mirror, Selected Chicano Literature*, eds. Octavio Romano-V. and Herminio Ríos C. (Berkeley: Quinto Sol Publications, 1972), pp. 232-33.

[2]Raymond Barrio, *The Plum, Plum Pickers*, (Sunnyvale, Ca.: Ventura Press, 1969), pp. 2-3. (All further citations from this novel will be indicated at the end of the citation with the page number only).

[3]Rudolfo A. Anaya, *Bless Me, Ultima* (Berkeley: Quinto Sol, 1972), pp. 91-92.

[4]Estela Portillo Trambley, "The Burning," in *Rain of Scorpions* (Berkeley: Tonatiuh International, 1975), p. 89.

[5]Ibid.

[6]Ibid., pp. 90-91.

[7]Ibid., p. 94.

[8]Ibid., p. 95.

[9]Ibid., pp. 95-96.

[10]Ibid., p. 95.

[11]Ibid., p. 96.

[12]Octavio Romano-V., "A Rosary for Doña Marina," in *El Espejo*, pp. 75-93.

[13]Portillo, "The Day of the Swallows," *El Espejo*, p. 169.

[14]Ibid., p. 185.

[15]Ibid., p. 186.

[16]Ibid., p. 188.

[17]Ibid., p. 189.

[18]Richard Vásquez, *Chicano*, translated by Rafael Zavala Piñón, (México: Editorial Novaro, S.A., 1972), pp. 382-383.

[19]Ibid., p. 384.

[20]Ibid., p. 389.

[21]Estela Portillo, "The Paris Gown," in *El Grito*, VI, No. 4 (Summer, 1973), p. 11.

[22]Ibid., p. 13.

[23]Ibid., p. 14.

[24]Ibid., p. 15.

[25]Ibid.

[26]Ibid., p. 16.

[27]Ibid., pp. 18-19.

[28]Jorge Alvarez, "Woman," *El Espejo*, p. 247.

[29]Bruce-Novoa, "La araña negra," *Inocencia Perversa/ Perverse Innocence* (Phoenix: Baleen Press, 1976). Also read at Popular Culture Conference, Chicago, April, 1976.

[30]Bruce-Novoa, "Inocencia perversa," originally published in *Inscape*, IV, No. 3 (1974), pp. 8-15.

[31]Bruce-Novoa, "Inocencia perversa," quotes and material from personal interview with author about book of the same name, Chicago, April, 1976.

[32]Bruce-Novoa, ". . .the more things stay the same," unpublished poem read in interview, Chicago, April, 1976.

[33]Anaya, *Ultima*, p. 247.

[34]Octavio Paz, "Hijos de la Malinche," *El laberinto de la soledad* (México: Fondo de Cultura Económica, 1970), pp. 59-60.

[35]Carlos Morton, "El Jardín," *El Grito Book Series*, VII, 4 (June-August, 1974), p. 7.

[36]Ibid., pp. 7-9.

[37]Ibid., p. 9.

[38]Ibid., p. 10.

[39]Ibid., p. 11.

[40]Ibid., p. 12.

[41]Ibid., p. 13.

[42]Ibid., p. 13.

[43]Ibid., pp. 19-20.

[44]Ibid., p. 20.

[45]Ibid., p. 22.

[46]Ibid., p. 33.

[47]Paz, *El laberinto*, p. 78.

Judy Salinas

[48]Rolando Hinojosa-S., *Estampas del valle y otras obras* (Berkeley: Quinto Sol, 1973), p. 80.

[49]Ibid., p. 82.

[50]Ibid., p. 141.

[51]Ibid, p. 139-40.

CONTEMPORARY CHICANO PROSE FICTION: A CHRONICLE OF MISERY

Charles M. Tatum

With the increasing militancy among blacks in this country has come the publication of a plethora of literature, giving testimony to the increasing awareness of a largely ignored cultural heritage. Until recently, no such rash of publications has coincided with the social movement among Mexican-Americans. However, within the last few years there has appeared with ever-increasing frequency a number of anthologies, collections of poetry, drama, short fiction, novels, and essays. As a body of Chicano literature begins to take shape, certain tendencies and characteristics are emerging that can be of value to the literary critic as he begins to define and describe this new wave of artistic creation.

A cursory examination of contemporary Chicano prose fiction, for example, reveals that the majority of novels and short stories published by Chicano authors within the last fifteen years deals directly with some aspect of the social reality of the community of Spanish-speaking people who began to emigrate to the United States shortly after the Mexican Revolution of 1910. Most of the writers turn back to the bitter experiences of these Mexican refugees, their arrival in this country, and their adjustment to an alien Anglo culture. While much of the literature resembles the direct Steinbeck style of social realism, it also contains several biographical and autobiographical accounts of discrimination, isolation and acculturation in a strange society. Considering Chicano fiction as a whole, it offers us a chronicle of a half-century of misery. Its effect is cathartic, providing a release for the accumulated suffering and frustration so that a new consciousness of *La Raza* might be formed from the experience.

Viewed historically, Chicano prose fiction covers a period that begins early in this century and continues now, in the urban *barrios* and in the agricultural fields of California and the Southwest. The depression, riots of the thirties and the forties, strikes, and the recent civil rights movement serve as the backdrop against which we see a whole culture in the process of transformation and adaptation to new ways and problems of existence. What is referred to euphemistically as "acculturation" and "assimilation" is refocused for us in these novels and short stories as survival based on the abandonment of traditions and language. The varied experiences of several generations are retold, allowing the reader to draw his own conclusions regarding the history of Chicanos in this country.

Several of the works trace the migration of refugees of the Mexican Revolution as they are uprooted from their homes and forced to undergo the abrupt transition from one culture to another. The novels, *Chicano* by Richard Vásquez and *Pocho* by José Antonio Villareal, and the autobiographical account, *Barrio Boy* by Ernesto Galarza, reflect various stages of this process of displacement. Galarza tells of his early boyhood in the isolated mountain village of Jalco in Central Mexico. Tradition dictates behavior in Jalco as the boy very early develops respect for the elders of the village and is slowly introduced into the community life of the town. Winds of the far-off revolution begin to blow harder when a local family receives word of a son who has fled north to the United States. Events take place in rapid succession thereafter as the boy and his family leave their village, join an uncle in Mazatlán, and then are forced to flee north again. Galarza poignantly describes his bewilderment upon arriving in the United States and, although he expresses no bitterness in retelling the events of his early boyhood, it is difficult for the reader to overlook the profound effect acculturation has on the child's perception of the world:

> Turning *pocho* was a half-step toward turning American. And America was all around us, in and out of the *barrio*. Abruptly we had to forget the ways of shopping in a *mercado* and learn those of shopping in a corner grocery or in a department store. The Americans paid no attention to the Sixteenth of September, but they made a great commotion about the Fourth of July. In Mazatlan Don Salvador had told us, saluting and marching as he talked to our class, that the Cinco de Mayo was the most glorious date in human history. The Americans had not even heard about it.[1]

A Chronicle of Misery

Chicano, like *Barrio Boy*, recounts the arrival of an unskilled refugee family—the Sandovals—in the United States. Having suffered equally at the hands of the *federales* and the revolutionaries, the family flees Mexico hoping to find security and prosperity in California. Instead, they are met with disillusionment. Like thousands of Mexicans, their entrance into this country is an inglorious one. Héctor Sandoval's initial impression sets the tone for the process of change he and his family will soon undergo. Expecting California to be green country, soft pastures, and farmlands, he finds, in contrast, rugged, rocky hills, barren except for brush, cactus, and an occasional group of stunted trees. "A great sense of being alone in unfriendly territory gripped the family."[2] Alone even among the Mexicans who, having preceded the Sandovals, are seen working the fields, scratching out a meager existence, Héctor is struck by the dismal living conditions of a refugee camp where he sees ragged children, barefoot, playing in the mud, and men sitting on street corners, victims of their own inactivity. He witnesses the legalized assassination of a countryman, shot down by American lawmen, the unashamed prostitution of teenage girls. The picture of the Promised Land is a tawdry one, filled with reminders of inferiority and shame.

Both *Chicano* and *Pocho* describe the profound effect immigration to the United States has on the Mexican male. Héctor Sandoval experiences a revived sexuality in his relationship to his wife Lita but at the same time suffers emasculation when he tries to earn a living as a picker. The constant humiliation in the fields drives him to heavy drink and he dies alone, one night, of a perforated ulcer.

The loss of dignity and masculinity is much more explicit in *Pocho* as the protagonist, Juan Rubio, is forced to abandon his role of a *mestizo* revolutionary to become lost in the wave of Mexican refugees flooding across the border. The Mexican-American anthropologist Octavio Romano describes this abrupt adaptation to Anglo culture in his essay "Goodbye Revolution, Hello Slum." For the first time in his history, the *mestizo* peasant had fought for a cause—personal, national, universal—and in so doing had developed a pride, a spirit that he was once again to be denied by the Texas Ranger, the symbol of his oppression in this country: "The Mexican refugee, called animal, traitor, and coward in Mexico, now in Texas is called greaser, spic, and bandit. For the refugees, this is for them the first step in the process known as acculturation."[3] Juan Rubio arrives in Juárez discouraged with the turn the revolution has taken but determined to join a new defensive. Instead, he is arrested in a barroom brawl and finds his way across the border into El Paso with the help of an old army friend. A once-proud Colonel who fought valiantly with Villa, Rubio is now reduced to running cattle for a rich American. For a time he lives with the hope he can redeem his past, by participating in the assassination of President Obregón, but when Juan learns of Villa's death, he becomes despondent, aware that the passing of this immortal demonstrates his own vulnerability.

The transition from the Mexican Revolution to the life of an immigrant, as described in Chicano fiction, is not a uniform one. It ranges from a young boy's reminiscences of a confusing series of changes to the bitter surrender of revolutionary status. However, if the revolution is not always looked on in a similar way, the three works thus far discussed do coincide in the protagonists' perception of an alien Anglo society and in their feeling of isolation and abandonment. The dreamed-of Utopia becomes (albeit in varying degrees) profound disillusionment.

The memory of Mexico, especially Mexico prior to the Revolution, remains strong for the older people who refuse to surrender their language and customs. Reacting instinctively to threats upon their culture, many of the refugee Chicanos band together in colonies, shutting out those elements that might threaten their solidarity in a strange land. In *Barrio Boy*, Galarza recalls the newly-arrived Mexicans who "were fond of identifying themselves by saying they had just arrived from *el macizo*, by which they meant the solid Mexican homeland, the good native earth. Although they spoke of *el macizo* like homesick persons, they didn't go back. They remained, as they said of themselves, *pura raza*."[4] Juan Rubio, in *Pocho*, dreams of the time when he will have saved enough money to return with his family to Mexico, a dream that helps him escape the misery that surrounds him.

If the old resist change, the incessant call of a seemingly better life coupled with a means of achieving equality begins to take its toll on another generation of Chicanos, the sons and daughters of the Juan Rubios and the Héctor Sandovals. *Barrio Boy*, subtitled "The Story of a Boy's Acculturation," gives us a glimpse of the initial stages of exchanging one's whole cultural background for another. Galarza describes this change in himself in terms of his experience in an Anglo-dominated educational system. He demonstrates the persistence and the means American society has at its disposal to obliterate deep cultural differences in the name of the mythical melting pot. The author's primary school experience probably represents the exception to the rule: his teachers are respectful of the racial and national diversity of their students. The young boy excels in school with the willing help of the teachers and his relationships with other Anglos are similar. The well-intentioned Mr. Howard, for example, encourages little Ernesto to read Horatio Alger and Blackstone's *Commentaries on the Common Law of England*. Mr. Charley, a neighbor, tells him of his charge up San Juan Hill with Colonel Teddy Roosevelt and how he dispatched dozens of Spaniards with his two horse pistols. Ernesto's adult friends are depicted as understanding and tender, but the result can only be viewed as catastrophic as gradually this young Mexican's past is bleached out by new values and customs.

Richard Rubio, in *Pocho*, represents a later and more complete stage of acculturation than the Chicano of *Barrio Boy*. The son of the revolutionary Juan, Richard is born in the United States and thus does not feel the same ties to Mexico as even the young Ernesto. Very early, he is led to question his Mexicanness, to develop a negative self-image, to begin to assume behavior patterns and characteristics he sees in his Anglo peers. Richard is ridiculed by his teacher for his curious mispronunciation of English. This eventually becomes a feeling of inadequacy on his part and a resolve to overcome what he sees as the source of his inferiority: "Although he liked his teacher he never forgave her for laughing at him, and from that day he was embarrassed whenever he was corrected by anyone."[5] Another element that contributes to his complex is the difference he observes between himself and those who hold themselves apart as *hispanos*, the offspring of the original Spanish conquerors and colonizers. Richard's own mother prefers to consider him of pure Spanish lineage rather than as an *indio*. He becomes self-conscious about his speech, the food served in the Rubio home, and his poverty; his escape becomes a fantasy world of books such as *Toby Tyler* and *Ten Weeks with the Circus*, books that take him far from the depressing effect his background has on him.

During the first years in the United States many of the young Chicano protagonists of the novels and short stories under consideration become more and more resentful of the values and traditions brought by their parents from Mexico. As they realize that the language and customs of their people are, by and large, unacceptable in an Anglo world, they reject what they are culturally, a process that often ends in personal psychological tragedy. However, not all of the authors view acculturation in the same light. Some manifest a less militant, more integrationist attitude.

Charles M. Tatum

José Antonio Villareal best represents this tendency in *Pocho*. As Ramón Ruiz points out in the introduction, the novel "can be studied as an historical piece that documents the intellectual-emotional evolvement of Mexican-Americans in a chronological sense."[6] That is, Villareal reflects the opinions of the forties and the fifties that Ruiz calls the assimilationist phase when most Mexican-Americans wanted to forget their past and join the American mainstream. In short, the novel is about an individual who tries to become totally Americanized while still struggling to reach a reconciliation with his cultural past.

Richard slowly begins to question the religious principles that formed an important part of his childhood, no longer taking literally his mother's Catholic beliefs nor accepting the cultural milieu out of which they came. As an adolescent he dates an Anglo girl and becomes more dependent on his fictional world of books; however, the vestiges of his Mexicanness still remain. He associates proudly with a gang of *pachucos* who, in their way, are searching for a means of expressing the frustration of their own truncated cultural past. For a time, Richard goes to the other extreme in his condemnation of whites and his defense of his new group of friends, but he decides he must break out of the *barrio* mold to fashion his own destiny. Richard joins the Navy, an act that is viewed by the novelist as tantamount to personal success.

Most of the other Chicano writers portray the *Pocho*, the Mexican who has assimilated into Anglo society, in a less favorable way. In the novel *Chicano*, the teenage Angelina Sandoval soon realizes that her relatively light skin can be an asset to her fading into white society. She is acutely sensitive to the taunts and insults of her peers at school who openly discriminate against the darker-skinned Mexicans such as her brother Gregorio. Angelina rebels openly against her parents, an act that shocks her own brothers and sisters who have never before openly questioned parental authority. She leaves home to establish herself in East Los Angeles, encouraging others in the family to do the same. Although the author, Richard Vásquez, does not suggest that the rigid, old country family ties must be preserved, he does imply that once the traditional family structure is broken down, the lot of these young Chicanos is a good deal worse. Los Angeles, symbol of urban progress, becomes the downfall of these men and women who abandon their own culture. Neftalí Sandoval, Angelina's father, senses why she has begun to behave in such a disrepectful way toward him: "I know, this never would have happened in Mexico. It's because you see all the *gringos* who have no sense of proper behavior. No one looks after the *gringas* to see that every man who happens by doesn't take advantage of them. It's because you've seen them in their loose way, that you no longer want to have propriety."[7] His daughter agrees, tearfully.

While Villareal would encourage the break from old ways, Vásquez sees the abandonment of traditional values as a tragic alternative. He never goes as far as condemning his characters for their attitudes and behavior; rather, he laments their having to choose between poverty and the retention of cultural identity. Anglo society, which is conceived as basically corruptive, forces the young Chicano into his dilemma by discriminating against the individual who continues to assert himself as a Mexican.

The *pocho*, the finished product who has accepted part-and-parcel American ways is satirized in the short "Cecilia Rosas" by Amado Muro. An autobiographical tale, Muro recreates his adolescent infatuation with a pretty salesclerk in an El Paso department store. While humorous in part, the overall effect of the story produces a vague uneasiness in the reader imparted by the author's description of Cecilia:

> Her beauty was Miss Rosas' only obvious vanity. But she had still another. She prided herself on being more American than Mexican because she was born in El Paso. And she did her best to act, dress, and talk the way Americans do. She hated to speak Spanish, disliked her Mexican name. She called herself Cecile Roses instead of Cecilia Rosas. This made the other salesladies smile derisively. They called her La Americana or the Gringa from Xochimilco every time they mentioned her name.[8]

Another important aspect of social reality that is described in Chicano prose fiction is the agricultural worker's experience. Historically, this experience begins with the large influx of Mexican war refugees, reaches its apogee during the twenties and thirties with the importation of *braceros*, and continues today on a seasonal basis in the fertile valleys of the Southwest, Midwest, and California. It fell to the lot of the recently arrived Mexican families to clear the desert lands, cultivate and irrigate the fields, and, finally, pick the crops. Carey McWilliams, the political scientist, gives a description of the circumstances under which these hapless individuals labored. The description can serve as a vivid introduction to this aspect of Chicano fiction:

> To appreciate what Mexican labor meant to the economy of the

Southwest, one simple, obvious fact needs to be stressed, namely, the desert or semi-desert character of the region. In the San Joaquín, Imperial, Salt River, Mesilla, and Lower Río Grande valleys, temperatures of 100, 110, and 112 degrees are not uncommon. Those who have never visited the copper mines of Morenci in July or the cotton fields of the San Joaquín Valley in September or the cantaloupe fields of Imperial Valley in June are hardly in a position even to imagine what Mexican workers have endured in these areas. It should be remembered that the development of the Southwest occurred at a time when the living and working conditions of American workingmen were undergoing rapid improvement. It was not easy to find in these years a large supply of labor that would brave the desert heat and perform the monotonous stoop-labor, hand-labor tasks which the agriculture of the Southwest demanded. Under the circumstances, the use of Mexican labor was largely non-competitive and nearly indispensable.[9]

Few Chicano authors deal in great detail with the early, pre-Depression years of the Mexican picker; however, there is enough to give us a reasonably complete picture of his generally pathetic situation. The Rubio family of the novel *Pocho* eventually settles in the Imperial Valley of California along with hundreds of other displaced and desperate refugees. Villareal focuses on the situation of the unfortunate melonpicker in this description:

The land had been reclaimed and the valley made artificially green and fertile, but the oppressive heat remained, and the people who tilled the fields, for the most part, came from the temperate climate of the central plateaus of Mexico and found it difficult to acclimatize. Every day, one or two or three of them were carried, dehydrated and comatose, from the field, placed in some shade, and administered cold-water spongings, until, revived and more than a little nauseous, they returned to the field to close the gap in the ranks made by their departure. Indeed, there were a few that year who died before they could receive help, and were carted off to El Centro, where they ended up in a pauper's grave or on a slab in some medical school in Los Angeles or San Francisco.[10]

The short story "Chronicle of Crystal City" recounts the early years of the importation of cheap Mexican farm labor to the cotton fields of the Río Grande Valley. Whole families would be put to work during the long, hot picking season and when the cotton had run out they would move slowly northward like a horde of homeless ants to Minnesota, North Dakota, and Wisconsin. The men, women, and children would be packed into open trucks with less care than normally given to livestock for a never-ending trek in search of a few day's pay.

Daniel Garza depicts part of the life of the cotton picker in his brief work "Saturday Belongs to the Palomía," the *palomía* referring to the gang of *pizcadores*, pickers, who would invade his town on weekends to escape the monotony and anguish of the fields. Even the Chicanos who are permanent residents are considered fortunate in comparison to the uprooted farm workers who find themselves far from homes and families. To try to break the never-ending cycle of work, the *palomía* engages in frenetic activity, brawling, and drunkenness during its short respite in the town. The narrator draws sharply the differences between whites and browns, owners and workers, those who must return to pick the cotton and those who enjoy the fruits of the pickers' toil.

Perhaps the work that most poignantly portrays the suffering and despair of the Mexican agricultural worker is *The Plum, Plum Pickers* by Richard Barrio, called by one critic the most significant novel of the decade in American literature.[11] Focusing on a proletarian way of life, Barrio presents a panorama of Chicano existence in dealing with the lives of a migrant couple, Manuel and Lupe Gutiérrez, who are caught in the crush of agricultural exploitation. Set in the imaginary migrant community of Drawbridge in California's Santa Clara Valley, the novel contains all the elements of the farm worker's struggle to free himself from the wall of indebtedness, hunger, and sickness that surrounds him.

Manuel, Lupe, and their two small children come north to the United States as thousands before them to seek the good life. Instead, they find themselves living in a miserable shack of the Western Grande Compound owned by the wealthy and powerful Mr. Frederick Y. Turner and operated by Morton J. Quill, a bigot whose livelihood depends on his ruthless exploitation of the Mexican fruit pickers. The lot of those who live in the Compound is a treadmill of hopeless exhaustion working from sun to sun, chasing the ripening crops from field to field, never saving enough to escape the year-in-year-out labyrinth of monotony and disappointment.

Mr. Frederick Turner has acquired his lands through the cynical manipulation of Anglo law, a legal system unfamiliar to the Spanish and Mexican settlers of California, the original owners of much of the territory. By tax defaults and sly but legal business deals he slowly puts together huge tracts of prime Northern California land on which his human chattel, mainly Mexicans, work themselves further into the debt of the Turner-owned country store. He is helped not only by Anglo officials but also by Mexicans themselves who sell out their own people to become *contratistas*, contractors of bodies, who are little better than slave traders.

It is Lupe Gutiérrez who suffers most deeply the constant insecurity and frustration of migrant life. Destined by her small children to spend the long and empty hours in a substandard shack that is her home, Lupe longs to return to Mexico, to bring to an end the hideous moving from north to south and back again, to find permanence for her family, to fulfill her dreams of being a good Mexican wife and mother:

> Would any of her dreams ever come true? No? Would she get a new dress? No? Ever? Never? When hair grew on trees perhaps. When would that be, Manuel, dear God, ay dios mío, Manuel out there, dios, dios, dios, picking all those tender cots, everybody and Roberto's crew, picking like filching idiots in the hot maniacal sun to the limit all summer long, storing away like squirrels for the hungry fall hunger and the starving winter, those long cold days, and for the nice rich people like the Turners, picking apricots, picking berries, picking pickles, picking luscious pears, picking prickly pears too, picking prunes, picking peaches, picking poison, picking grapes, stooping over to pick ripe tomatoes too, Ponderosa and those meaty tomatoes. Maybe they really did want her to become a prostitute. Maybe that was all there was to it. Mother, prostitute, and wife. Ay dios.[12]

As we have seen, a number of Chicano writers chronicle the dislocation, abandonment, discrimination, and suffering of their brown brothers in an often hostile Anglo world. The process of leaving one culture to adapt to another has taken its toll, not only in the fields and urban slums but also in the minds of men who have seen fit to reject their Mexicanness in exchange for acceptance. Implicit in the recalling of the past is a demand for change, a change based on a new awareness on the part of Chicanos of themselves and of their history, on developing a pride and an identity, on resisting substandard conditions in all areas of society. Some writers, however, express no hope for the future and their works betray a deep negativism that precludes a significant break from patterns of the past.

"The Week of the Life of Manuel Hernández" by Nick Vaca suggests this attitude. Following the formula of success proposed by one generation of educators, social scientists, and politicians, young Hernández "improves" himself through education, reaches the highest level of achievement by Anglo standards to become a university professor. Interspersed with quotes from Kierkegaard and Kropotkin, the reader follows his rise through the ranks of academia only to find, at the end, what he already knew as a child: the terrible bitterness of being different and thus not accepted. When Manuel is criticized by his colleagues for publishing articles that are socially relevant but not sufficiently professional, he suffers a breakdown that ends in suicide.

Contrasted to this despair is an acceptance of the status quo, a resignation to the process of acculturation as seen in the short story "Back to Bachimba" by Enrique López. The protagonist, like Manuel Hernández, has been Americanized in the schools and realizes on a visit to Mexico that it is impossible to retrace his steps, to be included in a circle of fellow Mexican intellectuals. He feels regret yet is content to conclude that "Much has been gained and will be gained from the multiethnic aspects of the United States, and there is no useful purpose in attempting to wish it away or to homogenize it out of existence. In spite of the race riots in Watts and ethnic unrest elsewhere, there would appear to be a kind of modus vivendi developing on almost every level of American life."[13]

There is pessimism and resignation but also anger and signs of a new militancy expressed by Chicano writers in their works. There is the anger of Carlos Vélez in his story "So Farewell Hope, and with Hope, Farewell Fear" in which a young man, returned from Vietnam, recalls the shame and indignity of his boyhood: the indignation of his father when he learns the school insists on changing his son's name from Ricardo to Richard, the deep-felt embarrassment of being singled out for punishment by his Anglo teachers, the pang of shame when he hears himself called Mexican. Ricardo remembers dropping out of high school to join the Marine Corps, being seriously wounded in Vietnam, and sent back to a hospital in the United States. The gun he has kept through the ordeal symbolizes his new-found determination to resist, to refuse to continue along the same path as those before him. The attitude expressed in this work is representative of that of a growing number of young Chicano men and women who, having experienced the same abuse as Ricardo, can no longer accept acculturation and assimilation as a viable alternative.

This new awareness and resolve to end the bitter period of Chicano history is reflected in other works as well. For example, there are several references in *The Plum, Plum Pickers* to the efforts of César Chávez to effectively organize the grape pickers for better working and living conditions. "The Coming of Zamora" by Philip Ortego retells, in the words of the New Mexican *campesino* Alarcón, the rise of Reies López Tijerina, the founding of the Alianza, the incident at

Charles M. Tatum

the Echo Amphitheater in the Carson National Forest, and finally his trial. Zamora, like Tijerina, is found guilty, but as the latter engendered a new hope in the rural Chicano dwellers of New Mexico and Colorado, the farmer Alarcón returns home to await his leader's release from prison.

Regarding the future, then, Chicano fiction runs the gamut from profound anguish and despair to faith in the new leaders. The novels and short stories discussed manifest the widely divergent attitudes found among Spanish-speaking people in this country: the weariness of the decades of struggle, the feeling of having achieved equal status, the opposition to those who would resist the adoption of Anglo values, the cries of *Basta!* The works provide a measurement of bitterness and militancy at one extreme and resignation and apathy at the other, the determination to forge a new consciousness as opposed to a willingness to accept the status quo.

Seen in perspective, recent Chicano prose fiction thus chronicles the arrival in the United States of a Mexican immigrant population, traces it through several periods of adjustment to an Anglo culture, and finally gives us a cross-section of how the country's second largest minority views the future of its race.

UNIVERSITY OF MINNESOTA

Notes

[1] Ernesto Galarza, *Barrio Boy* (Notre Dame, Indiana: University of Notre Dame Press, 1971), p. 207.

[2] Richard Vásquez, *Chicano* (Garden City, New York: Doubleday and Company, 1970), p. 37.

[3] Octavio Romano, "Goodbye Revolution, Hello Slum," *El Espejo-The Mirror* (Berkeley, California: Quinto Sol Publications, 1969), p. 78.

[4] Galarza, p. 200.

[5] José Antonio Villareal, *Pocho* (Garden City, New York: Doubleday and Company, 1970), p. 34.

[6] Ibid., p. vii.

[7] Vásquez, p. 62.

[8] Amado Muro, "Cecilia Rosas," *The Chicano* (New York: Mentor Books, 1971), p. 280.

[9] Carey McWilliams, *North from Mexico* (New York: Greenwood Press, 1968), pp. 177-178.

[10]Villareal, pp. 28-29.

[11]Richard Barrio, *The Plum, Plum Pickers* (Sunnyvale, California: Ventura Press, 1971). The comment was made by Dr. Philip Ortego, Assistant Professor of English at the University of Texas at El Paso.

[12]Barrio, p. 12.

[13]Enrique López, "Back to Bachimba," *The Chicanos* (Baltimore: Penguin Books, 1971), p. 270.

"LOSS OF INNOCENCE" IN
CHICANO PROSE

Ted Lyon

Chicano literature is new! Even though enthused critics are fond of going back to the "corridos" of the nineteenth century or to the stories of suffering in the many Spanish-language newspapers of the Southwest, the emergence of contemporary Chicano fiction can more realistically be established around 1960, or perhaps in 1959, with the publication of the novel *Pocho*. Since that date eighteen years ago, Chicano prose has symbolically struggled through childhood and adolescence to its present "coming of age" status. Tomás Rivera postulates that the Chicano "wishes to invent himself in the labyrinth," and that "Chicano literature and the Chicanos in fiction are simply *life in search of form*" ("Into the Labyrinth: The Chicano in Literature," *South Western American Literature*, Vol. II [1972], p. 91). The Chicano reflected in literature, therefore, is not a fully-formed, completed individual, but a searching soul, seeking to find form and meaning in life. The Chicano writer plays a vital role in creating a form that aids in self-expression, fulfillment, awareness.

Although written in the United States, Chicano literature, like Chicano life and culture, has not always meshed well with North American literature. Chicano authors usually hail from different backgrounds and social experiences and hence do not link themselves with the traditions of most North American writers. Few Chicano authors, for example, have been able to break into the New York publishing circles. Chicano writers obviously find roots in and derive inspiration from Mexican literature and art. Yet neither their language, subject matter, nor theme harmonize fully with the Mexican source. Feeling rejected by both Anglo American and Mexican traditions, the Chicano writer himself has rejected both literary parents, desiring to find identity in the newness of self-expression and artistic autonomy. Chicano literature has now reached such quantity and quality that it must be examined as an independent body, existing between and among two other strong literatures, but not of their "generation." Similar to an adolescent, caught in an age when he has left childhood but has not yet reached full maturity, the Chicano prose writer frequently reflects an individual or group identity crisis, often through the mind of a youth.

It is no surprise, therefore, that much of contemporary Chicano prose creates a child or adolescent as protagonist, narrator, or focus character and examines problems typical to that age: how to get along with society, how to harmonize one's past with his present and future, how to become an individual without totally rejecting family and friends, and how to harmonize one's interior feelings with the exterior world. In this search for identity, the concept of "loss of innocence," typical to many adolescents in real life, becomes a basic theme for Chicano fiction. Indeed, all the following works are strongly based in the world of youth, adolescence, and search for self-expression:

Novels:	Anaya, Rudolfo	*Bless Me, Ultima*
	Galarza, Ernesto	*Barrio Boy*
	Salas, Floyd	*Tatoo the Wicked Cross*
	Vásquez, Richard	*Chicano*
	Villareal, José	*Pocho*
	Villaseñor, Edmund	*Macho!*
	Zeta Acosta, Oscar	*The Autobiography of a Brown Buffalo*
Short Stories:		
	Rivera, Tomás	*". . .y no se lo tragó la tierra"*
	Romano, Octavio	"Strings for a Holiday"
	Vaca, Nick	"Martín"
		"The Week of the Life of Manuel Hernández"
	Arias, Ron	"The Interview"

Ted Lyon

| Guerrero, Miguel | "The Little, Little Guy" |
| Portillo Trambley, Estela | "Rain of Scorpions" |

"Loss of innocence" is defined as the state of passing from youthful trust and confidence in others to doubt and dependence on self, from acceptance of the world in which one has grown up to anger and rebellion toward that world. In each of the above-mentioned novels and short stories, an immature or youthful protagonist is permitted to experience the world in new ways, thereby deriving the knowledge or experience necessary to pass from his initial state of innocence to a more "sophisticated," but usually less satisfying, existence in the adult world. This does not imply that the authors or their protagonists desire to return to the simple happiness of childhood but rather express their deception and dismay at the world of adulthood. The theme of "loss of innocence" in Chicano prose is here studied in three main categories: (1) loss or rejection of religious belief, (2) exposure to the cruelties of the adult and Anglo world, and (3) experimentation with sex, drugs, and alcohol. Other categories for the study of a new awareness by a young Chicano protagonist could be examined: acquisition of knowledge, discovery, rejection of parents, etc., but these cannot be dealt with here.

Loss of Religious Belief

The twelve short stories of Rivera's *". . .and the earth did not part"* are actually woven together by a single type of protagonist—a child. Whether this youth is the narrator of the story, which is usually the case, or the focus character, his experiences of the imaginary year (12 anecdotes = 12 months) unify the stories. He is seen in the fields, in school, in church, in the barrio. Four of the stories center upon the failure of conventional religion to fulfill its expected function in the life of the boy. A maturing deception results from this failure. The most obvious example is the title story in which a young boy, a day laborer, finally musters the courage to curse the land and God because of his father's sunstroke. Contrary to all he had been taught ("Upon cursing he felt the fear instilled in him by time and by his parents"), the earth did not swallow him up. Nothing out of the ordinary happened. The narrator concludes the story with the words of lost innocence: the adolescent protagonist "was experiencing a peace that he had never known before. . .for the first time he felt himself capable of doing and undoing whatever he chose. He looked toward the ground, kicked it and said to it, 'Not yet, you can't eat me yet. Someday. But I won't even know it' " (p. 79).

"It Was a Silvery Night," from the same collection of stories, recalls a "coming of age" experience in which the youthful protagonist is counseled against trying to call up the devil; traditional and religious belief suggest that to do this will cause insanity. Feeling strength within himself he rejects tradition and attempts to summon the evil spirit but Lucifer does not appear. The result is a moment of rapid mental growth in which he concludes "there is no devil. There is nothing," and falls asleep peacefully, "watching the moon among the clouds and the trees. . .extremely happy about something" (p. 63). The happiness is obviously the result of throwing off a past belief and discovering what he now considers his own reality—the happiness that comes from rejecting religious dogma.

The story "First Holy Communion," instead of recounting the deeply spiritual experience of that ordinance, is made mundane as the boy-narrator witnesses a couple making love in the tailor shop next to the church. The experience opens eyes of understanding, causing him to think and reorder his world. He runs toward the church, symbolically, but recalls: "It was then that I realized that those must be the sins of the flesh. . ." After the mockery of the confession the boy even "imagined the priest and the nun on the floor (naked)," and recalls that "I even forgot that I had lied to the priest" (pp. 90, 91). He discovers that he now has a desire to know everything, as if he were a primitive Adam, ready to partake of the tree of knowledge after losing his pristine innocence.

Similar doubts and rejection of religion evidence themselves in "A Rosary for Doña Marina" (Octavio Romano), and especially in the better-known Chicano novels, *Pocho* and *Bless Me, Ultima.* Richard's conflict with religion in *Pocho* stems from his desire for more knowledge and a church which blocks that quest. Discord increases until Richard finally insists, "Please, mamá. I do not wish to make you unhappy, but you are forcing me to do so. I have left the Church. . . .I no longer believe in God" (p. 172). Like so many other young protagonists in Chicano literature, he has experienced his own self-awakening, and in the process feels he must reject religion. Significant to note is that religion in Chicano literature is only practiced by pious women. As soon as boys (and there are practically no girl protagonists) reach adolescence, they find out what their fathers have already learned—that freedom and growth come only when the fet-

Ted Lyon

ters of conventional religion are cast off and replaced by hard work and dependence on self.

Cruelties of the Adult or Anglo World

The majority of Chicano prose, especially that written during the first ten years (1959-69) of its emergence, presents the Chicano protagonist in direct confrontation with the surrounding Anglo society. From this encounter he learns rapidly, sometimes rejecting his own past and kin (a "vendido," or a "Tío Taco"), at other times retreating farther back into the security of home or barrio, but usually gaining the confidence to face new circumstances. Nick Vaca's excellent "The Week of the Life of Manuel Hernández" follows a child, adolescent, and young adult through twenty-five years of growth and conflict. As a young boy Manuel begins to feel mild discontent with himself and the world but is unable to verbalize reasons for this uneasiness. Years slip away as days of a single week (Manuel is still a child in this sense) during which he passes through the pressures of being drunk, final exams in the university, existential philosophy, foreign study, a college teaching career, denial of tenure, and a near-suicidal car accident. Through these harsh experiences Manuel realizes that life holds no good for him; his youthful hope in the future is lost in hatred and condemnation of society. He very quickly learns too that he must "eat" others to keep from being "eaten" by them. Criticizing his university professors for not finding solutions to man's dilemma, he falls into the same game of making life hard for others. The professors "crumble those things I hold sacred and inviolable. With what do they replace my sacred beliefs? With nothing but tentative conclusions. . ." (p. 134, *El Espejo*). Manuel is a loser; not only does he lose his innocence very early in life but also gives up the struggle entirely.

Other characters fare better than Manuel Hernández. Richard, in *Pocho*, faces racial and religious discrimination in a northern California town. After lengthy bouts with despair he comes to a new understanding of self and history, realizing that he cannot escape his race and culture, and joins the army, an obvious attempt to work within the Anglo system. Yet the reader is let down; he had expected and hoped that Richard, with his highly-developed sensitivity and understanding, would fight to retain his father's culture. The opposite takes place. Through unjust interrogation by the police Richard apparently loses his childhood candor, gives up the quiet cam-

258

paign to be "different," and falls into the accepted pattern of the day —join the army, the false panacea of acceptance. Unfortunately the novel ends at this point, without ever completely showing or affirming the results of the Anglo society on the protagonist; the reader can only conclude that one more life is wasted, stripped of its individuality and Chicano uniqueness.

Nick Vaca's poignant story "Martín" presents a different view of the world's cruelties. Chicano children torment a new arrival to the neighborhood, Martín, because of his bulgy stomach, supposing him to be grossly overfed. After numerous youthful torments, the young narrator follows Martín to his battered home and is dramatically awakened to the need for compassion, realizing the effects of extreme hunger and poverty on the tormented Martín. This is a reversal from most Chicano literature where the Anglo world swallows the struggling downtrodden. Here a young Chicanito comes to understand not only the cruelties of the world, but his own arrogant behavior. He makes no comment on his future behavior after this "awakening" but the reader recognizes that he has quickly passed from the childish cruelty of his small world to a much deeper understanding of human suffering.

The difficulties of the working world, particularly stoop labor, become harsh teachers for the Chicano. Rivera's "The Children Were the Victims" and "When We Arrive" introduce children and adolescents to the heat, pain, and monotony of field labor. Boys are quickly turned into men as they learn the necessity and at times even the nobility of work. Pete Sandoval of *Chicano* leaves the Army, still a directionless drifter. He finds a job as a cement finisher and here discovers real pleasure in hard labor. Indeed, the best parts of the novel are those which describe the details of working with cement—the profession, by the way, of the author Richard Vásquez (*Chicano*, pp. 166-72). Unlike characters in other Chicano stories and novels, Pete is not oppressed or broken by the work. He rapidly convinces himself and others that he is a "man" and can take the rough knocks of the job. He is one of the few Chicano literary characters who harmoniously unites with his work. His realization of the Anglo world's inhumanities comes later, when he attempts to integrate a "white" neighborhood.

The Anglo and the adult world in general are schoolmasters for the adolescent Chicano. They take him from his previous state of limited experience, of familial security, of economic dependence, and brusquely push him into knowledge and maturity. He learns that his parents disagree and even fight (*Pocho; Bless Me, Ultima; Chicano*); he finds the only way he may be able to exist in Anglo society is by accepting its absurdities ("Strings for a Holiday") or that respect of others only comes through hard work (*Macho!*). With this discovery of the adult Anglo world, the adolescent is either forced to abandon or voluntarily realizes that he must forsake childhood dreams: Richard (*Pocho*) was urged to be a writer and to go to college but the novel ends in conflict and entrance into the military—abandonment of childhood dreams. In "It is Painful" by Rivera, the focus character is expelled from school for fighting and realizes that his intended career with the phone company is lost. Antonio (*Bless Me, Ultima*) does not openly give up his dreams to go into the clergy, but he has seen enough to know that he will never be able to base his faith in the Catholic Church. Dreams and plans are lost in the harshness of the adult Anglo world.

Experimentation with Sex, Drugs, Alcohol, etc.

Like much of contemporary North-American literature which deals with adolescent sex, Chicano literature also explores this theme. Yet no Chicano novel or short story is based exclusively on sex (as are many novels in the United States); rather, sex is present merely as a break with a naive or protected past. Through it the characters are made aware of their past innocence and supposedly introduced into manhood. While it may justifiably be questioned whether sexual experimentation really brings any new manhood, protagonists and authors alike postulate that it does.

The clearest example of loss of innocence through sex is seen in *Pocho*. Sometime later than his friends, Richard discovers masturbation and in an initial frenzy utters, "I'm a father! I'm a father" (p. 114). At confession the following day he begins to realize that religion is losing out as a vital force in his life. A few days later Zelda, previously just part of the neighborhood gang, initiates him in the sex act. Returning home late, his father asks:

> "Where have you been?"
> "Walking, Papá."
> "Walking? You know you are not allowed to be out after nine o'clock, do you not?"
> "Yes, sir. But I must live my life," answered Richard.
> "Your life! Your life belongs to us, and will belong to us even after you marry, because we gave it to you" (p. 129).

For the first time in his life, Richard dares to question his father.

From this point he continues to assert his autonomy, largely as a result of his experimentation with Zelda. He "felt like a man" now, capable of facing another man, his father, the world.

Through his frequent and perhaps too obvious dreams, Antonio (*Bless Me, Ultima*) realizes that innocence is lost through sex and knowledge of worldly ways. Ultima points to the simple life and the land as the source for the innocence Antonio should feel. But his older brothers counter Ultima and drag him to a house of prostitution; he resists, shouting "I cannot enter, I cannot think those thoughts. I am to be a priest" (p. 65). An interior dialogue/debate takes place in Antonio's mind over how one loses innocence. The boy withstands the temptation but vicariously experiences his brothers' degrading actions and obvious loss of innocence.

The Autobiography of a Brown Buffalo introduces both sex and drugs as the way through which the protagonist/narrator allegedly opens up and expands his world. Although chronologically no longer an adolescent, the "Buffalo" is still an immature, timid soul. Drink, drugs, and sex confirm a courage he finds at no other time. He has little innocence to lose but he does convince himself that he is "macho" through alcohol and women. The novel ends with an extremely erotic but near-metaphysical situation. This specific Chicano finds meaning in a house of prostitution, in Juarez, Mexico, a type of mystical return to roots (language, culture, etc.).

Similar discoveries of supposed manhood achieved through sexual experiences and drugs abound in *Chicano, Macho!, Tatoo the Wicked Cross*, etc. Chicano writers, in general, have been wise enough to avoid lurid sensationalism, sexual descriptions, specific details, and obscenity; sex is generally not used as an end in itself, that is, eroticism, but as an indicator of an adolescent's loss of innocence.

The repeated motif of a youth, usually a male, passing through shocking new experiences which almost too rapidly thrust him into incipient manhood is a constant in Chicano prose. Although the loss of religious belief may signal future spiritual tragedy, or the clash with the adult world may result in life-long bitterness, or initiation into illicit sexual pleasures may be morally demeaning, Chicano literature passes no judgment on these acts. It merely records them as part of the life of the Chicano. Rarely is this new status as satisfying to the protagonist as the earlier stage of innocence and security. But just as any adolescent in life or literature must give up certain childish behavior to enter into the adult world, initiation into manhood is an essential and unavoidable step. Similar to rites of passage among

Ted Lyon

primitive tribes, contemporary society has evolved, just as irrationally, methods by which a youth may be considered an adult. Rejection of religious dogma, direct confrontation with the adult world, and indulgence in sex and drugs appear as constants in Chicano literature for accomplishing this "coming of age" status. Chicano prose writers have carefully recorded the important occasions when their characters make rapid strides away from the unbeguiled innocence of youth to initiation and full integration into manhood and society.

BRIGHAM YOUNG UNIVERSITY

Works Cited

Anaya, Rudolfo A. *Bless Me, Ultima*. Quinto Sol. Berkeley, 1972.
Rivera, Tomás. *". . .and the earth did not part."* Quinto Sol. Berkeley, 1971.
Vaca, Nick C. "The Week of the Life of Manuel Hernández," *El Espejo*. Quinto Sol. Berkeley, 1972.
Vásquez, Richard. *Chicano*. Doubleday. Garden City, New York, 1970.
Villareal, José A. *Pocho*. Doubleday, Anchor. Garden City, New York, 1970.

THE LITERARY STRATEGEMS AVAILABLE TO THE BILINGUAL CHICANO WRITER

Gary D. Keller

Introduction

This paper is dedicated to both the theory and the praxis of bilingual Chicano literature, and by extension of any multilingual or multidialectal literature. With respect to theory, my primary concern is with the establishment of critical standards that will be useful for evaluating bilingual literature. As part of this concern I will not only critique, constructively I trust, the axiological assumptions of critics of bilingual texts who have come before me, but offer a number of evaluative standards of my own.

With respect to praxis, I shall attempt to illustrate the rich variety of literary strategies available to bilingual Chicano writers. Bilingual writers are able to depict characters, explore themes, express ideologies or messages, and fashion rhetorical devices in unique ways.

I should note that most of my examples are taken from Chicano bilingual poetry. There are two reasons for this. The primary one is that code-switching is evident to a far less extent in Chicano prose (and most certainly in prose fiction), which I take to be additional evidence for what the reader will soon appreciate to be a fundamental guidon of this paper, namely that code-switching in literature need not, and usually does not reflect code-switching in society. Clearly, poetry is the most "arty" of the literary forms, the one generically most remote from the community; and yet, Chicano poetry displays more code-switching than Chicano prose. I believe that this fact has mostly to do with the poet's heightened need for concision and linguistic innovation in comparison to the essayist, novelist, or short story writer. The second reason for citing poetry over prose is that since poetry is more concise, I am able to include more examples in a paper constrained with respect to length.

One other observation is in order. The reader may find it curious that certain well-known, excellent Chicano texts are not cited, while others, less-known, are mentioned. This is the case because my paper does not deal with Chicano literature per se, only *bilingual* Chicano literature. Some Chicano texts have been written either wholly in English or wholly in Spanish, and therefore, on the basis of their monolingualism do not qualify for inclusion in this paper.

A Philology of Code-Switching

In 1976 I published an article, "Toward a Stylistic Analysis of Bilingual Texts: From Ernest Hemingway to Contemporary Boricua and Chicano Literature,"[1] which among other goals, attempted from a linguistic vantage point, to analyze some of the dynamic processes involved in bilingual literature. At the same time I expressed dismay at the fact that while much attention has been paid to bilingual texts from the point of view of philology and even sociology, there were only one or two studies worth mentioning that attempted to analyze the literary dynamics that are evident in bilingual texts. Happily, this period of neglect seems to be coming to an end, for in the past two years there have appeared at least four articles that do offer such attention.

Timm's paper, "Code Switching in *War and Peace*"[2] analyzes a large number of mostly French-Russian alternations, correlating them with the syntactical constraints that Gumperz and others[3] have detected in various speech communities. Yet, even though Tolstoy is an acknowledged master of literary realism and Timm's literary code-switching data in *War and Peace* consist of either outright dialogue or quasi-dialogue (e.g. a character "talking" to himself), there are occasions, significant for the esthetic pursuits of this paper, where, as the researcher puts it, "the use of code-switching for literary effect. . . has crashed through one of the usual [syntactic] barriers to conversational switching."[4] Beardsmore's "Polyglot Literature and Linguistic Fiction," focusing on the French, Flemish, and Dutch literatures of the Lowlands, distinguishes between:

1. Polyglot writings of specific authors such as Jan Van der Noot who produced parallel Dutch-French editions of some of his works.
2. Polyglot texts such as Shakespeare's *Henry V* and Tolstoy's *War and Peace,* marked by a "discreet use of a second language in a text."
3. Literary creations such as those of the regional literature of Belgium in which "languages are mixed in a very marked fashion and which, by this token, is destined for a public which operates code-switching in its own speech or else finds itself in a social setting where such operations are frequently to be encountered amongst others. This third type of polyglot literature implies the presence of relatively stable and widespread bilingualism."
4. Linguistic fiction, such as that to be found in Molière's *Malade imaginaire,* where macaronic Latin is placed in the mouths of certain doctors. The German poet, Stefan George, for example, invented a "lingua romana," an original language, albeit based on the Romance languages, as the following extract shows:

> La sera vola circa me con alas taciturnas
> El di ha pasato con suo violente túrben
> Suo furioso e insaciable ager.
> En veloz e insana capcia
> Se precipitaron copiosamente meas ideas
> Las unas devorando las altras. . .[5]

Beardsmore goes on to relate these textual taxa to different socio-cultural contexts and it is at this point that I move afield since my paper is involved with artistic techniques rather than the sociology of literature.

Much closer to home are two articles by Guadalupe Valdés-Fallis, "The Sociolinguistics of Chicano Literature," and Code-Switching in Bilingual Chicano Poetry."[6] I detect two separate analytic concerns in Valdés's inspiring articles; sometimes they appear to be at cross purposes. It is because Valdés raises important linguistico-literary considerations that can potentially and hopefully lead not only to a fuller critical appreciation of literary code-switching, but can provide us the criteria to perform a praxis of the alternation phenomena, that I will summarize and evaluate her theories with all necessary attention to detail. In an important sense Valdés "raises the ante" by performing not only elucidatory but judicial criticism of bilingual literature as well.

Does "Good" Code-Switching in Literature Need Be "Authentic" Code-Switching in the Bilingual Community?

One line of analysis that Valdés undertakes is to construct an axiology of bilingual literature by correlating the literary variety of code-switching with the variety found in actual speech communities. The correlation makes equal use of the types of social determinants of code-switching (identity markers, contextual switches such as those related to language domain, and so on[7]) as well as the syntactic constraints on communal code-switching that several researchers have found to exist. For example, code-switchers in society typically abhor switching between pronominal subjects or objects and the finite verbs to which these pronouns are immediately adjacent, between finite verbs and adjacent infinitive complements, or within negated verb sequences; but typically they do switch between subject and predicate, and between noun phrase or prepositional phrase modifiers of other noun phrases or prepositional phrases.

The axiological schema constructed by Valdés in this particular line of analysis runs in approximately the following manner:

I. Community code-switching, while certainly not definitively analyzed by linguistic methods at this time, does yield certain patterns of syntactical constraints or rules. Similarly, code-switching can be classified from the perspective of sociology by a number of motivating categories.

II. Bilingual literature often displays the same syntactical patterns and causal categories of code-switching that we find in flesh and blood communities.

III. One could criticize the esthetic worth of those literary examples of code-switching which clearly violate the syntactical norms of the code-switching community. In this regard, Valdés judges that:

> My reading of Chicano poetry shows that while certain poets are masters at combining English and Spanish, other poets,. . .have produced a large quantity of poetry which, in a linguistic sense, not only does not reflect normal or accepted use, but seems to be based on a random sprinkling of English or Spanish here or there. In many cases, the poets themselves do not code-switch in their everyday speech, and thus it is almost impossible for them to produce authentic examples of such use.[8]

A bit further on Valdés gives the following examples of inferior bilingual poetry:

1. Let us gather in a flourishing way
   contentos llenos de fuerza to vida

2. let us offer our hearts a saludar our águila rising
   freedom

3. corazón de venado
   blaze of dawn walking

         weave us a rain green

4. máscara máscara
   pobre man
   hombre rich
   pregnant mujer
   niño aborted[9]

She states of these examples:

> While superficially the alternating use of English and Spanish resembles that of the [superior] poetry analyzed previously, it is clear that these poets have less control over the use of language than the poets studied earlier. It is possible that they are in fact *attempting to create new images based on their two languages* and simply do not have a clear feeling for the actual alternation of English and Spanish in natural speech.[10] [Italics mine. I will reexamine the last passage of this series of four citations later in this paper, in light of the discussion that immediately follows.]

Before offering some hopefully constructive criticisms of the axiological implications in the scheme I have outlined, I should hasten to add that there is a second evaluative component in Valdés's axiology. She also maintains the esthetic value of code-switching on grounds other than its reflection of communal norms. Indeed, in accordance with two concepts utilized by the Prague school of linguistics, Valdés presents some samples of code-switching that exemplify artistic foregrounding as compared to mere routine language usage, defined by the concept of automatization. Thus Valdés is led to observe: "the bilingual poet, as opposed to the poet who confines himself to one language, can at any point in the poem choose to foreground in the language, which to him, offers the greatest possibilities. He does not have to sacrifice the aesthetic potential of *either* of his codes. In fact, very often he exploits them simultaneously."[11] Elsewhere Valdés indicates that code-switching between languages is "definitely related to a specific feeling for the language that a speaker may have or his momentary need; languages are clearly used metaphorically for emphasis or contrast."[12] Finally, in a separate passage she asserts:

> language alternation can be poetically significant or it can be of little or no importance to poetic meaning. Indeed, it may frequently be used simply because it has become increasingly identified with Chicano poetry. In many cases such alternation may be quite different from the actual speech norms of the bilingual community. For that reason this bilingual poetry must be studied not only for the strength of one or the other of its languages, but also for the possibilities of combined imagery which can be produced. There is indeed adequate and inade-

quate, good and bad, artistic and unartistic use of language in the poems in print today.[13]

Thus, if I read correctly, the two axiological currents that Valdés utilizes perhaps are reconciled in the following manner:

I. We can attach positive value to literary code-switching that reflects the norms of the bilingual community.

II. We can also attach positive value to literary code-switching that may not reflect bilingual communal norms but that does create "powerful bilingual images."

III. We cannot attach positive value to literary code-switching that neither reflects bilingual communal norms nor creates "powerful bilingual images."

In addition, we need to distinguish between a "strong assertion" and a "weak assertion" with respect to bilingual communal norms. The "strong assertion," much more difficult to defend, would be that "good" code-switching would need to sound natural to the bilingual community.

The more sensible "weak assertion" would state that code-switching could be "good" provided it created "powerful bilingual images" and sounded "acceptable" to the community even though the community itself would be unlikely to exercise such alternation. In the following passage, in spite of the "reflects the norms of the community" allegation (personally, I don't believe that the cited example does so reflect), Valdés appears to espouse the weak assertion in her literary exegesis:

. . .the poetic strength of

> mi padre también salió
> solito
> and crawled a gatas

cannot be duplicated by *crawled on all fours,* or by *anduvo a gatas.* Here is therefore a prime example of foregrounding, that is, of a creation of a live image. The poet creates this live metaphor by utilizing both languages simultaneously. His foregrounding is based on the linguistically different, but incorporates and reflects the norms of the community of which he is a part.[14]

To the axiological scheme that I have outlined above I need to suggest some significant modifications in order to separate and clarify, for the purpose of forming value judgments, the particular disciplines, respectively, of sociology (or sociolinguistics) and esthetics. In addition, I intend to argue against the esthetic validity for the purpose of the judicial evaluation of literary texts of both the "strong assertion" and the "weak assertion."

Distinguishing between Sociological Value and Esthetic Value

In my judgment proposition I. is applicable strictly to the field of sociology. That is, it is relevant only for researchers interested in the value that literary texts may have for them in analyzing synchronically (or diachronically) the bilingual speech norms of a given speech community. Thus the literary text provides raw data from which we can make sociolinguistic analyses and this raw data is valuable to the degree that it approaches flesh and blood social speech. This is an important service that literature has provided sociology as the research studies of Timm, Beardsmore, and Valdés-Fallis herself have borne out.

However, the converse, that code-switching which merely reflects communal speech norms but does not create "powerful bilingual images" is esthetically valuable, I believe to be fallacious. Literary code-switching, in order to be esthetically appreciated, must have something else, it must be poetically significant, it must be harmoniously integrated into the language system established by the patterns of the literary text. In other words, if the code-switch contributes to metaphor, characterization, irony, alliteration, anaphora, theme, or any other of a host of rhetorical, structural, thematic, etc., *literary concerns,* then, and only then, would code-switching be valuable for literature.

We need to return to the commonplace that literature is different from life, although what makes literature so fascinating is its ability to evoke reality by means of patterns of fictions. Systems and regularities such as realism—reality miniaturized, documented and dissected; surrealism—reality evoked through the kaleidoscope of dream work and disinhibition; or the thematics of the absurd—reality set free from the stricture of cause and effect relationships: these styles of fiction in the hands of the master writer all produce heightened intimations of reality that the experience of reality itself usually cannot muster.

Let us put code-switching into the picture. I judge not only that there may be but that there *must be* significant differences between literary code-switching and real-life code-switching. The differences are the sort that figure in distinguishing life from art. Art may reveal the nature of the social phenomenon but it does so only as a by-product of its own concerns, as an instrumentality in achieving a literary goal such as irony, characterization, cross-cultural comparisons, double entendres, puns, and so on.

Literary writing contains certain characteristics that do not conform with the normal conventions of communication. For example, all other uses of language are set within a general social matrix; they develop from antecedent events and presuppose consequent events; they are the products of a social continuum. To account for messages in a conventional text some cognizance must be made of their social environment. Literary texts, however, while they may be related to contexts, are separate from them. They are complete in themselves, and their textual significance is accordingly enclosed within the limits of the form they take. Moreover, literary messages are not only notable for their autonomy from social context, but for their idiosyncratic deployment of language resources. It has frequently been pointed out that literature contains a good deal of language that is grammatically and semantically deviant. Similarly, literary critics have been able to isolate poetic devices (e.g., the metrical line) or rhetorical figures that rarely if ever occur in other uses of language.

It is instructive in order to avoid the fallacious axiological confounding of sociological or sociolinguistic criteria with esthetic criteria to survey a parallel field, psychological literary criticism. A common tendency in literary critics, whether they be psychologists or psychoanalysts (such as Ernest Jones or Otto Rank) or academics (such as A. C. Bradley) has been to treat characters as if they were real people. In contemporary literary criticism, this confounding, analogous in our context to treating poetry, drama or fiction (with or without code-switching) as if it were real speech, has been decisively rejected. As Kenneth Muir points out, "characters are not real people: they are characters in a play, called forth by the role they have to act, and determined by the plot."[15] Norman Holland, the contemporary psychoanalytic critic notes that the original error arises from failing to recognize that a play (or a poem or story) "is an ordered and structured work of art, not like everyday reality. This order and structure impose changes on the literal representation of reality."[16]

To what absurdities this myopia can lead us! For example, the fact that Shakespeare's characters must speak verse has led a variety of nineteenth- and twentieth-century critics to label Macbeth, Othello, Iago, Richard II, etc., as "great poets." But surely this is nonsense—"If characters in poetic drama speak poetry," notes F. R. Leavis, "we ought to be able to notice the fact without concluding that they are poets."[17]

Yet certainly there are circumstances where the sociolinguistic goal of an accurate data base or where the psychological or psycho-analytic goal of authentic characters for the purpose of clinical study coincides with the esthetic goal. This ought to be the case when the literary text embraces the esthetic philosophy of realism or natural-ism or the like; where the desired artistic effect is a fiction of mimesis, where art aspires to become the microcosm and mirror of the social macrocosm. Here we can argue that textual code-switching that re-flects communal code-switching is "good" in itself since the esthetic philosophy of the text is realized to the degree that the text becomes a social document, a reflection of social reality. Yet even here both the writers and critics of realism must concede that the text achieves "documenthood" not by servile and indiscriminate copying of social life, but by considered exercise of craftmanship, in order to evoke life. The realistic work of art is a hieroglyph, a pictograph of reality, not an exhaustive series of social snapshots. Reality is boundless and het-erogeneous and therefore indigestible, and any realistic work of art, be it the anthropology of Oscar Lewis, or the realistic and neo-realis-tic novels of the nineteenth and twentieth centuries, must cut and paste, evoke and render, submit the untoward data base to editorial constraints.

Even the renowned Marxist critic, Georg Lukács, states flatly: "The live portrayal of the complete human personality is possible only if the writer attempts to create types." For a Marxist, character-ization must show "the real intrinsic totality of the decisive driving forces which determine the social process."[18]

Criticism of the novel, writes Mark Schorer, "must begin with the base of language, with the word, with figurative structures, with rhe-toric as skeleton and style as body of meaning. . . .A novel, like a poem, is not life, it is an image of life; and the critical problem is first of all to analyze the structure of the image."[19]

In short, realism, as Karl Mannheim said, means different things in different contexts.[20] The one thing it seems not to mean is a literal, photographic portrayal of reality. In fact, such a thing hardly seems possible, since every portrayal, by the mere fact of its being one, in-volves the intervention of some personality. Artistic portrayals of reality inevitably depend on the dialectic between reality itself (and who even agrees on that?) and the particular representation of reality made by the artist.

So then, while I encourage the sociolinguist to exploit literary verisimilitude in order to expand the data base on code-switching or any other community phenomenon, in short, to conduct a sociolinguistic of literary texts, I must also argue that the criteria for determining "good" data cannot be extended to determine "good" poetry, drama, or fiction. What criteria, then, are we left with in pursuit of assigning value to bilingual fiction, in the enterprise of distinguishing between artistically superior code-switches and mediocre or unaesthetic code-switches? We need to return to Valdés-Fallis's other criterion of "powerful bilingual images" which should be accepted as a shorthand or abbreviation for the exigencies of a literary axiology that is based fundamentally on the characteristics of the text itself. The guiding principles of literary evaluation are themselves quite varied. For example, merely from the point of view of linguistics we have concepts such as the Prague school's *foregrounding* and *automatization* which Valdés puts to good use; Michael Riffaterre's variation thereof, appealing to stylistic facts (style "stresses") versus linguistic facts (language merely "expresses"); or the esthetic usage of Mukařovský and Shklovsky, who point to the need for art to make language "novel," "surprising," to "barbarize" it, to "deform" it, to "stylize it either in the direction of the archaic or the remote," to "make it new," to "make it strange," etc.[21] This criterion of the Russian formalists is admittedly relativist. Mukařovksý notes that there can be no esthetic norm for it is the essence of the esthetic norm to be broken. In addition, over time no poetic style can remain forever familiar. Works can lose their stylistic novelty, and then, perhaps, later regain it. Moreover, it is not my intention to argue for a purely formalist theory of literature. Indeed, I find myself in agreement with T. S. Eliot that, "The 'greatness' of literature cannot be determined solely by literary standards, though we must remember that whether it is literature or not can be determined only by literary standards."[22] Or as Eliot put in the mouth of B. in "A Dialogue on Dramatic Poetry":

> You can never draw the line between aesthetic criticism and moral and social criticism; you cannot draw a line between criticism and metaphysics; you start with literary criticism, and however rigorous an aesthete you may be, you are over the frontier into something else sooner or later. The best you can do is accept these conditions and know what you are doing when you do it. And, on the other hand, you must know how and when to retrace your steps. You must be very nimble.[23]

The world is somewhere related to the work of art, however tenuously (or overtly). Yet the world, including worldly language, has been assimilated into the art form. While the "raw materials" of artistic literature must include, on one level, social life and inter-course, communal language, human behaviors, experiences, emo-tions, attitudes, and so on, all of these, as Wellek and Warren put it have been "pulled into polyphonic relations by the dynamics of aes-thetic purpose."[24]

Finally, we ought to be aware of the fact that when language serves a social purpose it does so by codifying those aspects of reality that a society wishes to control; when language serves an artistic or religious purpose it is inclined to represent a reality beyond the bounds of common communication and social sanction. Language can be regarded as a socially sanctioned representation of the exter-nal world. Without such a representation, the external world is a chaos beyond human control. In the beginning was the Word. The members of a society accept the codification which their language provides because it gives them a necessary sense of security. Reality is under control because they share a common attitude toward it by sharing a common means of communication. Communication can only take place if there are conventionally accepted ways of looking at the world.

Nevertheless, simply because we as members of a society accept a conventional view of reality, it does not follow that as individuals we are not aware of a reality other than that represented by our lan-guage. Indeed, the existence of religion and art is evidence that we are very much aware of reality beyond the bounds of common communi-cation and social sanction. Social conventions supply people's needs insofar as they are members of society, but they have needs as indi-viduals which such conventions by their very nature are incapable of satisfying. Every society has some form of art and some form of religion, and these serve as a necessary outlet for individual attitudes whose expression would otherwise disrupt the ordered pattern of reality which society promotes and upon which its survival depends. Art and religion are a recognition that there is a reality apart from the one which is officially recommended. What then is the nature of this reality?

This other reality is related to that which is conventionally recog-nized in the same way as literary language is related to conventional language. What literature, and indeed all art, does is create patterns out of deviations from normality; these patterns then represent a dif-ferent reality from that represented by conventional language. Thus literature gives formal expression to the individual's awareness of a world beyond the reach of communal communication.

The Bilingual Chicano Writer

The unique mode of language organization that is found in literary texts is indistinguishable from the significance these texts have as messages. Since the texts create their own systems of language, they inevitably create a different reality, and our awareness of one necessarily entails our awareness of the other.

Acknowledging the separate reality of all literary texts carries with it a crucial complication for understanding bilingual literature. The bilingual language of literary texts is not the same as the language of a given bilingual community. To presume that bilingual literature directly corresponds to usage in a given bilingual community entails a total misapprehension about the relationship between literary language and communal language.

In passing, let me note that a fine example of literature leaping the bounds of reality from the perspective of the very special context of bilingual literature can be found in what Beardsmore has aptly coined "linguistic fiction" (to which I have referred earlier). In point of fact this sort of literature is typically quasi-polyglot in nature; it is a sort of bilingual fiction, making use of language varieties that do not exist in flesh and blood language communities. The relationship between the fictional language and the social language is analogous to the creation of a pidgin from languages sharing the same speech community.

Esthetic Potential of Socially Unnatural Code-Switching: An Example

Forearmed with these considerations pertaining to the relationship between communal code-switching and literary code-switching, and more generally, which criteria *ought not* be the basis for a theory of literary value (I fully concede that the question of which criteria *ought to* provide such a basis is a much more difficult and subjective matter), let us return to the passages (pp. 266-7) which Valdés exposes as poor examples of code-switching. Are they undoubtedly inferior literature? My answer is that I am unsure. On the one hand they certainly don't appear to be paragons of art, and I am inclined to accept, on the face of it, Valdés's judgment, but on the basis of her critical intuition, not her avowed standard of evaluation. Yet, on the other hand, Valdés has lifted these examples from their literary context. She does not give us the whole poem, the preceding and subsequent passages into which these code-switches are related. Thus trying to evaluate these passages is a task rather like the one set before the three blind savants who attempted to characterize the elephant by dint of the feedback of the palms of their hands. If we accept my contention—the contention generally of critics who take the linguistic approach to literary criticism—that literary texts create a secondary language system that is the result of organizing deviations from the communal language into patterns that are critically discernible in those very texts, then it becomes futile to attempt a systematic or substantial literary criticism, whether it be judicial or simply elucidatory. Indeed, one consequence of my description of literature, from the linguistic point of view, is that the text subsumes, or rather, replaces, the functions of what in sociolinguistics would be distinguished as code and context. And if in fact the principal (I don't go so far as to say only) context for the evaluation of the text resides in the text itself, it simply won't do to evaluate the aforementioned examples of code-switching as Valdés has done, by separating them from their textual contexts and substituting in their stead a sociolinguistic context, "accuracy" from the communal standpoint.

Therefore I honestly can't say if the cited passages are good or not; I don't have enough substance to go on (and Valdés has not cited the sources), although the last and longest example begins to achieve patternings that for me hold definite interest. Let us reproduce it:

> máscara máscara
> pobre man
> hombre rich
> pregnant mujer
> niño aborted

About this example, Valdés alleges: ". . .the poet is evidently attempting to modify Spanish nouns with English adjectives, and English nouns with Spanish adjectives. I would very much doubt that combinations such as *pregnant mujer* and *pobre man* would be considered 'acceptable' by Mexican-American speakers who code-switch themselves. Indeed the above examples do not reflect actual speech among bilingual speakers nor do they seem to create powerful bilingual images."[25] Yet to me it is evident that the poet is attempting to accomplish much more than merely modify Spanish nouns with English adjectives, and vice versa. For example:

1. After the anaphora of the first line the poem is structured according to a strict syntactical pattern once we control for language. All of the lines of verse are noun clauses and each line alternates the position of the modifier in relationship to the head noun. The resulting pattern is:

    Adj. + Noun
    Noun + Adj.
    Adj. + Noun
    Noun + Adj.

In my opinion, based on the context that I have been given, it is this formal syntactical quality that is the most important artistic point of the passage.

2. In addition to a syntactic pattern which reveals itself when we control for language, there emerges a language pattern, albeit less rigorously symmetrical, when we control for syntax. It is the following:

    Sp. + Sp.
    Sp. + Eng.
    Sp. + Eng.
    Eng. + Sp.
    Sp. + Eng.

Somewhere in this poem, perhaps in the "missing" line which follows, I would venture to predict that an Eng. + Eng. combination appears, in order to complete the set.

3. The second and fourth lines, respectively, pobre man/pregnant mujer, have a number of relationships *worth* analyzing. They are good examples of bilingual parallelism since in addition to the aforementioned syntactical parallels (Adj. + Noun), they expose a semantic equivalence; a "pobre man" at least in the context of this poetic passage at a certain level equals a "pregnant mujer." These paratactical relationships are of course effectively reinforced by the strict, and once again, parallel pattern of alliteration that has structured each line. Moreover, counterposed to the marked parallelism of the lines in question is the semantic opposition between man and *mujer* and between *pobre* and pregnant. These semantemes are forced parallels, they are "novelties" in the Russian formalist sense, the associations are "strange" to the everyday world. Moreover, this forcing achieves artistic tension and resonance which is further heightened by the already noted alternating language pattern, Sp. + Eng. vs. Eng. + Sp.

Similar although less marked formal patterns can be detected between the third and fifth lines (hombre rich/niño aborted).

The examples that I have provided of patterned properties within the minimal context of the poetic passage cited by Valdés-Fallis do not cause me to now pronounce that poem an artistically "good" example of bilingual poetry. However, I am even less inclined to pronounce it as "bad" after having found, for my taste at least, rather exciting dictional, syntactic, and prosodic patterns and complexities which if integrated into similar features on the level of imagery, thematics, tone, plot, etc., would appeal to my esthetic sense and win my enduring admiration. Moreover, since I bring prosody into the discussion at this point, I believe it worth noting that this passage that Valdés has cited as lacking "control over the use of language" because the poet has not penned code-switches " 'acceptable' by Mexican-Americans who code-switch themselves," has about it a type of overall metrical scheme which does not at all lend itself to an analysis that is based on everyday language. Could we really ever expect a series of two-word lines of verse to reflect communal language in the *barrio?* Are we not being unfair to the poet here, by evaluating his self-contained literary text through recourse to assumptions that lie totally outside that framework? I am reminded at this point of Matisse's answer to an ingenuous critic who, visiting his studio, complained, "Surely the arm of this woman is too long." Replied Matisse, "You are mistaken. That is not a woman, that is a picture. *Avant tout, je ne crée pas une femme, je fais un tableau.*"[26]

"Good" Literary Code-Switching that Violates Social Norms: More Examples

Let us now provide some actual examples of textual code-switching which clearly don't obey the constraints of social code-switching but which, in my humble and subjective opinion *are* good literature. These are examples which appear to me to violate the "weak assertion"; they would not only be unnatural in social discourse, but unacceptable to bilinguals except for the extraordinary context of literature which licences such eccentricities.

Fenimore[27] has observed that Hemingway, in *For Whom the Bell Tolls* utilizes the terms "rare" and "much" idiosyncratically. Here are some examples:

1. the blond one with the rare name. . .
2. "Very rare, yes, " Pablo said. "Very rare and very drunk. . ."
   He's rare all right, R. J. thought, and smart and very complicated.
3. much horse. . .
4. thou art much woman. . .
5. He went much with gypsies. . .
6. Four Fingers, a cobbler, who was much with Pablo then. . .

The occurrence of "rare" and "much" in the contexts above can not be accounted for by reference to normal conventions of the language code as recorded, say, in a dictionary of English. We are confronted with a deviation from the code of standard English. Yet the pattern of deviation, that is, the intra-textual relations set up between "rare" and "name," "much" and "horse" and so on throughout the book is able to achieve two literary goals of great consequence. First, a significance is created beyond that which the item carries in the standard code. "Rare name" in standard English is not quite intelligible, but it does evoke for the reader "weird name" or "strange name." "Much horse" makes no sense outside of the internal, literary context of *For Whom the Bell Tolls,* but the pattern of this and similar occurrences causes us to realize that a quantitative estimate has been transferred to a qualitative plane, so that semantically, we take it to mean a "fine horse," a "grand horse," etc. The recognition by the reader of the contextual implications of the words "rare" and "much" involves a revision of their dictionary meanings, in this case, in the form of an extension. Second, an appeal is made to a new code: standard Spanish. "Rare" is a direct transfer (as distinguished from a calque)[28] from the Spanish "raro." (Occasionally Hemingway will cue even the most ingenuous reader to this fact by including the standard Spanish sentences in the novel: "the deaf man nodded, 'Sí, algo raro, pero bueno.' ") The words "rare" and "much" have a certain echo value. Their English surface is readily recognizable but nonsensical, but since they are "bounced off" Spanish they become endowed with more than one meaning. Here again the reader's recognition of the contextual implications of the text causes him to realize that his decoding task has been extended, or rather, doubled, for the writer is expressing himself in a dual code.

The amazing thing about the examples I have provided is that they are code-switches without even using Spanish in a manifest way. I believe that as code-switches they are unique to literature, although the same sort of linguistic phenomena exist in the community as well, in the form of loans. For example, Spanish expressions such as *estar supuesto a, dámelo para atrás,* and other calques are clearly loans from English: to be supposed to, give it back to me. Also, *la norsa, la marqueta* (direct transfers) come from English: nurse, market. However, although not every linguist would agree with me, I don't consider these phrases to be code-switches, but rather, examples of United States vernacular Spanish, that is, they were borrowed from English, they are now a part of a Spanish vernacular. On the other hand, the examples of "rare" and "much" are literary, part of the writer's imaginative invention, and aren't taken from a Spanish Civil War variety of language. Therefore, I consider the literary examples to be truly bilingual although they exist within the text at the strictly idiolectal level. They didn't have communal, socially sanctioned meanings during the Spanish Civil War, but they retain their artistic value, their "strangeness," "novelty," "barbarism," etc., now and for always.

Let us summarize what Hemingway has specifically achieved with such locutions.

1. Semantically, while he is able to *evoke* standard English, he presents the esthetic novelty of *expressing* himself in non-standard English filtered through a clarifying and resonating grid of underlying Spanish.

2. Semantically, he is able to evoke standard Spanish meanings without (in the specific locutions I have used as examples) once using a Spanish word. Note also that Hemingway is very discreet here; he merely limits himself to anomalous semantic usages, eschewing syntactic irregularities. He could have said "name rare," thereby directly reflecting Spanish word order, but in this case it is not necessary nor esthetically sound. He is able to evoke Spanish less radically.

3. Syntactically, he is able to express himself in the esthetically novel medium of both English and Spanish: a medium which is *manifest* non-standard English and *latent* standard Spanish.

4. He is able to make personal metalinguistic observations and implications concerning certain semantico-syntactic relationships between Spanish and English. He puts such observations, comparisons, contrasts, etc., to the service of characterization, irony, and so on. Here not only bilingualism is involved but biculturalism and cross-cultural contrasts. Consider again the example given earlier: "Very rare, yes" Pablo said. "Very rare and very drunk..."/ He's rare all right, R. J. thought, and smart and very complicated.

Pablo expresses his passage "straight," without ironic or reflexive implications of any kind. He's talking about a very rare (standard English=strange) person, himself.

Jordan's use of "rare" is not the non-standard English = latent standard Spanish usage of Pablo. He uses "rare" in a normal, albeit ironic and idiomatic English manner, thereby implicating his bilingualism and biculturalism and also setting himself apart from Pablo. Curiously enough this *idiomatic* usage of English is equivalent to the *standard* use of Spanish "raro." Jordan, who is engaged in a private joke based on the word rare is thinking something like, "Pablo is 'rare' all right, a 'rare' bird or s.o.b. and a dangerous one as well." (Of course, the equivalence is not "really" curious at all since it provides the psychological rationale for this particular stream of associations and private joke-making in the first place.) The whole passage becomes even more intriguing if we take a psychological approach, trying to create the situation as it "actually is," that is, if we reify the characters. Having performed this operation we realize that Pablo has never said "rare" at all, since he knows no English. He has said "raro" and Jordan has intentionally turned the word into a false cognate (equivalent to intentionally making *largo* mean large) in order to have his private joke. From this point of view it is only Jordan who thinks "rare." Truly, bilingualism is a two-way street. No matter which way we analyze the passage we have a pun and an irony. And also, clearly, the "game" that is being played is far removed from the mimetic representation of reality since what Pablo has said, Pablo has not said. Hemingway is having fun somewhere in the interstice of two languages, and from that cranny-vantage is creating a bilingual literature that is self conscious, that is often bicultural and/or cross-cultural, that reflects upon itself in a metalinguistic way, and that is often used for ironic or satirical purposes. And it is partly for these reasons that I think *For Whom the Bell Tolls* and other bilingual works evincing similar qualities are great.

Roman Jakobson has pointed out that in literary writing, unlike other forms of expression, we find language which deliberately draws attention to itself, and this is what much of Hemingway's work does, bilingually.

Similar linguistico-literary phenomena occur, here in a Chicano context, in El Huitlacoche's poem, "Searching for La Real Cosa."[29] The title itself, which also functions as a refrain in the poem, is a borrowing from English, "The Real Thing," which to my knowledge is not a *barrio* expression, although numerous linguistically analogous loans exist in United States vernacular Spanish. In the poem, which uses coincidental, false English-Spanish cognates (dime, sea, pie, once, etc.) for thematic purposes, the expression, "¡Dime, dime, por amor de Dios!" later appears changed as, "A dime, dime for the love of God."

In his novel, *Figuraciones en el mes de marzo,* Emilio Díaz Valcárcel parodizes vernacular Spanish that is heavily influenced by English by taking it to such extremes that it is no longer anything like the communal language. What results is a hilarious caricature. This reduction to absurdity through the creation of a macaronic language has a long, illustrious tradition. Examples can be found in the classical Latin writers as well as in Molière. Díaz Valcárcel has a "prize winning" Puerto Rican poet discourse in the following way:

> ¿quál siendo la rola de la poetría? Questiona halto difísil a reportal, pero me adelanto a sugestil que la labol del poheta eh la de reflectar asquitaradamanti la realití de su mah profoundo sel. ¿No lo habéis dicho ya crazymente el gran Hale? ¿And quáleh suh palabrah para la hehtoria? Rememberarlah, señoreh: Sel u no sel, that is el lío.[30]

A bit further on:

> ¿Habéih pensado deepmente en el grasioso fruto del tamarindo, sí u no? ¡Qué cosita agria y dulse a same tiempo, que pretóricamente llenita de poetría anchantadora mot propio y to! ¿Conocíaies la pohetrí of el poheta ofisial? ¡Tan frutimante colorfula and fullita de tamarindous![31]

Díaz Valcárcel also accomplishes a very effective series of parodic code-switches that make use of the adjective "nice." Once again some of these usages we would not expect to see in social discourse, but they do make for effective comedy. For example, one character is described as a "gallinita nice." In another passage a character asserts, "Padecemos de pseudobilingüitis aguda, muy nice."

A final example of switched-on literature in its own right is the poetic drama, *Dawn*, by the noted Chicano writer, Alurista. I have not found any syntactic elements in this play that would violate the "weak assertion," that is, which would be syntactically unacceptable to Chicano bilinguals in everyday discourse. Nevertheless, the language is worth analyzing here, for it reveals a number of interesting literary techniques. The play, featuring characters such as Mexicano, Chicano, Quetzalcóatl, Cihuacóatl, and the archvillains, Pepsicóatl and Cocacóatl, is a sort of contemporary *Everyman,* an allegory of economic imperialism that makes extensive use of ritualized and ceremonial language. The play is entirely "dialogue," but none of it could possibly have occurred in society. For example, when Quetzalcóatl first speaks, he utters the following lines:

> i bring light to the darkness
> mestizaje of bloods pounds
> in my veins
> i am the morning star
> and the navel of earth
> feathers and scales
> color my face, Quetzalcóatl
> i am Meshicano Mazateca
> Meshicano Zapoteca
> Chicano, Chicano
> cheekbone to ankle

> bronze
> is
> my
> skin
> and my heart
> moves in balance to the stars
> in the north
> the Huelga thunderbird
> in the south
> the Chilean condor
> Kukulcán cracks
> dawn open
> i wake through
> la raza every morning
> la raza wakes
> through my star
> every dew[32]

Spanish is introduced for at least three separate reasons in the play, the base language of which is English:

(1) To emphasize the Chicano roots of specific language domains. In other words, Spanish terms or locutions are used to express emphatically Hispanic concepts; occasionally these words become artistically necessary since the vocabulary item or concept is nonexistent in the English language. For example, Alurista makes use of overt Hispanic identity markers such as *órale, ése, ésa,* and political or kinship or social lexicon such as *Chicano, Aztlán, ruca, huelga, danza, mestizaje,* and *raza.* As Valdés has clearly shown, this is a common function of code-switching in Chicano poetry. As a matter of fact, Valdés analyzes this usage in another of Alurista's works, the poem, "We Played Cowboys."

(2) To enhance the ritual flavor of the language. Here, in contrast to (1), the techniques are best analyzed through recourse to traditional rhetorical analysis. In order to achieve that hypnotic effect so often strived for in ritual language (D. H. Lawrence strove for this effect in *The Plumed Serpent,* a novel which has distinct similarities to *Dawn*), Alurista often uses anaphoras to create overt syntactic parallelisms. For example:

> huelga
> red and black
> huelga
> justice will be done
>
> danza
> riding over justice

danza
riding over peace
danza
danza of bare feet
danza of people
danza of day
danza of spirit
danza of bronze
danza, danza
danza, danza. . . . .

i wake through
la raza every morning
la raza wakes
through my star[33]

As a matter of fact, these anaphoristic and/or parallelistic construc-
tions are spread extensively through the play, not only in Spanish-
English repertoire, but also exclusively in English as well:

genocide
genocide
killer of children
biocide
biocide
polluter of earth[34]

(3) If we accept the Náhuatl words that I have cited from the
play as currently part of contemporary Mexican Spanish, Alurista
creates at least two bilingual portmanteau words in *Dawn*: Pepsicóatl
and Cocacóatl. Neither of these have any consensual meaning in the
Chicano community, but they are emblematic of key thematic concepts in the author's play.

One Axiological Principle for Evaluating Literary Code-Switching

There is, in sum, one abiding principle that we can follow in assigning value to code-switches in bilingual literature. The very act of
switching from one language to another constitutes a radical moment of foregrounding (substitute equivalent terms referring to the
deviation from normal language, at your pleasure). Code-switching
is so radical a phenomenon that in itself it constitutes foregrounding.
It is one of the most overt ways of having language call attention to
itself, and as such, each and every code-switch must have a definite
(be it explicit or implied, thematic or stylistic, etc.) esthetic function
in order to justify itself. I believe this to be part of a general pattern in
art: the more radical the departure from the commonplace, the more

necessary for the text to show adequate cause. By and large what we seek from a writer is an overt, compelling sense of difference. That is part of what makes for notable art, a unique signature, a distinctive voice. The task is to make it stick, to make the voice just, the signature valid.

Valdés has stated, "...language alternation can be poetically significant or it can be of little or no importance to poetic meaning. Indeed, it may frequently be used simply because it has become increasingly identified with Chicano poetry."[35] I go one step further, judging that when language alternation is esthetically significant it is "good" and when it is of little or no esthetic importance, it is "bad." Random code-switching or code-switching for its own sake can be justified only by recourse to the torturous "vanguard" arguments that have been used to justify the one poem out of untoward printouts produced by the insouciant computer going through its programmed paces. And if code-switching is indeed "strong medicine," then it stands to reason that it should be used sparingly, because code-switching carries with it the solemn duty of providing for its esthetic adequacy.

Moreover, in point of fact, it has been my experience that code-switching *is* used relatively sparingly. Bilingual literature is more often than not characterized by strategic emplacements of the non-base language rather than wholesale language alternation. At the same time we need to note there are at least two occasions when only constant alternation will suffice, both, of course, precisely for esthetic reasons. One is in the interest of characterization, typically to portray what in linguistics has traditionally been called a compound bilingual (a controversial designator): a person whose code-switching is beyond conscious or voluntary control. The other esthetic project is a more subtle one, and hence, harder to justify. Here the writer constantly switches between languages in order to relate to his or her natural bilingual constituency of readers. In this fashion, the writer at one level serves up the text as a global, or totalistic, integrated "identity marker" in the sociolinguistic sense. The text naturally does not have to reflect the community's bilinguality nor even be semantically or syntactically acceptable in the ordinary sense. Nevertheless it is offered as a sort of a secret, a cipher that can only be decoded by those who are communally initiated. For this reason, as well as for many others, José Montoya's poem, "El Louie," emerges as one of the finest in contemporary Chicano literature. I quote a pertinent passage:

Y en Fowler at Nesei's
pool parlor los baby chooks
se acuerdan de Louie, el carnal
del Candi y el Ponchi—la vez
que lo fileriaron en el Casa
Dome y cuando se catió con
La Chiva

Hoy enterraron al Louie.

His death was an insult
porque no murió en acción—
no lo mataron los vatos,
ni los gooks en Korea.
He died alone in a rented
room—perhaps like a
Bogard movie.

The end was a cruel hoax.
But his life had been
remarkable!

Vato de atolle, el Louie Rodríguez.[36]

The motivation for code-switching apparent in Montoya's poetry does not exist for Hemingway, for example. The distinction lies in the critical question of readership. Hemingway's code-switching has a basic esthetic premise: the evocation of Spanish by means of a fluted, fashioned, and rendered English. The result is manifest, surface, deviant English that evokes latent, underlying Spanish. Hemingway's fancied readership is English monolingual. Hence, one of his prime concerns is to evoke Spanish by means of English. On the other hand, Montoya's combination of English and Spanish results in a secondary language system that contains revealing departures from the linguistic medium of Hemingway. One of the crucial differences is readership. Fenimore, in attempting to answer the question: To what extent is knowledge of Spanish necessary for a full reading of *For Whom the Bell Tolls,* observes that "in such cases as 'much horse' and in short, all phraseology which is not colloquial English and hence may be reflected Spanish, knowledge of that language is immaterial to the important thing—the tacit assumption that it *is* Spanish, and, based upon this assumption, our acceptance of a non-colloquial English."[37] Fenimore's observation is valid when associated with the readership that Hemingway had in mind: English monolinguals who would need to approach the uniqueness of the secondary language system by making certain general assumptions about its manifest and underlying nature. The relationship between Chicano or Boricua writers and their expected readerships is substantially different. The authors in question take for granted that at least a significant portion of their readership is English-Spanish bilingual. They assume that their readers are actively involved (or at least are linguistically competent to be involved) in the fusion of English and Spanish in order to derive novel effects. Their style parallels certain aspects of the language production of the living bilingual community. Hence, the literary outcomes often combine English and Spanish directly, without explanation, circumlocution, compensation or any other form of linguistic allotment for the monolingual. Only the bilingual author writing for a bilingual reader is capable of justifying expressions such as Eduardo Rivera's, "tough teta," "hard-up jíbaro," and "good grass"[38] (meaning *yerba buena* and marihuana at the same time).

Here resides, I believe, a significant departure between Valdés's critical approach and the one I take. She appears to judge that the code-switch must be comprehensible to the reader; I say more. Of course most code-switches are comprehensible and syntactically acceptable to the reader. Many even come from the community's own language usage, for it is certainly true that much spoken code-switching is performed for stylistic reasons and thus there is substantial overlap between literary and communal code-switching. Yet there is so much more to be evaluated; what of those code-switches that at a certain level are unfathomable, mystifying (to monolingual readers such as Hemingway's, to bilingual ones such as Montoya's), but, how beckoning! They inspire us to travel that extra distance into the writer's home turf, an esthetic bilingual idiolect. The trick for the writer is to make engagé the ineluctable bilingual image. In the case of one that is merely hermetic, the writer has gone too far into him/herself, and the switch holds no resonance nor interest for the reader. Moreover, the justification of massive code-switching as an offering to the switched-on community is not sufficient if the alternations do not have something else to recommend them, if they are not overdetermined esthetically by additional considerations of diction, characterization, or what not. It is precisely the vernacular authenticity together with the fashioning of deep feelings into a hard, tough, and unique idiolect that makes "El Louie" a poem as remarkable as the *vato* to whom it is dedicated. And more: no one has a signature quite like El Louie, the persona in the poem, and how unfathomably intertwined is that signature with the *separate* voice of the eulogizing poetic narrator. Contrast "El Louie" with a poem that goes about alternating extensively without forging additional esthetic bonds; for me the latter simply becomes a boring muddle. Foregrounding without compelling motive is esthetic anathema.

Finally, we should pursue another logical consequence of the principle that I have asserted. If code-switching in itself constitutes a radical act of foregrounding, and requires esthetic self-sufficiency, even when the code-switch either directly imitates or at least would sound natural to the bilingual who includes such alternation in his or her social repertoire, then those code-switches which break the established syntactic patterns of society, because of their very extremity require more compelling justification on esthetic grounds. This follows from my statement that the more radical the departure from the commonplace, the more necessary that the text evince adequate reason for that departure. We are strictly responsible for our rule-breaking. We have to show that what *seems like* gibberish has ulterior purposes; if not, then in fact we have simply produced artless gibberish. Take for example the beginning of Cortázar's famous short story, "Las babas del diablo": "Si se pudiera decir: yo vieron subir la luna, o: nos me duele el fondo de los ojos, y sobre todo así: tú la mujer rubia eran las nubes que siguen corriendo delante de mis tus sus nuestros vuestros sus rostros. Qué diablos."[39]

In this passage we are confronted not with aberrant code-switching, for the story is all in Spanish, but with the subversion of subject/verb, gender, and number agreement. Yet the passage works (this is the consensus of critics) because it functions thematically within the whole mosaic of the story. Other such experiments may not have such felicitous results. And perhaps due to the need to satisfactorily justify them, I have not found such radical syntactic alternations in bilingual literature. I can attest to examples such as "tough teta," "hard-up jíbaro," "sel u no sel, that is el lío," "muy nice" but not *teta tough; *hard jíbaro up; *sel u no sel, that lío es el; or *nice muy.

The former set still respects the constituent phrase structures of both English and Spanish, while combining them in linguistically novel ways. The latter hypothetical set remains gibberish, both in art and society, at least until such time as some vanguard literary genius presses them into a justifiable textual language system.

Toward a Praxis of Bilingual Composition

We are now in a position to turn from the thorny complications of assigning literary value to various categories of bilingual literature —in short, the problems of judicial evaluation. Let us turn to a

The Bilingual Chicano Writer

more descriptive concern, the simple elucidation of a variety of bilingual techniques that I have unearthed during the course of my readings in Chicano and other literatures. In so doing, I will be classifying examples under separate headings related to theme, characterization, or style (often in categories provided by traditional literary rhetoric). In proceeding in this manner I don't mean to imply that a given bilingual example has purely the literary function to which it has been assigned. In addition, I fully concede the deficiency of using short passages to exemplify literary techniques, the more so having criticized Valdés for the same procedure. I certainly don't wish to imply that theme is easily separable from character or from stylistic figures, much less to resurrect the long-surpassed dichotomy between form and content. The method is being used exclusively as a heuristic device, in order to register a substantial number of code-switching examples without extending the length of this paper unduly.

Thematic Code-Switching

As Valdés has well seen, much code-switching serves the special function of highlighting the theme, message, ideology, and so on, of the author. Certainly the most common example of this sort of alternation in Chicano literature reflects a sharp division of domains signaled by the use of English and Spanish. As Valdés shows, the English language is used to represent the Anglo world, the Spanish language, the Chicano world. As we have seen, Alurista's *Dawn* displays good examples of this type of code-switch. Another clear example can be found in Ernesto Galarza's moving autobiography, *Barrio Boy*.

> Crowded as it was, the *colonia* found a place for these *chicanos,* the name by which we called an unskilled worker born in Mexico and just arrived in the United States. The *chicanos* were fond of identifying themselves by saying thay had just arrived from *el macizo,* by which they mean the solid Mexican homeland, the good native earth. Although they spoke of *el macizo* like homesick persons, they didn't go back. They remained, as they said of themselves, *pura raza.* So it happened that José and Gustavo would bring home for a meal and for conversation workingmen who were *chicanos* fresh from *el macizo* and like ourselves, *pura raza.* Like us, they had come straight to the *barrio* where they could order a meal, buy a pair of overalls, and look for work in Spanish. They brought us vague news about the revolution, in which many of them had fought as *villistas, huertistas, maderistas,* or *zapatistas.* As an old *maderista,* I imagined our *chicano* guests as battle-tested revolutionaries, like myself. . . .Beds and meals, if the

newcomers had no money at all, were provided—in one way or another—on trust, until the new *chicano* found a job. On trust and not on credit, for trust was something between people who had plenty of nothing, and credit was between people who had something of plenty. It was not charity or social welfare but something my mother called *asistencia,* a helping given and received on trust, to be repaid because those who had given it were themselves in need of what they had given. *Chicanos* who had found work on farms or in railroad camps came back to pay us a few dollars for *asistencia* we had provided weeks or months before.[40] [Italics are the author's.]

Alurista uses Spanish basically in order to signal where his ideals, politics, values, allegiances, etc., lie. There is nothing to suggest that the poet can not think of the English equivalent of certain words or expressions and therefore uses Spanish. On the other hand, Galarza uses Spanish precisely when he is confronted with a concept or domain that is alien to Anglo culture. At this point Galarza uses the Spanish word or expression and then immediately elucidates it with an English definition. In this fashion, while Galarza is a Chicano writer, his procedure does not differ from authors writing for Anglo readers. Steinbeck, for example, often uses a Spanish concept, and then, in "anthropological" fashion goes on to explain it for his monocultural reader. Alurista is bicultural in the sense that, even though the English language usually represents the adversary, he switches between the two languages with a bilingual's natural ease; Galarza's procedure is cross-cultural, taking his reader by the hand through the esoteric or unknown world of the Chicanos. Yet both have in common the same semantic field for their use of Spanish—it represents the Chicano domain. The same sort of characteristic can be seen when the base language is Spanish. In the poem by Pedro Ortiz Vásquez, "Quienes somos," English is the language consigned to express strangeness, alienation:

> it's so strange in here
> todo lo que pasa
> is so strange
> y nadie puede entender
> que lo que pasa aquí
> isn't any different
> de lo que pasa allá[41]

A special category of thematic code-switching should be established for those expressions in literature which reflect what sociolinguists analyzing normal social discourse have termed "identity markers." As in communal language, literary "identity markers" such as

The Bilingual Chicano Writer

the examples of *órale, ése, ésa,* that we have seen in Alurista, are used to establish rapport in Spanish between the author and his Chicano readers. In Luis Valdés's classic *acto, Las dos caras del patroncito,* the farmworker manages to trick the *patrón.* The play ends this way:

> Farmworker: Bueno, so much for the patrón. I got his house, his land, his car—only I'm not going to keep 'em. He can have them. But I'm taking the cigar. Ay los watcho. (EXIT)[42]

"Ay los watcho" is the perfect ending for this sort of consciousness-raising and rapport-establishing exercise, a theater the avowed intention of which is to motivate the migrant worker to join the union. At the end of El Huitlacoche's poem, "Searching for La Real Cosa," after having debunked the conventional identifications of the Chicano, the poet asserts:

> Por fin, ¿eh? ¡Ya estuvo!
> ¿Quién es la real cosa?
> A dime, dime for the love of God!
> ¡Madre! Ese vato, ¡qué sé yo![43]

The identity markers *¡Ya estuvo!, ¡Madre!, Ese vato, ¡qué sé yo!* are all pressed into a plea for a vision of Chicanismo that transcends stereotyping.

In addition to the code-switching that allots separate domains to English and Spanish for various thematic reasons, there are literary texts that incorporate additional registers *within* the English and/or Spanish language. It is common that once the writer has consciously made the decision to create literary texts in a bilingual medium, that this decision leads to added sensitivity to the levels of register within language. Thus *interlinguistic* literary texts lead naturally to a richer *intralinguistic* expressivity. Hemingway's *For Whom the Bell Tolls* provides a clear example of the phenomenon. The novelty of Hemingway's style is a function not only of Spanish, but archaic, Elizabethan English as well. And this archaic, Elizabethan element reinforces the epic qualities of the novel. *For Whom the Bell Tolls* is an epic and the Elizabethan tone enhances the breadth of the epic language. The *thee, thou, thine* is not only English calculated to conjure up *te, tú, tuyo,* but the singular pronoun used by John Donne and other classical English writers. Seen in this light, the epigraph from whence the title takes on new dimensions, both linguistic and thematic. Both in the epigraph and in the actual usage of *thee, thou,* etc., is implied Spanish and also English in the grand, epic manner, with the consequent implication, thematically, of the novel's relevance across cultures and over time. All this is facilitated by a bilingual medium, one which permits the addition of an archaic, epic and biblical register within the portion of the novel alloted to English code.

The bilingual literature of Eduardo Rivera, El Huitlacoche, and José Montoya provides parallel examples. The base language of these writers is English, so that Spanish is used sparingly and strategically. On most occasions, the Spanish they choose is taken from the vernacular—the language is emotional, intimate, popular.[44] In this sense these writers reflect the traditional bilingual dichotomy. The classic bilingual uses one language for commerce, education, and public duties in general; the second language for falling in love, being angry, having a good time, family life, and so on. The Spanish of all three writers is almost exclusively of the latter domains. Nevertheless, with respect to English the situation is quite different. As shown below, the English repertoire runs the gamut from the most formal register to the most colloquial and popular. It also includes loan translations, the sort of thing that Hemingway was so adept at.

Registers and Language Switching in Eduardo Rivera, El Huitlacoche, and José Montoya

Ex. of Formal Eng.	1. ...poetaster...
	2. ...a tangle of tropical weeds, smooth and hilly, precipitous and sloped, the monotony of greens relieved only by bald patches of soft red clay...
	3. ...a large mural depicting angels in multicolored flowing gowns, puffed cheeks blowing celestial notes from golden horns and trumpets, pliant fingers plucking harps...
	4. If I did not forgive my father his naive belief in his omnipotence then I would have succumbed to his logic and in condemning him would validate his credo of an ultimate, personal accountability. The vicious circle; the double bind.
	5. The end was a cruel hoax. But his life had been remarkable!
Ex. of Colloq. Eng.	1. ...good and bad-ass neighborhoods...
	2. ...grimy-pawed tot...
	3. ...Fwop! Like sugar cane.
	4. Extreme Unction, that last-ditch sacrament...
	5. ...sex-in-the-brain stares...
	6. the gut-shrinking love-splitting, ass-hole-up tight-bad news—
	7. Eight worthless daughters and one half-ass son.

The Bilingual Chicano Writer

Loan Translations	
Formal Eng. repre-senting Span.	Chalito and I went to college where after many peripeteias [Spanish, *peripecias*] I eventually majored in sociology.
Colloquial Eng. repre-senting Span.	Papa Santos would give her a concoction of boiled milk with ginger and some wild herb called "good grass" [Spanish, *yerba buena,* but also evokes *marijuana*].
Compound Structures	

Eng. colloq. & Sp. colloq.	1. no lo mataron los vatos,
	   ni los gooks en Korea.
	2. It was tough teta for any simple-minded jíbaro...
	3. Pues, I'm just a vato loco man
	   but if I had my way again
	   I'd ask for 'Miliano Zapata's rise
	   Steinbeck claims he never died
	   I crave that dude at my side

Eng. colloq. & Sp. formal	None: formal Spanish not used by these writers

Eng. formal & Sp. colloq.	1. And Louie would come through—
	   melodramatic music, like in the
	   mono—tan tan tarán—Cruz
	   Diablo, El Charro Negro!
	2. Is this a binary hoodwink?
	   Schizophrenia or stereoscopy?
	   ¿mala fe? or merely ¿mala leche?[45]

Eng. formal & Sp. formal	None: formal Spanish not used by these writers

The opposite is the case of Emilio Díaz Valcárcel's *Figuraciones en el mes de marzo.* This book, which has the structure of an album of various sorts of documents and letters, is basically written in Spanish with the inclusion of a scattering of English. As I have observed earlier (pp. 280-1), when English is used it is almost always directly combined with Spanish to produce hilarious effects. The Spanish, however, covers the whole set of registers from the oratorical (and pseudo-oratorical) to the semi-formal (cocktail party language), colloquial, and regional. Indeed, the utilization of phonological, lexical and idiomatic features that are peculiar either to Madrid or to Puerto Rico is a significant element in the novel. These regionalisms are used often for humor—as in the Puerto Rican poet's combining of mangled English and mangled Spanish. Moreover, in order to achieve these humorous, burlesque effects, the author is wont to exaggerate. No person in the Puerto Rican (or any other) community speaks like Valcárcel's poet-protagonist. Regionalisms are also used for cross-cultural contrasts in this novel: the Madrilenian way of expressing oneself is contrasted with the Puerto Rican custom.

292

Gary D. Keller

Of course, not only registers within English or Spanish need be involved. Particularly, in Chicano literature we see an incorporation of lexicon (no syntax that I have been able to detect) from pre-Colombian, Amerindian languages. The examples that I have cited from Alurista (both "straight" lexicon such as *Quetzalcóatl* and *Cihuacóatl,* as well as the portmanteaus, *Pepsicóatl* and *Cocacóatl*) are clear cut. El Huitlacoche uses terms such as *esquintles, huaraches, Netzahualcoyotl,* and *Huitzilopochtli,* among others. Jesús Maldonado (el flaco) writes an "Oda al molcajete." In the poetry of Lorenza Calvillo Schmidt and Adaljiza Sosa Riddell the powerful figure *Malinche* is evoked. *La Malinche* can only stir up deep and ambivalent feelings, since in the Chicano mythos this "Eva mexicana,"[46] as Octavio Paz has termed her and José Clemente Orozco has painted her, represents at least three major motifs:

(1) She is the "Indian woman" par excellence.

(2) She is a "traitor" to the Indians since she joins with the Spaniards. Indeed, *Malinche* is commonly used as an antonomasia for traitor. But she is also the "romantic lover and rebel," inasmuch as she is enamoured of Hernán Cortés and becomes his mistress.

(3) She is the "mother" of the mestizo—that is, the Chicano, José Vasconcelos's "raza cósmica"—since she bears out of wedlock the fruit of the sinful yet exalted sexual congress between herself, aristocratic Indian maiden, and Cortés, Spanish adventurer and conquistador.

Both of the women poets mentioned above refer to their *malinchismo,* the *malinchismo* of the Chicana woman. For Sosa Riddell it is part of Chicano transculturation (or perhaps, if we care to be more optimistic in the interpretation of the poem, merely biculturalism):

> Malinche, pinche
> forever with me
> . . . .
> Pinche, como duele ser Malinche
> Pero sabes, ése
> what keeps me from shattering
> into a million fragments?
> It's that sometimes,
> You are muy gringo, too.[46]

For Calvillo Schmidt this treachery is partly the result of the exploitation of the Chicano male, who has been sent to Korea, Vietnam, barber's school, anywhere far away from the more "docile" Chicana who is permitted to attend college but who is also coopted by the white male:

> A Chicano at Dartmouth?
> I was at Berkeley, where
> there were too few of us
> and even less of you.
> I'm not even sure
> that I really looked for you.
>
> I heard from many rucos
> that you
> would never make it.
> You would hold me back;
> From What?
> From what we are today?
> "Y QUE VIVA"
> Pinche, como duele ser Malinche.[47]

In the popular and anonymous folk poem "Los animales,"[48] collected by Américo Paredes, a number of pre-Columbian terms (in origin) for animals, plants, foods, etc., are referred to: *huacales, coyote, zopilote, tlacuache, jicote, mitote, pinacate, mayate, guajolote, mole, pozole, huitlacoche,* and so on. These Amerindian terms are essential to evoke the folkloric, Chicano themes of the poems in question. They serve as the mortar for the creation of a Chicano folklore with unique, distinguishable features.

The thematic purposes for expanding the variety and levels of register and for incorporating elements of additional languages such as Náhuatl are as varied as the thematic concerns of the authors themselves. For many Chicano writers, and specifically in the examples that I have cited from Alurista, Jesús Maldonado, Calvillo Schmidt, Sosa Riddell, El Huitlacoche, and the anonymous author(s) of "Los animales," the added Amerindian lexicon represents an effort to recuperate Chicano history and create or recreate a Chicano mythos based on the four essential ethnic progenitors of Chicanismo: the Indian, the Spaniard, the Mexican, and the Anglo. Whether in reference to a glorious past (*Quetzalcóatl*) or a painful one (*Malinche*), multilingualism is a way to give each ancestor his (or her) due.

For José Montoya, at least in "El Louie," using highly vernacular Spanish together with highly vernacular English (but also formal English) is an essential part of composing a psychologically accurate portrait of a particular type of compound bilingual, the *pachuco.* Nevertheless, the poem has complex resonations since it is a *pachuco* poem about a *pachuco,* and yet it transcends simple folk or popular poetry. The poem convinces us as a character study; we are also convinced that the voice of the poet (or narrator) is authentically *pachuco,* yet in several passages, and particularly at the end, the voice transcends unselfconscious *pachuquismo* and manifests a sensitivity to myth, history, and ethics, expressed in formal English. In a sense José Montoya does without telling us what Jorge Luis Borges tells us he is going to do in the short story, "La intrusa," when he alleges that he is going to tell us a straightforward story, a sort of "diamond in the rough" but that he is also going to yield to the "tentación literaria de acentuar o agregar algún pormenor."[49] It is the emergence of the self-conscious image of the artist that is made possible by the expansion of the poetic diction to include formal English in "El Louie."

For Díaz Valcárcel, the wide spectrum of Spanish registers that he utilizes serves perfectly to cultivate the "problem" of whence the Puerto Rican in the Hispanic world.

Finally, it is important to note that the artistic variation of registers is not even confined to bilingual literature, but is commonly found in monolingual literature as well. A clear example of the phenomenon is to be found in the American novel of the South. Faulkner and Styron are good cases in point. While limits on the scope of this paper don't permit me to dwell on this phenomenon, I will cite one example. The main protagonist of Faulkner's *Light in August* is the mulatto, Joe Christmas, whose racial condition ultimately determines his fate:

> ". . . .It would not be either one or the other and let his body save itself. Because the black blood drove him first to the negro cabin. And then the white blood drove him out of there, as it was the black blood which snatched up the pistol and the white blood which would not let him fire it. And it was the white blood which sent him to the minister, which rising in him for the last and final time, sent him against all reason and all reality, into the embrace of a chimera, a blind faith in something read in a printed Book. Then I believe that the white blood deserted him for the moment. Just a second, a flicker, allowing the black to rise in its final moment and make him turn upon that on which he had postulated his hope of salvation. It was the black blood which swept him up into that ecstasy out of a black jungle where life has already ceased before the heart stops and death is desire and fulfillment. And then the black blood failed him again, as it must have in crises all his life. He did not kill the minister. He merely struck him with the pistol and ran on and crouched behind that table and defied the black blood for the last time, as he had been defying it for thirty years. He crouched behind that overturned table and let them shoot him to death, with that loaded and unfired pistol in his hand."[50]

Register-switching is a way analogous to the "blood" metaphor to signal the implacable oppositions in the novel:

> [Formal] The car had overshot him, slowing; now he passed it at his swift, silent, steady pace; again the car speeded up and passed him, the men leaning out and looking ahead. He was going fast too, silent, with the delicate swiftness of an apparition, the implacable undeviation of Juggernaut or Fate.

> [Vernacular] "Jesus Christ!" Grimm cried, his young voice clear and outraged like that of a young priest. "Has every preacher and old maid in Jefferson taken their pants down to the yellowbellied son of a bitch?"

> [Formal] For a long moment he looked up at them with peaceful and unfathomable and unbearable eyes. Then his face, body, all, seemed to collapse, to fall upon itself, and from out the slashed garments about his hips and loins the pent black blood seemed to rush like a released breath. It seemed to rush out of his pale body like the rush of sparks from a rising rocket; upon that black blast the man seemed to rise soaring into their memories forever and ever. They are not to lose it, in whatever peaceful valleys, beside whatever placid and reassuring streams of old age, in the mirroring faces of whatever children they will contemplate old disasters and newer hopes. It will be there, musing, quiet, steadfast, not fading and not particularly threatful, but of itself alone serene, of itself alone triumphant.

> [Vernacular] "Durn the luck. Just when I had to get started for home. I'm already late."
> "Excitement?" Byron says. "What excitement?"
> . . ."I thought maybe you hadn't heard. About an hour ago. That nigger, Christmas. They killed him."[51]

Spanish Used to Express the Alien

As we have seen, when one aspect of the theme revolves around what is intimate and known versus what is alien, typically Spanish expresses the former and English, the latter. Yet this does not necessarily have to be the case. Occasionally, under special circumstances, the tables can be turned and Spanish can be used to express that which is alien. Take for example a passage from El Huitlacoche's "The Urban(e) Chicano's 76." The poet is criticizing a moment in John Steinbeck's famous screenplay, *¡Viva Zapata!*, which featured Marlon Brando in the main role. The scene in question has Brando-Zapata dressed in his pajama bottoms on his wedding night, lamenting to his bride that he can't read or write. The bride then offers to educate him. At this moment a group of Zapata's followers congregate below the nuptial balcony and Zapata comes out in pajamas to address them:

> Zapata comes out on the wedding night

in pajama bottoms, he yearns to read and write
I love you Johnny, the way you write
but shit, you stink, babosísimo fool
that's my boy up there in striped bottoms
addressing armed campesinos in broad-rimmed sombreros
from the balcony railing with Arabesques
¡el frito bandito![52]

The words, "campesinos," "sombreros," and "frito bandito" (instead of *bandido*) are all examples of Spanish lexicon that are well-known to English speakers and have actually been partially assimilated into English. What the poet does is to show how these words have been used in the Anglo world to stereotype the Hispano. Thus they become "alien" to the Hispanic world to the degree that they are used by the Anglo to characterize (and caricaturize) the Hispano. In another poem by the same author the following lines appear:

You turned el chile into preprocessed velveeta
and Tiburcio Vásquez into el frito bandito
You made Emiliano Zapata
Marlon Brando who went to bed
in his pajama bottoms on the wedding night.[53]

A similar example of this process of alienation, this time not in literary language but in communal language, is the term *caramba*. Having been stereotypically associated with Hispanics for several decades now in the English language, virtually no Hispanic ever uses it. A somewhat related example appears in the passage of Sosa Riddell's poem which I have quoted earlier:

It's that sometimes,
You are muy gringo too.

Here the Spanish word, *gringo,* used to depict the sociocultural Other, is now directed to what is (or perhaps was) alien in one's own cultural makeup. Thus a special sort of tension, one that is highly productive from an artistic point of view, is set up in the code-switch involving a Spanish designator for an Anglo sort of otherness having established itself in a Hispanic persona.

Having described two polar and antithetical usages, the first where Spanish is used for what is familiar, the second, in special circumstances, where Spanish expresses that which is alien, namely, Anglo, we are obliged to round out the dialectic and exemplify a code-switch depicting the creative synthesis between the self and the Other. In Angela de Hoyos's poem, "Café con leche," the poet ambivalently observes that she has seen a male Chicano friend coming out of a motel with a *gringuita*. The final stanza encapsulates a stirring and subtle irony:

> No te apenas, amigo:
> Homogenization
> is one good way
> to dissolve differences
> and besides
>   what's wrong
> with a beautiful race
> café con leche?[54]

The expression *café con leche* serves many functions, only two of which are to evoke the beauty of the prior *mestizaje,* the fruit of Spaniard and Indian, and second, to prefigure the potential new *mestizaje,* between Chicano and Anglo. In addition, the image lends itself admirably to the central conflict: we can think of *café* and *leche* as separate entities, and identify each with the skin color of each race (milk walking with coffee from the motel), or we can think of that cappuccino color that they make in the blending.

Code-Switching Between Title and Text

I shall conclude this section on code-switching for thematic purposes with one last subcategory, in the domain of poetry. A large number of poems have been written with a second language title. Only the title is non-English; the poem itself is written exclusively in the English language, although occasionally the choice of lexicon may tilt toward English words which originate in the second language (e.g., chateaux, demoiselles, etc.). In this sort of poem even more attention is drawn to the title than normally, because of the language switch. This category of code-switch is quite common with English language poets who are associated with the symbolist, and above all, imagist schools. Thus, among many other examples that could be mentioned, we have Ezra Pound's "Blandula, Tenulla, Vagulla," "Erat Hora," "Portrait d'une Femme," "Siena mi fe'; disfecemi Maremma," and "Yeux Glauques"; Lawrence Durrell's "Bere Regis"; J.M. Synge's "Notre Dames des Champs"; Arthur Symons, "Clair de Lune" (evoking Verlaine's famous poem); Oscar Wilde's "Les Ballons"; T. S. Eliot's "La Figlia che Piange"; Wallace Steven's "Cy Est Pourtraicte, Madame Ste Ursule, et Les Unze Mille Vierges," "Le Monocle de Mon Oncle," "Anglais Mort à Florence," and "Esthetique du Mal"; and William Carlos Williams's "Aux Imagistes," and "El Hombre."

The existence of such English-language compositions with titles in other languages does not deny the fact that some of the poets mentioned above, such as Pound, wrote other poems characterized by a good deal of code-switching in the text itself, or wrote poems entirely in another language, as did Eliot, who penned a number of very humorous compositions in French ("Le directeur," "Mélange adultère de tout," etc.) in a droll, doggerel style that emphasizes rhyme to a burlesque extreme.

Herminio Ríos thinks that this sort of bilingual poetry (he mentions specifically T. S. Eliot and Ezra Pound) is "simply a device to create an atmosphere,"[55] but this is just as fallacious as his belief that, in contrast, Chicano poetic code-switching is merely "a reflection of every day speech, in which the social situation determines, to a large extent, the frequency and location within the sentence where the changes from one system to another will occur."[56] My close reading of a substantial number of poems composed by non-Chicano code-switchers leads me to judge that the phenomenon in question usually reflects very definite thematic concerns. These switches typically serve to foreground the poetic message—which in no way denies the exigencies of "atmosphere," once we realize that this latter quality is not "simply a device" but is just as integrated into the poetic whole as any other aspect which we may want to arbitrarily sift out for the purpose of literary analysis. Moreover, what I claim for the textually switched-on poetry of, say, Pound or Stevens holds even more for the poems that I have cited earlier, characterized by one, isolated code-switch between title and text. Constraints on the length of this paper permit me to give only one example of the significantly thematic import of title/text code-switches in non-Chicano poets. Wallace Stevens entitles "Le Monocle de Mon Oncle" so as to highlight by means of French two concerns which are central to the poem: 1. That we need a subjective "glass piece" with which to view reality. Life should be a series of "revealing aberrations,"[57] to be imposed on reality, for it is these imaginative distortions of the perceived world that permit us, quixotically, to face up to reality. As counterpoint to the "Oncle" there is a draft of a poem in Stevens's *Opus Posthumous* called "The Naked Eye of My Aunt." The Aunt is a perceptual failure because she tries to face the object too squarely. 2. At the same time that the poem presents an "aberrant" or "poetic" perception of reality, which is both distorted and necessary, the poem also is intended to deflate the pretensions of poetry itself. This ambivalence between the necessary distortion that is at the same time pomp, poetic petulance, is nicely evoked by the comic-burlesque word play: *monocle/ mon oncle.*

Now let us turn to some examples of title/text switches in Chicano poetry. The text of raúlsalinas's poem, "Los caudillos," is written in English with the exception of one line which appears as a quote from Tijerina's followers ("¡esta tierra es nuestra!"[58]). The poem may be in English but *caudillos* is highly appropriate for the title since the text evokes not leaders, chiefs, bosses, honchos, etc., but authentic Hispanic *caudillos* (Chávez, Tijerina, Rodolfo "Corky" Gonzales, etc.) although they are living and leading in an Anglo world (hence the English language text). El Huitlacoche's short poem, "¡Hostias!"[59] satirizes the secularization of religion by parodying the three-in-one concept (a steak sauce? a multipurpose lubricating oil? and so on). The title has at least two references: the denotative divine wafer and the connotative blasphemy. Only Spanish could possibly render this multivalence. Imagine how ridiculous the poem would sound if it were entitled either, "Holy Wafer!" or "Damnation!"

In conclusion, I should note that bidialectical title/text code-switching has also been cultivated. For example, the textual selection of lexicon in Wallace Stevens's "Like Decorations in a Nigger Cemetery" is almost exclusively formal. A similar Chicano bidialectical example is Jesús Maldonado's "Loa al frijol." The *loa* is a classical dramatico-poetic form which expresses a eulogy to some illustrious figure, usually by means of allegory. Here we are confronted with a "frijolito lindo" that "reinas cuando frito" and "matas hambrecito."[60] A great deal of caustic social satire is packed into this bidialectical, poetic language/vernacular usage code-switch.

Code-Switching for Characterization

The one Chicano character that counts for much, with respect to code-switching, is the compound bilingual. The term compound bilingual in sociolinguistics is somewhat controversial. Here I define it merely as someone who is incapable (either chronically or temporarily, because of some specific, say, traumatizing, circumstance) of separating out the two codes. Thus the individual mixes languages (and/or registers) constantly, typically within phrases and sentences. The opposite, the coordinate bilingual, while certainly capable of producing compound structures, does so as a reflection of his or her conscious volition, is not involuntarily forced to alternate codes. The coordinate bilingual is not particularly worth investigating in this paper on bilingual literary strategies because when functioning coordinately such an individual will be speaking either in English or Spanish exclusively. Conversely, when functioning in a compound fashion, the coordinate bilingual's potential for language separation would be masked. Hence it is not possible to distinguish the coordinate bilingual from a compound bilingual as a literary character on the mere basis of a literary text.

The psycholinguistic nature of the compound bilingual has received attention from the Chicano writer, who, naturally, must use code-switches to reflect that phenomenon. As I have pointed out, the poem, "El Louie," functions at one level as a reflection of a compound bilingual as well as of a *pachuco*. (I don't mean to imply that all *pachucos* are compound bilinguals. This probably is not the case, but as Adalberto Aguirre has pointed out, the general matter of sociolinguistically describing such self-designators as *pachucos, manitos, hispanos, texanos,* etc. requires much research which has yet to be accomplished.[61]) Nick Vaca's story, "The Purchase," a prayer cum free associations, is intended to psychologically portray a compound bilingual episode.

> Ave María Purísima, I must make another pago hoy or else it'll be too late. Sí, too late, and then what would I do. Christmas is so close, and if I don't hurry con los pagos, I'll have nothing to give any of mis hijos. If that should happen, it would weigh muy pesado on my mind. Even now, con el pensamiento that I may not be able to give them anything, I have trouble durmiendo en la noche. And, Santo Niño de Atocha, if Christmas should come and catch me sin nada, I would never sleep well por el resto de mi vida.[62]

Whether or not the story is in fact a "high fidelity" reflection of the real-life compound bilingual, or simply an artistically licensed evocation of the same is a separate question, and a very difficult one that could be answered only after much more sociolinguistic research into the real-life phenomenon has been conducted. Personally, I doubt the fidelity of the code-switches. They have too patterned and pat a quality (e.g., . . .it would weigh muy pesado on my mind. Even now, con el pensamiento that. . .).

This brings me to an additional point. Even though I have given two examples in this section of literary code-switching in the service of characterization, as the reader surely recalls I have spent much effort in the refutation of the so-called esthetic expectation (or worse, requirement) that literary code-switching be "true to life." A corollary should be stated here. Much code-switching that has been thought by readers or critics to be high fidelity renditions of the "real stuff" simply isn't and doesn't have to be. One of the most common mistakes for the critic to incur, particularly with reference to Chicano poetry, but also with prose, is to confuse the literary voices. It is one thing to evaluate code-switching when it occurs in dialogue, in a novel or short story or as dramatic dialogue (but here again most Chicano theater tends to be Brechtian in its political consciousness-raising and therefore, allegorical in nature); it is quite another to consider the voice of a poet, or rather, narrator in a poem, to be "talking" or even to be ruminating in an unselfconscious, free-associative way. Which brings us once again to the requirement that we carefully analyze the context in which literary code-switches appear. Such analyses will require distinguishing between various sorts of dialogues such as socially mimetic versus allegorical, as well as various types of interior monologues or processes of associations.

Code-Switching as a Function of Style

Let us begin by noting that much code-switching that occurs in the community reflects considerations which are basically stylistic. Identity markers, contextual switches, triggered switches (due to the preceding or following item), sequential responses (speaker uses language last used, thereby following suit), and so on[63] have clear stylistic purposes. Therefore, we can say, without in any way contradicting my judgment that literary and real-life code-switching need to be evaluated by different criteria, that there is much stylistic overlap between social and literary code-switches. At the same time we note that the stylistic possibilities available to literature far surpass those found in society.

Let me also state that I am convinced that bilingual literature in theory can display all of the stylistic features that have been unearthed in the literary analysis of monolingual literature at all levels, whether structure, the sound-stratum, imagery, rhetorical devices, diction, tone, or whatever, as well as some additional features not available to monolingual texts, as our analysis of certain cross-cultural and bicultural word plays has shown. This is not to say that in practice we shall find them all, for writers express themselves within a certain literary space, a *hic et nunc* more or less expanded, yet definitely subject to constraints, particularly cultural ones. In short, while allegorical verse plays exist in Chicano literature, I have yet to find a bilingual Chicano sonnet, although I'm sure one could be written.

302

Tone

As Luis Leal, Joseph Sommers, Carmen Salazar Parr, and others whose papers appear in this volume have attested, Chicano themes revolve around a number of different loci, some of the major ones being social protest against Anglo, or more rarely, Mexican oppression, consciousness-raising of the "naive" Chicano, usually a migrant worker and/or Mexican newly arrived in the United States, the recuperation of Chicano history (the Treaty of Guadelupe Hidalgo, the Mexican Revolution, the Zoot Suit incidents, etc.), the creation or recreation of a Chicano mythos (*Aztlán, La Raza,* Emiliano Zapata, etc.), the emancipation of the Chicana from both Anglo and Hispano male dominance, and the quest for a personal identity within the bicultural Mexican-American milieu. All of these thematic categories can be and usually are evoked by means of differing tones. Take for example the charge of Anglo oppression. The tone can run from the Ginsbergian *rant* or *howl*, as in Ricardo Sánchez's "smile out the revolú,"

> smile out the revolú,
> burn now your anguished hurt,
>
> crush now our desecrators,
> chingue su madre the u.s.a.
>
> burn cabrones enraviados,
> burn las calles de amerika[64]

or El Huitlacoche's, "From the Heights of Macho Bicho,"

> Tell US marines
> que aquí 'tamos nomás
> a las justas alturas
> de las circunstancias
> con el quetzal y la anaconda
> los de bicho alto
> y los de palo alto
> aquí nomás nomás
> We're waiting for US marines
> los meros justos
> los justos meros
> los meros meros
> los meros machos
> los mandamás.[65]

to the humorous parody in the "Advertisement" where Mexican-Americans for all occasions are offered for sale,

> (1) a familially faithful and fearfully factional folk-fettered fool

(2) a captivating, cactus-crunching, cow-clutching caballero
(3) a charp, chick-chasing, chili-chomping cholo
(4) a brown-breeding, bean-belching border-bounder
(5) a raza-resigned, ritual-racked rude rural relic
(6) a peso-poor but proud, priest-pressed primitive
(7) a grubby but gracious, grape-grabbing greaser[66]

to the upbeat, emphatically rhymed "La Causa," by Abelardo Delgado, reminiscent of the folksong:

what moves you, chicano, to stop being polite?
nice chicano could be patted on the head and wouldn't bite
and now, how dare you tell your boss, "Go fly a kite"?
es la causa, hermano, which has made me a new man.[67]

Those poems which cultivate the theme of self-identity, in keeping with the subject at hand typically have a more reflective, self-absorbed tone. For example, Estupinián's "Sonido del Teponaztle,"

Y antes de llamarme Chicano. . .
there was a mirror
in my guts that could not
be put down
with light penetrated
through the years
of *mi madre es. . .?*[68]

or Alurista's "We've Played Cowboys."

We've played cowboys
    not knowing
nuestros charros
    and their countenance
con trajes de gala
    silver embroidery
on black wool
    Zapata rode in white
campesino white
    and Villa in brown
y nuestros charros
    parade of sculptured gods
on horses
    —of flowing manes
proud
    erect
they galloped
and we've played cowboys
    —as opposed to indians
when ancestors of mis charros abuelos
indios fueron[69]

Yet all of these examples that I have cited have in common the fact of language switching, an alternation of codes that adjusts itself to the tone that the writer is seeking.

Imagery

The term imagery has been used variously in literary criticism. I restrict my usage in this portion of my paper simply to metaphor and simile, both of which appear in abundance in bilingual Chicano literature.

Examples of bilingual metaphors:[70]

> Brother, oh brother *vendido*
> you are hollow inside.
> [Raymundo Pérez, "Hasta la victoria siempre."]

> *la tierra* is *la raza*'s kissing cousin,
> [Abelardo Delgado, "La tierra."]

> Reluctant awakenings a la media
> Noche y la luz prendida.
>
> PRRRRRRINNNNGGGGGG!
>
> A noisy chorro missing the
>   Basín.
> [José Montoya, "La jefita."]

Examples of bilingual similes:[71]

> Transparente como
> Una jolla, opaca como
> El Carbon, heavy like
> A feather—carga fija
> Del hombre marginal.
> [José Montoya, "Lazy Skin."]

> I am speaking of
> Entering Hotel Avila
> Where my drunk compadres
> Applaud like hammers,
> [Gary Soto, "The Vision."]

> sousing himself to perdición
> on gabo's gratis spirits
> at the well-lit crap table
> while he tarries for the man
> to develop his picture and
> his querida—two brown persons
> standing tween one million laminated smackers
> como el Cristo plastificado entre los dos ladrones.
> [El Huitlacoche, "Searching for La Real Cosa."]

The Bilingual Chicano Writer

The anonymous folk-poem, "The Night Before Christmas," a parody of the original, written in doggerel verse, is quite well known in the Southwest. It yields an additional bilingual simile:

> When Santa will come in un manner extraño
> Lit up like the Star Spangled Banner cantando,[72]

Rhetorical Devices

This paper has already pointed to a great number and variety of literary devices, including some, such as calques, which are unique to bilingual literature. With one or two exceptions I won't go over ground already covered, but rather, will present a sample of additional categories of rhetorical devices.

CONGERIES. (Accumulation of phrases that say essentially the same thing)

> Unable to speak a tongue of any convention, they gabbled to each other, the younger and the older, in a papiamento of street *caliche* and devious calques. A tongue only Tex-Mexs, wetbacks, *tirilones, pachucos* and *pochos* could penetrate.[73] [El Huitlacoche, "The Man Who Invented the Automatic Jumping Bean."]

> i respect you having been:
> > My Loma of Austin
> > my Rose Hill of Los Angeles
> > my West Side of San Anto
> > my Quinto of Houston
> > my Jackson of San Jo
> > my Segundo of El Paso
> > my Barelas of Alburque
> > my Westside of Denver
>
> Flats, Los Marcos, Maravilla, Calle Guadalupe, Magnolia, Buena Vista, Mateo, La Seis, Chiquis, El Sur and all
> > Chicano neighborhoods that now exist and once existed[74]
>
> [raúlsalinas, "A Trip through the Mind Jail."]

ANAPHORA. (Repetition of a word or phrase at the beginning of a literary segment)

> Preso
> Locked inside a glass-like
> Canopy built of grief[75]
> [José Montoya, "In a Pink Bubble Gum World."]

Bilingual anaphoras (if you accept this designator for the phenomenon under consideration) are different from the monolingual variety in that, with the exception of identical cognates, the word that is repeated has two different spellings and pronunciations. Thus the anaphora is mostly at the semantic level. And yet the repetitive quality still remains. Bilingual anaphoras can be distinguished from mere word plays based on repetition. Consider, for example, the following, also from the poem cited above:

> Pero armado con estas palabras
> De sueños forged into files—
> "Las filas de la rebelión"
> Cantaban los dorados de Villa.[76]

This latter example, apart from the fact that it does not occur at the beginning of a passage, is properly classified a word play, not an anaphora. It is my contention that the bilingual anaphora will conserve some, although usually not all, of the phonic and rhythmic qualities of this rhetorical device.

CHIASMUS. (A contrast by reverse parallelism)

> pobre man
> hombre rich
> [cited earlier, see p. 267]

VERSE FILLER. (*Ripio*; element used to complete a line of verse, often to satisfy the requirements of rhyme; typically used in doggerel)

> Tis the night before Christmas, and all through the casa
> Not a creature is stirring, Caramba ¿qué pasa?
> The stockings are hanging con mucho cuidado,
> In hopes that Saint Nicholas will feel obligado
> to leave a few cosas, aquí and allí
> For chico y chica (y something for me).
> Los niños are snuggled all safe in their camas,
> Some in vestidos and some in pajamas,
> ["The Night Before Christmas," see footnote 72]

ALLITERATION.

> under lasting latigazos[77]
> [Ricardo Sánchez, "and it. . ."]

See also a relevant passage from "The Advertisement," cited on pp. 303-304.

INTERROGATIO. (The "rhetorical" question that is posed for argumentative effect and requires no answer)

> —¿A dónde voy?—, pregunta.
> ¿A los *cucumber patches* de *Noliet*,
> a las vineyards de *San Fernando Valley*,
> a los *beet fields* de Colorado?

> Hay ciertas incertidumbres ciertas:
> lo amargo de piscar naranjas
> lo lloroso de cortar cebollas[78]
> [Tino Villanueva, "Que hay otra voz."]

> How to paint
> on this page
> the enigma
> that furrows
> your sensitive
> brown face
> a sadness,
> porque te llamas
> *Juan,* y no *John*
> as the laws
> of assimilation
> dictate.[79]
> [Angela de Hoyos, "Chicano."]

METONOMY. (Naming a thing by substituting one of its attributes or an associated term for the name itself)

> Zapata rode in white
> campesino white
> and Villa in brown
> [cited earlier, see p. 304]

APOSTROPHE. (Speaking to an imaginary or absent person)

> Come, mother—
> Your rebozo trails a black web
> And your hem catches on your heels
> You lean the burden of your years
> On shaky cane, and palsied hand pushes
> Sweat-grimed pennies on the counter.
> Can you still see, old woman,
> The darting color-trailed need of your trade?
> The flowers you embroider
> With three-for-a-dime threads
> Cannot fade as quickly as the leaves of time.
> What things do you remember?[80]
> [Rafael Jesús González, "To An Old Woman."]

HYPERBOLE. (An exaggeration or overstatement intended to produce an effect without being taken literally)

> stupid america, remember that chicanito
> flunking math and english
> he is the picasso
> of your western states
> but he will die

with one thousand masterpieces
hanging only from his mind.[81]
[Abelardo Delgado, "Stupid America."]

UNDERSTATEMENT. (A statement deliberately worded so as to be unemphatic in tone, often for ironic purposes)

Sometimes he bragged
He worked outside Toluca
For americanos,
Shoveling stones
Into boxes.[82]
[Gary Soto, "A Few Coins."]

GRADATIO. (A progressive advance from one statement to another until a climax is achieved)

Last week,
I had been white
. . .we were friends

Yesterday,
I was Spanish
. . .we talked. . .
once in a while.

Today,
I am Chicano
. . .you do not know me.

Tomorrow,
I rise to fight
. . .and we are enemies.[83]
[Margarita Virginia Sánchez, "Escape."]

Spelling Innovations for Stylistic Purposes

Bilingual Chicano literature, mostly in the area of poetry, displays a significant number of spelling variations for literary purposes. The spelling may be used to evoke a typical or normal state of affairs, socially or psychologically. For example, it may show the accent of a specific Hispano or Anglo character, evoke English-Spanish interference effects in societal bilingual speech, or represent a language variety or dialect within Spanish or within English. In Tomás Rivera's "El Pete Fonseca," one of the characters comments:

En la labor también nos acercábamos a ella o ella se acercaba a nosotros y el Pete se soltaba con sus canciones. A veces hasta en inglés *sha bum, sha bum o lemi go, lemi go, lober. . .*[84]

Jesús Maldonado uses the terms, "alcaweta," "weras," and "logo"[85] in his poetry, and Estupinián utilizes "los wíkens"[86] in one of his poems. The other basic reason for spelling license is for some thematic purpose. Often a political statement is involved. In Alurista's *Dawn* we have the following two passages:

> you call it profitable investment
> i call it yanki colonization
> your foreign aid[87]
>
> now, now
> you don't want to be
> like the meskins
> you in amerikkka now[88]

A common device in Chicano literature is to write English in lower case where the standard spelling would call for capitals. The intention is usually to undermine the oppressive status of English, to put it on a par with Spanish, which rarely uses capitals. In addition to Alurista, whom I have just cited, this sort of usage is typical of Ricardo Sánchez, Abelardo Delgado, and many others.

Of course the spelling variations employed to portray a character or set of social circumstances may also serve a second, thematic function. This is the case with the example of "meskins" (uttered by the treacherous Cocacóatl) from Alurista, or in the following from the play, *Noo Jork,* by Jaime Carrero.

Mother: *Es importante.*
Cop: Not here in New York.
Mother: Very important in Noo Jork.
Cop: *(Smiling and correcting her pronunciation.)* New York. N E W Y O R K.
Mother: That's what I say: NOO JORK!
Cop: *(To Gladys.)* Tell your mother that she's not saying it right.
Gladys: Ma, *se dice* NEW YORK.
Mother: *No me da la gana.*
Cop: *(To Gladys.)* What's that?
Gladys: Never mind.
Cop: *(To the Mother.)* I must show you how to pronounce it. Say YOKE.
Mother: JOKE.
Cop: No, no, no. Yoke. New York.
Mother: Noo Joke!
Cop: No. *(Smiles.)* Say YELLOW.
Mother: Jello. *(Fast.)* Hey, I get this one. Your head is full of *jello* hair.
Cop: No. *(Slow.)* My head is full of YELLOW hair.
Mother: You're full of jello.
Gladys: Ma, *tú no entiendes.*
Mother: Sure. I understand. He wants me to become Irish.[89]

Gary D. Keller

Conclusion

In the first part of this paper I have attempted to clarify the axiological underpinnings of literary criticism directed toward that aspect of Chicano literature characterized by code-switching. I have described the sociolinguistic antecedents of such literary criticism and have attempted to distinguish between those sociolinguistic assumptions which can be validly transposed to the esthetic domain and those which can not. This task has led me to judge that code-switching *per se* constitutes a radical way for artistic language to draw attention to itself, to foreground, in the parlance of the Prague school. Moreover, precisely because code-switching is a radical, overt stylistic occurrence, it requires adequate literary justification in order to be deemed valid or successful.

In the second part of this paper I have sought to establish the beginnings of a corpus or dictionary of bilingual literary entries. I have used these paradigmatically to exemplify how code-switching serves the development of theme, the portrayal of character, the establishment of either a cross-cultural or bicultural literary space, the expression of a tone or literary voice, the depiction of images, the expansion of artistic license to spelling, and the fashioning of a wide variety of rhetorical devices.

THE WILLIAM PATERSON COLLEGE OF NEW JERSEY

Notes

[1]Gary D. Keller, "Toward a Stylistic Analysis of Bilingual Texts: From Ernest Hemingway to Contemporary Boricua and Chicano Literature," in *The Analysis of Hispanic Texts: Current Trends in Methodology,* ed. Mary Ann Beck, Lisa E. Davis, José Hernández, Gary D. Keller, and Isabel C. Tarán (New York: Bilingual Press, 1976), pp. 130-149.

[2]Lenora A. Timm, "Code-Switching in *War and Peace,*" in *Aspects of Bilingualism,* ed. Michel Paradis (Columbia, South Carolina: Hornbeam Press, 1978), pp. 302-315.

[3]See: M. Clyne, *Perspectives on Language Contact Based on a Study of Germans in Australia* (Melbourne: Hawthorne, 1972); J. J. Gumperz, "The Sociolinguistic Significance of Conversational Code-Switching," in *Papers on Language and Context,* ed. J. Cook-Gumperz and J. J. Gumperz (Berkeley: Language Behavior Research Laboratory [Working Paper 46], 1976; N. Hasselmo, "Code-Switching and Modes of

The Bilingual Chicano Writer

Speaking," in *Texas Studies in Bilingualism,* ed. G. Gilbert (Berlin: Gruyter, 1970), pp. 179-210; D. Shaffer, "The Place of Code Switching in Linguistic Contacts," in *The Second LACUS Forum,* ed P. Reich (Columbia, South Carolina: Hornbeam Press, 1975), pp. 487-496.

⁴Timm, p. 306. See also p. 313.

⁵Hugo Baetens Beardsmore, "Polyglot Literature and Linguistic Fiction," *International Journal of the Sociology of Language,* No. 15 (1978), 98, citing Stefan George. See also, J. Forster, *The Poet's Tongues: Multilingualism in Literature* (Cambridge: Cambridge University Press, 1970), p. 56.

⁶Guadalupe Valdés-Fallis, "The Sociolinguistics of Chicano Literature: Towards an Analysis of the Role and Function of Language Alternation in Contemporary Bilingual Poetry," *Point of Contact / Punto de contacto,* 1, No. 4 (1977), 30-39; Guadalupe Valdés-Fallis, "Code-Switching in Bilingual Chicano Poetry," *Hispania,* 59 (1976), 877-886.

⁷See: Guadalupe Valdés-Fallis, "Social Interaction and Code-Switching Patterns: A Case Study of Spanish/English Alternation," in *Bilingualism in the Bicentennial and Beyond,* ed. Gary D. Keller, Richard V. Teschner, and Silvia Viera (New York: Bilingual Press, 1976), pp. 53-85; Guadalupe Valdés-Fallis, "Code Switching and the Classroom Teacher," [Pamphlet], (Arlington, Virginia: Center for Applied Linguistics, 1978); Guadalupe Valdés-Fallis, "Code-Switching Among Bilingual Mexican-American Women: Towards an Understanding of Sex-Related Language Alternation," *International Journal of the Sociology of Language,* No. 17 (1978), 65-72; Wendy Redlinger, "Mothers' Speech to Children in Bilingual Mexican-American Homes," *International Journal of the Sociology of Language,* No. 17 (1978), 73-82; Lenora A. Timm, "Spanish/English Code Switching: el porque y how-not-to," *Romance Philology,* 28 (1975), 473-482; Carol Pfaff, "Syntactic Constraints on Code-Switching," (ERIC ED 127 828). See also the bibliography cited in footnote 3.

⁸Valdés, "The Sociolinguistics of Chicano Literature," p. 37.

⁹Ibid.

¹⁰Ibid.

¹¹Valdés, "Code-Switching in Bilingual Chicano Poetry," pp. 884-5.

¹²Ibid., p. 885.

¹³Valdés, "The Sociolinguistics of Chicano Literature," p. 38.

¹⁴Ibid., p. 36.

¹⁵Kenneth Muir, "The Jealousy of Iago," *English Miscellany,* II (Rome, 1951), 65-83, 67.

¹⁶Norman N. Holland, *Psychoanalysis and Shakespeare* (New York: McGraw-Hill, 1964), p. 297.

¹⁷F. R. Leavis, "Diabolic Intellect and the Noble Hero: A Note on *Othello,*" *Scrutiny,* VI (1936), 259-283, 266.

¹⁸Georg Lukács, *Studies in European Realism,* trans. Edith Bone (London: Hillway Publishing Co., 1950), pp. 8 and 123.

¹⁹Mark Shorer, "Fiction and the 'Matrix of Analogy,'" *Kenyon Review,* XI (1949), 539.

²⁰Holland, p. 300.

²¹See: Valdés, "Code-Switching in Bilingual Chicano Poetry," p. 884; Bohuslav Havránek, "The Functional Differentiation of the Standard Language," in *A Prague School Reader on Esthetics, Literary Structure and Style,* ed. Paul L. Garvin (Wash-

ington, D.C.: Georgetown University Press, 1964); Michael Riffaterre, "Describing Poetic Structures: Two Approaches to Baudelaire's 'Les chats,' " in *Essays in Stylistic Analysis,* ed. Howard S. Babb (New York: Harcourt Brace Jovanovich, 1972), 362-392; René Wellek and Austin Warren, *Theory of Literature*, 3rd ed. (New York: Harcourt, Brace and World, 1956), pp. 242-245; and Dorothy Walsh, "The Poetic Use of Language," *Journal of Philosophy,* XXXV (1938), pp. 73-81.

[22]T. S. Eliot, *Essays Ancient and Modern* (New York, 1936), p. 93.

[23]T. S. Eliot, *Selected Essays* (New York: Harcourt, Brace & World, 1964), p. 42.

[24]Wellek and Warren, p. 241.

[25]Valdés, "The Sociolinguistics of Chicano Literature," p. 37.

[26]Henri Matisse, "Notes d'un peintre sur son dessin," *Le Point IV,* XXI (1939), 14.

[27]Edward Fenimore, "English and Spanish in *For Whom the Bell Tolls,*" in *Ernest Hemingway: The Man and His Work,* ed. John K. M. McCaffery (New York: Cooper Square Publ., Inc.). Originally published in *A Journal of English Literary History,* X (1943).

[28]By "direct transfer" I mean that the phonological substance is more or less borrowed from one language to another, in contrast to a calque or other such semantic borrowing, where the phonological component is not transferred to the other language. *La hamburguesa* is an example of a direct transfer (from English hamburger) whereas *el rascacielos* (from English skyscraper) is a calque. For a fuller discussion see, Howard Fraser, "Languages in Contact: A Bibliographical Guide to Linguistic Borrowings Between English and Spanish," *The Bilingual Review/La revista bilingüe,* II, Numbers 1 and 2 (1975), 138-172.

[29]El Huitlacoche, "Searching for La Real Cosa," *The Bilingual Review/La revista bilingüe,* V, Numbers 1 and 2 (1978), 139-142.

[30]Emilio Díaz Valcárcel, *Figuraciones en el mes de marzo* (Barcelona: Seix Barral, 1972), p. 287.

[31]Ibid.

[32]Alurista, *Dawn,* in *El Grito* (Chicano Drama) Book 4, Year VIII (1974), p. 57.

[33]Ibid., p. 64 and p. 57.

[34]Ibid., p. 65.

[35]Valdés, "The Sociolinguistics of Chicano Literature," p. 38.

[36]José Montoya, "El Louie," in *Literatura chicana: texto y contexto,* ed. Antonia Castañeda Shular, Tomás Ybarra-Frausto, and Joseph Sommers (Englewood Cliffs, New Jersey: Prentice-Hall, 1972), pp. 173-176.

[37]Fenimore, pp. 210-211.

[38]Eduardo Rivera, "Antecedentes," in *New American Review,* No. 13 (1972).

[39]Julio Cortázar, "Las babas del diablo," *Ceremonias,* 3rd ed. (Barcelona: Seix Barral, 1970), p. 201.

[40]Ernesto Galarza, *Barrio Boy* (New York: Ballantine Books, 1972), pp. 196-197.

[41]Pedro Ortiz Vázquez, "Quienes somos," *The Bilingual Review/La revista bilingüe,* II, No. 3 (1975), 292.

[42]Luis Valdez, *Las dos caras del patroncito,* in *Literatura chicana: texto y contexto,* ed. Antonia Castañeda Shular, Tomás Ybarra-Frausto, and Joseph Sommers (Englewood Cliffs, New Jersey: Prentice-Hall, 1972), p. 53.

[43]El Huitlacoche, "Searching for La Real Cosa," p. 142.

[44]See Keller, "Toward a Stylistic Analysis of Bilingual Texts. . ." pp. 140-141 for a breakdown of the six semantic areas in which appear the Spanish words used by Eduardo Rivera and El Huitlacoche.

The Bilingual Chicano Writer

[45]These examples have been taken from: Eduardo Rivera, "Antecedentes," José Montoya, "El Louie," El Huitlacoche, "Searching for La Real Cosa," El Huitlacoche, "The Man Who Invented the Automatic Jumping Bean," *The Bilingual Review/La revista bilingüe,* I, No. 2 (1974), 193-200, and El Huitlacoche, "The Urban(e) Chicano's 76," *The Bilingual Review/La revista bilingüe,* III, No. 2 (1976), 185-186.

[46]Adaljiza Sosa Riddell, "Malinche," *El Grito* (Chicanas en la literatura y el arte) Book 1, Year VII (1973), p. 76.

[47]Lorenza Calvillo Schmidt, "Como duele," *El Grito* (Chicanas en la literatura y el arte) Book 1, Year VII (1973), p. 61.

[48]Anonymous, "Los animales," collected by Américo Paredes, in *Literatura chicana: texto y contexto,* ed. Antonia Castañeda Shular, Tomás Ybarra-Frausto, and Joseph Sommers (Englewood Cliffs, New Jersey: Prentice-Hall, 1972), pp. 129-132.

[49]Jorge Luis Borges, "La intrusa," *El informe de Brodie* (Buenos Aires: Emecé Editores, 1970), p. 15.

[50]William Faulkner, *Light in August* (New York: Random House, 1959), pp. 424-425.

[51]The quotations have been taken, in order of appearance, from Faulkner, p. 435, p. 439, pp. 439-440, and p. 418.

[52]El Huitlacoche, "The Urban(e) Chicano's 76," pp. 185-186.

[53]El Huitlacoche, "From the Heights of Macho Bicho," *The Bilingual Review/La revista bilingüe,* II, Numbers 1 and 2 (1975), 192.

[54]Angela de Hoyos, "Café con leche," *Poems for the Barrio* (Bloomington, Indiana: Backstage Books, 1975), no pagination.

[55]Herminio Ríos, "Introduction," *El Grito* (La voz poética del chicano), Book 3, Year VII (1974), p. 7.

[56]Ibid.

[57]Eugune Paul Nassar, *Wallace Stevens: An Anatomy of Figuration* (Philadelphia: University of Pennsylvania Press, 1965), p. 150.

[58]raúlsalinas, "Los caudillos," in *We Are Chicanos,* ed. Philip D. Ortego (New York: Washington Square Books, 1973), 194.

[59]El Huitlacoche, "¡Hostias!" *The Bilingual Review/La revista bilingüe,* II, Numbers 1 and 2 (1975), p. 193.

[60]Jesús Maldonado, "Loa al frijol," in *Literatura chicana: texto y contexto,* ed. A. Castañeda Shular, T. Ybarra-Frausto, and J. Sommers (Englewood Cliffs, New Jersey, 1972), p. 121.

[61]Adalberto Aguirre, "Chicano Sociolinguistics: A Review and Proposal," *The Bilingual Review/La revista bilingüe,* V, Numbers 1 and 2 (1978), 96.

[62]Nick Vaca, "The Purchase," in *Mexican-American Authors,* ed. Américo Paredes and Raymund Paredes (Boston: Houghton-Mifflin, 1972), 144.

[63]See footnote 7 for references discussing the terms to which I have alluded.

[64]Ricardo Sánchez, "smile out the revolú," *Canto y grito mi liberación* (New York: Anchor Books/Doubleday, 1973), p. 139.

[65]El Huitlacoche, "From the Heights of Macho Bicho," p. 193.

[66]Steve Gonzales, "The Advertisement," in *Literatura chicana: texto y contexto,* ed. A. Castañeda Shular, T. Ybarra-Frausto, and J. Sommers (Englewood Cliffs, New Jersey: Prentice-Hall, 1972), p. 128.

[67]Abelardo Delgado, "La Causa," in *We Are Chicanos,* ed. Philip D. Ortego (New York: Washington Square Books, 1973), 219.

[68]Estupinián, "Sonido del Teponaztle," in *El espejo-The Mirror: Selected Mexi-*

can-American Literature, ed. Octavio Ignacio Romano-V. (Berkeley: Quinto Sol, 1969), p. 194.

[69]Alurista, "We've Played Cowboys," in Literatura chicana: texto y contexto, ed. A. Castañeda Shular, T. Ybarra-Frausto, and J. Sommers (Englewood Cliffs, New Jersey: Prentice-Hall, 1972), p. 31.

[70]The examples, in order of appearance, are from the following: Raymundo Pérez, "Hasta la victoria siempre," in We Are Chicanos, ed. Philip D. Ortego (New York: Washington Square Press, 1973), p. 202; Abelardo Delgado, "La tierra," in We Are Chicanos, ed. Philip D. Ortego (New York: Washington Square Press, 1973), p. 218; and José Montoya, "La jefita," in El espejo-The Mirror, ed. Octavio I. Romano-V. (Berkeley: Quinto Sol, 1969), p. 188.

[71]The citations, in order of appearance, are from the following: José Montoya, "Lazy Skin," in El espejo-The Mirror, ed. Octavio I. Romano-V. (Berkeley: Quinto Sol, 1969), p. 184; Gary Soto, "The Vision," The Tale of Sunlight (Pittsburgh: University of Pittsburgh Press, 1978), p. 58; and El Huitlacoche, "Searching for La Real Cosa," p. 139.

[72]The Chicano version of "The Night Before Christmas" is often published in newspapers in the Southwest during the Yuletide season. However, there are a number of variations. The one that I am familiar with is the following:

> Tis the night before Christmas, and all through the casa
> Not a creature is stirring, Caramba, ¿qué pasa?
> The stockings are hanging con mucho cuidado,
> In hopes that Saint Nicholas will feel obligado
> to leave a few cosas, aquí and allí
> For chico y chica (y something for me).
> Los niños are snuggled all safe in their camas,
> Some in vestidos and some in pajamas,
> Their little cabezas are full of good things
> They esperan que el old Santa will bring.
> Santa is down at the corner saloon,
> Es muy borracho since mid-afternoon,
> Mamá is sitting beside la ventana
> Shining her rolling pin para mañana
> When Santa will come in un manner extraño
> Lit up like the Star Spangled Banner cantando,
> And mamá will send him to bed con los coches,
> Merry Christmas to all and to all buenas noches.

[73]El Huitlacoche, "The Man Who Invented the Automatic Jumping Bean," p. 195.

[74]raúlsalinas, "A Trip Through the Mind Jail," in We Are Chicanos, ed. Philip D. Ortego (New York: Washington Square Press, 1973), p. 200.

[75]José Montoya, "In a Pink Bubble Gum World," in El espejo-The Mirror, ed. Octavio I. Romano-V. (Berkeley: Quinto Sol, 1969), p. 184.

[76]Ibid., p. 185.

[77]Ricardo Sánchez, "and it. . . ," in Canto y grito mi liberación, p. 39.

[78]Tino Villanueva, "Que hay otra voz," cited by Valdés, "The Sociolinguistics of Chicano Literature," p. 33.

[79]Angela de Hoyos, "Chicano," Revista Chicano-Riqueña, Año tres, Número cuatro (1975), 23-24.

[80]Rafael Jesús González,"To An Old Woman," in We Are Chicanos, ed. Philip D. Ortego (New York: Washington Square Press, 1973), p. 170.

The Bilingual Chicano Writer

[81]Abelardo Delgado, "Stupid America," in *We Are Chicanos,* ed. Philip D. Ortego (New York: Washington Square Press, 1973), p. 216.

[82]Gary Soto, "A Few Coins," *The Tale of Sunlight* (Pittsburgh: University of Pittsburgh Press, 1978), p. 52.

[83]Margarita Virginia Sánchez, "Escape," in *We Are Chicanos,* ed. Philip D. Ortego (New York: Washington Square Press, 1973), p. 208.

[84]Tomás Rivera, "El Pete Fonseca," *Revista Chicano-Riqueña,* Año dos, Número uno (1974), 18.

[85]Jesús Maldonado, "Oda al molcajete," in *Literatura chicana: texto y contexto,* ed. A. Castañeda Shular, T. Ybarra-Frausto, and J. Sommers (Englewood Cliffs, New Jersey, 1972), pp. 119-120.

[86]Estupinián, "Sonido del Teponaztle," p. 194.

[87]Alurista, *Dawn,* p. 68.

[88]Ibid., p. 69.

[89]Jaime Carrero, *Noo Jork,* in *Revista Chicano-Riqueña,* Año dos, Número 4 (1975), pp. 6-7.

LA PROSA CHICANA: TRES EPIGONOS
DE LA NOVELA MEXICANA
DE LA REVOLUCION

Guillermo Rojas

Tres son los prosistas méxicoamericanos, mejor conocidos por chicanos en los Estados Unidos, que en la actualidad escriben en español y que siguen una modalidad que nosotros denominaríamos continuación de la novela mexicana de la Revolución. A saber son Tomás Rivera, autor de *Y no se lo tragó la tierra*, obra que ganó el primer premio Quinto Sol en 1970, Rolando R. Hinojosa-S., a cuya obra *Estampas del Valle y otras obras* le fue otorgada el primer premio Quinto Sol en 1973, y Miguel Méndez M., autor de *Peregrinos de Aztlán*, novela que se publicó en 1974.

Al hablar de la novela mexicana de la Revolución uno inmediatamente piensa en las obras que hoy se conocen como obras clásicas, es dicer *Los de abajo, La sombra del caudillo* y *Mi caballo, mi perro y mi rifle*. Incluimos en este grupo *El águila y la serpiente*, obra que para nosotros no es novela aunque muchos la consideren novela *sui generis*, y muchas otras obras que se salvan del anonimato por haber demostrado alguno de los cuatro elementos narrativos esenciales, la trama, el desarrollo de personajes, el estilo, y los problemas y soluciones a éstos que el autor plantea.

Beryl J. M. McManus en su estudio, "La técnica del nuevo realismo en la novela mexicana de la Revolución", ya había señalado algunos de los rasgos característicos de esta prosa, que son los siguientes:

1. La novela carece de protagonista; ahora es el pueblo el personaje más importante.

La prosa chicana: Tres epígonos

2. Por lo general los novelistas no enfocan el interés ni en la trama ni en el estilo.

3. El nuevo realismo se destaca por el número de personajes provincianos, típicos de las regiones de las cuales provienen, ya sean de Chihuahua, de Michoacán, de Sonora o de otros estados.

4. El habla típica de esta gente forma parte del lenguaje literario.

5. El paisaje se describe extensamente.

6. La obra es breve; todos sus capítulos o divisiones son cortos.

7. La técnica descriptiva, ya bien sea para describir personajes o la naturaleza, es concisa y rápida.

8. El estilo es cortado y directo.

9. Muchas obras contienen cierto espíritu satírico, cuyo único valor es la crítica social.

Además de estos rasgos característicos de la novela mexicana de la Revolución, McManus nos da cuatro etapas de desarrollo de la novela: "1) causas del conflicto, 2) descripción de la vida revolucionaria durante el período de lucha activa (1910-1916), 3) el conflicto político y el trastorno entre los elementos civiles, 4) los problemas de la reconstrucción que son el problema político, la cuestión religiosa, el problema obrero, el problema agrario y el problema de la educación".[1]

Los rasgos arriba mencionados han sido resucitados por los escritores chicanos quienes han ido fraguándolos para forjar su propia estilística y medio literario. Esos rasgos ahora se vinculan a los problemas sociales estadounidenses, y con esto los escritores exponen las luchas políticas, sociales y económicas del pueblo hispanoparlante americano.

Tomás Rivera nació en Crystal City, Texas, en el año de 1935; estudió en Southwest Texas State University y en la Universidad de Oklahoma donde le confirieron el título de Doctor en Literatura en 1969. Ha sido profesor en las escuelas elementales de Texas, en Southwest Texas Junior College y en la Universidad de Sam Houston en Huntsville, Texas. Ahora es decano en la Universidad de Texas, El Paso.

En 1970 se publicó *Y no se lo tragó la tierra*, una colección de cuentos estructurada en catorce cuentos breves y sencillos. La lectura es rápida, las descripciones de los campos donde trabajan los campesinos son breves; su función es ubicar a los personajes anónimos en un ambiente antihigiénico, sin agua potable, sin retretes, trabajo en soles brutales y viviendas que por lo general son gallineros.

Los personajes de los cuentos por lo común carecen de nombres; se les conoce por papá, la madre, el hijo o algún otro nombre que distingue el género del personaje. En esto Rivera logra la anonimidad que es rasgo característico de muchas obras mexicanas de la Revolución.

Aunque Rivera descuida el estilo—es decir, el uso del lenguaje figurado es mínimo—sí presta gran atención a la estructura de sus cuentos y a toda la obra en general. El cuento pasa de la descripción del ambiente a la introducción del tema y finalmente al desenlace que en la mayoría de los cuentos es inesperado y sorprendente. Los cuentos carecen no sólo de caracterización de los personajes sino también de trama. Rivera omite estos dos elementos para atacar los problemas sociales, como lo hacen Gregorio López y Fuentes en *Tierra* (1932) y Mauricio Magdaleno en *El Resplandor* (1937).

La unidad de la obra se logra a través del punto de vista del niño narrador quien ve y oye los sucesos que se tratan en los cuentos. El primer y último cuento sirven de marco a la obra; los otros doce cuentos entre el primero y el último, configuran los doce meses del año.

El título del primer cuento es "El año perdido". El tema de éste así como los temas de los otros doce aparecen en un resumen en el último cuento, "Debajo de la casa". Vemos a través de dos monólogos interiores pasar ante nosotros un trozo de cada uno de los trece cuentos anteriores. Concluye el niño narrador que ha logrado aprender muchísimo a pesar de haber fracasado como alumno en la escuela. Con este broche de oro cierra Rivera su obra: "Y no se lo tragó la tierra".

Ahora pasaremos a discutir cuatro de los cuentos. "El año perdido", el primer cuento, se desarrolla en una serie de tiempos trastornados. Es probable que el autor esté jugando con su propia imaginación y pensamientos. Elabora un juego de tiempos verbales que no relatan más que la confusión de los pensamientos del personaje anónimo. La narración es en tercera persona y la trama consiste sólo de lo que el personaje escucha, oye y piensa: Cree oír que le llaman, pero se da cuenta que él mismo se ha llamado. Todo lo que transcurre ocurre en la imaginación del personaje.

En el segundo cuento, "Los niños no se aguantaron", nos enteramos de los problemas del campesino. El cuento se desarrolla rápidamente, la caracterización es breve y anónima. Con pocas palabras el autor define el problema del trabajo brutal bajo el sol y cómo el campesino tiene que hacer el trabajo sin ninguna seguridad o garantía de su bienestar. Contrabalancea Rivera el problema campesino con la codicia del dueño cuya meta es lograr las ganancias máximas. La

La prosa chicana: Tres epígonos

acción se limita a las faenas campestres de los niños, a la sed de los niños movida por el solazo infernal y al susto que el dueño quiere meterles con un rifle a los niños que se han ido a beber agua a un estanque vacuno.

El autor no tiene interés en las descripciones excesivas. Parsimoniosamente caracteriza niños y adultos, contrapone la sed contra la codicia y se precipita al desenlace trágico, la muerte del niño por un balazo en la frente. No hay interés por el lenguaje figurado, ni la descripción, ni la caracterización. Es el problema social el que lleva el mayor relieve en las consideraciones artísticas, y con esto Rivera es fiel a uno de los preceptos de la prosa de la Revolución mexicana, atacar los problemas sociales.

El cuento "Es que duele" expone las penas, la vergüenza y los contratiempos que tradicionalmente han conocido los chicanos en sus primeros días escolares. Rivera pone de relieve los problemas sicológicos que impiden el progreso del alumno que forzosamente tiene que sufrir el espulgo con lápices o tales útiles llevado a cabo por profesores que buscan a los niños piojosos. Otro problema señalado es la cohibición y sufrimiento que padecen los niños chicanos ante los aguijones racistas lanzados por los niños anglosajones. La trama del cuento revela cómo las habladas culminan en un pleito entre un chicano y un anglosajón. El chicano es expulsado y se va a casa pensando en los acontecimientos de la escuela que le causan dolor. El niño no sabe enfrentarse con ese dolor y sufrimiento, y en un monólogo interior nos enteramos de cómo piensa resolver sus problemas: "Yo creo que es mejor estarse uno acá en el rancho, aquí en la mota con sus gallineros, o en la labor se siente uno a lo menos más libre, más a gusto".[2]

El autor chicano ha ido forjando un lenguaje que por lo general consiste en español mezclado con el inglés. Cito los casos siguientes: La maestra espulga al niño "con el palito de paleta o de *ésquimo pie*" (22). Después del pleito el niño interroga a la profesora: "¿Me va a llevar usted con la *principal*?" (22). Una vez expulsado el niño se va a casa con el *report card* (26).

La experiencia infantil de Rivera, llena de supersticiones y creencias transmitidas por los chicanos adultos, forma material propicio del cual Rivera extrae temas literarios. En el cuento "Y no se lo tragó la tierra" Rivera expone la creencia popular, "quien maldice a Dios la tierra se lo traga". Hábilmente unce Rivera el problema del trabajo brutal en temperaturas calurosas que conduce a la insolación con el deseo del hijo quien quiere maldecir a Dios por la mala fortuna en la vida y el estado jornalero que los hunde en la miseria.

La trama se desarrolla alrededor del padre y los hijos que trabajan en el campo. El padre se enferma y el hijo lamenta el estado de la familia, que ya ha perdido a dos tíos tuberculosos. El niño quiere rebelarse contra Dios pero la madre lo calma. Al día siguiente se enferma el hijo menor. Con esto revienta de cólera el hijo major:

> Luego empezó a echar maldiciones. Y no supo ni cuándo, pero lo que dijo lo había tenido ganas de decir desde hacía mucho tiempo. Maldijo a Dios. Al hacerlo sintió el miedo infundido por los años y por sus padres. Por un segundo vio que se abría la tierra para tragárselo. Luego se sintió andando por la tierra bien apretada, más apretada que nunca. Entonces le entró el coraje de nuevo y se desahogó maldiciendo a Dios.

Con esto logra echar abajo el niño otra creencia más que impide su desarrollo normal. Se siente fuerte y seguro de sí mismo, listo para desafiar al sol, a la tierra y a toda la vida:

> Tenía una paz que nunca había sentido antes. Le parecía que se había de hacer y deshacer cualquier cosa que él quisiera. Vio hacia la tierra y le dio una patada bien fuerte y le dijo—Todavía no, todavía no me puedes tragar. Algún día, sí. Pero yo ni sabré (70).

El cuento "Y no se lo tragó la tierra" nos presenta como tema "el empirismo contra la ignorancia". Como el cuento "La noche plateada", deshace las viejas creencias del pueblo chicano, y a la vez la obra lleva cierta didáctica. Al final de ambos cuentos los niños pueden luchar mejor con sus mundos, y pueden triunfar en la vida. En "La noche plateada" el niño pierde el temor al diablo. En el cuento "Y no se lo tragó la tierra" el niño ya no teme a la muerte y también se resigna al trabajo brutal del campo.

Rolando R. Hinojosa nació en Mercedes, Texas. Estudió en la Universidad de Texas, la Universidad de Highlands (Las Vegas, Nuevo México), y se le confirió el grado de Doctor en Filosofía en la Universidad de Illinois. Sus experiencias de trabajo han sido diversas: jornalero en una planta química, cantinero, gerente de oficina para una compañía manufacturera de ropa, empleado del servicio civil oficial, y profesor de escuela secundaria. Ha enseñado en la Universidad de Trinity (San Antonio, Texas), y fue jefe del Departamento de Lenguas Modernas y luego decano en la Universidad Texas A & I en Kingsville. Ahora es jefe de Estudios Chicanos en la Universidad de Minnesota.

La prosa chicana: Tres epígonos

La obra de Rolando Hinojosa, *Estampas del Valle y otras obras*, se publicó en 1973. El tomo consiste de cuatro obras, "Estampas del Valle", "Por esas cosas que pasan", "Vidas y milagros" y "Una vida de Rafa Buenrostro".

"Estampas del Valle" es una serie de narraciones breves que por lo general son bosquejos de tipos representativos de la sociedad chicana del Valle de Texas. En ella vemos camioneros, comerciantes, criadas, cantineros, prostitutas, curas, amantes, niños, adultos, abogados, estafadores, policías y estudiantes. La obra no tiene tema unificador. Como en *El águila y la serpiente*, de Martín Luis Guzmán, encontramos cuentos perfectos que sí tienen trama, por ejemplo "Al pozo con Bruno Cano" que después discutiremos.

La prosa de Hinojosa difiere de la de Tomás Rivera por su ironía y humorismo. Hinojosa es retratista como muchos de los novelistas de la Revolución Mexicana. Sus descripciones son más extensas que las de Rivera, pero aún son breves. Su estilo realista es sencillo y a veces grosero. Hinojosa, no como Rivera que prefiere el personaje anónimo, da nombres a sus personajes, y éstos pasan de "Estampas del Valle" a las otras obras del tomo. Rivera se preocupa por los problemas sociales, mientras Hinojosa quiere captar la esencia humorística del pueblo chicano. En la nota preliminar ya se trasluce el humorismo del autor cuando se mofa de su propia obra: "Estas estampas son y están como las greñas de Mencho Saldaña: unas cortas, otras largas y todas embadurnadas con esa grasa humana que las junta y las separa sin permiso de nadie".[3]

Entre los personajes de mayor relieve tenemos a la tía Chedes, que es una mujer simple: "Cuando Vicky [la hija] le avisó a mi tía Chedes que dejaba la escuela para irse con una carpa de maromeros, . . .mi tía Chedes lloró que fue un encanto: se desmayó, luego chilló, pataleó, se peyó, gritó y le dio el hipo; vamos, lo de siempre cuando se ponía nerviosa" (22). Uno de los maromeros se nos presenta en esta forma: "Leocadio Tovar (en las tablas don Chon) soplaba la trompeta y el trombón, y tocaba la marimba de botellas con más ganas que talento. A veces donde falta una cosa hay que suplirle con otra" (27). Doña Panchita Zuárez era "sobandera, partera al pasito, y remendona fina de jovencitas no muy usadas y todavía en servible estado de merecer" (35). Melitón Burnias aparece como especie de idiota en el barrio: "Era algo sordo, flaco, chaparrito, de oficio desconocido y más seco que cagarruta de cabra en agosto" (35). Por último tenemos a la güera Fira:

Sin rodeos: La güera Fira es puta. No la hace de puta (como las criadas) ni putea (como las amas de las criadas); no. La güera Fira es puta y ya. Hay más. La güera Fira tiene los ojos azules, el pelo corto y no tiene que pintárselo y tiene unas formas que le quitaron el hipo al cura don Pedro Zamudio.

La güera Fira no es de aquí ... Hija de mujer mexicana de Jones-ville y de un soldado bolillo de Fort Jones: no fue la primera que saliera ni la última, pero la verdad, seguramente tiene que ser la mujer más hermosa del Valle.

La güera Fira es una mujer que lleva su putería como las chicas de escuela llevan los libros: con naturalidad. Al bañarse, huele a agua y jabón y cuando sale a la calle rumbo a su trabajo, todavía le quedan húmedos los ricitos en la sien (43).

"Al pozo con Bruno Cano" es un cuento excelente, bien estructurado y con una trama desarrollada: La muerte y el entierro de Bruno Cano. Un diálogo entre el cura don Pedro Zamudio y un amigo del difunto introduce el cuento. El cura rehúsa llevar los sacramentos al entierro porque Bruno Cano le había mentado la madre a "todo un sacerdote de la santa madre iglesia" (35). Por fin el amigo convence al cura y la narración pasa a la muerte de Bruno Cano. En retrospectiva sabemos cómo Cano, con la ayuda de Melitón Burnias, pensaba sacar un tesoro a medianoche del solar de doña Panchita Zuárez. El cuento es muy gracioso por el juego de palabras y el malentendido que culmina en la muerte de Bruno Cano. Habían concordado los amigos que al dar con el tesoro Melitón Burnias rezaría unos rezos para ahuyentar al fantasma que supersticiosamente se cree cuida el tesoro. Cuando Cano toca algo firme con la pala, le anuncia al sordo de Burnias que están por sacar el tesoro, pero como Burnias no oye muy bien se precipita el siguiente malentendido:

> ¿Melitón, Melitón, no oíste? Creo que vamos cerca.
> ¿Que si no oí? ¿Que si no oí qué?
> Te digo que vamos cerca.
> Ah, sí, pues entonces, ¿qué rezo yo?
> ¿Qué?
> ¿Que qué rezo yo?
> ¿Cómo que qué resolló?
> ¿Qué resolló algo?
> ¿Que resolló algo dices?
> ¿Qué resolló? ¡ay, Diosito mío! (36)

Burnias corre y deja a Bruno Cano en el hoyo donde, después de maldecir al cura, muere supuestamente de un infarto.

La descripción donde el pueblo chicano aparece como personaje es la siguiente, donde el autor describe el entierro de Bruno Cano:

La prosa chicana: Tres epígonos

> El entierro estuvo muy concurrido. La cosa duró cerca de siete horas. Hubo doce oradores, cuatro coros, (uno de varoncitos y uno de chicas, otro de mujeres de la Vela Perpetua, y el cuarto de hombres del Sagrado Corazón de Jesús; todos de blanco). Los Vega trajeron el cuerpo de Bruno en la carroza morada con la cortinita gris a fleco. Además de don Pedro, fuimos los doce monaguillos cada uno vestido en casulla negra y blanca bien almidonada. La gente de los otros pueblos del Valle pronto se dio cuenta que algo había en Flora y se dejó venir en troque, en *rides*, en bicicletas y unos de Klail hasta alquilaron un Greyhound que ya venía repleto de gente procedente de Bascom.
>
> Aparecieron tres dulceros y empezaron a vender raspas para combatir aquel sol que derretía las calles de chapapote. La concurrencia, y yéndose por lo bajo, no era menos de cuatro mil almas. Unos, de seguro, ni sabían a quién enterraban; los más ni conocieron a Cano; lo que pasa es que a la gente le gusta la bulla y no pierde ripio para salir de casa.
>
> Don Pedro tuvo que aguantarse y rezó no menos de trescientos Padrenuestros entre Aves y Salves. Cuando se puso a llorar (de coraje, de histeria, de hambre, vaya usted a saber) la gente, compadecida, rezó por don Pedro. Los oradores repiteron las elegías varias veces y los de la raspa, cada uno, tuvieron que comprar otras tres parras de hielo de cien libras para dar vasto a toda la gente. En casos ni sirope echaban ya. La gente se comía el hielo con o sin agua. De su parte, los coros pronto disiparon su repertorio; para no desperdiciar la oportunidad se echaron el *Tantum Ergo* que no venía al caso y, menos, el "Ven, Buen Pastor, Redentor Celestial" que se oía sólo en Pascuas. Por fin los cuatro coros se juntaron y entonces la cosa se puso más fina (37-38).

La descripción del entierro de Bruno contiene un tono exagerado que tiende hacia lo surrealista.

Hinojosa también emplea como medio literario la mezcla del inglés y el español y esos giros que provienen del inglés. En vez de escribir "llanta ponchada" usa *flat* (23); por "gato" (*jack* en inglés) usa *yaque* (23). Hablando de los ancianos que participaron en la Revolución mexicana, dice que ahora son "prisioneros en esas *rest homes*" (121). Un chicano pierde sus tierras por no haber entendido "el papelaje que le encajaron los *land developers*" (124). En el cuento costumbrista "Un domingo en Klail" Hinojosa describe el partido de béisbol, diversión popular en los barrios chicanos durante los años cuarenta y cincuenta. Arturo, uno de los jugadores, "no entiende muy bien eso de *nobody hurt*" (125). El equipo es uno de esos que se conoce por *good field, no hit* (125). Los trabajadores migratorios de Texas que se van al norte, van a trabajar a la *cherry* (129). Los chicanos toman "café en el *coffee lounge*" (132). Cuando Burnias lleva un puerco a vender y el inspector lo rechaza, Burnias pregunta, "¿pero pos *why?*" (159). Los chicanos compran *donas* en vez de rosquillas o buñuelos fritos. (170). Uno de los estudiantes chicanos se roba una *jersey de football* (181).

Miguel Méndez nació en Bisbee, Arizona, en 1930. Pasó sus primeros años adolescentes en un ejido en el estado de Sonora, México, y estudió seis años en los Estados Unidos donde desempeñó varios trabajos. Es albañil y en la actualidad vive en un barrio de Tucson, Arizona.

De los tres autores Méndez cuida más de su estilo y su descripción narrativa. Es la obra suya la cual manifiesta el mayor grado de influencia de la novela mexicana de la Revolución. La técnica es muy semejante a la de Mariano Azuela: Humaniza a la naturaleza y deshumaniza al hombre.

Peregrinos de Aztlán pone de relieve el mundo lleno de hambre y dolor que acompaña siempre a los chicanos que luchan cotidianamente para alimentarse, haciendo el trabajo más duro con los soles aguerridos que los mata o los enferma. La trama algo débil trata de sufrimientos de un viejo indio yaqui, Loreto Maldonado, que a los ochenta años trabaja de lavacoches y guardacoches. Méndez usa el monólogo interior para llevarnos a los recuerdos jóvenes del indio que participó en la Revolución mexicana, sus años de bracero en los Estados Unidos y su vejez en su tierra natal, México, donde muere solo y triste.

Entre los monólogos interiores Méndez intercala escenas que aportan grabados de los problemas sociales que confrontan al chicano: Falta de trabajo, falta de atención medica, falta de enseñanza, viviendas asquerosas y poco higiénicas, trabajo brutal, desamparo de las autoridades, problema de las drogas, alcoholismo y pérdida de los valores sociales positivos.

Al hablar de la técnica narrativa mendeciana me limitaré a dos elementos, la caracterización de los personajes y del ambiente, y el lenguaje pachuquista, que es un elemento nuevo en la prosa chicana.

La caracterización de los personajes es cruda, agria y deshumanizadora. El nombre del personaje principal, Loreto Maldonado, en sí lleva simbólicamente el epíteto de mal aventurado, mal dotado o mal afortunado. En la Revolución había perdido una pierna: "Loreto caminaba con las dificultades que lo hacen las hormigas después de haber sufrido el refregón de una pata sádica".[4] El hambre continua de Loreto lo desatinaba y "las tripas le maullaban chillonas como gatas violadas en la oscuridad" (18). A Loreto le brincaba el corazón "como sapo rocanrolero" (14). Al lavar los autos y al cobrar su dinero extendía "la mano extrañamente abierta como una araña" (19).

A pesar que la caracterización de Loreto Maldonado contiene rasgos deshumanizadores, el autor se preocupa por realzar la nobleza del protagonista, atribuyéndole cualidades de trabajador honrado y orgulloso, de hombre valiente y compasivo. "Para el anciano Loreto Maldonado, vivir significaba luchar a muerte; como si la fluidez de su condición temporal fuera un potro negro, el más bronco, empeñando en azotarlo contra pedregales, desde su lomo resbaladizo" (14). Al salir de la iglesia una dama le entrega cinco pesos de dádiva y Loreto contesta: "Yo trabajo, no acepto limosnas de naiden" (15).

Es por los ojos de Loreto que el autor logra mostrar la compasión del personaje, y a la vez sirve de portavoz de los problemas sociales: "Loreto, con su visión amarga de viejo, que conoce los mecanismos de la vida, lo contemplaba todo sin mostrar ningún asombro. Intuía que habitaba una dimensión gris purulenta de heridas gangrenosas. Su mundo era oscuro, vedado a la luz de la alegría". Loreto veía "los seres desgraciados que morían de hambre...los míseros [que] lloraban sumidos en el olvido, y los débiles [que] andaban semidesnudos y sucios" (60-61). Por medio del contraste Méndez le da a Loreto un relieve de superioridad: "Otros seres que lo rodeaban vivían en su gloria como parásitos, pagando dádivas con payasadas grotescas" (31).

Ejemplos de otros personajes deshumanizados son los siguientes. La mujer rica que le ofrece la limosna a Loreto vestía "sombrero de los llamados 'bacinica', en el brazo izquierdo tantas pulseras ceñía como cascabeles que arrastran las víboras muy viejas, su maquillaje era muy espeso, el necesario para planchar los surcos que deja el arado del tiempo" (15). El Cometa, nombre que aporta la raíz del verbo comer, se destaca por su glotonería:

> [Era] gordo como gato carnicero, con los ojillos bailarines límites de sendos cachetes inflados; nariz hecha al desgane, apelotada y una frente peluda; acortinada con cabellos que servían de trapecios para que los piojos se trenzaran en reñidos torneos de acrobacia. Usaba pantalones de pechera prendidos de un solo tirante, gruesos de grasa y mugre; pues tenía el tal "Errante" la venia del chicharronero que se decía llamar "Musulini," para servirse de los asientos de la deliciosa fritanga de marrano, que se untaba al fondo del caso (31).

Tenía poca amistad con el calzado, "más que pies servíanle de base dos enormes tortas esponjadas" (31). Al parecer no cuidaba de su pelo, "su greñero no conocía el peine ni retratado" (32).

A la vez que Méndez deshumaniza a sus personajes y los describe con rasgos repulsivos, humaniza a la naturaleza. A la ciudad, terruño de los peregrinos, le atribuye Méndez rasgos humanos despreciables. Al describir una caminata del viejo Loreto por la ciudad, escribe: "El viejo Loreto rebanaba la niebla que se había encasquetado de cachucha sobre la cara sucia de la ciudad" (17). En otras ocasiones la ciudad aparece con rasgos femeninos con los cuales Méndez personifica los vicios nocturnos: "La ciudad va vistiendo sus arreos de alcahueta coquetona con que seduce a los incautos. Como una diosa mitológica, cínica y desvergonzada, se va aprovechando la ciudad de las debilidades humanas para llenar sus últimos rincones" (20). Al describir el problema de las prostitutas, el alcoholismo y el uso de las drogas vemos la siguiente descripción: "Va la ciudad nocturna sonsacando amargados; sinvergüenza, descalzonada, nalgas de fuera, impúdica; con su vestido de noche adornando con letreros de neón; tronando palmas a los parranderos, como damisela descocada" (21).

El desierto se humaniza. Méndez lo describe en tonos líricos y exhortadores. En el desierto la tierra es "pálida como una amada muerta" (89). El desierto es "cádaver de mar disecado". La vegetación puede comunicarse con el ser humano: "Arbustos y árboles escuálidos nos dijeron con su aislamiento que luchaban a muerte con el maldito desierto". Los "mesquites esqueléticos ... pintaban sombras desnutridas". Los cactos son "como guerrilleros que no transan", o "Ejércitos ... ariscos que no distinguen adversario" (90).

Ahora hablaremos del lenguaje chicano, el español mezclado con el inglés. Tomás Rivera, Rolando Hinojosa y Miguel Méndez lo utilizan, especialmente en los diálogos, pero es Méndez quien hace mayor uso de este habla. Así como Azuela quien introduce el habla mexicano en la novela mexicana de la Revolución, Méndez introduce el habla del pachuco chicano como medio literario y lo logra bien.

> —Orale, mi buen Chuquito, qué milagro que anda usted por aquí.
> —Nel, carnal; pos acá echándole una birria en Mexicles ¿sabes qué, ése? ando bruja ves? aliviáname con un toleco, camita, pa' ver si apaño avión.
> —... vale más borrarse uno de esta pinchi life, ése, pos se lo acaban a uno y ya ni camello le dan... pos aquí camarón, me la paso en Tijuas (26-27).

Aquí tenemos la transposición al español entendido por todos.

> —¿Cómo estás? mi buen Chuquito, qué milagro que anda usted por aquí.

La prosa chicana: Tres epígonos

—No, hermano; pues vine a México a tomarme una cerveza. ¿Sabes qué, hermano? No traigo dinero. Préstame 50 centavos, hermano, para ver si me pongo en estado eufórico.

—...vale más abandonar esta miserable vida, hermano, pues a uno se lo acaban, y ya ni trabajo le dan ... Pues aquí hermano, me la paso en Tijuana.

La jerigonza del pachuco es difícil de comprender, pero en la boca de los personajes mendecianos recobra un rasgo realista y revelador del mundo pachuco de antaño. Mendez conoce bien el caló y lo emplea con gran éxito.

En conclusión, la sencillez del estilo, el uso de la técnica descriptiva de personajes y ambiente, la preocupación por problemas sociales, la innovación y uso del inglés y el español como medio literario, y la falta de trama y temas unificadores demuestran que Tomás Rivera, Rolando Hinojosa y Miguel Méndez han seguido las huellas de la novela mexicana de los años 1915 al 1940, y por eso muy justamente se les considera epígonos de la novela mexicana de la Revolucion.

UNIVERSITY OF CALIFORNIA, DAVIS

Notas

[1] Beryl J. M. McManus, "La técnica del nuevo realismo en la novela mexicana de la Revolución," en *Memoria del Cuarto Congreso del Instituto Internacional de Literatura Iberoamericana* (La Habana, 1951), 318.

[2] Tomás Rivera, *Y no se lo tragó la tierra* (Berkeley: Quinto Sol, 1970), 22. Todas las citas subsiguientes llevarán sólo el número de la página.

[3] Rolando R. Hinojosa-S., *Estampas del Valle y otras obras* (Berkeley: Quinto Sol, 1973), 15. Otras citas de esta obra sólo llevarán el número de la página.

[4] Miguel Méndez M., *Peregrinas de Aztlán* (Berkeley: Editorial Peregrinos, 1974), 14. Otras citas de esta obra sólo llevarán el número de la página.

JOSE ANTONIO VILLARREAL
AND RICHARD VASQUEZ:
THE NOVELIST AGAINST HIMSELF

Rafael F. Grajeda

> Yes, the first duty of the native poet is to see clearly the
> people he has chosen as the subject of his work of art. He
> cannot go forward resolutely unless he first realizes the
> extent of his estrangement from them. We have taken
> everything from the other side; and the other side gives us
> nothing unless by a thousand detours we swing finally
> round in their direction, unless by the thousand wiles and a
> hundred tricks they manage to draw us toward them, to
> seduce us, and to imprison us. Taking means in nearly
> every case being taken: thus it is not enough to try to free
> oneself by repeating proclamations and denials.
>
> Frantz Fanon

José Antonio Villarreal's *Pocho* and Richard Vásquez' *Chicano*[1]
are the first novels published in the United States which are both
written by Mexican American authors and attempt a rendering of
their Mexican American experience. Their significance lies in marking respectively the first and second literary voices to be raised in
behalf of the question of cultural identity of the Mexican American
people. That this theme is of profound dimensions is clear. That an
honest treatment of such a theme has to make formidable demands
on the literary imagination is equally clear. One is thus not surprised
to discover that the first two novels to attempt this demanding task

Rafael F. Grajeda

fail to penetrate very deeply into the full complexity of the experience which they purport to treat. Both novels promise more than they deliver; both are replete with so many glaring defects that judged *as novels* they must be said to constitute rather unmistakable failures. And it is as failures that they have their significance in this study.

The contention of this analysis is that while some of the weaknesses of *Pocho* and *Chicano* are technical—that is, the over-explicitness, the sentimentality, the flaccid journalistic style and the tendency to assert rather than to render—the more serious of the difficulties in these books derive from the writers' failures in that "first duty of the native poet..., [which is] to see clearly the people he has chosen as the subject of his art." Such failure, this study insists, is not unrelated to the general enervating condition that in the past has informed the American citizen of Mexican ancestry, a condition that in stark detail mirrors the psychological effects of colonialism.[2] As literary failures, the two novels are significant, for in a close analysis of the very terms of their artistic weaknesses can be seen the "real life" analogues, and authentication, perhaps, if such is felt necessary, of the literary figure of the Mexian American as a colonized person.

The worlds of both *Pocho* and *Chicano* are, in telling detail, one. It is the North American social environment, replete with contradictions for the immigrant and his offspring. It is a world in which individualism is espoused but where conformity is pressured: in which equal opportunity is preached as an ideal but where such opportunity is denied unless pursued in prescribed manner; in which equality is taught but inequality is practiced. It is, in a word, the North American world where the ideal, in all of its utopian humanitarianism, is so compelling that it facilitates a hypocrisy as blatant as it is at times unconscious.

And it remains a world with an extraordinary absorption capability, so that, for the immigrant father, it becomes difficult, and ultimately impossible, to "keep" his children. Sensing what is happening to his family, Juan Rubio, the Mexican father in *Pocho*, thinks:

> A man must have a house, place his family within it, and leave no room for authority but his own, for it was the only place a man could have authority. He wanted to return to Mexico, and he would one day do so. In another five years definitely, but for now he must reclaim his family before it was too late (p. 122).

For the children in this world it becomes difficult for them to affect a gradual movement into the new social environment, holding on to the old culture as a base while that movement is made. The protagonist of *Pocho*, as he feels the pull of his social world in conflict with that of his father,

> thought of himself, and starkly, without knowledge of the words that would describe it, he saw the demands of tradition, of culture, of the social structure on an individual. Not comprehending, he was again aware of the dark, mysterious force, and was resolved that he would rise above it. It was nighttime, and black under the figtree where he lay and he suddenly sat up and said:
> "Mierda! Es pura mierda!"
> And he knew that he could never again be wholly Mexican . . . (p. 95).

The cultural limbo implied here defines the world of the "pocho." It is the world inhabited by Villarreal's young protagonist and by two generations of Mexican Americans in Vásquez' novel, a world, finally, that is devoid of possibility or alternative. And it signals a dead-end.

That both *Chicano* and *Pocho* share so many similarities in content attests to the similarity of the historical and social experience of Mexican American people. Both novels, for example, begin with life in Mexico; both trace the immigration north at approximately the same time—during the Mexican Revolution of 1910; both novels depict the relative economic success of the families, first doing farm labor and later doing other kinds of work; and both books show the gradual disintegration of the family as a social unit.[3]

José Antonio Villarreal and *Pocho*

Pocho fits rather easily into the category of initiation novels in which the path of the youthful hero is traced as he makes his tentative moves "into life." All of the characteristics of the type are present in Villarreal's novel: the super-bright, ultra-sensitive but confused protagonist; the unknowing and insensitive society; the hostile environment, opposing, it seems, at every point, the well-being of the hero; the protagonist's gradual shucking off of—for him—meaningless and confining religious, social, and cultural impedimenta; and the emergence ultimately of "the emancipated self," a bit scarred by disillusionment, for sure, but nevertheless, ready to confront experience on a "higher" level than has been possible before. And if we remember that Richard Rubio, the "pocho" protagonist of this novel, desires to become a writer, the book begins to assume the shape of caricature—of itself as initiation story, and of the literary type which it accepts as its model.

Rafael F. Grajeda

The world of this novel is predominantly social. It contains within itself the major contradictions between the "Melting Pot" ideal (" 'My teacher says we are all Americans,' said one of the girls who was in the first grade"), and the "white-is-right" reality. It is a world that facilitates the holding, with varying degrees of seriousness, of these two premises at the same time. How the inhabitant of this world reconciles or otherwise blunts the disturbing edge of the contradiction depends on the personal need of the moment. In this world, the focus falls on Richard Rubio's personal development during his first eighteen years. Yet this development is linked with broader historical and cultural themes by means of the father's participation in the Mexican Revolution, the unrest of the workers during the thirties, the arrival in California of the Okies, the emergence of the Pachucos (Mexican Zootsuiters), and the relocation of Japanese Americans during World War II.

From the beginning there is a sharp contrast between the way that others see Richard and the way that he sees himself. He knows who his father is, but so too does he "know" that he is different from his father. He is an American; his father is a Mexican. "This is America, Father," says Richard. "If we live in this country, we must live like Americans." As others see him, however, his name, his complexion, his accent, and his diet identify him as a "Mexican," as a "Frijoley bomber!" or a "Tortilla strangler!"; as "scum" and as a "pocho."

In the midst of the different demands that others attempt to place on him, Richard begins to feel the urge to be recognized on his own terms. At several points in his development he resolves not to allow himself to be confined and limited by tradition, by custom, by culture, by social pressure, or by the expectations that others might have of him. "I can never be changed by that which is outside of me," he says near the end of the novel. Renouncing, then, his traditional responsibility as the eldest son of a Mexican family, he refuses any longer to support his mother and sisters and in desperation escapes into the Navy and the Second World War, for it seems to him that only by leaving the confinements of his past can he attain the "freedom" that he needs—as a future writer and as an individual. His father's life has been lived in accordance with values appropriate for *him* in *his* time and place. Each generation undertakes the same quest. The urge to assert one's self and to shape and live out one's own destiny is universal. That urge inevitably involves the severing of ties with the family.

This meaning, however, does not come through quite as simply as that. Actually the ambivalence of the plot, as well as the absence of any context of felt belief—other than a vague sort of commitment on Richard's part to expressing his individuality—inhibit any attempt at defining a coherent meaning that grows out of the narrative.

The novel begins, appropriately enough, with Juan Manuel Rubio, ex-colonel Rubio, father of Richard, the "pocho" identified in the book's title. At the beginning of chapter one, Juan arrives from Mexico City at Ciudad Juarez, on the northern border of Mexico. His arrival, though unknown to him, marks the first step of his participation in "the great exodus that came of the Mexican Revolution" (p. 15). From the second chapter on, the plot focuses on Richard's personal development through which is seen also the gradual effect of the northern environment on the the entire family.

In the midst of boys older than he, Richard is quick to learn not only that he is different from others (that is, Anglo Americans), but he also hears them saying that "everybody knew that a Spaniard was better than a Mexican any old day" (p. 41). He is called "cholo" and "chilebeans," and he is made fun of because he eats tortillas. This he has a hard time understanding, mainly because of the strong Mexicanness of his father and because of the enjoyment that he himself experiences in the midst of "the ever-present odor of a pot of pink beans boiling, freshly cooked tortillas filling the close, warm room," as he listens to his father tell "the tales of that strange country which seemed to him a land so distant" (p. 43). From other Mexicans who come to Santa Clara during the summer work season, he learns the songs and the dances of the traditional Mexican fiesta. Still, when he is eight years old, in 1931 during the Depression, when the prune pickers attempt to organize a union and strike for higher wages, Richard's sympathies go rather obviously to the blond teenage daughter of one of the growers when she insults the Mexican strikers and shouts at them, "Okay, then, you Goddamn bastards!. . .Get the hell off our property, and don't come back until you're ready to go to work" (p. 55).

Thus begins a pattern in Richard's behavior that continues through much of the novel: on the one hand he is aware of himself as a Mexican and "sometimes, when he was alone, he got kinda funny proud about it," and on the other hand, if he does not have actual feelings of rebellion against this Mexicanness, he begins to feel opposed to anything—social rules, traditions, and religious doctrines—which he feels somehow limiting and molding him to fit a pattern. Throughout he is acutely aware of the expectation that others have of him: his father wants him to be a "man" and a Mexican; his mother wants him to be a provider and a good Mexican son; the boxing-match promoter wants him to box because "It's the only way people of your nationality can get ahead"; the high-school counselor wants him to study auto mechanics or welding "because he was a Mexican"; the police detective urges him to work for the police because "There's a lot you can do for your people that way"; and liberal whites "insist he dedicate his life to the Mexican Cause." Valuing only his own individuality, he attempts to wind his way through the many obstacles that he sees as attempts at stifling him as a person.

Gradually the family changes. And in spite of his own Americanization, Richard is sensitive to this change, especially as it is affecting his mother, who is less and less willing to accept her position as subservient Mexcian wife and mother. The gradual assimilation of the family continues. Even Juan, the revolutionary, begins to change. At the moment when he discusses with his wife the possibility of buying a house in Santa Clara, the family's return to Mexico is wholly forgotten except as an illusion to cling to; and the process of Americanization, for the rest of the family, if not for Juan himself, becomes almost total.

Juan is able to bend just so much. There comes a time when he can no longer tolerate the disintegration of the family as he has known it; and hence he leaves home to start another family with a woman recently arrived from Mexico. This leaves the family responsibilities to the eldest son in a Mexican family. Automatically, therefore, the mother assumes that Richard, now having graduated from high school, will remain at home and support the family. Torn between his desire to "go to college" and the responsibility he knows is his, he remains in Santa Clara for a while and enrolls in a creative writing course at night school, where he has a brief encounter with some white Marxists who he soon realizes are also threatening his "individuality." Finally, seeing his friends leave for the Armed Forces in 1941, and hearing from his Japanese-American friend of the wartime plans to relocate Japanese-Americans in detention camps, Richard decides to "get out." He joins the Navy and "knows" at the end of the book that "for him there would never be a coming back" (p. 187).

The world of this novel is one of ambiguities that ultimately remain unresolved. It is the world of the pocho—that is, of the Mexican American who, having assimilated society's judgments of himself as a "Mexican," attempts to remake himself in the image of "an American." It's hero is the outsider who gradually comes to some

awareness of his equivocal position in society and "defends himself"
as best he can by falling back on an individualism that is at best spe-
cious, because—as a real possibility—it is pursued within a cultural
vacuum. He is, in other words, the hero as dupe.

Many details of the hero's face emerge in spite of the writer's hand-
ling of his character, for in large degree Richard Rubio remains un-
convincing. He is not brought to life, but remains, throughout most
of the novel, at a distance removed from the reader. As literary character, Richard Rubio suffers from the inherent danger of the young
protagonist in the *Bildungsroman*. While being the kind of character
truly capable of experiencing significant development, he must also
be credible. Throughout this novel Richard's chronological age is
given but cursory attention. When his age is referred to, the reader
cannot but be surprised that Richard is so young, for he often reveals
an understanding well beyond his years and the precocity that might
explain this understanding is unsustained. When he is eight or nine
years old, for example, he is determined to remain in school, but not
in order to learn a trade or "to become something," as his father
expects, but rather "to live." "Ah, Mama! Try to understand me," he
says: "I want to learn, and that is all. I do not want to be something—
I am. I do not care about making a lot of money and about what
people think. . ." (p. 64). When he is thirteen years old, he discovers
that there are always alternatives.

> Everything had another way to it, if only you looked hard enough,
> and he would never be ashamed again for doing something against the
> unwritten code of honor. Codes of honor were really stupid . . . and
> what people thought was honorable was not important, because he
> was the important guy (p. 108).

And when he was fourteen years old, "he refused to accept sexual
satisfaction as the sublime effort of life. There must be more than just
that" (p. 129).

Suspending disbelief and accepting the hero with this degree of
maturity, the reader is disappointed in his expectations for consistency. When thirteen, Richard makes one of several gestures in the
book aimed at freeing himself from the confines of his parents' religion. During this period of his life all of his religious doubting and
questioning reaches a moment of resolution during communion. Instead of taking the "paper thin white wafer," Richard rises from his
kneeling position at the altar, and deliberately walks out of church.
Doing so, he feels exhilarated, "happy with his freedom." The paragraph that immediately follows this scene is quoted here in full to

Rafael F. Grajeda

suggest that the symbolic gesture in church is as consistent with the hero's extraordinary maturity, as his behavior afterwards fits the ordinary thirteen-year-old, not unlike Ricky or any of the protagonist's other friends to whom he feels comfortably superior.

> A few days later, his father was suddenly ill. It is only a coincidence, his mind said, but in a moment of panic he repented and promised God his abstinence of everything carnal for life, if only He would make his father well. He abstained until the third day, when a faith healer came to the house and cured his father. That night, Richard did it [masturbated] three times to make up for what he had missed (p. 117).

And this incident is never mentioned again!

In similar fashion the consistency of Richard's characterization breaks down at the end of the novel when talking with Thomas Nakano, whose family is about to be "relocated" during the war. In what turns out to be a curious understatement Nakano says that he is glad they are going away because "things are getting kinda rough for Japanese people around here." Richard tries to "show how things come to pass," but the best that he can do—given not only his supposed awareness, but also his personal experience with racism during his eighteen years—is to tell Nakano that "people are funny about things anyway, without wars to make them funnier" (p. 183).

That this novel has all of the characteristics of the American initiation novel and that at the end the author seriously implies that the hero now is ready to undertake that significant quest for selfhood must suggest that the form of *Pocho* is ironic. Such, however, is not the case. The moral judgments are almost wholly made through a hero who, because he is unbelievable, cannot be trusted. When one considers that, as unbelievable as he is, the hero has the full sympathy of the author, the reader finds himself in the position of having to judge on more than literary grounds. Neither fictive character nor creator of the fictive character can be trusted. Literature and life, in this regard, touch at most significant points, and ultimately art is the liability.

However mishandled the theme of *Pocho* may be, and however inconsistent the characterization, the novel still commands our interest and our serious consideration, for in the pocho's attempts at confronting his experience in the United States can be seen the universal urge of human beings—displaced by history and circumstances—to clutch on to some sense of self that will offer a feeling, at least, of having a "place."

For Richard, who is caught between two worlds, each of which makes conflicting demands on him, this "place" increasingly assumes the form of the self, entire within itself, and in that form, it is thought full of possibilities. In the guise of "individualism"—a value legitimized, and in theory, at least, encouraged by the society in which he lives—this self-indulgence serves him well to subvert the opposing demands of his sense of betrayal involved in leaving the family. He has no "place" to which he can easily "go," therefore he goes within himself. In one of the most significant scenes in the novel, he and his friends are arrested and taken to the police station where they are beaten and individually interrogated about attacks that have been made on white girls by the "goddam pachucos." Because Richard is the only Mexican American in the group he receives "special" treatment. After it becomes clear to the police that the boys are innocent, the interrogating detective, alone in the room with Richard, offers him a job with the police department. "We can use someone like you," he says to Richard. He continues:

> "There's a lot of your people around now, and someone like you would be good to have on the side of law and order."
> Jesus Christ! Another one, thought Richard. Aloud he said, "No thanks. I don't want to have anything to do with you guys."
> "Think about it.... There's a lot you can do for your people that way."
> His sincerity surprised Richard. He seemed to mean it. "No," he answered. "I'm no Jesus Christ. Let 'my people' take care of themselves" (p. 162).

The detective reminds Richard that a few minutes earlier he had been defending "his people," and Richard answers, "I was defending myself!" Afterwards with his friends he senses that because he remained in the interrogation room longer than the others, they suspect him of betraying their trust and hold it against him that they were arrested and beaten, for "if he had not been there, they would not have been accused by association." He knows that things can't ever be the same between him and the group. He cries about this and then thinks that it is not worth crying for people. The description, then, of his reaction—carrying with it the authority of the omniscient narrator—is significant because it suggests the extent to which he is able to deceive himself. Villarreal writes, "He withdrew into his protective shell of cynicism, but he recognized it for what it was and could easily hide it from the world" (p. 164).

Except for this specific situation, Richard's "protective shell,"

Rafael F. Grajeda

earlier in the novel or hereafter, can in no way be described as "cynicism." On the contrary, this "protective shell of cynicism" is merely another pose which he strikes, one consistent with the image of himself as a disillusioned, sensitive soul in search of personal freedom. It is not cynicism that we see in his reaction to his father's desertion of the family a few pages later. It is not cynicism that informs his words to his mother when she tells him that he is now the head of the family.

What Richard recognizes as a "protective shell of cynicism" is actually a self-deception twice removed: throughout most of the latter half of the novel he is motivated by what he understands as his need to be emancipated, his need to be himself, and surely, as he perceives this, it has little to do with a "protective shell." In actuality his behavior constitutes a recoil into the self. He is aloof, unattached, the hero as narcissist-observer. In his relationship with Mary, with Zelda, with the pachucos, and with his best friend, Ricky, his personal involvement is minimal.

The extent of his alienation from persons and experience can be measured by the manner in which he defends his new "friends" to his old buddies. "Those pachuc's you were talking about," he says, making them sound more like boy scouts than the angry street dudes who they really are, "are real nice guys." And the homosexuals, "they're real intelligent and good people," who, he says "just happen to like that, that's all. Like a guy with only one leg, or a deaf-and-dumb guy. . ." (p. 177).

This lack of commitment is to be understood in the total context in which the pocho finds himself. In a quandary one recoils, finds refuge, temporary justification, and meaning within the self. He is the "mock-intellectual," full of himself and confident, but in his confidence totally failing to understand the causes of his confusion. To the end of the novel he maintains that he cannot ever be changed by forces which exist outside of him. What a close reading of the novel reveals is that to an extraordinary degree Richard *has* been molded and continues to be molded by what is outside of him.

Though the emphasis through most of the novel is on Richard's subjective experience, always present are the externals of the world in which he moves, and those surfaces reflect an ethnocentric and racist rigidity whose full force can best be appreciated by the ironic edge of the "We are all American" ideal which Richard learns at school. As it turns out, this is a surface hard for Villarreal to disclose, but one, nevertheless, that makes itself felt in moments of ironic intensity: there is Richard on the street of his childhood play being called a "dirty meskin" and in the high school counselor's office being advised to be "realistic"; there is Richard's best friend, Ricky, determined to get himself "an American name" like "Malloy or something," because "Malatesta's too Dago-sounding"; there is the casual reference to the friend of the Rubio family who is arrested on a drunken charge and later found dead in jail; there are the second-hand accounts of what parents teach their children: " 'My mother's right about this lousy town. No decent people at all—just a bunch of Mexicans and Japs and I don't know what kind of crud!' " (p. 139). And finally there is Thomas Nakano's pained awkwardness as he says to his friends near the end of the book: " 'I got nothing to do with the war, fellas. . . .I'm an American, just like you guys. I just come to say goodbye, 'cause we gotta go away to a relocation center in a few days . . .' " (p. 182).

The extent to which Richard has been molded by that which is outside of him of course determines how many of these "externals" he can see and the manner by which he accommodates himself to these as realities.

It is, of course, a utopian myth that "We are all Americans" and that therefore Richard, as well as his Japanese American friend, Thomas Nakano, is an American in the same important sense in which his Anglo friends are Americans, a myth that "all people are his people" or that he "can be a part of everything because he is the only one capable of controlling his destiny." It is a myth that racism is "due more to the character of a handful of men than to the wide, almost organized attitude of a society." All of these are illusions that Richard can continue to hold only at the expense of the painful reality that stares him in the face, a reality that at least in part the novel demonstrates.

The figure of the pocho here represents a variation of "the colonized man." That he also represents the rebel and the outsider does not signal any contradiction. If anything, surely, it intensifies the sense in which he can be said to endure the scars of colonization. The white mask remains. His "rebellion" and the sense in which he elects his outsidedness are both functions of the mask. They are both stances that, however meaningful they might be for the Anglo American hero in the initiation novel, are for the pocho exercises in self-deception. His rebellion is meaningless; it is, in fact, further enslaving because it is based upon what the social reality, in contrast to the social forms, of the novel defines as utopian myths. In his attempts to find some accommodation for himself as Mexican and as American, the hero here recoils into the nullity of the abstraction, "individualism." The pattern of his encounter with experience finally is a false one, for it suggests an external neatness that does not exist. To the end he remains the dupe, seduced by some of the very forces and pressures against which he posits his commitment to individualism.

Richard Vásquez and *Chicano*

The very title, *Chicano*, for a novel purporting to treat the Mexican American experience and published in 1970, would seem to indicate a thematic development beyond that of *Pocho*. By itself, the title would seem to mark a successive step in the development of consciousness traced by three cultural figures: the Mexican father; the first generation Mexican American, the pocho; and the Chicano. If Juan Rubio, the Mexican, is destined to live out his life in "another country," defending chauvinistically what he cannot understand; and if the son, Richard, the pocho, must forever walk that precarious line that distinguishes self-hood from betrayal and self-hatred; then the grandson—the Chicano promised by Vásquez' novel—would be expected to have worked out some accommodation with his Mexican past and his North American present. "What the son wishes to forget the grandson wishes to remember": Richard Rubio, the pocho, in the name of "individualism," wishes to escape his Mexicanness. His movement is a conscious one away from his father, and into himself, a movement which Villarreal's novel identifies as involving also, in a most significant sense, assimilation into the dominant culture, by definition a one-way movement marking what is left behind for extinction.

The "Chicano" announced by Vásquez' title, however, never appears. What does appear is but a variation of the pocho experience, manifested, as in Villarreal's work, *in spite* of the writer. The irony in the book works on at least two levels and is rarely the conscious result of craft. Characterization is thin, inconsistent, and, at times, incredibly motivated; scenes are weakened by obvious marks of contrivance; and development of plot is sketchy with only a semblance of dramatic progression.

The contention of this analysis is that the "bad writing," in part at least, is the result of the writer's perspective. By "perspective" here is meant not only the ideological position of the author—that position, as it is revealed through the narrative, surely is confused—but also the pervasive absence of "feeling for" and understanding of his subject matter. To a significant degree the failures in *Chicano* as a literary work derive from the writer's tenuous hold on his subject. Had this novel been written by someone other than a Mexican American, the critic's job would be made easier. He could ascribe the distortions and the confusions to an outright ignorance—however well-intentioned—having its source in ethnocentric or racist attitudes.[4] That the writer's name is "Vásquez" lends added significance to the novel, for as with *Pocho*, a close scrutiny of the work's flaws reveals the extent to which the socialization of the Chicano consciousness has been successful in the United States of America.

Three generations are traced in *Chicano*, having their origin in Héctor and Lita Sandoval of Agua Clara, a small village in Northern Mexico. The following diagram will facilitate reference to family members:

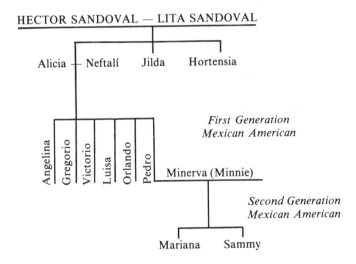

HECTOR SANDOVAL — LITA SANDOVAL

Alicia — Neftalí   Jilda   Hortensia

Angelina Gregorio Victorio Luisa Orlando Pedro   Minerva (Minnie)

First Generation Mexican American

Second Generation Mexican American

Mariana   Sammy

Narrated in rather strict chronological sequence, the story is divided into two unequal parts: Part one concentrates on the family's move from Mexico to Southern California where the children of Neftalí and Alicia are born and where twins, Marina and Sammy, are born to Pedro and Minnie Sandoval; Part two focuses on the Mariana Sandoval-David Stiver story.

Chicano begins with Hector Sandoval's arrival at Agua Clara in Northern Mexico where he meets and marries Lita, and subsequently fathers three children: Jilda, Hortensia, and Neftalí. During the Revolution of 1910, the family moves north to the United States and settles in a small community close to Los Angeles. There Héctor and his son Neftalí get jobs picking oranges, and the two daughters begin by working as maids in Anglo households and end as prostitutes. Upon Héctor's death, Lita returns to Mexico, and Neftalí, now alone, moves to Irwindale, where he buys some land on which he builds a house, marries Alicia, and in the next ten years has four sons and two daughters. During World War II, Gregorio, the eldest son, is killed, and on the occasion of his funeral, the rest of the sons and daughters rebel against their father, Neftalí, and leave home. Angelina, the eldest, starts a small cafe in Los Angeles and develops her business into an elaborate lounge and restaurant. The youngest brother, Pete, returns from the War and marries Minnie. They have twins (Mariana and Sammy), and Pete becomes a successful concrete contractor.

As the youngest son of Neftalí, Pete has often felt neglected. For this reason he and his wife, Minnie, decide that in their family the Mexican tradition which grants privilege, authority, and responsibility to the eldest son will not be observed. The attention and devotion will not be concentrated on Sammy, the male member of the twins. As it turns out, Mariana is the brighter of the two, and very quickly Sammy is identified as the "slow one" in school. In an attempt to do the best possible for his children, Pete moves his family out of the East Los Angeles barrio and into an all-white suburb. There they encounter the predictable hostility from their neighbors, all of whom fear the devaluing of their property. Sammy, alone, deprived now even of the companionship of his barrio friends who were also failing in school, does even worse in the suburban school than in the barrio. Under pressure from the neighbors and concerned for Sammy's well-being, the family moves back to East Los Angeles, where Sammy drops out of school, becomes a drug addict and pusher and is finally arrested; and where his sister Mariana graduates from high school and enters business college.

Chronologically, the novel progresses no further. Mariana, now eighteen years old, meets sociology student David Stiver, with whom she falls in love and by whom she becomes pregnant. At Stiver's insistence she agrees to an abortion. She contracts an infection, and, at the end of the novel, dies.

In the novel's treatment of these three generations, almost all of the figures important in the Mexican American experience are presented: there is the Mexican immigrant, the *pocho*, the *vendido*, the revolutionary, the peon, the *abuelitos* (the elders), the farm workers, the school "dropout-addict-criminal," the boxer, the World War II victim and veteran, the rising entrepreneur, the newly educated, the racist as well as the patronizing and the sympathetic Anglo American, and the candidate (potentially at least) for marrying into the white, North American society.

Though the novel includes all of these characters, the main thread of the narrative winds from Héctor Sandoval to his son, Neftalí, two of his grandchildren, Angelina and Pete, and ultimately to his great-grandchildren Sammy and Mariana. In a sense, the main thrust of the book points in the direction of Mariana, who at the end of the novel dies. In this sense, an overview of the book suggests a movement, south to north, and in more than literal terms. That journey begins in the south with Héctor and ends in the north with Mariana. That the journey from Mexican to "American" takes more than half a century, that it covers hundreds of miles, and that on the way children are born who in turn bear children, can be misleading, for it suggests—in what is perhaps a uniquely American way—an appropriate, if not rather sluggish, evolution from the old culture to the new.

The conditions of the lives of two generations of Mexican Americans in this novel belie that impression. That there will be an evolution, that change *will* occur as they move north from Mexico, is clear. That the American society pressures a "change" to take place in an inordinately brief period of time is attested to by this novel. Such pressure encourages *assimilation* rather than *integration*. Such pressure creates the *pocho*.

The movement in *Chicano* is from south to north. Figuratively speaking, the journey from generation to generation marks a progressively deeper incursion into the north, to the point where Mariana Sandoval, great-granddaughter of Héctor Sandoval, Mexican immigrant, attempts—through love—the most significant of entries into that northern white world. That effort finally is thwarted by a racial prejudice motivated, in part at least, by personal ambition. The new life inside of her, bearing the blood of both south and north and perhaps lending *one* meaning to the journey—that new life is aborted. And Mariana dies the empty death of the sacrificial victim, affirming nothing more significant than an apology for having "inconvenienced" David Stiver!

Mariana finally appears to be the character through whom Vásquez attempts to reconcile the racial and cultural conflict of the novel, and through whom meaning is to be ascribed to the movement

Rafael F. Grajeda

north from Mexico. Of all the Mexican American characters in this
novel, she, surely, is the one most capable of carrying the burden of
affirmation in *Chicano*. She is the most self-conscious of all the
characters, and the one most capable of understanding the issues involved. In addition, she is the only American-born Mexican in the
novel who appears consciously to maintain some substantive connection with her past, signaled not only by her periodic visits to the
home of her grandparents where she reads to Neftalí and in turn
learns the old values and traditions, but also by her attempts at
"teaching" David Stiver about Mexicans. The reader's expectations
that she be the carrier of affirmative values in the novel, however, are
ultimately frustrated.

She chooses to sacrifice herself and is sure to exonerate the name
of Stiver before she dies. In this role she is neither admirable, nor even
pathetic, for her sacrifice—being in the service of a character who is
despicable in himself—is devoid of significance. Her death, finally, is
a mere contrivance. It serves no end besides "freeing" Stiver to the
new life that he anticipates enjoying among the "smart, intellectual
debutantes," in upper-class suburbia, Illinois. Her death is literarily
gratuitous; it does not grow out of the novel; it serves no consistent
thematic purpose that the book can sustain.

It is not a meaningless universe in which Mariana lives. Her
world is not governed by shadowy substances that play havoc with
what the heart desires. It is not an "inherited unfairness," in the metaphysical sense, that informs her situation. Rather, hers is a world of a
predominantly social contour and as such—given her perceptions
and inclinations, is to some degree manipulable.

If Villarreal's novel can be said to represent the hero as dupe, then
Chicano depicts its characters as eagerly jumping into the American
madness of "making it." Both novels illustrate the condition of the
pocho. And in spite of some surface differences between the characters in both books, they in fact share more than is perhaps apparent:
victimized emotionally and intellectually by a social ethic that judges
them inferior, they, consciously or otherwise, set out to remake themselves in the image of that which is "right," and end up in cultural
limbo.

How much awareness do Vásquez' characters have? To what
extent do they know what it is they are moving into? To what extent
is their movement the result of conscious effort, to what extent is it
merely the natural result of living in the midst of the society? Surely
there is less consciousness on the part of these characters than there is

in Richard Rubio, who lives continuously, it seems, with a finger on his pulse. Still, in the characters of *Chicano* we see a definite turning away from themselves *as they are*, a recoil from the self that can best be seen by their behavior, since Vásquez does not deal explicitly or at length with the sense in which his characters "feel themselves."

Long before leaving Mexico, Héctor, for example, knows what every immigrant knows of America: that it is the land of opportunity and the land of gringo dollars. At the same time, though, he knows that "they don't let Mexicans drive locomotives in the United States" (p. 12). Upon his arrival with his family in California, one of the first things he notices is the imposing figure the *americano* cuts.

> They were americanos and wore badges. He noted that their horses were magnificent, well-fed, large and muscular, well-trained. The saddles were of rich leather, and the men wore soft hats, riding boots, and huge pistols at the hip (p. 38).

And one of the first lessons he gets is on gringo justice. The lawmen come looking for a Mexican whom they want to question "about the knife fight he had in the americano town." The Mexican sees them, starts to run, and is shot.

> The tattered man clutched his breast and swayed, and the rider took careful aim and fired again. The man collapsed. The lawman rode up to the fallen man and, pointing his pistol almost directly down, put another bullet into the still form.
> The other lawman came ..., examined the body briefly, went to his mount and the pair rode off at a casual trot (p. 38).

As the first glimpse that Héctor has of the americanos, this scene is significant only in that it illuminates the topography of the North American world in which he and his children now live. There aren't any more guns in the story, until fifty-odd years later when the Los Angeles police, in attempting to "keep law and order," threaten the people with shotguns. But the racist attitude seen in the early shooting continues to be very present throughout. There is the baiting of Gregorio at school because he was so "dark" and "squatfeatured... non-Anglo looking;" the Thompson party to which Julio Salazar is invited to play his guitar and sing but from which he is then quickly dismissed when the birthday cake and ice cream are brought out. There are the obstacles that Pete encounters when he attempts to buy a house in the suburbs; the reactions of the white neighbors in Dow Knolls Prestige Homes tract when they learn that they have a Mexican neighbor. And there are Sammy's public school experiences during which he quickly learns that when Miss Clark, the teacher, said

Rafael F. Grajeda

" 'we' she meant all the others, the Anglos, the Americans, and when she said 'you' she meant 'you people' " (p. 202).

Neftalí is the only character who is represented as having intimations that perhaps it was a mistake to leave Mexico. He notices, for example, that when the family is struggling to survive, his father is present and the family offers a strong sense of security, but that as the father's earnings increase and as his sisters get jobs that provide additional family income the sense of *familia* wanes. He has, then "fleetingly," the impression "that the family had come into a giant trap" (p. 49). When he discovers that his two sisters are, and have been, prostitutes all the time he thought they were working as maids in Anglo households, he is told by his sister Hortensia: "You don't know what the hell this country's all about...I make ten times as much money as housekeeping, and put in half the hours. And have time to go places and do things which you'll never do, because you pick oranges from dawn to dark" (pp. 52-53). Neftalí is shocked and says, "It . . .it would have been better had we stayed in Mexico. . ." (p. 53).

This is nothing more than idle musing and is recognized as such by his sisters, for already the Sandovals have seen enough of the United States that they have most definitely been brought into it. Jilda's response to Neftalí is trenchant; it suggests the reality of the lived experience, over and above any intellectualizing or glib morality, and it offers a glimpse at the extraordinary absorption capability of the United States of America. "Like hell it would," she replies to Neftalí:

> "Don't you remember, brother, the hunger, the nothing we had, no clothes, beans and corn every day, a big occasion when we had a chicken? Well, now I eat chicken whenever I want. Hortensia and I have a room all our own, on the edge of the barrio, where we buy things we like, that we never dreamed we could own in Mexico" (p. 53).

A little later during the same conversation, she says:

> "it's hard enough to be a Mexican in this country without being honest. You either have to be a maid and screw the patrón, or marry an orange picker and live in a shack in the barrio bajo" (p. 53).

Whether or not that dilemma is a real one is beside the point; the real import of Jilda's words lies in the perception there reflected, as that perception becomes a motivating force of behavior. Referring as it does to an exchange that on the one hand holds out the enticement of power, money, and convenience, it can be understood as delineating in broad strokes the dialectics of assimilation. When, as a prostitute, she accuses Neftalí of not knowing what "this country's all about," she demonstrates an understanding of America that is borne out in much of the novel. Just as one does not have to be in jail to be a prisoner, one does not have to be in a whorehouse to be a prostitute.

And with these Sandoval whores at the beginning of the North American experience, prostitution becomes a motif that generalizes the experience in various forms. Julio Salazar, Johnny Rojas, and Officer Raúl are the characters in this novel that most clearly invite the designation of *vendidos*: those who have "sold" themselves—in significant ways parallel to Hortensia and Jilda's prostitution, and for, essentially, an identical kind of exchange.

In this world, who are the "misfits"? Mariana, perhaps, but even she, through her relationship with Stiver, moves in the direction of that world. The question about "misfits," though, is more complex than this. In the world of *Chicano*, Blacks, Japanese, and Mexicans are "misfits." To David Stiver, Mariana is "exotic." And he agrees with her that "exotic means alien. . . It means different from yourself. Like you were from some place far off" (p. 249). And it is this feeling of being "alien," that the Mexican American characters in this novel attempt to somehow reconcile. The feeling is assuaged by "joining." Richard Rubio, in *Pocho*, puts it well: "This is America, Father. . . . If we live in this country, we must live like Americans."

In *Chicano*, both generations of American-born Sandovals join: Angelina; Pete and his wife Minnie; and their twin children Mariana and Sammy. The cruel irony is that having "joined," they find out they don't "belong."

In a curious way, these characters share some of the plight of Richard Wright's Bigger Thomas. What James Baldwin says about Bigger applies to the characters of *Chicano* and illuminates, perhaps, a wider context in which the pocho can be seen. Baldwin writes:

> Bigger has no discernible relationship to himself, to his own life, to his own people—*in this respect, perhaps, he is most American*—and his force comes, not from his significance as a social (or anti-social) unit, but from his significance as the incarnation of a myth.[5]

Vásquez' characters are, in fact, in cultural limbo. While in Tijuana, Sammy "noticed the American tourists taking him for granted as part of the scenery, while the natives spotted him for a tourist" (p. 333). These characters hold perhaps, as Pete does, the dollar prize for having joined in the prescribed manner, but they have little else.

Rafael F. Grajeda

Having come a considerable distance north—that is, away from their father, Neftalí and their grandfather, Héctor—they find themselves in the precarious position of being rejected by the very world which they thought they were joining. Yet the only differences between the Sandovals and the inhabitants of the Dow Knolls Prestige Homes is skin-color, last name, and Pete's accent. The Sandovals are perhaps, no more alienated than the Nuemans and Miss Ann Clark of Dow Knolls. Surely they are no more cultureless than the Anglos of the novel! In this debilitating sense, then, the Sandovals (Pete, Minnie, Sammy, Mariana) are perhaps "most American," with the only missing items being a white skin and a "sophistication"—acquired at the university, as David Stiver has—that allows one to "recognize a symphony from an overture, or discuss Maria Montessori and progressive education, or baroque and renaissance art," or decorate a home "in French Colonial or contemporary Mexican!" (p. 249).

Ultimately, the sense of emptiness that remains in the novel is pervasive, by implication affecting, as it does, more than the life-experience of one family. Yet in spite of the absence of any catharsis at the end, and in spite of other flaws in the novel, *Chicano*, like *Pocho*, does manage, as a first step, to deal literarily and seriously with the wide range of the pocho experience. Here, that experience runs the gamut from the *vendido* to the nihilistic hustler. Weak as it is as literature, the novel has perhaps a more significant value as a historical and sociological document.

The Writer-as-Pocho

> The bad narrator:
> slovenly language,
> he confuses words;
> swallows them, speaks indistinctly.
>
> (From Náhuatl poem)

> The good painter is wise
> God is in his heart.
> He puts divinity into things:
> He converses with his own heart.
>
> He knows the colors, he applies them
> and shades them;
> He draws feet and faces
> He puts in the shadows, he achieves perfection.
>
> (From Náhuatl poem)

Ultimately the quality of *Pocho* and *Chicano* is locked into the writers' point of view as members of a people who have in the past been colonized. Some of the technical flaws in the books have already been enumerated; they are obvious and hence would be easy to document methodically and in detail. Such analysis, however, would not enrich an understanding of the novels, nor would it carry their social or psychological meaning to any new depths of perception. The other weaknesses, however—those that might be ascribed to the writers' very perception and understanding of the experience—have considerable importance, since the very nature of the flaws appears to be caused by a confusion not unlike the one experienced by the protagonists of these books.

Assuredly, the dichotomy between technique and perception is false, for they are inextricably joined, one to the other, in the creation of art. Technique affects perception as perception affects technique. The "perfection" that the "good painter" achieves is the perfection not only of the painter who "knows the colors" and "applies them and shades them," but also of that of the "wise" man who "converses with his own heart."

"Personal point of view," broadly conceived, of course, touches the center of what has always been the writer's true function, namely to depict life as it is, rather than as it appears to be, or, as James put it nearly a century ago, "to consider life directly and closely, and not be put off with mean and puerile falsities, and be conscientious about it."[6] And for reasons which are perhaps best analyzed by the social sciences, the performance of such a task in the modern period has often placed the writer on the periphery of society, if not altogether outside the mainstream of conventional thought.

In a special sense, then, it is possible to refer to the contemporary writer in a post-industrial society as a "misfit," caught up in a social situation whose values he is forced to reject. With *Pocho* and *Chicano*, the source of the problem lies in the fact that, like the characters in their books, the writers appear to have been absorbed by their society to the extent that they share many of its premises, particularly as those premises affect them personally as Mexican Americans. That at its center their society is informed by racist and ethnocentric attitudes, appropriately, if only half-heartedly, demonstrated in their novels, is of clear significance.

For the non-white writer in the United States of America, writing of the racial/ethnic experience poses particular problems. While, like all writers, his art is dependent upon his own "willingness to discover his true self, upon his defining himself—for the time being at least—against his background,"[7] his very history as a "colored" person,

Rafael F. Grajeda

imposes on him the discipline of cleansing himself of the debilitating, self-denying effects of colonialism. "I can be free," writes Ellison, "only to the extent that I detect and grasp the complex reality of my circumstances and work to dominate it."[8]

In Ralph Ellison's brilliant Tar Baby metaphor in *Shadow and Act* can be read much of the anguish involved in the peculiar situation that the non-white writer in America occupies. Ellison writes:

> Let Tar Baby . . . stand for the world. He leans, black and gleaming, against the wall of life—utterly noncommittal under our scrutiny, our questioning, starkly unmoving before our naive attempts at intimidation. Then we touch him playfully and before we can say Sonny Liston! we find ourselves stuck. Our playful investigations become a labor, a fearful struggle, an *agon*. Slowly we perceive that our task is to learn the proper way of freeing ourselves. . . .
>
> Sensing this, we give him our sharpest attention, we question him carefully, we struggle with more subtlety; while he, in his silent way, holds on demanding that we peceive the necessity of calling him by his true name as the price of our freedom. It is unfortunate that he has so many, many "true names"—all spelling chaos; and in order to discover even one of these we must first come into the possession of our own names. For it is through our names that we first place ourselves in the world. Our names, being the gift of others, must be made our own (p. 147).

The passage is quoted at length because in its terms can be read the formidable demands which experience and art make on the Mexican American writer. The contention of this essay is that having "playfully" touched this "tar baby," José Antonio Villarreal and Richard Vásquez "find themselves stuck" so conclusively that they remain incapable of extricating themselves. Further, that perhaps they wrote their first novels before giving that tar baby their sharpest attention and before putting to him their most careful questions. Indeed, so lightly do they take the powers of the tar baby, that they miss even the perception that in order to free themselves, they must first learn to call him by his true name.

At its worst this self-denying stance wears the mask of the grubby but harmless frito-bandito type who takes care of the white patrón's horse, bowing excessively and saying "sí señor, I theeenk." In *Pocho*, for example, during the 1930's strike-confrontation with the white grower, it is not only Richard Rubio who sympathizes with Jamison and his daughter as she berates the Mexican farmworkers. Villarreal describes Jamison as a good man, one who "was not averse to taking his workers into his immaculate living room on cold mornings, where

his wife would serve them hot coffee and a jigger of his good brandy"
(p. 52). In addition, at the end of the work season Jamison bought the
wine for a worker's party and even got drunk in their [the Mexican
workers'] company. He is in fact such a good patrón, that he had
raised his daughter "to be the kind of girl who would go with him,
Jack Perreira [a Mexican], to the high school senior prom" (p. 55).
The point is not that the depiction of a non-racist white boss-man is
incredible. Rather the significance lies in the narrator's attitude
which this and similar passages reveal towards the self as a Mexican
American in comparison with the Anglo American. Unfortunately,
such a groveling attitude *is* part of the pocho experience, but what is
rendered here is not revealed through a fictional character; it is the
serious account of an omniscient narrator who, potentially at least, is
capable of exerting narrative control over the scene that would
allow the reader some degree of understanding of the pocho's behavior. No such narrative distance is established, though. The description is presented seriously, and carries the understanding of the
pocho to areas most assuredly unintended by the author. The writer
ultimately is at one with the characters. Since white is right in situations where white relates with brown, white is accepted as the norm—
brown being inferior. If Mr. Jamison is the kind of americano who
gets drunk with his fieldworkers and will even allow his daughter to
go to the prom with a Mexican, he must *really* be a good man. In full-
blown detail this is the peon mentality of the pocho—an attitude that
Rodolfo Gonzales has characterized as "mental stoop-labor."

This same attitude is shown in *Chicano*. The absence of narrative
distance and control is suggestive of the real sense in which the narrator is at one with his characters. In the scene where Mariana and
her mother are invited by Elizabeth and Mrs. Jameson to shop in the
supermarket in the "gringo neighborhood," Vásquez shows Mariana's astonishment at the difference between that store and the one in
the barrio where they live. The parking lot is clean and landscaped,
the store is spacious, orderly, and immaculate, the vegetables and
fruit are fresher, and the prices are the same as in the barrio. The initial intention of the scene is obvious: an instance of "separate and
unequal." Yet, sight of that intention is lost when the reader perceives
that "separate and unequal" involves an acceptance of that state of
affairs—translated into white is right; brown is wrong—not only by
the characters but by the narrator himself. Mariana, he says, "suspected this store was not unique, that in the gringo neighborhoods everything was a little better" (p. 181). And earlier, while at the home of

Rafael F. Grajeda

Elizabeth, her Anglo friend, Mariana, who is accustomed to baking cakes only from cakemixes is told that that's no fun: "The fun," her friend tells her, "is doing everything just right...the main thing is to do everything exactly right" (p. 178). And "exactly right" means, in every respect, the opposite of the way her family does it. Vásquez agrees: in the Jameson home "everything appeared planned"; in the Sandoval home "there was little scheme"; Mrs. Jameson is an attentive, understanding, and patient mother; Minnie is impatient, self-conscious, and defensive; the Jamesons aren't well-off financially, but in their home "everything had a use and was in good condition and attractive"; the Sandovals are well-off economically but they lack "taste," understanding, and education—all they have are the possessions: the biggest and most modern TV set available, the "gleaming white automatic washer and dryer, far more luxurious and expensive than the apartment-sized washer and dryer in the Jameson house"; the expensive, complicated camera; the console hi-fi set with the $40 needle; the Cadillac; and those capri pants and dresses that Minnie is always described in, "a size too small."

Again, the issue here is not that his rendering of the Mexican American experience is absolutely inauthentic; it does perhaps hold some truth. Rather the argument is that in the very manner of presentation (that is, through the selection of detail and the tone) the narrator reveals agreement with a point of view expressed by Elizabeth later when, talking with David Stiver, she glibly announces that "Everybody in East L.A. falls into the culturally deprived category."

Looked at out of context it is perhaps incredible that such a character as Elizabeth Jameson, facilely uttering this socialese, is to be taken seriously; earlier she has rendered similar conclusive judgments, such as: " 'At first it seems these people have no manners or consideration. But actually it's just a way of thinking. Or not thinking' "; and: " 'It's very typical this business of having something secret to discuss. Interrupting others to go off and whisper. It stems from a deep-rooted feeling of inferiority' " (p. 263). Elizabeth, we must remember, is Mariana's life-long friend, the "good Anglo" whose family, out of choice, has elected to live in the barrio with the people. Hence, however incredible she may appear to the reader, it is clear that Vásquez takes her seriously as a mouthpiece—clear that whatever he intends through her, her judgments surely are not rendered in the ironic sense that would enable the reader to hear *one*—the outsider's—point of view about the Mexican American experience in contradistinction to what that experience really is. No, if her point of view, in this respect, is not identical to the narrator's, it is an outlook respected and in fact supported by the novel's rendering of the barrio experience. Existing doubts about Vásquez' use of Elizabeth Jameson are dispelled when, in the same scene in which Elizabeth is quoted above, we hear Mariana—the character closest to being a heroine in the book—herself echoing a similar point of view. In response to Stiver's question about why people at the party don't introduce others, she answers:

> "That's just one of the stupid ways of the chicanos.... This party isn't so bad, because almost everyone knows each other. But usually, half the people don't know anybody, and unlike the gringos, nobody has the courage or whatever it is to walk up and introduce himself, so everyone just stands around, hoping conversation will develop somehow" (p. 268).

The matter of the pocho, though, as already suggested in the discussions above, is rather more complex than involving merely attitudes and feelings of self-rejection. The pocho, it must be remembered, is not usually, nor only, blind; he "sees" and he does not "see." The mask he wears, he feels—sometimes with anxiety and pain. And it sometimes slips. After all of the societal conditioning, and after all conscious efforts to forget the past or ignore the incipient threat of the present, the father's presence is felt; and too, the racist contour of the present imposes itself at the most inopportune moments reminding him that in spite of the exchanges and compromises, he still does not "belong." Hence his confusion, his being "in" and his being "out," his desire to run away and his need to remain. In the writer, this confusion is reflected in the ambiguous rendering of the Mexican father and of the barrio experience in general. They are not simply rejected, for to do that there is too much of the social reality that he must ignore. Yet neither are they embraced, for the pocho—by definition being a product of the North American environment—while often feeling the abstract bonds of his southern cultural heritage, at the same time (and with varying degrees of intensity) suspects that different as his Mexican heritage is from the americano culture, that heritage is inferior: what's more, it's highly inappropriate to the North.

In *Pocho* and *Chicano*, this ambiguity of point of view is pervasive and ultimately affects the meaning of the works, not in the sense in which ambiguity often functions in a work of literature, to enrich the quality of the art, but rather to confuse and garble meaning. If in

Rafael F. Grajeda

these novels can be found instances of the peon mentality referred to above, there are as many scenes where an association is sought and made to the Mexicanness of the father and to a recognition of the injustices of the social system. Those injustices are not easily denied.

The impression one derives from reading these novels is that these injustices insistently intrude themselves into the context of these experiences, and impose on the writer the necessity of somehow "dealing" with them. In *Pocho*, Richard, time and again, is assigned the function of "defending humanity," which in this context means defending the system against the charges of racism. Racial and ethnic discrimination—aimed at himself; at the pachucos; at his Japanese American friend, Nakano; at his Italian American friend, Ricky Malatesta—all of it, Villarreal has him learn, "was due more to the character of a handful of men than to the wide, almost organized attitude of a society" (p. 151).

In *Chicano* there is a similar attempt on Vásquez' part to shy away from the full implication of racism as it affects members of the Sandoval family, Julie Salazar and other Mexican Americans in the East Los Angeles barrio. Ineffectual and incredible as they sometimes appear, the members of the Jameson family, Judge Morganthau, Don Cameron of Dow Knolls and Stiver's father and sister serve the purpose of offsetting their racist and destructive counterparts in the novel, and hence blunting the sharp edge of an injustice that seemingly insists on making itself known. Judge Morganthau's humane concern for Angelina, for example, offsets the heavy-handed tactics of the police during the arrest of Jorobado and the meatcutter; the members of the Jameson family and Don Cameron, as liberal whites, counter the racism of the Dow Knolls neighbors who are finally successful in driving the Sandoval family back to the barrio; Mrs. Eva Weimer, Sammy's bilingual second-grade teacher in the barrio, offsets his bigoted fourth-grade teacher in suburbia, Miss Clark; and finally Mr. Stiver and his daughter, Marge, qualify perhaps a bit of David Stiver's self-serving actions.

In both novels the movement of the pocho is from Mexican to American. In both he moves progressively deeper and deeper into a social context that he fails to understand, and by which he is ultimately seduced. He is duped. This innocence constitutes his major flaw. Unquestioningly he renounces the old culture to which he feels but a tenuous sort of connection, and in hopes of finding true acceptance in "his" country, resolves to do what is necessary to gain full membership. His goal is never attained, nor is there any kind of significant

354

reconciliation achieved. His encounter with experience leads to an alienation that is as American as it is unrecognized by him. At the end he has little more than his utopian dreams and/or the mere trappings of a success for which he willingly renounces his father. Caught up in the midst of the noise and confusion of American society, he fails to learn "to wear his name."

In both of these novels the pattern of action on the part of the pocho appears relatively closed to change or liberation. The socialization of consciousness has been so fully determined that only through some extraordinary occurrence is anything other than the continual process of assimilation foreseeable.

Reading their novels one would get the impression that the Mexican American is indeed cultureless. In *Chicano* particularly there is a curious rendering of the barrio experience as totally devoid of integrity: even in the fiestas (the wedding scene, the birthday gathering, the moving party, the party with Jorobado) the sense of any real "celebration" is missing, as is the sense of *la vida buena*, or even of *la vida dura*. Instead the description is limited to the externals of noise, confusion, drunkenness, and gluttony. This is a distortion of reality which, again, is to be explained by the author's perspective.

To say that the Mexican American experience, to large degree, has been informed by the feelings of marginality peculiar to the pocho as described here is not to say automatically that the barrio is a cultural wasteland. For, in spite of the pressures to assimilate, and in spite of—perhaps *because of*—discriminatory practices against Mexican Americans in the society, the barrio experience has, to a stubborn degree, maintained some sense of the people's past: the language, the music, *los cuentos de los viejitos*, the *fiestas patrias*, customs and traditions—all of the efforts made by the Chicanos "to describe, justify, and praise the action through which that people has created itself and keeps itself in existence."[9] The new consciousness around which the contemporary Chicano Movement is organized constitutes a recognition of an alternative to assimilation which is conspicuously absent in *Pocho* and *Chicano*. The social movement is, in fact, based on the felt need—particularly by the youth—to search out, embrace, and continuously renew the Chicano culture.

In contemporary Chicano literature, that new awareness begins to be articulated and dramatized. If the pocho remains a recognizable figure in this literature, his presence is based on Octavio Paz' perception that the shortest way home is often around the world. Translating this into North American terms: to come home, first you must

Rafael F. Grajeda

take the risk of leaving; this necessarily involves looking closely at the North American past.

Notes

[1]José Antonio Villarreal, *Pocho* (New York, 1959). Richard Vásquez, *Chicano* (New York, 1970). All references to *Pocho* are from the Anchor paperback edition, 1970; references to *Chicano* are from the Avon paperback edition, 1970.

[2]For a cogent historical study of the colonization of the Chicano, see Rodolfo Acuña's well-documented work, *Occupied America: The Chicano's Struggle Toward Liberation* (San Francisco, 1972).

[3]Generally speaking, these are similarities in the experience of most Mexican Americans who trace their immediate ancestry to Mexico. Carey McWilliams, in *North From Mexico* (New York, 1968), points out that after 1900 approximately ten percent of the total population of Mexico immigrated to the Southwest, and that between 1900 and 1930 the number of Mexican immigrants was more than a million. For an autobiographical treatment of life in Mexico and subsequent immigration during the Mexican Revolution of 1910, see Ernesto Galarza's *Barrio Boy* (Notre Dame, 1971). See also Manual Gamio's *The Mexican Immigrant: His Life Story* (Chicago, 1931), and *Mexican Immigration to the United States: A Study of Human Migration and Adjustment* (New York, 1971). For a novelistic treatment of the Mexican American farm worker experience, see Raymond Barrio's *The Plum Plum Pickers* (Sunnyvale, California, 1969), Edmund Villaseñor's *Macho* (New York, 1973), and the excellent *"... y no se lo tragó la tierra"—"And the Earth Did Not Part"* by Tomás Rivera (Berkeley, 1970). For works of fiction treating essentially the same cultural experience see Miguel Méndez M., *Peregrinos de Aztlán* (Tuscon, 1974) and Rolando R. Hinojosa-S., *Estampas del valle y otras obras - Sketches of the Valley and Other Works* (Berkeley, 1973).

Omitted from this common experience are those Mexican Americans (for the most part, those born in New Mexico who identify as Hispanos) who trace their ancestry back to the New Mexico territory of the late 16th century. For a fictionalized rendering of that experience, see the prize-winning novel, *Bless Me, Ultima* (Berkeley, 1972) by Rudolfo Anaya.

[4]For a thorough and detailed analysis of the tratment of the Mexican and the Mexican American by Anglo American writers, see Cecil Robinson's excellent study, *With the Ears of Strangers*: *The Mexican in American Literature*. Robinson writes: "In many cases the various types of Mexicans to appear in American writing in different periods have been significant principally in revealing the psychic needs of the writers who have produced them. The American writer, especially in recent years, has often turned to the Mexican out of a sense of his own deficiency or of the deficiencies of the society in which he grew up. In either case, the Mexican and his culture have been

used as compensation. Furthermore, under the compulsion of a sense of guilt in the name of his own race-proud society, the modern American writer has tended to oversimplify his Mexican characters in the direction of some stoic or primitive ideal. The resultant literary images of the Mexican as one of the various types of noble savage, or as the emotionally unhampered, picaresque product of an unsterilized society, or yet as a graceful representative in the New World of the mellower culture of traditional Europe are often as unreal in their overemphasis as the earlier stereotypes of the brutal, dirty, cowardly Mexican of the border chronicles and first novels of the Southwest" (p. 68).

[5]*Notes of a Native Son* (Boston, 1955), pp. 34-35.

[6] "The Great Form," *Critic* (New York), Aug. 17, 1889. Included in *Literary Opinion in America*, ed. Morton Dawen Zabel, rev. ed. (New York, 1951).

[7]Ralph Ellison, *Shadow and Act* (New York, 1953), p.xix.

[8]Ellison, p. 214.

[9]Frantz Fanon, *The Wretched of the Earth* (New York, 1963), p. 233.

INTERNATIONAL LITERARY
METAPHOR AND RON ARIAS:
AN ANALYSIS OF
THE ROAD TO TAMAZUNCHALE

Carlota Cárdenas de Dwyer

> The work of Jorge Luis Borges is a species of internation-
> al literary metaphor. He knowledgeably makes a transfer
> of inherited meaning from Spanish and English, French
> and German, and sums up a series of analogies, of con-
> frontations, of appositions in other nations' literatures.
> His Argentinians act out Parisian dramas, his Central
> European Jews are wise in the ways of the Amazon, his
> Babylonians are fluent in the paradigms of Babel.
>
> Anthony Kerrigan[1]

These remarks about Borges seem pertinent as one prepares to
approach an unpretentious, slim volume bearing the label "*The Road
to Tamazunchale*—a novel by Ron Arias."[2] While it is not the point of
this discussion to establish Arias as a second Borges, consideration of
this passage does highlight the degree to which this young Chicano
writer echoes and reinvents a variety of previous literary antecedents
in a process aptly named "international literary metaphor" by Anthony Kerrigan in his introduction to Borges' collection of stories entitled *Ficciones*. For one might as easily write of Arias that his Chicanos parody a German *Faustbuch*, a chivalric romance, and a picaresque novel; that his vatos are as sagacious as any Central European
Jew; and that his East Los Angeles *barrio* is as various and as complete a complex as cosmopolitan Buenos Aires.

Yet, in spite of his far flung associations, Ron Arias is thoroughly recognizable as a "Chicano writer." His narrative of the last peregrinations of a dying old man is full of realistic detail from contemporary Chicano life. From the devoted niece Carmen with her unrelenting patience and the self-styled curer Cuca with her salubrious *ponche* to the street-smart Mario and the respectful Jesús, who prefers to be called "Jess," from the Cuatro Milpas restaurant and Los Feliz theatre to the vintage *mariachi* records and the mute parakeet called Tico-Tico, everything rings true to the Chicano reader who shares memories of a corresponding familial and social structure.

While the authentic detail of Chicano life is vividly captured by the author, that is not what is most intriguing to the modern reader. This tale of Fausto Tejada, seemingly more of a novella in many ways, engages the reader's concern on two basic levels of interest. The first level of intrest focuses on the aging Fausto as he embarks on a series of imaginative forays into the world of his inner-consciousness in order to explore various stages of post-terrestial existence. In each successive encounter with an aspect of his approaching death, i.e., wake, burial, etc., Fausto confronts and dispels the frightening and threatening qualities of death. At the end, his journey complete, all his anxieties are resolved and he is able to rest in peace: "Fausto set himself down beside his wife, clapped some life into his cold hands, then crossed them over his chest and went to sleep" (p. 107). Yet, the reader follows the peripatetic old man to this point of peaceful and perdurable reconciliation only after a series of bizarre and sometimes baffling experiences. These excursions into the inner world, with their fusing of the local and the exotic, the literary and the historical, furnish the second basic level of interest. Within this elaborate narrative structure, the character of Fausto Tejada and his overriding concern about his impending death are of major thematic significance and furnish the essential lines of coherence and continuity.

Fausto Tejada, with a tenacious grip on his failing/fleeing mortality, sports many guises as he ventures forth. At one moment he is a shabby Doctor Faustus, a retired door-to-door book salesman rather than the Old World scholar, but nonetheless seeking experience itself as much as knowledge or truth. However, like his namesake in the early *Faustbuch*, the German store of Faust legends from which sprang the Faust of Marlowe and Goethe, he conjures images and exploits to satiate his thirsting imagination. At the next moment Fausto proclaims himself "Don Fausto Tejada," and donning cape and staff he pursues with unwavering commitment his quests, both minor and major. At times, he seems to follow in the irregular footsteps of the first quixotic knight as he marshals alpaca instead of armies and when his staff is described as a rusty hoe. Yet, his picaresque journey contains many elements of the pure Romantic, as he nobly befriends and harbors the displaced Peruvian shepherd, Marcelino Huanca.

Fausto, with his flickering shades of Doctor Faustus and Don Quixote, is Everyman now quaking before the apparent nothingness of death. He is also a contemporary, urban Chicano surrounded by *curanderas* and *vatos*. Additionally, the very form of the narrative establishes him as a modern man, liberated from the confining categories of nineteenth-century realism. Just as Fausto shares the traditions of the Germanic legend, the medieval romance, and the Spanish picaresque, so is Ron Arias, as a modern Chicano author, wedged between the parallel traditions of modern United States writers and the so-called magic-realists of contemporary Latin American fiction.[3]

Here in *The Road to Tamazunchale* one may observe many of the implicit attitudes and explicit qualities common to the writings of Kurt Vonnegut, William Burroughs, John Barth, and Thomas Pynchon, as well as to Alejo Carpentier, Jorge Luis Borges, Juan Rulfo, Carlos Fuentes, Mario Vargas Llosa, and Gabriel García Márquez. For writers in both groups display the same genius for creating a glittering jewel-work of intricate narrative pattern, underpinned, in some ways also undermined, by a fundamental ontological dilemma. The ambiguous conflict in Alejo Carpentier's *El reino de este mundo* (1949) between the perspective of the European imperialists who view Mackandal as a vanquished renegade and that of the indigenous inhabitants who perceive him as triumphant messiah is not unlike the unresolved questions in Thomas Pynchon's *The Crying of Lot 49* (1965) of whether Oedipa's theory of the Tristero conspiracy is delusion or discovery, insanity or insight. Despite their many differences, the works of all these writers move in concert to challenge seemingly rational approaches to the absurdities and tragedies of twentieth-century life and to voice disdain for simplistic solutions.

Because the personality of Juan Tejada and his pervasive concern about his impending fate are of major thematic significance and furnish the essential lines of continuity and coherence in the narrative frame, it is possible, in the last analysis, to separate the pathways of his spiritual odyssey from those of his fabulous journeys, for the events of the latter produce the terms of the former. Therefore, it is necessary to examine carefully the entire text of the work to apprehend its unified literary dynamics. While a complete exegesis of the novel would be rather lengthy to include in this discussion, a close reading of the first two chapters is offered here to illustrate precisely the nature of the interplay between the spiritual odyssey and the corresponding series of fabulous journeys. From the first moment, the template of Fausto's mental activity provides the associative pattern of his various wanderings. Fausto's disassociation of his psychic powers from corporeal confines is dramatized with startling intensity in the opening scene when he, in effect, disengages himself from his "human coil."

The first chapter begins with a matter of fact description of Fausto quietly and deliberately removing a layer of skin from his infirm and wrinkled body. The procedure is conveyed in precise terms and likened to such a mundane and unnoteworthy occurrence as the removal of nylon hose. "It bunched at the knuckles, above the fingernails. Carefully he pulled each fingertip as he would a glove" (p. 13). Yet while Fausto's removal process and even the neatly folded "wad of skin" are of seemingly convincing veracity, Fausto's niece Carmela enters and perceives nothing unusual about the old man, indicating concern solely about his relative well-being. Then, after unfolding the dry tissue and displaying the "feather-light suit" on the bedding, Fausto is disappointed when his niece registers no surprise. Indeed, she seems to notice nothing unusual at all. Oblivious to her uncle's grotesque design to call her attention, Carmela only recalls his previous attacks in the past. The disconcerting image she remembers is that of him in the hospital "straining to speak, with a tube in one arm and another up a nostril" (p. 13).

It is morning and Carmela is looking in on her uncle before leaving for her job. Assured that he is comfortable she leaves him, telling him that his breakfast is on the table. Fausto arises and reminisces briefly about his life since his retirement:

> For six years he had shuffled to the window, to the bathroom, down to the kitchen, through gloomy rooms, resting, listening to the radio, reading, turning thin, impatient, waiting for the end. Six years ago she had convinced him to stop work (p. 14).

Abruptly, with no introduction or preparation, Carmela's voice from that scene in the past is heard. In fact, the entire short scene between the two is given as if it were being replayed in the present. Fausto's compliant and slightly resigned "I'll stay" in response to her plea that he retire and stay home echoes with almost ringing clarity.

Then, a transition to the present is provided—"Now, years later. . ."—and Fausto is overwhelmed with the awful sensation of his body becoming a decaying and dying thing: "He felt as if his muscles were finally turning to worms, his lungs to leaves and his bones to petrified stone" (p. 14). He responds to this thought of death with fury and outrage. For the first time Fausto is seen involved with the unavoidable present and the unwelcome anticipation of his eventual, if not imminent, death:

> Suddenly, the monstrous dread of dying seized his mind, his brain itched, and he trembled like a naked child in the snow. No! he shouted. It can't happen, it won't happen! As long as I breathe, it won't happen. . . .(p. 14).

Fausto's desperate yearning for an alternative to his fated demise is answered by what he perceives as "the song of life." The mysterious sound "beckoned with the faint, soft sound of a flute" (p. 14). The chapter closes with the dying end of the enticing sound.

Chapter two begins with Fausto's firm conviction that he will embark immediately—his destination Peru, his armament a sword with buckler. Meanwhile, before going down to the kitchen, he dresses himself in his customary smoking jacket and khaki trousers. Hurrying towards the stairs, his thoughts roam excitedly to his imagined journey to Peru. His mind fills with thoughts of an Old World viceroy, a garrison, and his goal, Cuzco, heart of the Inca civilization. Steadying himself on the bannister, he considers various means of transport and finally decides on the bus, concluding reasonably that "he was never the best of horsemen" (p. 15).

At this point Fausto seems to be overcome by his own emotions and collapses on the floor: "Excitement rose in his throat, and suddenly his fingers had sunk into the carpet" (p. 15). With his physical collapse his fantastic journey begins as he hurries through Lima toward a bus. After arriving in Cuzco and settling in a hotel, he is surprised to find Carmela in his room in a very uncharacteristic attitude: "At first her beauty left him speechless. She sat on the edge of the bed with her back to the afternoon light, her long black hair spread over her shoulders" (p. 18). However, when Fausto addresses this beguiling figure as "Carmela," she maintains that her name is Ana. She promises to take him to a mountain visible in the cloudy distance. They set off by train, but soon are walking through a steamy Amazon valley.

Becoming increasingly fatigued, Fausto begins to lose consciousness. Seeing a vague but menacing figure in the thick brush, he charges, like Don Quixote toward the windmills. The unarmed Fausto speculates, "If it were death, he would impale the monster to the hilt" (p. 20). Succeeding only in entangling himself in the vines of a tree, he is rescued by Ana, who cuts him free with a machete.

The two continue their journey through an exotic and lush valley, halting briefly at a pool to bathe and refresh themselves. They resume their trek again, now moving upward toward the barren promontory above the valley. Passing through a "cloud-forest of weird, root twisted shrubs and moist, darkened hollows" (p. 20), the strange and unreal atmosphere gives way to an eerie one, slightly gothic in its threatening undertones. "The gnarled branches of these stunted, phantom trees seemed to reach out and block the trail" (p. 20). The extraordinary and preternatural character of the area is further defined when Ana asserts that stranded travelers live on here "as insects, bats, even rocks" (p. 20).

With the gradual descent of nightfall, the two approach a torch-light processional that is ascending the mountain. Ana rushes ahead. Clutching his chest in a spasm of pain, Fausto calls out, but he is answered only by a child's beckoning gesture. Dragging himself forward, he observes people engaged in a ritualistic ceremony. The men dance, "their ponchos whirling in one great circle around the women who kneeled in the center, sending their wails to the rocky crags above" (p. 21). Nearing a "crude platform" with Ana's assistance, Fausto reclines and becomes the object of the mourning rite. "Too tired to refuse their grief" (p. 21), Fausto nevertheless questions and, in effect, refuses the role of corpse assigned to him.

At this point Fausto's two frames of reference converge as he addresses Ana and is answered by his niece, Carmela. The "crude platform" is now his own bed and he is, once again, at home.

After suffering a physical collapse and imagining himself as the central figure in a wake ceremony, Fausto maintains his staunch refusal to capitulate his spirit to the forces of death, and he hears again, while lying prostrate on his bed, the mysterious flute with its tantalizing song of life. He remarks to Carmela, "It's beautiful. . . .I can't think of anything more beautiful" (p. 21). Like Juan Dahlman in Borges' "The South," who escapes from spending his last moments in the boring dreariness of an antiseptic institution by virtue of his imagination and memory, so does Fausto here flee from inglorious collapse. Weakened but not overcome, he withstands the shock of near death and is able, in the next chapter, to play-act at death.

While the exploits of Juan Tejada may initially exhibit a daz-

Carlota Cárdenas de Dwyer

zling display of technical mastery and creative virtuosity, there lies beneath the glittering surface of this imaginative account a profound and substantive core. Although some of the seemingly incongruous and unexpected elements may appear arbitrary, none is without its ideational justification or relevance. From start to finish, Fausto doggedly pursues the spectres of his own subconscious. Traversing borders of consciousness as well as of geography in the first eleven chapters, he repeatedly returns to the Elysian Field near his own backyard. Finally forgoing his struggle in chapter thirteen, he declines, for the first time, to participate in the climactic fantasy of metamorphoses in which movement is not from one area to another but from one form of being to another.

In conclusion, it is important to note that the character of Ron Arias' realism is deep and thoughtful. Unlike the short-lived Realists of the nineteenth century, Arias strives to portray not the slick surface of experience, but the varied texture of inner response to that experience. Closer to *Tristram Shandy* than to many of its Chicano predecessors, *The Road to Tamazunchale* reveals, as in Fausto's incident with the filmmakers, that after the revolution is over, life and the universal search for psychic survival persist.

UNIVERSITY OF TEXAS, AUSTIN

Notes

[1]Jorge Luis Borges, *Ficciones*, translated with an introduction by Anthony Kerrigan (New York, Grove Press, 1962), p. 9.

[2]Ron Arias, *The Road to Tamazunchale* (Reno, Nevada: West Coast Poetry Review, 1975). All subsequent references will be to this text and will appear in parentheses.

[3]See, for example, Angel Flores, "Magical Realism in Spanish American Fiction," *Hispania*, 38, 2 (1955), 187-92; Luis Leal, "El realismo mágico en la literatura hispanoamericana," *Cuadernos Americanos*, 153 (julio-agosto 1967), 230-35; and Floyd Merrell, "The Ideal World in Search of Its Reference: An Inquiry into the Underlying Nature of Magical Realism," *Chasqui: Revista de Literatura Latinoamericana* 4, 2 (1975) 5-17.

LO MEXICANO Y LO CHICANO EN
EL DIABLO EN TEXAS

Salvador Rodríguez del Pino

Aristeo Brito, quien ha clasificado su primera novela como "literatura chicana", es uno de los pocos escritores chicanos que escriben fundamentalmente en español. Tomando en cuenta y aceptando la autoclasificación de la novela, no discutiré las razones por las cuales Brito así denominó su primer libro; el problema que me concierne es encontrar hasta qué punto la lengua empleada por un escritor chicano, que tiene la habilidad de escoger entre dos lenguas, influye en su psique creador para representar un mundo de experiencia inconfundiblemente chicano. José Antonio Villarreal, novelista "chicano-mexicano", nos dice en su entrevista con Juan Bruce-Novoa: "En resumen, yo no creo que jamás habrá una literatura chicana que pueda ser separada de la literatura americana y, a causa de ello, directamente vinculada con la literatura inglesa".[1] Villarreal llegó a esta conclusión diciendo que la mayoría de los escritores chicanos escriben en inglés y cuando no lo hacen, se les traduce. Además, sigue Villarreal, ". .nosotros nos adherimos muy fuertemente a la tradición de las letras americanas".[2] Supongo que esto sucede especialmente cuando el escritor chicano ha pasado formalmente por la instrucción de los departamentos de inglés de las universidades americanas y que consequentemente, toda su formación literaria ha sido dentro de esa tradición. Pero, ¿qué pasa entonces con los escritores que se han formado dentro de la tradición de las letras hispánicas? Obviamente, esta pregunta supone una dicotomía para los escritores chicanos: si éstos escriben en inglés, su obra será clasificada dentro de la literatura americana; si escriben en español, se considerará como literatura mexicana porque, de acuerdo con esta observación, no existe una literatura chicana autónoma. Si como en este caso, la lengua se establece como único factor para designar lo escrito, entonces ¿cuál sería la clasificación de un escrito bilingüe o la de una obra escrita en lo que se determinará "español chicano"? Eso es puro experimento, nos diría Villarreal. Pero la realidad es otra. Lo bilingüe es tan parte del habla del chicano como lo es su herencia mexicana. Los escritores chicanos ya no experimentan; emplean el bilingüismo para autentificar lo chicano. Este bilingüismo hoy día empleado por los escritores chicanos no es una simple alternación de palabras o expresiones en dos lenguas, ni tampoco es uso arbitrario o caprichoso. Los conceptos e imágenes expresados en forma bilingüe son reflejos de un mundo diferente al americano o al mexicano aunque indudablemente provenga de los dos. Es tan compleja a veces esta lengua única que no basta ser bilingüe para comprenderla; en muchos casos es imprescindible haber vivido dentro de la experiencia chicana para captar por completo el sentido de las metáforas.

El lenguaje, más que el comportamiento social, es el índice por medio del cual se representan de una manera fiel los conceptos y valores del universo chicano. El conocimiento de la lengua del autor es el pasaporte al mundo que él describe. Por esta razón, el escritor chicano no puede más que usar su propia lengua para hacer vivir y vibrar el mundo de su experiencia. Sin embargo, al escribir en español, el escritor chicano es también partícipe de su herencia hispánica, como lo es de la americana al escribir en inglés; por medio de las dos, participa de lo universal involucrando su chicanismo dentro de un marco más amplio y extenso de lo que aparece a primera vista. El mundo de la experiencia chicana fue forjado por las circunstancias americanas y mexicanas, pero éste ya no pertenece ni a lo netamente mexicano ni a lo netamente americano. Tal vez este desprendimiento sea causado por otro extremismo mexicano no mencionado por Octavio Paz.[3]

Con *El diablo en Texas* tenemos la primera novela chicana que se expresa en dialecto chicano, en español mexicano, en inglés y en forma bilingüe. Las otras novelas chicanas escritas en español no han empleado la expresión chicana en su forma inglesa, y muy poca la bilingüe. Obras como *Peregrinos de Aztlán* de Miguel Méndez y *Caras viejas y vino nuevo* de Alejandro Morales están escritas completamente en español. Méndez emplea varios niveles lingüísticos dentro de la misma lengua y recrea la jerga fronteriza, mientras que el español de Morales, que no usa expresiones bilingües o netamente chicanas, ha sido criticado en cuanto a la "calidad" del castellano empleado.[4] Sin duda, el español empleado por estos escritores tiene que reflejar el mundo en que viven ellos y sus protagonistas y esto incluye experiencias vitales de diferente orden del mundo mexicano. Si lo aseverado es razonable, entonces es imperante, para poder tener un acercamiento a la novela chicana escrita en español, tratar de separar lo mexicano para que lo chicano quede claramente al descubierto y susceptible al análisis. Si el mundo chicano brota del mexicano, ¿dónde podremos trazar la línea de separación entre estos dos mundos? Uno de los recursos que tenemos es de ir a la literatura mexicana y ver cómo pintan este mundo sus propios novelistas.

Con la publicación en 1947 de *Al filo del agua* de Agustín Yáñez, se inicia un período en el cual se puede identificar un mundo mexicano desprovisto de lo épico y legendario que había pintado la Novela de la Revolución, un mundo que se ofuscaba dentro de una novela de ambiente idealista y tremendista. Y en 1950 Octavio Paz publica *El laberinto de la soledad* en cuyos ensayos se identifica el carácter mexicano para toda una generación de escritores que toman su libro como santo y seña de lo mexicano. Carlos Fuentes lo autentifica y Juan Rulfo lo mitifica. Es precisamente este mundo mexicano de Paz el que tiene trascendencia para los escritores chicanos. Octavio Paz ha tenido y tiene todavía mucha influencia en la literatura chicana, que parece necesitar una autoridad que señale lo que es mexicano. Además de ser uno de los autores más estimados por el chicano, Paz es el más citado después de Vasconcelos. Pero Octavio Paz no es solamente apreciado por su análisis del mexicano y su mundo, sino que su "manera de entrelazar la literatura en términos de escritor y lenguaje, realidad y lenguaje, el escritor y la mitología ha sido adoptado y desarrollado por los escritores chicanos".[5]

La Revolución Mexicana ha sido el hecho identificador como trasfondo de lo mexicano. Pero aunque la Revolución esté presente en las novelas de Yáñez, Rulfo y Fuentes, ya no ocupa el primer plano de la novela, sino que el relato, de trama contemporánea, analiza con marco histórico a la Revolución y determina las consecuencias de ella en el presente. Trasladando la Revolución a la novela chicana, Juan Bruce-Novoa nos dice que la Revolución Mexicana ha sido el punto de partida histórico en la novela chicana, "point zero for the Chicano Novel".[6] Pero no todo lo mexicano nació con la Revolución. La Revolución logró el desgarramiento para que el mexicano penetrara en su historia. La identificación, el auto-conocimiento y los mitos empezaron a brotar por la fisura humeante que dejó aquel desgarramiento violento. El mexicano empezó a verse a sí mismo por esa vio-

Salvador Rodríguez del Pino

lencia. Samuel Ramos, Octavio Paz y José Vasconcelos—es su mundo el que se perfila como mundo mexicano en la literatura chicana.

Por ejemplo, el mundo de Presidio, el lugar en donde acontece la novela de Brito, es un mundo mexicano y chicano entrelazado no sólo por la proximidad a México, ya que se encuentra en la frontera, sino porque su historia y destino están influenciados por los acontecimientos de los dos países y manipulados por un diablo que siempre trama su curso. Presidio-Ojinaga se extiende entre los Estados Unidos y México, dividido por el Río Bravo, fuente de vida y muerte. La historia de Presidio es una historia de opresión continua proveniente de circunstancias de los dos lados. Esa opresión lo tiene muerto en vida sin redención aparente. Brito nos invita a rezar por Presidio en su introducción en la cual condensa toda su historia. La introducción termina con una invocación: "Presidio mal aventurado, a tí y a vos padre que eres de Presidio, Amén".

> Yo vengo de un pueblito llamado Presidio. Allá en los más remotos confines de la tierra surge seco y baldío. Cuando quiero contarles cómo realmente es, no puedo, porque me lo imagino como un vapor eterno. Quisiera también poderlo fijar en un cuadro por un instante, así como pintura pero se me puebla la mente de sombras alargadas, sombras que me susurran al oído diciéndome que Presidio está muy lejos del cielo. Que parir allí es parir medio muerto; que trabajar allí es moverse callado a los quehaceres y que no se tome a mal el miedo del turista cuando llega a Presidio y sale espantado al escuchar el ruido vacío de las almas en pena. . .[7]

Al leer estas palabras que introducen el relato de la novela *El diablo en Texas*, no puede uno más que pensar en el mundo de Comala en la novela de Juan Rulfo, *Pedro Páramo*. Presidio, al igual que Comala, está mitificado, suspendido en el tiempo y en el espacio. Poblado de ánimas en pena que impiden contar "la verdadera historia", Presidio tiene que ser descrito desde una perspectiva que requiere elementos fantásticos y surrealistas para poderse comprender. Pero en este caso, existen dos Presidios: el Presidio verdadero, real, que existe geográficamente en Texas y el Presidio mitificado del relato. Esta yuxtaposición de realidades crea el problema de que cada una influya sobre la otra dentro y fuera de la novela, porque el que haya ido a Presidio, Texas, y leído la novela, no dejará de sentir la influencia del Presidio mítico. Sin embargo, lo que interesa es el Presidio de la novela creado por el autor con rasgos parecidos a los de Comala. Comala está en "la boca del infierno"[8] y Presidio "muy lejos del cielo". Los dos mundos están poblados de ánimas en pena, de recuerdos, de rencores vivos, de angustias porque sus historias son oídas y contadas y esto le da al espacio una calidad de vida-muerte, de tiempo petrificado y de distintos niveles de realidad. Esta analogía Presidio-Comala se extiende más allá de las perceptibles características míticas y fantásticas: los dos mundos están arraigados en el concepto mexicano de la muerte, a la cual se considera una extención de la vida y cuyas fuentes las podemos encontrar en el pensamiento indígena: "La muerte no era el fin natural de la vida sino fase de un ciclo infinito". . ."La vida se prolongaba en la muerte".[9] Paz traduce este concepto indígena a lo mexicano: "Si no morimos como vivimos es porque realmente no fue nuestra la vida que vivimos: no nos pertenecía como no nos pertenece la mala suerte que nos mata".[10] Brito lo traspone a lo chicano: ". . .en Presidio nunca se muere. Se afirma y se hace sustento como pan de cada día, hasta el punto de convertirse en párasito eterno".[11]

Escogí *El diablo en Texas* como ejemplo de novela chicana porque en ella la influencia de lo mexicano es evidente; sin embargo, esa influencia no altera el mundo chicano de la obra. Es más, la presencia del mundo mexicano yuxtapuesto a lo chicano hace que éste último sobresalga por medio de la expresión lingüística que se emplea para novelar al elusivo mundo de la experiencia chicana. Ese mundo implícito en *El diablo en Texas* proveniente de lo mexicano es también el mundo de obras como *El luto humano* de José Revueltas, *Pedro Páramo* de Juan Rulfo, *Al filo del agua* de Agustín Yáñez, *Confabulario* de Juan José Arreola y *La muerte de Artemio Cruz* de Carlos Fuentes. En otras palabras, Aristeo Brito sigue una tradición novelística mexicana ejemplificada por la generación de los autores mencionados. *El laberinto de la soledad* de Octavio Paz tuvo profunda influencia en varios de estos escritores, influencia basada en su examen y descripción de la psique del mexicano, así como los símbolos culturales que emplea Paz para explicar el comportamiento y conciencia del mexicano y las raíces de su soledad. Las máscaras, el machismo, el carácter de oprimido y servil a causa de la colonización, la interpretación de las fiestas, el cacicazgo, la conformidad y el estoicismo ante la muerte son rasgos mexicanos expuestos por Paz que después aplicaron a sus relatos estos escritores y que Brito también evoca como mexicano. El mundo mexicano de Paz es el mundo mexicano de Brito.

Presidio, en la novela de Brito, es pueblo mexicano y chicano a la vez, mitificado, historificado e imaginado por medio de diferentes tiempo-espacios sin cambiar la esencia o el alma particular de Presi-

Salvador Rodríguez del Pino

dio-mundo. Relatos fragmentados cuentan la historia de Presidio: un feto que habla desde su semilla pura en la prisión del vientre, lo imagina; el diablo, en diferentes formas y máscaras, trama su suerte y las almas asesinadas en el Fortín quedan aprisionadas en Presidio para burlarse de él. Pero Presidio sigue igual, inmutable a través de tres etapas en el tiempo-espacio de la novela. Es la soledad de un pueblo entero que, a través de su historia, soporta una opresión calcinante sin alivio y sin esperanza, manipulado por destinos ajenos a su voluntad y tratando siempre de burlar los designios del diablo que eternamente está en acecho como si el pueblo fuera su única diversión. El "patas de chivo" se disfraza de Rinche (Texas Ranger), de cacique oportunista y asesino; toma forma de galán en los fandangos, de guardagujas para llevarse por medio de engaños a los pasajeros del tren con destino a la gloria; se vuelve víbora, conejo, chapulín, dinero y sigue un sin fin de transformaciones para engañar al pueblo que ya lo conoce y sabe de sus tretas. Y el pueblo en su semilla grita: "Soy hombre de noche, soy vida de noche. Soy hijo de la llorona y me llamo Reyes, hijos de la tal por cual. Yo soy hermano de Jesús del río".[12]

Al principio, el río unía a Presidio-Ojinaga; el pueblo era uno: mexicano. Pero llegó el puente separando a Presidio de sus raíces, transformándolo en otro, en "de este lado del río":

> ¿Te acuerdas, antes que hicieran el puente, cómo llevaba gente de un lado pa'l otro? Yo me divertía mucho con él. Entonces todos éramos iguales. No es que no séamos, pero ha cambiado desde que pusieron el puente. Qué curioso, Vicke. La gente se siente separada. ¿Qué no los puentes son para que haiga menos de eso? Antes podíamos ir a que los agüelitos sin... ¿pa' qué son esos papeles? ¿Por qué los piden esos hombres todo el tiempo? ¿Quiénes son? ¿Y el diablo los ha visto? ¿Es cierto que estamos en el infierno?

Aquí podemos ver el desprendimiento de Presidio de México por medio de un elemento que debería unir y no separar. Esa separación no es solamente de sus raíces sino que también lo es del cielo. Las alusiones comparando a Presidio con el infierno o con cementerios son numerosas: "Presidio, prisión, infierno"..."Sólo les falta a las casitas una cruz al frente para que sean cementerios"...etc. Esta es la descripción del espacio incambiable cuya historia se cuenta en tres partes divididas por tiempos desiguales: 1883, 1942 y 1970, y cuyo narrador siempre está presente ya sea en energía seminal, en feto dentro de la madre o en precoz recién nacido que no más esperaba nacer para contar la historia que se había acumulado en su mente durante muchos años y que estaba lista para ser contada al emerger del útero.

Lo mexicano y lo chicano

Se podría decir que el mundo mexicano es predominante en la primera parte, 1883, y el chicano es activo en la etapa de 1970, pero para apreciar mejor esa transformación de lo mexicano a lo chicano, tenemos que valernos de la introducción. En la introducción, Brito condensa la historia del relato en forma parecida al último cuento de Tomás Rivera, "Debajo de la casa", en . . .*y no se lo tragó la tierra*; sólo que Brito lo hace aquí en forma de letanía que trata de comprometer al lector para que pida y ruegue por Presidio. La forma lingüística de la introducción es también importante puesto que empieza con un español poético de elementos fantásticos reminiscentes de Rulfo; después, poco a poco, se van perdiendo los signos de ortografía condensando paulatinamente la historia en sucesos cristalizados y mitificados. La prosa se vuelve activa pasando de nuevo a lo poético que evoca algo tal vez imaginado, tal vez real y así se van introduciendo voces inglesas, expresiones chicanas, hasta que la prosa explota en una jerga dinámica completamente chicana para terminar en un tono irónico de fatalidad que pide perdón a Dios por algo que quizá no tenga remedio pero que vale la pena tratar de rogar por ello:

Prosa poética:
Cuanto quiero contarles cómo realmente es no puedo, porque me lo imagino como un vapor eterno.

Mundo mexicano:
porque en los corrales de este lado las vacas flacas de Ojinaga se compran a muy buen precio para engordarlas a expensas de otros y la iglesia mientras tanto se cae de ojos tristes en los días que no hay domingos. . .

Mundo de Presidio:
. . .noche, noche larga como el infinito, noche pesada monótona como la historia puta mentirosa así como las del zumbido, pero éstas tienen razón, la historia no. . .

Voces regionalistas:
pero en las boticas no se venden medecinas ya que no hay dotores sólo hojas de laurel, romero, ruda y yerbabuena para los niños que voltean los ojos legañosos y las madres paren cuates cuando comen los churupes los frijoles con quelites. . .

Mundo chicano:
. . .el agua se la robaron las bombas traca traca trac toda la santa noche hasta que agarraba aire y se morían pero el gin no se paraba con su whooooooo sorbía las treilas a la Chancla y a la Mocha y a la Golondrina nombres puestos por la raza para indicar sello de posesión. . .

Jerga chicana
los batos locos no se aguantaban tampoco en las boticas donde hay vi-

Salvador Rodríguez del Pino

trolas con Elvis Presley Fats Domino Little Richard and the blob that
creeps and you ain't nothing but a hound dog finding your thrill on
Blueberry Hill bailando solos con zapatos puntiagudos con taps tapping tap tapping chalupas down the street unpaved no sound carros
con colas arrastrando sus dos pipas with fenderskirts.

Invocatoria:
Dios perdónalos, porque al cabo allá en el otro cachete la vida perra,
caray mi amigo ¿de dónde? desde Michoacán vestido con la ropa hecha de costales de harina y huaraches de hule marca goodyear que
nunca conoció Presidio, Presidio mal aventurado, a tí a vos padre que
eres de Presidio, Amén.

En esta primera novela de Aristeo Brito se ha tratado de explorar
lo que podría ser el prototipo de la novela chicana escrita en español
empleando lo que él mismo persigue: "la búsqueda de la expresión
auténtica". La búsqueda de la autenticidad en la narrativa por medio
de diferentes modelos, direcciones y técnicas causa que esta novela
parezca paradójica y experimental, rebuscada y simple a la vez. La
obra de Brito marca una nueva dirección y posible modelo para la
novela chicana que aún busca en los modelos tradicionales de la literatura hispánica y estadounidense una brecha de salida, de escape,
para respirar el aire auténtico de su mundo. La búsqueda de esta autenticidad, dentro de la literatura chicana actual, es el signo de su universalidad.

UNIVERSITY OF CALIFORNIA, SANTA BARBARA

Notas

[1] Juan Bruce-Novoa, "Interview with José Antonio Villarreal". *Revista Chicano-
Riqueña*, IV, 2, págs. 40-48. (Traducción mía.)
[2] Bruce-Novoa, pág. 43.
[3] "Queramos o no, estos seres son mexicanos, *uno* de los extremos a que puede llegar el mexicano". Octavio Paz, *El laberinto de la soledad* (Fondo de Cultura Económica, México, 1959), pág. 13. Subrayado mío.
[4] Marvin Lewis, "*Caras viejas y vino nuevo*: Essence of the Barrio". *Bilingual Review*, IV, 1 & 2 (1977), págs. 143-44.
[5] Federico A. Sánchez, "Raíces mexicanas". *Grito del Sol*, Year One, Book Four
(Oct-Dec. 1976), págs. 75-87. (Traducción mía.)
[6] Bruce-Novoa, pág. 40.
[7] Aristeo Brito, *El diablo en Texas* (Editorial Peregrinos, Tucson, 1976), pág. 7.

[8]Juan Rulfo, *Pedro Páramo* (Fondo de Cultura Económia, México, 1973), pág. 9.

[9]Paz, pág. 49.

[10]Paz, pág. 48.

[11]Brito, pág. 97.

[12]Brito, pág. 20.

[13]Brito, pág. 19.

DEGRADACION Y REGENERACION
EN *BLESS ME, ULTIMA*:
EL CHICANO Y LA VIDA NUEVA

Roberto Cantú

Introducción

El problema que nos presenta la lectura de *Bless Me, Ultima* (1972) es, ante todo, el de su exégesis textual. A diferencia de otras novelas escritas por autores chicanos, la obra de Rudolfo A. Anaya permite, o quizá sería mejor decir que exige, varios acercamientos interpretativos. Al ser una novela de iniciación o de formación en su sentido más lato, se une a otras en las que la misma estructura aparece como factor integrante. Novelas como *Pocho* (1959), de José Antonio Villarreal, o *Barrio Boy* (1971), de Ernesto Galarza, ejemplifican la vida de un jovencito de ascendencia mexicana quien se ve ante una inevitable prueba iniciadora; a saber, la aculturación sajona. *Bless Me, Ultima* (BMU) no se aparta de esta tradición, por lo visto bien establecida en la novelística chicana.

Pese a esta obvia homología estructural, podríamos afirmar que existen grandes diferencias entre estas tres novelas, incluso en lo que respecta al substrato ideológico de cada una de ellas.[1] En primer lugar, en *Pocho* observamos una actitud progresivamente iconoclasta, tanto hacia la cultura mexicana como a la que impera en el contexto norteamericano; Ricardo Rubio, el joven protagonista, reniega de la tiranía del pasado cultural y angustiado por lo que podríamos denominar su "inautenticidad existencial", se marginaliza del grupo, se ensimisma y se opone, al fin, a cualquier forma de asimilación, no obstante la ironía de su final reclutamiento en la fuerza naval de los Estados Unidos, decisión trágica que más bien parece una liberación del ambiente rural que le asfixiaba. En *Barrio Boy*, por otra parte, hay una tácita aceptación de la cultura norteamericana, y una explícita fe en la educación escolar. O sea, que el mensaje de la obra parece ser que por medio de la "educación" el chicano podrá sobrevivir en esta nueva cultura que le rodea. Como se podrá inferir de lo anterior, entre estas dos novelas existe una radical polarización en cuanto a las ideas relacionadas con la efectiva aculturación, o posible asimilación, del chicano; y la razón es obvia: en *Pocho*, Villarreal hace patente su crítica mordaz de cualquier proceso colectivista, especialmente de aquellas tradiciones que tienen como efecto la nivelación espiritual del hombre. Odia la mediocridad y añora la grandeza de antaño que muere en la actualidad. El perfil de los intelectuales en *Pocho* es uno de marginalización, de fracaso.[2] Galarza, en cambio, cree a pie juntillas en la escuela y en lo que, por extención, ella representa.[3]

BMU es, en varios aspectos, la "des-polarización" de la disyuntiva anterior, o si se quiere, la obra que sintetiza magistralmente las dos posturas adoptadas por Villarreal y Galarza. Y esto en sí es un gran adelanto en el desarrollo ideológico del chicano, según su manifestación en la novelística chicana. En la obra de Anaya, encontramos el mismo impulso iconoclasta de *Pocho*, junto con un parecido optimismo en cuanto a la facultad del hombre de aprender y emprender nuevos modos de vida. Por consiguiente, Antonio Márez y Luna, el protagonista de BMU, se libera del peso ancestral al igual que Ricardo Rubio, pero a diferencia de éste, no se pierde en un mundo carente de convicciones firmes. Antonio, a diferencia de Ernesto (*Barrio Boy*), no encuentra su camino en la escuela, pero sí tiene, al igual que Ernesto, un horizonte trazado; los dos, pues, son jóvenes encausados hacia una meta.

Si nos limitamos al plano meramente narrativo, el argumento de BMU no mostrará tener mucha correlación con la problemática actual del chicano. Hoy día nos preocupan el barrio, la ciudad, los conflictos urbanos: nos preocupa nuestro futuro. En muchos aspectos, BMU refleja la supervivencia de lo rural en nuestro mundo; es expresión de todo aquello que se ha vuelto anacrónico a fuerza de tanto avance efectuado por nuestra época de cambios continuos. El argumento o diseño externo de BMU es ya conocido: trata de un jovencito quien tiene la fortuna de conocer a una curandera durante el primer momento crítico de su vida, antes de cumplir la edad de siete años. Ultima, que así se llama la guía espiritual de Antonio, le advierte de los peligros que le acechan en el mundo (e.g., Tenorio Trementina), le da a conocer la belleza de la Creación, y le enseña, por medio de su ejemplo y consejos a vivir una vida nueva. Al morir Ultima, el aprendiz se encuentra preparado para enfrentarse a las contingencias de un futuro que sólo él podrá estructurar en destino propio. Dentro del argumento encontramos brujas, hechizos, poderes sobrenaturales, etc. Consecuentemente, poco que diera testimonio de la lucha socio-cultural del chicano contemporáneo. No obstante, hay en BMU algo que podríamos llamar un *sentido subyacente*—aquello que se nos escapa en la primera lectura de la obra pero luego nos viene de golpe en sucesivas lecturas—que sí tiene mucho que ver con la encrucijada actual del chicano. Precisamente esto quisiéramos analizar en el presente trabajo. Para eso observaremos de cerca ciertos elementos del diseño interno que consideramos significativos, o que por lo menos parecen ser claves para una intelección unitaria de la novela.

Degradación y regeneración

El diseño de BMU se divide en un andamiaje de tres niveles: Universo, Mundo y Hombre.[4] Cada uno de estos niveles parece obedecer una trayectoria que se proyecta a través de tres momentos o tiempos: un pasado mítico, un presente de degradación progresiva, y un futuro de regeneración total. Esta homología entre los tres niveles establece lo que hemos calificado de *sentido subyacente*. En forma gráfica lo representaríamos de la siguiente manera:

Diseño Interno y Sentido Subyacente de BMU

	Pasado	*Presente*	*Futuro*
1. Universo	La Carpa Dorada Génesis	Diluvio Inminente	Nuevo Universo
2. Mundo	Grandeza de Antaño	Degradación	Regeneración
3. Hombre (Antonio)	Herencia Ancestral	Crisis	Nueva Vida

Por razones de claridad expositiva, presentaremos cada uno de estos niveles por separado.

1. *Universo*

En BMU hay dos variantes respeto al génesis del Universo: una es la de la Carpa Dorada (lo pagano), y la otra es la establecida por el Génesis bíblico (lo cristiano, por extensión). La leyenda de la Carpa Dorada la escucha Antonio por parte de Samuel, otro jovencito quien se encarga, junto con Cico, de iniciar a Antonio en el nuevo culto. La leyenda se relaciona con la fortuna de los primeros habitantes de la tierra. Estos viven en un lugar edénico en el que no carecen absolutamente de nada; sólo resta sobre ellos una interdicción divina que les prohibe comer carpas del río. Con el tiempo este protopueblo es puesto a prueba, y pronto da muestras de su flaqueza: hambrientos, se olvidan de la interdicción y se comen las carpas, haciéndose merecedores de la ira y castigo divinos. A punto de ser muertos, un dios intercede por ellos y los salva de la muerte. Se les castiga, no obstante, transformándolos en carpas y desterrándolos a vivir para siempre en el río. Como prueba de amor, el dios que intercede por estos primeros hombres pide a los demás dioses que le permitan transformarse en carpa con el fin de que pueda vivir al lado de esta raza caída. Este dios es la Carpa Dorada.

De lo anterior podemos entresacar dos puntos esenciales: primeramente, la leyenda de la Carpa Dorada tiene varias coordenadas similares a las del Antiguo y Nuevo Testamento (e.g., la creación de la tierra y del hombre, el Edén y la interdicción divina: la figura redentora, etc.); en segundo lugar, los primeros habitantes dialogan con los dioses, hasta que son castigados. El hombre, después de su caída, se desgarra de lo divino; queda, podemos decir, "incomunicado". Como resultado de esto, la segunda creación del hombre da muestras de la progresiva degradación humana. Según Cico:

> many years later, a new people came to live in this valley. And they were no better than the first inhabitants, in fact they were worse.[2] They sinned a lot, they sinned against each other, and they sinned against the legends they knew.[5]

La creación del hombre, a diferencia de lo encontrado en libros "sagrados" como el *Popol Vuh*, no lleva a un progresivo mejoramiento. Por el contrario, con el pasar del tiempo y con los nuevos projectos divinos, el hombre va degenerando. De aquí que en el presente narrativo encontremos preocupados a Antonio y a Cico debido a la inminencia del Diluvio, forma en que, según la profecía de la Carpa Dorada, terminará el mundo. Esta preocupación se agrava cuando Cico y Antonio se dan cuenta de que el pueblo de Guadalupe está rodeado de agua (110). En páginas anteriores a esto, leemos:

> That year we waited for the world to end. Each day the rumor spread farther and wider until all the kids were looking at the calendar and waiting for the day. "It'll be on fire", one would say, "it'll be in water", another would argue. "It's in the Bible" (69-70).

De un pasado mítico, legendario, pasamos a la imagen de un presente degradado y profano, y seguimos hacia un futuro de regeneración. La revelación de este proceso la ve Antonio en uno de sus sueños (IX), en el cual se ve cumplida la profecía de la Carpa Dorada. Cito del sueño:

> [the golden carp] had been witness to everything that happened, and he decided that everyone should survive, but in new form. He opened his huge mouth and swallowed everything, everything there was, good and evil. (. . .) he became a new sun in the heavens. A new sun to shine its good light upon a new earth (168).

Dado el valor profético de los sueños de Antonio, queda aquí en forma explícita el destino del Universo y su próxima regeneración.

2. *Mundo*

El nivel ocupado por el mundo es exclusivo de todo lo que le pertenece al hombre, o sea, todo aquello fabricado o inventado por él, desde la cultura más primitiva hasta el complejo cultural más refinado, incluyendo dentro de esto subdivisiones varias. Para nuestros propósitos, y por razones de economía y claridad, hemos limitado el Mundo de BMU a tres subdivisiones: 1) el lenguaje, 2) la religión, y 3) la familia. Cada una de éstas que podríamos llamar "invenciones" del hombre, atraviesa por los mismos momentos aquí estudiados. Por consiguiente, cada invención degradará a lo largo del relato; su regeneración quedará en varios casos solamente en forma implícita, como es el de la familia y el lenguaje. Veamos en seguida las subdivisiones que hemos propuesto.

2.a. *El lenguaje.* En BMU hay, primeramente, el consabido fenómeno lingüístico; a saber, la interpolación de palabras en español dentro del discurso en inglés. De esta manera, leemos:

> "the hot beans flavored with chicos and green chile were muy sabrosos" (39)
> "Only the ricos could afford school" (51)
> "Muchacho (. . .) I need confession" (162), etc.

Esto que a primera vista nos parecería algo idiosincrásico a la narrativa chicana, y por ende, como algo de poca aportación al sentido de la obra que estudiamos, será, en verdad, esencial para nuestra subsiguiente apreciación del narrador. Por el momento dirijámonos al análisis de dos problemas relacionados con el lenguaje: uno es el del discurso propio a la narración, y el otro es el idioma o el habla de los personajes novelísticos, quienes se expresan en español o en inglés

Hay en BMU una modulación que fluctúa según la circunstancia u objeto referencial del narrador. En la mayoría de los casos en que la narración va hilando progresivamente el diseño externo de la obra, el discurso es más bien sencillo, incluso en casos en que se interpolan giros en español. Lo que cambia el tono de la voz narrativa es 1) la mágica presencia de Ultima, y 2) el objeto que ocupa la atención del narrador, ya sea la naturaleza, el tiempo o el espacio. Un ejemplo del cambio narrativo influido por la circunstancia lo encontramos al principio de la obra, en el cual leemos:

> Ultima came to stay with us the summer I was almost seven.
> When she came the beauty of the llano unfolded before my eyes, and the gurgling waters of the river sang to the hum of the turning earth. The magical time of childhood stood still, and the pulse of the living earth pressed its mystery into my living blood. She took my hand, and the silent, magic powers she possessed made beauty from the raw, sunbaked llano. . . (1)

Este encuentro entre, digamos, maestra y aprendiz, muestra ser desde el principio de decisiva influencia en el joven protagonista. La presencia y el contacto con Ultima tienen un efecto revelador en Antonio, y marcan en él, a la vez, un tipo de "renacimiento". Esto se infiere de lo que añade el narrador inmediatamente después de lo citado anteriormente: "Let me begin at the beginning (...) but the beginning that came with Ultima" (1).

Esto expresa claramente la importancia de Ultima dentro del relato; también, explica la fluctuación dentro del discurso textual, y vemos que toda narración que involucre a la maestra y al aprendiz tendrá este tono poético, mientras que el discurso que se aparte hacia otra circunstancia (e.g., el grupo formado por el Horse, etc., y Tenorio Trementina), degradará y consistirá básicamente de interjecciones e injurias. Lo anterior comprende, desde luego, el "lenguaje" empleado por los personajes novelísticos; en cuanto al narrador, éste oscila entre un discurso sencillo—en las circunstancias narrativas de carácter ordinario—y otro henchido de imágenes. En fin, Ultima, como circunstancia, ennoblece; separarse de ella y situarse en otro contexto (e.g., el burdel de Rosie, la cantina o peluquería de Trementina, etc.), trae consigo el envilecimiento, la degradación.

Como precisamos anteriormente, la narración cambia también de tono cuando el objeto que ocupa la atención del narrador es la naturaleza, el tiempo o el espacio. El cambio se debe, claramente, al efecto que tiene Ultima en la percepción sensorial, de orden óptico o táctil, de su aprendiz: "The summer came and burned me brown with its energy, and the llano and the river filled me with their beauty" (76). Texto sencillísimo que encubre el sentido de la obra: por lo mismo, texto complejo. Estación del año (verano) que estimula y madura al fruto; fruto (Antonio) que se llena de la savia (sabiduría) proveniente de raíces ancestrales; el llano y el río (tierra y agua) que en antiguas mitologías eran conjunción de polos contrarios, originadores de la vida, ahora se convierten en signos, en alegoría, en historia. El llano y el río: los padres de Antonio; Ultima: puerta y espejo, incitación al autoconocimiento, rito de iniciación.

Hay en BMU otro conflicto lingüístico que trasciende la problemática del texto; este conflicto es el del aprendizaje del inglés por parte de hispanoparlantes. En esta encrucijada tan común a miles de chicanos, observamos la misma degradación que se lleva a cabo en otros planos de la obra. Un ejemplo bastante revelador de este conflicto lo vemos cuando Antonio nos dice que sus padres se expresan en español, al igual que todos los "viejos" del pueblo, mientras que la juventud, una vez ingresada en la escuela, habla solamente en inglés. Leemos: "All of the older people spoke only in Spanish, and I myself understood only Spanish. It was only after one went to school that one learned English" (9).

Uno de los principales deberes de la escuela es, obviamente, el de enseñarle al chicano el idioma inglés, facilitando de esta manera una sana adaptación al medio ambiente; ahora bien, en vez de mejorar su situación, o por lo menos de ampliar las facultades comunicativas del mismo, "incomunica" al chicano, separándole de su familia y de su cultura (lengua, historia), a la par que le mantiene a cierta distancia de la cultura sajona (lengua, historia + privilegios sajones). En otras palabras, no lo asimila totalmente: abusa de su condición y lo usa eficazmente. Lengua ajena que enajena, que barbariza: esto explicaría el aparente "salvajismo", digamos, de niños como el Bones o el Horse, infantes que están, por decirlo así, en estado o condición silvestre, in-humana. Respecto a las hermanas de Antonio, leemos: "Deborah had been to school two years and she spoke only English . . . .She was teaching Theresa and half the time I didn't understand what they were saying" (10).

Refiriéndose de nuevo a Deborah, leemos más adelante: "She said that in school the teachers let them speak only in English. I wondered how I would be able to speak to the teachers" (30). La escuela abre sus puertas y recibe a Antonio, quien va con el temor de alguien que se aproxima a un recinto sagrado. Va en busca de conocimiento, queriéndose apoderar del secreto mágico de las palabras y de los nú-

meros, pero encuentra algo muy diferente: el prejuicio y la incomuni-
cación. Las ilusiones bajan, pues, a un nivel degradante:

> The strangeness of the school and the other children made me
> very sad. I did not understand them. I sneaked around the back of the
> school building, and standing against the wall I tried to eat. But I
> couldn't. A huge lump seemed to form in my throat and tears came to
> my eyes. I yearned for my mother, and at the same time I understood
> that she had sent me to this place where I was an outcast. I had tried
> hard to learn and they had laughed at me. I had opened my lunch to
> eat and again they had laughed and pointed at me.
>
> The pain and sadness seemed to spread to my soul, and I felt for
> the first time what the grown-ups call, la tristeza de la vida (54-55).

Como sería de suponer, hay otros jovencitos que sufren de la
misma marginalización, y esto tiene una derivación lógica: la agru-
pación de seres afines. La dinámica sicológica de un gran número de
movimientos sociales está aquí patentemente expresada: "We band-
ed together and in our union found strength. We found a few others
who were like us, different in language and custom, and a part of our
loneliness was gone" (55).

En suma, el lenguaje o discurso del relato manifesta varias fluc-
tuaciones, determinadas mayormente por factores circunstanciales.
La presencia de Ultima, como he dicho anteriormente, ennoblece el
discurso narrativo, mientras que lo contrario a ella, de signo opuesto,
lo degrada. En cuanto a los personajes (e.g., los "vatos" de los Jaros),
observamos un progresivo olvido del español, junto con el efecto
nocivo que tiene en ellos la escuela, en tanto que ésta funciona como
ineficaz medio de aculturación del chicano, amén del achatamiento
espiritual que efectúa en el alumnado. Una palabra sobre el narrador:
el hecho de que se exprese en inglés, empleando en ocasiones algunas
palabras en español, es testimonio de que el joven Antonio olvida pos-
teriormente el español, o por lo menos que se expresa mejor en inglés.[6] Huelga decir que en este caso nos referimos al Antonio adulto
quien nos narra episodios de su juventud, episodios cuyas delimi-
taciones biográficas estructuran el relato en BMU. La regeneración
de esta realidad degradada quedará en el texto solamente en forma
implícita. Pero la imagen del chicano que balbucea interjecciones y
frases entrecortadas, incomunicado totalmente del contexto, nos
lleva a identificarlo con el pueblo caído al cual nos referimos anteriormente. Y he aquí un ejemplo de la estética de Anaya: de un conflicto hondamente chicano, se eleva a un plano universal en el que se
presenta en forma discernible la condición humana. Pero lo universal

Roberto Cantú

de esta condición no justifica el hecho; no nos engañemos. Las raíces del Movimiento Chicano están aquí claramente articuladas.

2.b. *La religión*. El joven Antonio vive en un hogar sumamente religioso, especialmente en lo tocante a la madre, María Luna. Desde un fondo histórico, precedido por los antepasados, surge la figura de un sacerdote, constructor de pueblos: el padre Luna. Este ascendiente de Antonio es aún un vivo recuerdo y modelo ejemplar para la familia, la cual ve en Antonio un aspirante al sacerdocio y un padre Luna en potencia. Según Antonio, su madre era:

> a devout Catholic, and so she saw the salvation of the soul rooted in the Holy Mother Church, and she said the world would be saved if the people turned to the earth. A community of farmers ruled over by a priest, she firmly believed, was the true way of life (27).

Pero éste es un sueño que, como el del padre de Antonio, no encaja en la realidad marcada por los tiempos; dicho de otra manera, ese estilo de vida ha perdido su vigencia. En el tiempo presente de la narración (infancia de Antonio), el padre Byrnes es el que dirige a los feligreses, al rebaño de Cristo. Y he aquí el cambio: de un pretérito legendario, regido por el sacerdote Luna, severo Moisés y respetado dirigidor de pueblos, pasamos a un presente en el que un padre descarría a su pueblo, imponiéndole un dogma como yugo y amedrentándolo con sus amenazas del infierno. La revelación que busca Antonio, la voz divina que él desea oír durante su primera comunión, en fin, su religiosidad, todo se esfuma ante el encanallamiento de este padre y, por extensión, de la Iglesia:

> the priest was talking to us. He said something about being Christians now, and how it was our duty to remind our parents to contribute to the collection box every Sunday so that the new school building could be built and sisters could come to teach us. I called again to the God that was within me but there was no answer. Only emptiness (211).

Como dijimos anteriormente, Antonio, para realizar el sueño materno, aspira al sacerdocio; sin embargo, ¿qué clase de feligreses le esperan? Una juventud que no abriga ningún espíritu de caridad o de hermandad. Con justificada razón Florence le dice a Antonio: "You could never be their priest" (206).

La religión, el sacerdocio, en suma, la Iglesia, se encuentran en una situación degradada. "Los dioses se están muriendo", le dice Florence a Antonio en uno de sus sueños (233). En un momento significativo de la narración, leemos: "Somehow everything changed. The priest had changed, so perhaps his religion could be made to change.

If the old religion could no longer answer the questions of the children then perhaps it was time to change it" (236).

2.c. *La familia.* A principios de la novela, Antonio-narrador nos confiesa lo siguiente: "Why two people as opposite as my father and my mother had married I do not know. Their blood and their ways had kept them at odds, . . ." (27). Y en efecto, hay entre ellos una continua pugna cuyas causas son las diferencias en cuanto a la visión del mundo y de la vida. Gabriel Márez y María Luna se unen en matrimonio, pero no unen sus metas, sus aspiraciones; la herencia ancestral pesa aún sobre ellos, haciéndolos, por lo mismo, personajes simbólicos de dos coordenadas históricas del chicano: el agricultor y el jinete. Estos personajes, como en verdad todos los de la obra, no son "personajes" en el sentido tradicional del término, sino que se convierten, dentro del texto, en signos—históricos, míticos—que se diseñan en función del mensaje o sentido subyacente de la obra. Un ejemplo del valor semiológico de estos "personajes" lo vemos en el caso en que éstos resumen la historia del chicano:

> Always the talk turned to life on the llano. The first pioneers there were sheepherders. Then they imported herds of cattle from Mexico and became vaqueros. They became horsemen, caballeros, men whose daily life was wrapped up in the ritual of horsemanship. They were the first cowboys in a wild and desolate land that they took from the Indians. Then the railroad came. The barbed wire came. The songs, the corridos became sad, and the meeting of the people from Texas with my forefathers was full of blood, murder, and tragedy. The people were uprooted. They looked around one day and found themselves closed in. The freedom of land and sky they had known was gone. Those people could not live without freedom and so they packed up and moved west. They became migrants (199).

En esta cita podemos observar dos momentos claves en el desarrollo paralelo de la familia Márez: a uno de plenitud sigue un momento de degradación. El cambio deriva de la invasión de diferentes y más sofisticados estilos de vida: al indio lo sucede el jinete, y a éste lo suplanta el hombre que monta un "caballo de hierro", o sea, la modernidad. Según Antonio:

> My father had been a vaquero all his life, a calling as ancient as the coming of the Spaniards to Nuevo Méjico. Even after the big rancheros and the tejanos came and fenced the beautiful llano, he and those like him continued to work there, I guess because only in that wide expanse of land and sky could they feel the freedom their spirits needed (2).

Roberto Cantú

Cuando Gabriel Márez se muda junto con su familia al pueblo de Guadalupe, y se aleja de sus antiguos compañeros, todo esto, junto con la calidad del nuevo empleo, le envilece:

> He went to work on the highway and on Saturdays after they collected their pay he drank with his crew at the Longhorn, but he was never close to the men of the town. Some weekends the llaneros would come into town for supplies and old amigos like Bonney or Campos or the Gonzalez brothers would come by to visit. Then my father's eyes lit up as they drank and talked of the old days and told the old stories. But when the western sun touched the clouds with orange and gold the vaqueros got in their trucks and headed home, and my father was left to drink alone in the long night (2-3).

Dada la condición del padre, no es de sorprender que en varias ocasiones la madre de Antonio muestre ser la figura dominante dentro de la familia. En cuando al resto de la familia—los tres hermanos y dos hermanas de Antonio—, también observamos un cambio: de un pasado en que la familia, unida, había construido su hogar, pasamos a un presente en el que los hijos ya no obedecen, ni respetan, a sus padres. A Gabriel Márez lo mantenía la ilusión de que, una vez que regresaran sus tres hijos de la guerra, entonces se mudarían a California. Sin embargo, al volver sus hijos, Gabriel se da cuenta de que sus sueños no imperan ya en el corazón de sus descendientes. Estos sueños irrealizados, junto con esta familia degradada, tienen una esperanza de reivindicación; si no en su forma original, por lo menos de una manera en que se adapten a las nuevas circunstancias. No tarda Gabriel en percatarse de que sus sueños ya no tienen vigencia en el mundo actual; por lo mismo, no se opone a que su hijo Antonio aprenda las tradiciones de los Luna (los agricultores no explotados); y leemos:

> Oh, I would have liked to have sent you to the llano, that is the way of life I knew, but I think that way of life is just about gone, it is a dream. Perhaps it is time we gave up a few of our dreams (. . .) we lived two different lives, your mother and I (. . .) We have been at odds all of our lives, the wind and the earth. *Perhaps it is time we gave up the old differences* (235; el subrayado es nuestro).

Con esto se augura una etapa de regeneración para la familia Márez Luna, una etapa de comprensión mutua, de transigencia y respeto; en suma, se sugiere el advenimiento de una "familia" (por lo menos en lo que toca a los esposos) en la que campeará la armonía y la comunión de objetivos vitales. Cambiando nuestra percepción interpretativa, y suponiendo que los padres de Antonio simbolizan el pasado étnico de México, se nos revelará la solución de este conflicto histórico: un cabal mestizaje—ideológico, cultural—que supera el meramente sanguíneo.

3. *Hombre (Antonio)*

Hasta ahora hemos intentado subrayar el sentido que, según nuestra interpretación, funciona como subsuelo ideológico en la o-bra, y sospechamos que no andamos del todo errados, mayormente cuando vemos que la relación binaria entre *degradación y regeneración* aparece anudada consistentemente al diseño interno de BMU. El nivel ocupado por el hombre no escapa a esta relación. Sin embargo, hay que adelantar una observación y notar que la presencia de Antonio en el texto cobra diferentes significaciones, según la lectura que se lleve a cabo. En esto no se aparta del carácter semiológico de otros personajes, tales como Ultima, Gabriel Márez, etc. De aquí que Antonio *signifique*: 1) el personaje que rememora con nostalgia sucesos importantes acaecidos en su infancia (nivel individual); 2) el pasado histórico del chicano (nivel colectivo); y 3) la aventura del héroe a través de varias pruebas iniciáticas (nivel universal). Debido al carácter del texto, todas estas significaciones se entrelazan con frecuencia.

La presentación detallada de estas tres posibles lecturas merece un estudio más extenso. Para nuestros intereses inmediatos, baste decir que si a Antonio lo interpretamos como signo histórico, colectivo, entonces sí podemos adjudicarle la presencia de una degradación y de una subsiguiente regeneración. Antonio sería el resumen de ciertas instituciones y estilos de vida que caducan y que luego surgen en forma remozada. Pero si vemos en Antonio un caso individual en el que se nos presenta la maduración de un infante, entonces nos alejaremos un poco de la relación binaria que aquí nos ocupa, y tendremos que admitir la existencia de otro proceso; en éste notaríamos las siguientes etapas: 1) los primeros siete años en la vida de Antonio, los cuales transcurren sin mayor novedad; 2) la llegada de Ultima y el "renacimiento" que ella causa en él; y 3) la desilusión y posterior integración sicológica de Antonio. Este problema nos ha ocupado en otro estudio, y a él remitimos al interesado.[7] Sólo quisiéramos añadir que este proceso tripartito no se aleja mucho del sentido subyacente de la obra, puesto que se puede entrever el mismo desarrollo, o sea, una etapa de postración y abatimiento, seguida de una de síntesis y renovación.

Para concluir, recordemos que en el título de este trabajo se hace

Roberto Cantú

mención del chicano y la vida nueva. ¿Cuál es la nueva vida que se sugiere o se recomienda en esta obra? El tiempo nos permite abordar este punto sólo de una manera muy breve, dejando detalles para otra ocasión.

El chicano y la vida nueva

Una relación que capta nuestro interés a partir de las primeras páginas es el obvio *mestizaje* de Antonio; su padre y madre significan, por así decirlo, el pasado indohispano del chicano. Esta historia, conflictiva como las puede haber, es el pasado que aún no se ha asimilado totalmente, debido a que renegamos de uno cuando no del otro. Y no es, en verdad, que Antonio reniegue de sus antepasados, sino que se siente dividido entre ellos. Hablando en sentido traslaticio, Antonio le dice a Ultima: "Now we have come to live near the river, and yet near the llano. I love them both, and yet I am of neither. I wonder which life I will choose?" (38).

Para esto, el lector ya ha empezado a asociar el río y la agricultura con la familia Luna, y el llano y el mar con los Márez. Por consiguiente, no nos sorprende la pregunta de Antonio; ni la repuesta de Ultima, quien le dice: "You have plenty of time to find yourself" (38). Y la obra en sí es esta búsqueda, este deseo de conocerse a sí mismo que marca tan singularmente toda novela de formación. Al final de la obra Antonio escucha de labios de su padre algo que le revelará una verdad: "Every generation, every man is part of his past. He cannot escape it, but he may reform the old materials, make something new" (236). Y precisamente en esta verdad, de perogrullo si se quiere, encontramos la semilla de la vida nueva, según vislumbrada por Anaya. Limitándonos al nivel colectivo que hemos propuesto anteriormente, en tanto que Antonio funciona como signo histórico, presentaríamos por el momento el siguiente esquema:

Historia de Antonio-Pueblo

Pasado

(1) Mundo precortesiano   } MITO
(2) El México rural

Presente

(1) Problemas de aculturación (USA-México)   } DEGRADACION
(2) Prejuicio racial + opresión

El chicano y la vida nueva

Futuro

(1) Adaptación a la circunstancia
(2) Invención de un estilo de vida   } REGENERACION
(3) Reivindicación étnica

Lo anterior carece de toda novedad, y en varias ocasiones indu-dablemente habrá alcanzado mejor expresión; no obstante, sigue siendo de sumo interés y de gran valía no sólo para el chicano sino, incluso, para el hombre hispanoamericano en general. Son preocu-paciones a escala continental que atañen a toda una cultura medio obsesionada con el modelo norteamericano. Experimento hispano-americano: el chicano como conejillo de Indias.

Nuestro acercamiento interpretativo a BMU nos ha facilitado una visión del mundo según la perspectiva que le hemos adjudicado temporalmente al autor, y nos ha permitido entrever una expresión sistemática, coherente, de su ideología, factor de extrema importan-cia para los que nos interesamos en el desarrollo histórico-intelectual de un pueblo. El mensaje de BMU es una verdad tan antigua como la vida del hombre, pero por lo mismo merecedora de ser revisada pe-riódicamente.

CALIFORNIA STATE UNIVERSITY, LOS ANGELES

Notas

[1]No incluimos *Macho!* (1973), de Edmund Villaseñor, debido a que se basa en la maduración de un indio tarasco quien, a causa de su breve estancia en los Estados Unidos, no alcanza a hacer propios los problemas socio-culturales del chicano.

[2]En su reciente novela, *The Fifth Horseman* (1974), encontramos el mismo moti-vo: el intelectual fracasado. Véase la traza pintada del español don Domingo Arguiú, y contrastarla con el panchovillista Heraclio Inés. En las dos novelas de Villarreal, la figura arquetípica de Pancho Villa se encuentra como presencia, ya sea en forma de recuerdo o de hecho. Pancho Villa, Heraclio Inés y Juan Rubio son todo lo contrario del intelectual decadente: son el México que pudo ser, pero que pereció en manos de los tinterillos e intelectualoides de la Revolución. Como crítico, pues, de esta guerra civil mexicana, Villarreal se une al coro formado por Azuela, Rulfo y Fuentes.

[3]Hay que recordar que *Barrio Boy* está escrita en forma autobiográfica y que muchos lectores argüirán que no deberíamos clasificarla como novela; en verdad no nos interesa la clasificación, sino, más bien, su estructura homóloga a las novelas de formación. Hay que hacer también la observación de que varios críticos consideran

Roberto Cantú

que *Pocho* es una obra autobiográfica (véase el prólogo a la novela por Ramón E. Ruíz; asimismo, el artículo de Arturo Madrid-Barela, "In Search of the Authentic Pachuco; An Interpretive Essay", *Aztlán*, Vol. 4 [Spring 1973], Núm. 1, 31-60), pese a que está escrita en tercera persona y, más aún, no obstante la enorme diferencia ideológica entre el narrador y el joven protagonista. Esto se verá claramente en nuestro estudio sobre la obra de José Antonio Villarreal (en preparación).

[4]Para la distinción entre Universo y Mundo, sigo aquí lo sugerido por Edmundo O'Gorman en su artículo "La historia como búsqueda del bienestar", *Plural*, Vol. III, Núm. 12, (15 de septiembre de 1974), 9.

[5]Rudolfo A. Anaya, *Bless Me, Ultima* (Berkeley: Quinto Sol Publications, 1972), pág. 110. Todas las citas provienen de la misma edición.

[6]En una ocasión nos damos cuenta de que la madre de Antonio le incita a que domine ambos idiomas. Ver pág. 171.

[7]Véase "Estructura y sentido de lo onírico en *Bless Me, Ultima*", *Mester*, Vol. V, Núm. 1 (noviembre de 1974), 27-41.

A SELECTED BIBLIOGRAPHY
OF CHICANO CRITICISM

Ernestina N. Eger

The criteria for selection of these critical articles on contemporary Chicano literature include availability and significance. Journal articles, theses abstracted in *DAI*, and articles from the ERIC collection of microfiche are listed; brief reviews, newspaper articles, and unpublished materials are omitted.

Bibliography

1. Castro, Donald F. "Chicano Literature: A Bibliographical Essay." *English in Texas* (Texas Joint Council of Teachers of English, Houston), 7, 4 (Summer 1976), 14-19. ED 134 986.
2. Lewis, Marvin A. "Toward a Bibliography of Chicano Literary Criticism." *N. A.I.E.S. Newsletter*, 1, 3 (April 1976), 9-12.
3. Lomelí, Francisco A., and Donaldo W. Urioste. *Chicano Perspectives in Literature: A Critical and Annotated Bibliography.* Albuquerque NM: Pajarito Pubs., 1976.
4. Salinas, Judy. "Recommended Resources for Teaching Chicano Literature and Culture." *Popular Culture Association Newsletter*, 6, 1 (March 1977), 62-75.
5. Tatum, Charles M. *A Selected and Annotated Bibliography of Chicano Studies.* [Manhattan KS: Kansas State Univ.], Society of Spanish and Spanish-American Studies, 1976.
6. Tatum, Charles. "Toward a Chicano Bibliography of Literary Criticism." *Atisbos*, No. 2 (Winter 1976-77), pp. 35-59.

General & Miscellaneous

7. Armas, José. "Role of Artist and Critic in the Literature of a Developing Pueblo." *De Colores*, 3, 4 [1977], 5-11.
8. Avendaño, Fausto. "Observaciones sobre los problemas de traducción de la

Ernestina N. Eger

literatura chicana." *Bilingual Review/ Revista Bilingüe*, 2, 3 (Sept.-Dec. 1975), 276-80.

9. Barrón, Pepe. "Introducción: Libertad de estilo lingüístico." *Fomento Literario* (Congreso Nacional de Asuntos Colegiales), 1, 3 (invierno 1973), 1-4.

10. Béjar Navarro, Raúl. "El mexicano norteamericano: Observaciones sobre su ubicación y surgimiento cultural." *Revista de la Universidad de México,* 31, 4-5 (dic. 1976-enero 1977), 20-23.

11. Blauner, Robert. "Chicano Writing." *Racial Oppression in America.* New York: Harper & Row, 1972. Pp. 162-81.

12. Brown, Carl R.V. "Cultural Democracy and Cultural Variability in Chicano Literature." *English Education*, 8, 2 (Winter 1977), 83-89.

13. Bruce-Novoa, John. "Literatura Chicana: Una respuesta al caos." *Revista de la Universidad de México*, 29, 12 (agosto 1975), 20-24.

14. Bruce-Novoa, John D. "México en la literatura chicana." *Revista de la Universidad de México*, 29, 5 (enero 1975), 13-18. Rpt. in *Tejidos*, 3, 3 (otoño 1976), 31-42.

15. Bruce-Novoa, Juan. "Research Notes: Round Table on Chicano Literature." *Journal of Ethnic Studies*, 3, 1 (Spring 1975), 99-104.

16. Bruce-Novoa, Juan. "The Space of Chicano Literature." In *The Chicano Literary World 1974.* Ed. Felipe Ortego and David Conde. Las Vegas NM: New Mexico Highlands Univ., 1975. Pp. 29-58. ED 101 924. Rpt. in *De Colores*, 1, 4 (1975), 22-42.

17. Cantú, Roberto. "The Crisis of Christianity in Chicano Literature." Audio cassette #BC 2042. Los Angeles: Pacific Tape Library, 1974.

18. Cárdenas de Dwyer, Carlota. "Chicano Literature." Audio cassette #70854. Urbana IL: NCTE, [1975].

19. Cárdenas de Dwyer, Carlota. "Chicano Literature 1965-75: The Flowering of the Southwest." *DAI*, 37, 3 (Sept. 1976), 1582-83A (SUNY at Stony Brook).

20. Cárdenas de Dwyer, Carlota. *Chicano Voices: Instructor's Guide.* Boston: Houghton Mifflin, 1975. 110 pp.

21. Cárdenas de Dwyer, Carlota. "Chicanos: Their Prose y Poesía." *Review*, No. 13 (Winter 1974), pp. 48-54.

22. Cárdenas de Dwyer, Carlota. "Westering and the Chicano Literary Tradition." In *The Westering Experience in American Literature: Bicentennial Essays.* Ed. Merrill Lewis and L. L. Lee. Bellingham WA: Western Washington Univ., 1977. Pp. 206-14.

23. Chambers, Bradford. "Why Minority Publishing: New Voices Are Heard." *Publishers' Weekly*, 199, 11 (15 March 1971), 35-50.

24. Dávila, Luis. "Chicano Fantasy Through a Glass Darkly." In *Otros mundos, otros fuegos; Fantasía y Realismo Mágico en Iberoamérica* (Memoria del XVI Congreso del Instituto Internacional de Literatura Iberoamericana). Ed. Donald A. Yates. East Lansing: Michigan State University, 1975. Pp. 245-48.

25. Dávila, Luis. "Otherness in Chicano Literature." In *Contemporary Mexico: Papers of the IV International Congress of Mexican History.* Ed. James W. Wilkie, Michael C. Meyer, and Edna Monzón de Wilkie. Berkeley: Univ. of California, 1976. Pp. 556-63.

26. de la Garza, Rudolph O., and Rowena Rivera. "The Socio-Political World of the Chicano: A Comparative Analysis of Social Scientific and Literary Perspectives." In *Minority Language and Literature: Retrospective and Perspective.* Ed. Dexter Fisher. New York: Modern Language Association, 1977. Pp. 42-64.

27. Elizondo, Sergio D. "Myth and Reality in Chicano Literature." *Latin American Literary Review*, 5, 10 (Spring-Summer 1977), 23-31.

28. Fry, William Albert. "Instructional Materials for a Community College Course in Chicano Literature." *DAI*, 37, 11 (May 1977), 7013A (Maryland).

29. García, Nasario. "Recent Anthologies of Chicano Literature." *Bilingual Review/ Revista Bilingüe*, 2, 3 (Sept.-Dec. 1975), 312-320.

30. Geuder, Patricia A. "Sociolinguistics and Chicano Literature." ED 082 585.

31. Gómez-Quiñones, Juan. "On Culture." *Revista Chicano-Riqueña*, 5, 2 (primavera 1977), 29-47.

32. González Gómez, Miguel. "La Literatura Chicana." *Fomento Literario* (Congreso Nacional de Asuntos Colegiales), 1, 3 (invierno 1973), 50-61.

33. Haslam, Gerald. "¡Por la Causa! Mexican-American Literature." *College English*, 31, 7 (April 1970), 695-709.

34. Hilton, Ronald. "Is Intellectual History Irrelevant? The Case of the Aztecs." *Journal of the History of Ideas*, 33, 2 (April-June 1972), 337-44.

35. Hinojosa, Rolando. "Mexican-American Literature: Toward an Identification." *Books Abroad*, 49, 3 (Summer 1975), 422-30. Rpt. in this volume, pp. 7-18.

36. Islas, Arturo. "Writing from a Dual Perspecitve." *Miquiztli*, 2, 1 (Winter 1974), 1-2.

37. Jiménez, Francisco. "Chicano Literature: Sources and Themes." *Bilingual Review/ Revista Bilingüe*, 1, 1 (Jan.-April 1974), 4-15.

38. Jonz, Jon G. "Language and La Academia, If English Works, ¿Por qué se emplea español?" *Journal of Ethnic Studies*, 5, 4 (Winter 1978), 65-79.

39. Keller, Gary D. "Toward a Stylistic Analysis of Bilingual Texts: From Ernest Hemingway to Contemporary Boricua and Chicano Literature." In *The Analysis of Hispanic Texts: Current Trends in Methodology*. Ed. Mary Ann Beck, Lisa E. Davis, José Hernández, Gary D. Keller and Isabel C. Tarán. Jamaica NY: Bilingual Press, 1976. Pp. 130-49.

40. Landy, Lino and Ricardo López Landy. "Literatura chicana." *Grito del Sol*, 1, 1 (Jan.-March 1976), 25-38.

41. Leal, Luis. "Mexican-American Literature: A Historical Perspective." *Revista Chicano-Riqueña*, 1, 1 (verano 1973), 32-44.

42. Lyon, Ted. "The Originality of Chicano Literature: A Comparison with Contemporary Mexican Writing." ED 122 987.

43. Madrid-Barela, Arturo, "Alambristas, Braceros, Mojados, Norteños: Aliens in Aztlán, An Interpretive Essay." *Aztlán*, 6, 1 (Spring 1975), 27-42.

44. Madrid-Barela, Arturo. "In Search of the Authentic Pachuco: An Interpretive Essay." *Aztlán*, 4, 1 (Spring 1973), 31-60.

45. Madrid-Barela, Arturo. "Pochos: The Different Mexicans, An Interpretive Essay, Part I." *Aztlán*, 7, 1 (Spring 1976), 51-64.

46. Mares, Ernesto A. "Myth and Reality: Observations on American Myth and Myth of Aztlán." *El cuaderno* (de vez en cuando), 3, 1 (winter 1973), 35-50.

47. Martínez, Max. "Prolegomena for a Study of Chicano Literature." *De Colores*, 3, 4 [1977], 12-14.

48. Moesser, Alba Irene. "La literatura mejicoamericana del suroeste de los Estados Unidos." *DAI*, 32, 5 (Nov. 1971), 2648A (Southern California).

49. Miller, Yvette Espinosa. "The Chicanos: Emergence of a Social Identity Through Literary Outcry." *Selected Proceedings of the 1st and 2nd Annual Conferences on Minority Studies* ("Identity and Awareness in the Minority Experience"). Vol.

Ernestina N. Eger

1. Ed. George E. Carter and Bruce L. Mouser. La Crosse WI: Univ. of Wisconsin, Institute for Minority Studies, 1975. Pp. 27-45.

50. Molina de Pick, Gracia. "Estudio crítico de la literatura chicana." *Fomento Literario* (Congreso Nacional de Asuntos Colegiales), 1, 3 (invierno 1973), 32-41.

51. Monsiváis, Carlos. "Literatura Comparada: Literatura Chicana y Literatura Mexicana." *Fomento Literario* (Congreso Nacional de Asuntos Colegiales), 1, 3 (invierno 1973), 42-49.

52. Morales, Alejandro Dennis. "Visión panorámica de la literatura mexicoamericana hasta el boom de 1966." *DAI*, 36, 10 (April 1976), 6731A (Rutgers).

53. Navarro, J. L. "Bum Literature?" *La Luz*, 7, 3 (March 1978), 13-15.

54. Ortego, Philip Darraugh. "Backgrounds of Mexican American Literature." *DAI*, 32, 9 (March 1972), 5195A (Univ. of New Mexico).

55. Ortego, Philip D. "The Chicano Renaissance." *Social Casework*, 52, 5 (May 1971), 294-307.

56. Ortego y Gasca, Philip D. "Chicanos and the Pursuit of a Literary Identity: An Introduction of Sorts. . ." and "Prolegomenon to the Study of Mexican American Literature." *English in Texas* (Texas Joint Council of Teachers of English, Houston), 7, 4 (Summer 1976), 3-14. ED 134 986.

57. Ortego, Philip D. "Which Southwestern Literature and Culture in the English Classroom?" *Arizona English Bulletin*, 13, 3 (April 1971), 15-17. Rpt. in *La Luz*, 1, 9 (Jan. 1973), 50-51. ED 052 180.

58. Ortego, Philip D., and José A. Carrasco. "Chicanos and American Literature." In *Searching for America*. Ed. Ernece B. Kelly. Urbana IL: National Council of Teachers of English, 1972. Pp. 78-94. ED 058 213.

59. Paredes, Raymund A. "The Promise of Chicano Literature." In *Minority Language and Literature: Retrospective and Perspective*. Ed. Dexter Fisher. New York: Modern Language Association, 1977. Pp. 29-41.

60. Pérez-Ponce, Jorge M., and Alberto Guerrero. "Sí, tenemos literatura." "La Cultura en México," suplemento cultural de *Siempre*, 23 dic. 1970, pp. ii-iv.

61. Pérez Sandoval, Rafael. "El eterno retorno y la literatura chicana." *Vórtice*, 1, 2 (otoño 1974), 68-77.

62. Phillips, Jean. "Flor y canto: Chicano Literature and Performance." *Speech Teacher*, 24, 3 (Sept. 1975), 202-8.

63. Powers, Lloyd D. "Chicano Rhetoric: Some Basic Concepts." *Southern Speech Communication Journal*, 38, 4 (Summer 1973), 340-46.

64. Rivera, Tomás. "Chicano Literature: Fiesta of the Living." *Books Abroad*, 49, 3 (Summer 1975), 439-52. Rpt. in this volume, pp. 19-36.

65. Rivera, Tomás. "Into the Labyrinth: The Chicano in Literature." In *New Voices in Literature: The Mexican American*. Ed. Edward Simmen. Edinburg TX: Pan American Univ., 1971. Pp. 18-25. Rpt. in *South-western American Literature*, 2, 2 (Fall 1972), 90-97.

66. Rivera, Tomás. "Literatura chicana: Vida en busca de forma." ED 058 808.

67. Rivera, Tomás. "On Chicano Literature." *Texas Books in Review*, 1, 1 [1977], 5-6.

68. Robinson, Cecil. "With Ears Attuned—and the Sound of New Voices: An Updating of *With the Ears of Strangers*." *Southwestern American Literature*, 1, 2 (May 1971), 51-59.

69. Rodríguez, Juan. "El florecimiento de la literatura chicana." In *La otra cara de México: El pueblo chicano*. Comp. David Maciel. México DF: Ediciones

"El Caballito," 1977. Pp. 348-69.

70. Sánchez, Federico A. "Raíces Mexicanas." *Grito del Sol*, 1, 4 (Oct.-Dec. 1976), 75-87.

71. Sánchez, José. "Chicano Movement." *De Colores*, 1, 3 (Summer 1974), 62-65.

72. Sánchez, Ricardo. "Chicano Literature: A Tertiary Perspective." *La Luz*, 1, 10 (Feb. 1973), 42-43.

73. Sánchez, Ricardo. "Chicano Literature: An Evolving Linguistic Pyramid." *Nosotros* (El Paso), 2, 3 (1972). Rpt. *Magazín* (San Antonio), 1, 8 (January 1973), 24-26. Rpt. *American Pen*, 6, 4 (Fall 1974), 52-60.

74. Segade, Gustavo. "Toward a Dialectic of Chicano Literature." *Mester*, 4, 1 (Nov. 1973), 4-5.

75. Sotomayor, Frank. "An Explosion of Chicano Literary Merit." *La Luz*, 2, 1 (April 1973), 52-53.

76. Steiner, Stan. *La Raza: The Mexican Americans*. New York: Harper, 1970. Pp. 324-38 et passim on Luis Valdez; pp. 378-92 on Rodolfo "Corky" Gonzales.

77. Torres, Luis. "Relevance in Chicano Literature." *Metamorfosis* (Univ. of Washington, Seattle), 1, 1 [1977], 36-40.

78. Treviño, Albert Dwight. "Mexican American Literature in the High School English Program: A Theoretical and Practical Approach." *DAI*, 35, 8 (Feb. 1975), 4997A (Univ. of Texas, Austin).

79. Trujillo, Marcela. "Chicano Writers and Poets." *La Luz*, 2, 3 (June-July 1973), 43-48.

80. Vaca, Nick Corona. "Sociology through Literature: The case of the Mexican-American." *DAI*, 38, 2 (August 1977), 1053A (Univ. of California, Berkeley).

81. Valdés, Richard A. "Aztlán: The Creation of Myth in Chicano Literature." *Selected Proceedings of the 3rd Annual Conference on Minority Studies: Essays on Minority Folklore*, Vol. 3 (1977), 111-28.

82. Valdés, Ricardo. "Defining Chicano Literature, or the Perimeters of Literary Space." *Latin American Literary Review*, 5, 10 (Spring-Summer 1977), 16-22.

83. Womack, John, Jr. "The Chicanos." *The New York Review of Books*, 19, 3 (31 August 1972), 12-18. Tr. and rpt. as "Los 'chicanos'." *Revista de Occidente*, 44, 132 (marzo 1974), 343-74.

La chicana

84. Gonzales, Sylvia. "The Chicana in Literature." *La Luz*, 1, 9 (Jan. 1973), 51-53.

85. [Hoyos, Angela de, y Susana de la Torre.] "Mujeres en el Movimiento: Plática de las mujeres de *Caracol*." *Caracol*, 4, 5 (enero 1978), 16-18.

86. Salinas, Judy. "The Image of Woman in Chicano Literature." *Revista Chicano-Riqueña*, 4, 4 (otoño 1976), 139-48.

87. Sánchez, Rita. "Chicana Writer: Breaking Out of the Silence." *De Colores*, 3, 3 (1977), 31-37.

88. Trujillo Gaitán, Marcela. "The Dilemma of the Modern Chicana Artist and Critic." *De Colores*, 3, 3 (1977), 38-48.

See also 93, 96.

Criticism

89. Martínez, Max. "The Necessity of Chicano Literary Critics." *Caracol*, 2,

9 (May 1976), 18-19.

90. Parr, Carmen Salazar. "Current Trends in Chicano Literary Criticism." *Latin American Literary Review*, 5, 10 (Spring-Summer 1977), 8-15. Rpt. in this volume, pp. 134-42.

91. Sommers, Joseph. "Critical Approaches to Chicano Literature." *De Colores*, 3, 4 [1977], 15-21. Also in *Bilingual Review/Revista Bilingüe*, 4, 1-2 (Jan.-Aug. 1977), 92-98. Rpt. in this volume, pp. 143-52.

92. Sommers, Joseph. "From the Critical Premise to the Product: Critical Modes and Their Applications to a Chicano Literary Text." *New Scholar*, 6 (1977), 51-80.

93. Zamora, Bernice. "The Chicana as a Literary Critic." *De Colores*, 3, 3 (1977), 16-19.

Poetry

94. Alegría, Fernando. "Introducción." *Hispamérica*, No. 2 (1972), pp. 37-39.

95. Campa, Arthur L. "Protest Folk Poetry in the Spanish Southwest." *Colorado Quarterly*, 20, 3 (Winter 1972), 355-63.

96. Cárdenas, Reyes. "Crisis in Chicana Identity." *Caracol*, 3, 9 (May 1977), 14-15.

97. Cárdenas de Dwyer, Carlota. "Chicano Poetry." *Literary Criterion*, 12, 1 (Winter 1975), 23-35.

98. Delgado, Abelardo. "Poetry as the New Source of Energy." *Caracol*, 2, 9 (May 1976), 7.

99. Delgado, Abelardo. "Yo digo que. . ." *La Luz*, 3, 8 (Nov. 1974), 6.

100. Flores, José. "Energía divina." *Caracol*, 4, 2 (octubre 1977), 9-11, 20.

101. Garza, Mario. "Duality in Chicano Poetry." *De Colores*, 3, 4 [1977], 39-45.

102. Gonzales, Sylvia. "National Character vs. Universality in Chicano Poetry." In *The Chicano Literary World 1974*. Ed. Felipe Ortego and David Conde. Las Vegas NM: New Mexico Highlands Univ., 1975. Pp. 13-28. ED 101 924. Rpt. in *De Colores*, 1, 4 (1975), 10-21.

103. González, Rafael Jesús. "Chicano Poetry: Smoking Mirror." *New Scholar*, Vol. 6 (1977), 127-38.

104. Hancock, Joel. "The Emergence of Chicano Poetry: A Survey of Sources, Themes and Techniques." *Arizona Quarterly*, 29, 1 (Spring 1973), 57-73.

105. Lomelí, Francisco, and Donaldo Urioste. "El concepto del barrio en tres poetas chicanos: Abelardo, Alurista y Ricardo Sánchez." *De Colores*, 3, 4 [1977], 22-29.

106. Ortega, Adolfo. "Of Social Politics and Poetry: A Chicano Perspective." *Latin American Literary Review*, 5, 10 (Spring-Summer 1977), 32-41.

107. Ortego, Philip D. "Chicano Poetry: Roots and Writers." *Southwestern American Literature*, 2, 1 (Spring 1972), 8-24. Also in *New Voices in Literature: The Mexican American*. Ed. Edward Simmen. Edinburg TX: Pan American Univ., 1971. Pp. 1-17.

108. Pérez, Arturo P. "Poesía chicana." *Cuadernos Hispanoamericanos*, No. 325 (julio 1977), pp. 123-31.

109. Pino, Frank. "Chicano Poetry: A Popular Manifesto." *Journal of Popular Culture*, 6, 4 (Spring 1973), 718-30.

110. Rodríguez-Puértolas, Julio. "Chicanos y corridos." *Papeles de Son Armadans*, 75, 224-5 (nov.-dic. 1974), 121-53. Rpt. as "La problemática sociopolítica chicana en corridos y canciones." *Aztlán*, 6, 1 (Spring 1975), 97-116.

111. Valdés-Fallis, Guadalupe. "Code-switching in Bilingual Chicano Poetry." *Hispania*, 59, 4 (Dec. 1976), 877-86.

112. Valdés-Fallis, Guadalupe. "The Sociolinguistics of Chicano Literature: Towards an Analysis of the Role and Function of Language Alternation in Contemporary Bilingual Poetry." *Punto de Contacto/Point of Contact*, 1, 4 (1977), 30-39.

113. Villanueva, Tino. "Más allá del Grito: Poesía engagée chicana." *De Colores*, 2, 2 (1975), 27-46.

114. Ybarra-Frausto, Tomás. "The Chicano Movement and the Emergence of a Chicano Poetic Consciousness." *New Scholar*, 6 (1977), 81-109.

Prose Fiction

115. Castro, Donald F. "The Chicano Novel: An Ethno-Generic Study." *La Luz*, 2, 1 (April 1973), 50-52.

116. Grajeda, Rafael Francisco. "The Figure of the Pocho in Contemporary Chicano Fiction." *DAI*, 35, 8 (Feb. 1975), 5402-3A (Univ. of Nebraska, Lincoln).

117. Islas, Arturo. "Can There Be Chicano Fiction? or Writer's Block." *Miquiztli*, 3, 1 (Winter-Spring 1975), 22-24.

118. Lewis, Marvin. "Ethnicity, Alienation, Identity: Themes in Hispanic Minority Fiction." ED 143-716.

119. Mickelson, Joel C. "The Chicano Novel Since World War II." *La Luz*, 6, 4 (April 1977), 22-29.

120. Monahan, Sister Helena. "The Chicano Novel: Toward a Definition and Literary Criticism." *DAI*, 33, 3 (Sept. 1972), 1175A (St. Louis Univ.).

121. Rodríguez, Juan. "El desarrollo del cuento chicano: Del folklore al tenebroso mundo del yo." *Mester*, 4, 1 (Nov. 1973), 7-12. Rpt. in *Fomento Literario*, 1, 3 (invierno 1973), 19-30, and in this volume, pp. 58-67.

122. Segade, Gustavo V. "Un panorama conceptual de la novela chicana." *Fomento Literario* (Congreso Nacional de Asuntos Colegiales), 1, 3 (invierno 1973), 5-18.

123. Simmen, Edward. " 'We Must Make This Beginning': The Chicano Leader Image in the Short Story." *Southwest Review*, 57 (Spring 1972), 126-33.

124. Somoza, Oscar Urquídez. "Visión axiológica en la narrativa chicana." *DAI*, 38, 7 (Jan. 1978), 4203A (Univ. of Arizona).

125. Tatum, Charles M. "Contemporary Chicano Prose Fiction: A Chronicle of Misery." *Latin American Literary Review*, 1, 2 (Spring 1973), 7-17. Rpt. in this volume, pp. 241-53.

126. Tatum, Charles M. "Contemporary Chicano Prose Fiction: Its Ties to Mexican Literature." *Books Abroad*, 49, 3 (Summer 1975), 431-38. Rpt. in this volume, pp. 47-57.

127. Valdés-Fallis, Guadalupe. "Metaphysical Anxiety and the Existence of God in Contemporary Chicano Fiction." *Revista Chicano-Riqueña*, 3, 2 (invierno 1975), 26-33.

128. Villaseñor, Edmund Victor, with Carl Mueller and Juan Gómez. "The Chicano Novel." Audio cassette #35604. North Hollywood CA: Center for Cassette Studies, n. d.

Theater

129. Alegría, Alonso. "El teatro chicano en California: un teatro necesario." *Amaru* (Lima), No. 12 (June 1970), pp. 29-30.

Ernestina N. Eger

130. Bagby, Beth. "El Teatro Campesino: Interviews with Luis Valdez." *Tulane Drama Review*, 11, 4 (Summer 1967), 70-80.

131. Boal, Augusto. "Hay muchas formas de teatro popular ¡Yo prefiero todas!" *Crisis* (Bs. As.), No. 19 (Nov. 1974), pp. 51-57.

132. Bravo-Elizondo, Pedro. "Symbolic Motifs in Two Chicano Dramas." *Selected Proceedings of the 1st and 2nd Annual Conferences of Minority Studies* ("Identity and Awareness in the Minority Experience"). Vol. 1. Ed. George E. Carter and Bruce L. Mouser. La Crosse WI: Univ. of Wisconsin, Institute for Minority Studies, 1975. Pp. 47-54.

133. Bravo-Elizondo, Pedro. "El teatro chicano." *Revista Chicano-Riqueña*, 1, 2 (otoño 1973), 36-41.

134. Bravo-Elizondo, Pedro J. "El teatro chicano: Espejo de una realidad." *Otros mundos, otros fuegos; Fantasía y Realismo Mágico en Iberoamérica* (Memoria del XVI Congreso del Instituto Internacional de Literatura Iberoamericana). Ed. Donald A. Yates. East Lansing: Michigan State University, 1975. Pp. 265-69.

135. Brokaw, John W. "Teatro Chicano: Some Reflections." *Educational Theatre Journal*, 29, 4 (Dec. 1977), 535-44.

136. Bruce-Novoa and David Valentín. "Revolutionizing the Popular Image: Essay on Chicano Theatre." *Latin American Literary Review*, 5, 10 (Spring-Summer 1977), 42-50.

137. Burger, Gerd, Arnulf Rating and Gerhard Riecke. "Erkenntnisse über den Abfall: El Teatro Campesino und sein Stuck 'La Carpa de los Rasquachis'." *Theater heute*, 18, 3 (März 1977), 31-35.

138. Cisneros, René. "Los Actos: A Study in Metacommunication." *Tejidos*, 2, 8 (invierno 1975), 2-13.

139. Copelin, David. "Chicano Theatre: El Festival de los Teatros Chicanos." *The Drama Review*, 17, 4 (Dec. 1973), 73-89.

140. Delucchi, Mary Phelan. "El Teatro Campesino de Aztlán: Chicano Protest through Drama." *Pacific Historian* (Univ. of the Pacific), 16, 1 (Spring 1972), 16-27.

141. Donahue, Francis. "Anatomy of Chicano Theater." *San José Studies*, 3, 1 (Feb. 1977), 37-48.

142. Donahue, Francis. "Teatro de guerrilla." *Cuadernos Americanos*, 32, 5 (Sept.-Oct. 1973), 17-33.

143. Drake, Sylvie. "El Teatro Campesino: Keeping the Revolution on Stage." *Performing Arts*, 4, 9 (Sept. 1970), 56-62.

144. Dukore, Bernard F. "The Brown Revolution." *Documents for Drama and Revolution*. New York: Holt, Rinehart and Winston, 1971. Pp. 211-25.

145. García, Nasario. "Satire: Techniques and Devices in Luis Valdez's 'Las Dos Caras del Patroncito'." In *The Chicano Literary World 1974*. Ed. Felipe Ortego and David Conde. Las Vegas NM: New Mexico Highlands Univ., 1975. Pp. 83-94. ED 101 924. Rpt. in *De Colores*, 1, 4 (1975), 66-74.

146. Harrop, John, and Jorge A. Huerta. "The Agitprop Pilgrimage of Luis Valdez and El Teatro Campesino." *Theatre Quarterly*, 5, 17 (March-May 1975), 30-39.

147. Huerta, Jorge A. "Algo sobre el teatro chicano." *Revista de la Universidad de México*, 27, 6 (feb. 1973), 20-24.

148. Huerta, Jorge A. "Chicano Agit-Prop: The Early *Actos* of El Teatro Campesino." *Latin American Theatre Review*, 10, 2 (Spring 1977), 45-58.

149. Huerta, Jorge A. "Chicano Theatre—A Background." *Aztlán*, 2, 2 (Fall 1971), 63-78.

150. Huerta, Jorge A. "Concerning Teatro Chicano." *Latin American Theatre Review*, 6, 2 (Spring 1973), 13-20.

151. Huerta, Jorge A. "Del templo al pueblo: El teatro chicano de hoy." In *La otra cara de México: El pueblo chicano.* Comp. David R. Maciel. México D.F.: Ediciones "El Caballito," 1977. Pp. 316-47. English version in this volume, pp. 90-116.

152. Huerta, Jorge. "From Quetzalcóatl to Honest Sancho: A Review Article of *Contemporary Chicano Theatre.*" *Revista Chicano-Riqueña*, 5, 3 (verano 1977), 32-49.

153. Huerta, Jorge A. "Ritual to rasquachi, and back: The history and evolution of Chicano theatre." Audiotape # 35757. North Hollywood CA: Center for Cassette Studies, 1974.

154. Huerta, Jorge A. "El Teatro de la Esperanza: Keeping in Touch with the People." *The Drama Review*, 21, 1 (March 1977), 37-46.

155. Huerta, Jorge A. "Where Are Our Chicano Playwrights?" *Revista Chicano-Riqueña*, 3, 4 (otoño 1975), 32-42.

156. "L'implication idéologique du Théâtre Chicano/The Ideological Implications of Chicano Theatre." *International Theatre Informations* (Paris), Spring 1975, pp. 22-27.

157. Jiménez, Francisco. "Dramatic Principles of the Teatro Campesino." *Bilingual Review/ Revista Bilingüe*, 2, 1-2 (Jan.-Aug. 1975), 99-111. Rpt. in this volume, pp. 117-132.

158. Kanellos, Nicolás. "Chicano Theatre to Date." *Tejidos*, 2, 8 (invierno 1975), 40-45.

159. Kanellos, Nicolás. "Folklore in Chicano Theater and Chicano Theater as Folklore." *Journal of the Folklore Institute* (Indiana Univ., Bloomington), 15, 1 (Jan.-April 1978), 57-82.

160. Kourilsky, Françoise. "El Teatro Campesino." *Travail Théâtral*, 7 (avril-juin 1972), 57-70.

161. Kourilsky, Françoise. "Approaching Quetzalcóatl: The Evolution of El Teatro Campesino." *Performance*, 2, 1 (Fall 1973), 37-46.

162. Major, Linda B. "Dramatic Search for Root of Chicanismo." *Agenda,* Summer 1974, pp. 7-13.

163. Morton, Carlos. "The Teatro Campesino: La Serpiente Sheds Its Skin." *The Drama Review,* 18, 4 (Dec. 1974), 71-76.

164. Projektgruppe Regensburg. "Das Befreiende Gelächter: Interview mit Luis Valdez über El Teatro Campesino." *Theater heute*, 13, 9 (Sept. 1972), 29-32.

165. Santibáñez, James. "El Teatro Campesino Today and El Teatro Urbano." In *The Chicanos: Mexican American Voices.* Ed. Ed Ludwig and James Santibáñez. Baltimore MD: Penguin, 1971. Pp. 141-48.

166. Shank, Theodore. "A Return to Mayan and Aztec Roots." *The Drama Review,* 18, 4 (Dec. 1974), 56-70.

167. Torres, Louis R. "A Profile of Jorge Huerta: A Look at the Status of the Chicano Theater." *La Luz*, 5, 9 (Sept. 1976), 17-18.

168. Valdez, Luis, "Notes on Chicano Theatre," in "Teatro Chicano: Two Reports." *Latin American Theatre Review*, 4, 2 (Spring 1971), 52-55.

169. [Valdez, Luis.] "Strassentheater revolutionär. Gespräch mit Luis Valdez, dem Chef des Teatro Campesino." *Theater heute*, 9, 4 (April 1968), 16-19.

Ernestina N. Eger

170. Weisman, John. *Guerilla Theater: Scenarios for Revolution.* Garden City NY: Anchor Press, 1973.

171. Ybarra-Frausto, Tomás. "Punto de Partida," in "Teatro Chicano: Two Reports." *Latin American Theatre Review,* 4, 2 (Spring 1971), 51-52.
See also 76.

Individual Authors

ACOSTA. 172. Martínez, Angélica. "The Cocky Cockroach, Acosta y su Macho Myth: A Book Review." *Tejidos,* 3, 4 (invierno 1976), 19-21.

173. Ramírez, Arthur. Review of *The Autobiography of A Brown Buffalo* and *The Revolt of the Cockroach People. Revista Chicano-Riqueña,* 3, 3 (verano 1975), 46-53.

174. Romero, Osvaldo. Review of *The Autobiography of a Brown Buffalo. Mester,* 4, 2 (abril 1974), 141.

175. Smith, Norman D. "Buffalos and Cockroaches: Acosta's Seige of Aztlán." *Latin American Literary Review,* 5, 10 (Spring-Summer 1977), 85-97.
See also 17, 230.

ALURISTA. 176. Kanellos, Nicolás. "La llorona de Alurista." *Otros mundos, otros fuegos; Fantasía y Realismo Mágico en Iberoamérica* (Memoria del XVI Congreso del Instituto Internacional de Literatura Iberoamericana). Ed. Donald A. Yates. East Lansing: Michigan State University, 1975. Pp. 261-64.

177. Maldonado, Jesús. *Poesía Chicana: Alurista el Mero Chingón.* Monografía #1. Seattle: Centro de Estudios Chicanos de la Univ. de Washington, 1971.

178. Rojas, Guillermo. "Alurista, Chicano Poet, Poet of Social Protest." *Otros mundos, otros fuegos; Fantasía y Realismo Mágico en Iberoamérica* (Memoria del XVI Congreso del Instituto Internacional de Literatura Iberoamericana). Ed. Donald A. Yates. East Lansing: Michigan State University, 1975. Pp. 255-60.

179. Ruffinelli, Jorge. "Alurista: Una larga marcha hacia Aztlán." *La palabra y el hombre* (U. Veracruzana), Nueva época, Núm. 17 (enero-marzo 1976), pp. 30-41.

180. Testa, David. "Alurista: Three Attitudes Toward Love in His Poetry." *Revista Chicano-Riqueña,* 4, 1 (invierno 1976), 46-55.
See also 105.

ANAYA. 181 Anaya, Rudolfo A. "A Writer Discusses his Craft." *CEA Critic,* 40, 1 (Nov. 1977), 39-43. Rpt. as "The Writer's Landscape: Epiphany in Landscape." *Latin American Literary Review,* 5, 10 (Spring-Summer 1977), 98-102.

182. Cantú, Roberto. "Degradación y regeneración en *Bless Me, Ultima:* el chicano y la vida nueva." *Caribe* (Univ. de Hawaii), 1, 1 (primavera 1976), 113-126. Rpt. in this volume, pp. 374-388.

183. Cantú, Roberto. "Estructura y sentido de lo onírico en *Bless Me, Ultima.*" *Mester,* 5, 1 (Nov. 1974), 27-41.

184. Dávila, Luis. Review of *Bless Me, Ultima. Revista Chicano-Riqueña,* 1, 2 (otoño 1973), 53-54.

185. Donnelly, Dyan. "Finding a Home in the World." *Bilingual Review / Revista Bilingüe,* 1, 1 (Jan.-April 1974), 112-18.

186. Pacheco, Javier. Review of *Heart of Aztlán. Rayas,* No. 1 (Jan.-Feb. 1978), pp. 10-11.

187. Rogers, Jane. "The Function of the *La Llorona* Myth in Rudolfo Anaya's *Bless Me, Ultima,* and review of *Heart of Aztlán. Latin American Literary Review,* 5,

Selected Bibliography

10 (Spring-Summer 1977), 64-69, 143-45.
    188. Testa, Daniel. "Extensive/Intensive Dimensionality in Anaya's *Bless Me, Ultima*." *Latin American Literary Review*, 5, 10 (Spring-Summer 1977), 70-78.
    189. Treviño, Albert D. "*Bless Me, Ultima*: A Critical Interpretation." *De Colores*, 3, 4 [1977], 30-33.
    See also 18, 122, 124.
    ARIAS. 190. Bruce-Novoa, Juan. "Interview with Ron Arias." *Journal of Ethnic Studies*, 3, 4 (Winter 1976), 70-73.
    191. Gingerich, Willard. "Chicanismo: The Rebirth of a Spirit." *Southwest Review*, 62, 3 (Summer 1977), pp. vi-vii, 302-4.
    192. Lewis, Marvin A. "On *The Road to Tamazunchale*." *Revista Chicano-Riqueña*, 5, 4 (otoño 1977), 49-52.
    193. Marín, Mariana. "*The Road to Tamazunchale*: Fantasy or Reality?" *De Colores*, 3, 4 [1977], 34-38.
    194. Martínez, Eliud. "Ron Arias' *The Road to Tamazunchale*: A Chicano Novel of the New Reality." *Latin American Literary Review*, 5, 10 (Spring-Summer 1977), 51-63.
    195. Salinas, Judy. Review of *The Road to Tamazunchale*. *Latin American Literary Review*, 4, 8 (Spring-Summer 1976), 111-12.
    BARRIO. 196. Geuder, Patricia A. "Address Systems in *The Plum Plum Pickers*." *Aztlán*, 6, 3 (Fall 1975), 341-46.
    197. Lattin, Vernon E. "Paradise and Plums: Appearance and Reality in Barrio's *The Plum Plum Pickers*." *Selected Proceedings of the 3rd Annual Conference on Minority Studies* (April 1975). Vol. 2. Ed. George E. Carter and James R. Parker. La Crosse WI: Institute for Minority Studies, Univ. of Wisconsin, 1976. Pp. 165-71. ED 125 799. Rpt. in *Critique: Studies in Modern Fiction*, 19, 1 [1977], 49-57.
    198. McKenna, Teresa. "Three Novels: An Analysis." *Aztlán*, 1, 2 (Fall 1970), 47-56.
    199. Miller, Yvette E. "The Social Message in Chicano Fiction: Tomás Rivera's *...and the earth did not part*, and Raymond Barrio's *The Plum Plum Pickers*." *Selected Proceedings of the 3rd Annual Conference on Minority Studies* (April 1975). Vol. 2. Ed. George E. Carter and James R. Parker, LaCrosse WI: Univ of Wisconsin, Inst. for Minority Studies, 1976. Pp. 159-64. ED 125 799.
    See also 230.
    BRITO. 200. Eger, Ernestina N. Review of *El Diablo en Texas*. *Latin American Literary Review*, 5, 10 (Spring-Summer 1977), 162-65.
    201. Febles, Jorge M. Reviews of *El Diablo en Texas* and *Cuentos i poemas de Aristeo Brito*. *Revista Chicano-Riqueña*, 5, 4 (otoño 1977), 55-58.
    BRUCE-NOVOA. 202. Ramírez, Arthur. Review of *Inocencia perversa/Perverse Innocence*. *Revista Chicano-Riqueña*, 5, 4 (otoño 1977), 58-60.
    CHAVEZ. 203. Huber, Robert. "Fray Angélico Chávez, 20th Century Renaissance Man." *New Mexico Magazine*, 48, 3-4 (March-April 1970), 18-23.
    204. Weber, Kenneth R. Review of *My Penitente Land: Reflections on Spanish New Mexico*. *Journal of Ethnic Studies*, 3, 2 (Summer 1975), 119-21.
    DELGADO. 205. Bruce-Novoa, Juan. "Interview with Abelardo Delgado," *Revista Chicano-Riqueña*, 4, 4 (otoño 1976), 110-18.
    206. Cárdenas, Reyes. "Abelardo's Poetry." *Caracol*, 2, 2 (Oct. 1975), 15, 22.
    See also 23, 105.
    DE LEON. 207. Cárdenas, Reyes. "Nephtalí's Purple Shirt." *Caracol*, 2, 6 (Feb.

Ernestina N. Eger

1976), 21.

208. Garza, Sabino. "I Will Catch the Sun: Nephtalí de León." *La Luz*, 6, 12 (Dec. 1977), 15-19.

ELIZONDO. 209. García Camarillo, Cecilio. "Entrevista con Sergio Elizondo." *De Colores*, 3, 4 [1977], 72-79.

GALARZA. 210. Arellano, Estevan, Antonio Luján and Shirley Baca. "Plática con Galarza." *El Cuaderno* (de vez en cuando), 1976 [4, 1-2], pp. 6-19.

211. Senior, Clarence. Review of *Barrio Boy*. *Revista/Review Interamericana*, 3, 2 (Summer 1973), 220-22.

See also 124.

GARCIA. 212. Lenson, David. "Richard García: *Selected Poetry*." *Margins*, No. 28/29/30 (Jan.-March 1976), p. 150.

GOMEZ-QUINONES. 213. Tovar, Inés H. " 'Roses are Rosas': Juan Gómez-Quiñones—A Chicano Poet." *Mester*, 5, 2 (abril 1975), 95-100.

GONZALES. 214. Pendás, Miguel. "An Epic Poem by Corky Gonzales: I Am Joaquín/Yo soy Joaquín." *Militant*, 37, 1 (12 Jan. 1973), 16.

See also 76.

HERRERA. 215. Sifuentes, Roberto. Review of *Rebozos of love we have woven sudor de pueblos on our back*. *Aztlán*, 6, 1 (Spring 1975), 128.

HINOJOSA. 216. Alvarez García, Imeldo. "*Klail City y sus alrededores.*" *Casa de las Américas*, No. 99 (nov.-dic. 1976), pp. 126-30.

217. Brox, Luis María. "Los límites del costumbrismo en *Estampas del Valle y otras obras*." *Mester*, 5, 2 (abril 1975), 101-4.

218. Bruce-Novoa, Juan. "Interview with Rolando Hinojosa-S." *Latin American Literary Review*, 5, 10 (Spring-Summer 1977), 103-14.

219. Pereira, Teresinha Alves. Review of *Estampas del Valle y Otras Obras*. *Revista Chicano-Riqueña*, 3, 1 (invierno 1975), 57-58.

220. Rojas, Guillermo. "La prosa chicana: Tres epígonos de la novela mexicana de la Revolución." *Cuadernos americanos* (México), 34, 3 (mayo-junio 1975), 198-209. Also in *The Chicano Literary World 1974*. Ed. Felipe Ortego y David Conde. Las Vegas NM: New Mexico Highlands Univ., 1975. Pp. 59-70. ED 101 924. Rpt. in *De Colores*, 1, 4 (1975), 43-57, and in this volume, pp. 317-28.

221. Tatum, Charles. Review of *Klail City y sus alrededores*. *Latin American Literary Review*, 5, 10 (Spring-Summer 1977), 165-69.

HOYOS. 222. Chazarra Montiel, A. Review of *Selecciones*. *Estafeta literaria*, No. 605 (1 feb. 1977), pp. 2709-10.

223. Islas, Maya. "*Selecciones*: Poesía de Angela de Hoyos." *Caracol*, 3, 9 (May 1977), 16-17.

See also 96.

LOPEZ. 224. SG [Sigfredo Gordón]. "Problema vivo" (review of *Chicano Go Home*, by Tomás López). *Hispanoamericano/Tiempo*, 22 nov. 1976, p. 47.

MALDONADO. 225. Alarcón, Justo S. " 'Under a Never Changing Sun' o el determinismo chicano." *Revista Chicano-Riqueña*, 5, 4 (otoño 1977), 33-42.

MONTALVO. 226. Garza, Sabino C. Review of *Pensamientos Capturados*. *El Maizal*, 1, 2 [Jan. 1978], 15.

MENDEZ. 227. Brito, Aristeo. "El lenguaje tropológico en *Peregrinos de Aztlán*." *La Luz*, 4, 2 (May 1975), 42-43.

228. Bruce-Novoa, Juan. "La voz del silencio: Miguel Méndez." *Diálogos*, 12, 3 (mayo-junio 1976), 27-30. Shortened and tr. as "Miguel Méndez: Voices of Silence."

De Colores, 3, 4 [1977], 63-69.

229. Flores, Lauro, y Mark McCaffrey. "Miguel Méndez: El Subjetivismo frente a la Historia." *De Colores*, 3, 4 [1977], 46-57.

230. Lewis, Marvin A. "*Peregrinos de Aztlán* and the Emergence of the Chicano Novel." In *Selected Proceedings of the 3rd Annual Conference on Minority Studies* (April 1975). Vol. 2. Ed. George E. Carter and James R. Parker. LaCrosse WI: Institute for Minority Studies, Univ. of Wisconsin, 1976. Pp. 143-57. ED 125-799.

231. Rodríguez, Juan. Review of *Peregrinos de Aztlán*. *Revista Chicano-Riqueña*, 2, 3 (verano 1974), 51-55.

232. Segade, Gustavo V. "*Peregrinos de Aztlán*: Viaje y Laberinto." *De Colores*, 3, 4 [1977], 58-62.

See also 124, 220.

MONTOYA. 233. Lint, Robert G. "Barrio Endowment to American Literature." ED 131 499.

See also 17.

MORALES. 234. Benavides, Ricardo. "Estirpe y estigma en una novela chicana." *Chasqui*, 6, 1 (Nov. 1976), 84-93.

235. Escalante, Evodio. "Escrito en chicano." "La cultura en México," suplemento cultural de *Siempre*, No. 1188 (31 marzo 1976), p. ix.

236. Lewis, Marvin A. "*Caras viejas y vino nuevo:* Essence of the barrio." *Bilingual Review/Revista Bilingüe*, 4, 1-2 (Jan.-August 1977), 141-44.

237. Ramírez, Arturo. "El desmoronamiento y la trascendencia." *Caracol*, 3, 11 (julio 1977), 22-23.

238. Sobek, María Herrera. Review of *Caras viejas y vino nuevo*. *Latin American Literary Review*, 5, 10 (Spring-Summer 1977), 148-50.

PORTILLO. 239. Castellano, Olivia. "Of Clarity and the Moon—A Study of Two Women in Rebellion." *De Colores*, 3, 3 (1977), 25-30.

240. Lattin, Vernon. Review of *Rain of Scorpions and Other Writings*. *N.A.I.E.S. Newsletter*, 2, 2 (Jan. 1977), 20-22.

241. Lewis, Marvin A. Review of *Rain of Scorpions and Other Writings*. *Revista Chicano-Riqueña*, 5, 3 (verano 1977), 51-53.

242. Valdés, Ricardo. Review of *Rain of Scorpions and Other Writings*. *Latin American Literary Review*, 5, 10 (Spring-Summer 1977), 156-62.

QUINTANA. 243. Kopp, Karl. Review of *Hijo del Pueblo,* by Leroy V. Quintana. *American Book Review*, 1, 1 (Dec. 1977), 19-20.

RECHY. 244. Lynch, Honora Moore. "Patterns of Anarchy and Order in the Works of John Rechy." *DAI*, 37, 3 (Sept. 1976), 1583A (Houston).

RIVERA. 245. Campos, Jorge. "Literatura chicana: Cuentos de Tomás Rivera." *Insula*, 29, 328 (marzo 1974), p. 11.

246. Menton, Seymor. Review of *. . .y no se lo tragó la tierra*. *Latin American Literary Review*, 1, 1 (Fall 1972), 111-15.

247. Pino, Frank, Jr. "The Outsider and 'El Otro' in Tomás Rivera's '. . .y no se lo tragó la tierra'." *Books Abroad*, 49, 3 (Summer 1975), 453-58.

248. Pino, Frank, Jr. "Realidad y fantasía en '. . .y no se lo tragó la tierra' de Tomás Rivera." *Otros mundos, otros fuegos; Fantasía y Realismo Mágico en Iberoamérica* (Memoria del XVI Congreso del Instituto Internacional de Literatura Iberoamericana). Ed. Donald A. Yates. East Lansing: Michigan State University, 1975. Pp. 249-54.

249. Rivera, Tomás. "Recuerdo, Descubrimiento y Voluntad en el Proceso Ima-

ginativo Literario." *Atisbos*, 1, 1 (Summer 1975), 66-77.

250. Rocard, Marcienne. "The Cycle of Chicano Experience in '. . .and the earth did not part' by Tomás Rivera." *Caliban*, XI, in *Annales de l'Université de Toulouse/* Le Mirail, Tome X, Fascicule 1 (1974), 141-51.

251. Rodríguez, Juan. "Acercamiento a cuatro relatos de . . .*y no se lo tragó la tierra*." *Mester*, 5, 1 (Nov. 1974), 16-24.

252. Rodríguez, Juan. "La embestida contra la religiosidad en . . . *Y no se lo tragó la tierra*." *PCCLAS Proceedings* (Pacific Coast Council on Latin American Studies): *Changing Perspectives in Latin America*, 3 (1974), 83-86.

253. Vélez, Diana. "The Reality of the Chicanos." *Bilingual Review/Revista Bilingüe*, 2, 1-2 (Jan.-Aug. 1975), 203-7.

See also 92, 116, 121, 122, 124, 199, 220, 230.

ROMANO. 254. Fraire-Aldava, Eugene. "Octavio Romano's 'Goodby Revolution, Hello Slum': A Study of Ironic Tone and Meaning." *Aztlán*, 3, 1 (Spring 1972), 165-69.

ROMERO. 255. Olvera, Joe. "Orlando Romero's *Nambé: Year One*." *Caracol*, 3, 1 (Sept. 1976), 20-21.

See also 124.

SALINAS. 256. Cambón, Glauco. "Raúl Salinas: A New Voice in American Poetry." *Entrelíneas*, 4, 1-2 (Spring-Summer 1975), 11-[13].

257. García-Camarillo, Cecilio. "Revolución artística y acción social: Platicando con Raúl Salinas." *Rayas*, No. 1 (Jan.-Feb. 1978), pp. 12, 9, 11.

SANCHEZ. 258. Cody, James. Review of *Canto y grito mi liberación*. *Margins*, No. 12 (June-July 1974), pp. 27-29.

259. Delgado, Abelardo. Review of *Hechizospells*. *Caracol*, 4, 4 (dic. 1977), 20-21. Also in *El Maizal*, 1, 2 [Jan. 1978], 8-9.

260. [Garza, Juan Leandro.] "México fuera de México: La condición humana." *Tiempo/Hispanoamericano* (México D.F.), 27 dic. 1976, pp. 8-10.

261. Lovato, Alberto J. "La burra no era arisca, cabrones, los chingazos la hicieron así. . ." *El Cuaderno* (de vez en cuando), 2, 1 (1972), 36-39.

262. "Platicando con Ricardo Sánchez." *Rayas*, No. 2 (March-April 1978), pp. 12, 4, 3.

263. Sánchez, Ricardo. "Mictla: A Chicano's Long Road Home." In *The Publish-It-Yourself Handbook*. Ed. Bill Henderson. Yonkers NY: Pushcart Book Press, 1973. Pp. 52-69.

See also 23, 105.

SOTO. 264. Paredes, Raymund A. Review of *The Elements of San Joaquín*. *Minority Voices*, 1, 2 (Fall 1977), 106-8.

265. Rodríguez, Juan. Review of *The Elements of San Joaquín*. *New Scholar*, 6 (1976), 269-73.

TORRES-METZGAR. 266. Geuder, Patricia A. Letter to Max Martínez, in response to review of *Below the Summit*. *Caracol*, 4, 1 (Sept. 1977), 5, 22.

267. Martínez, Max. Review of *Below the Summit*. *Caracol*, 3, 8 (abril 1977), 20-22.

268. Olvera, Joe. Review of *Below the Summit*. *Caracol*, 3, 11 (julio 1977), 22-23.

269. Valdés, Ricardo. Review of *Below the Summit*. *Latin American Literary Review*, 5, 10 (Spring-Summer 1977), 156-62.

See also 118.

ULIBARRI. 270. Ramírez, Arturo. "Un mosaico vital, " review of *Mi abuela fumaba puros/My Grandma Smoked Cigars. Caracol*, 4, 6 (feb. 1978), 7.

271. Ramos, Charles. Review of *Tierra Amarilla. Southwestern American Literature*, 2, 1 (Spring 1972), 60.

272. Sackett, Theodore A. Review of *Tierra Amarilla. Modern Language Journal*, 56, 8 (Dec. 1972), 515-16.

VASQUEZ. 273. Ginzburg, Francine. "*Chicano* Revisited/*Chicano* se visita de nuevo." *Entrelíneas*, 4, 1-2 (Spring-Summer 1975), 7, 10, [13].

274. Moesser, Alba. "Notas sobre dos autores mejicoamericanos de California." ED 063 829.

275. Ríos, Herminio. Review of *Chicano. El Grito*, 3, 3 (Spring 1970), 67-71. See also 116, 124, 198.

VILLANUEVA. 276. Pereira, Teresinha Alves. "Entrevista a Tino Villanueva." *Revista Chicano-Riqueña*, 3, 3 (verano 1975), 30-34.

See also 15.

VILLARREAL. 277. Alarcón, Justo S. "Hacia la nada. . .O la religión en Pocho." *Minority Voices*, 1, 2 (Fall 1977), 17-26.

278. Bruce-Novoa, Juan. "Interview with José Antonio Villareal." *Revista Chicano-Riqueña*, 4, 2, (primavera 1976), 40-48.

279. Bruce-Novoa, Juan. "*Pocho* as Literature." *Aztlán*, 7, 1 (Spring 1976), 65-77.

280. Dimicelli, Judith M. "A Chicano Twentieth-Century Book of Genesis," review of *The Fifth Horseman. Bilingual Review/Revista Bilingüe*, 3, 1 (Jan.-April 1976), 73-77.

281. Jiménez, Francisco. "An Interview with José Antonio Villarreal." *Bilingual Review/Revista Bilingüe*, 3, 1 (Jan.-April 1976), 66-72.

282. Luedtke, Luther S. "*Pocho* and The American Dream." *Minority Voices*, 1, 2 (Fall 1977), 1-16.

See also 116, 122, 124, 274.

VILLASEÑOR. 283. Donnelly, Dyan. "The Making and Unmaking of a Macho." *Bilingual Review/Revista Bilingüe*, 3, 2 (May-August 1976), 194-96.

284. Sánchez, Marta Ester. Review of *Macho. Latin American Literary Review*, 3, 6 (spring-summer 1975), 99-100.

See also 43, 124, 128.

ZAMORA. 285. Bruce-Novoa, Juan. Review of *Restless Serpents*, by José A. Burciaga and Bernice Zamora. *Caracol*, 4, 1 (Sept. 1977), 15, 20. Rpt. in *Latin American Literary Review*, 5, 10 (Spring-Summer 1977), 150-54.

CARTHAGE COLLEGE

INDEX

Index

Index

Index

Acknowledgments, *continued*

The following papers first appeared in *The Bilingual Review/La revista bilingüe:* Francisco Jiménez, "Dramatic Principles of the Teatro Campesino," II, 1 & 2 (1975), p. 99; Joseph Sommers, "Critical Approaches to Chicano Literature," IV, 1 & 2 (1977), p. 92; Salvador Rodríguez del Pino, "La novela chicana de los setenta comentada por sus escritores y críticos," IV, 3 (1977), p. 240; Egla Morales Blouin, "Símbolos y motivos nahuas en la literatura chicana," V, 1 & 2 (1978), p. 99; Carlota Cárdenas de Dwyer, "International Literary Metaphor and Ron Arias: An Analysis of *The Road to Tamazunchale,*" IV, 3 (1977), p. 229.